Dementia Care With Black and Latino Families

A Social Work Problem-Solving Approach

Delia J. González Sanders, PhD, LCSW, is an assistant professor and field coordinator at Central Connecticut State University, Department of Social Work, a research co-investigator at the Center on Aging, University of Connecticut Health Center, and an adjunct professor at Smith College School for Social Work in Northampton, Massachusetts. Dr. González Sanders's research interests include diverse caregivers of Alzheimer's disease and related irreversible dementia; eliminating health disparities among Latinos and other ethnically diverse populations; cultural competence in social work; translating social work research into clinical practice; and examining Latino caregiver problem solving and resilience. She received her PhD in Social Work from Smith College and her MSSW from the University of Texas, Austin.

Richard H. Fortinsky, PhD, is a professor at the UConn Center on Aging and Department of Medicine, University of Connecticut School of Medicine, where he holds the Physicians Health Services Endowed Chair in Geriatrics and Gerontology. Dr. Fortinsky conducts applied research with the goals of preserving and improving health status, and improving health and social care, for community-dwelling older adults and their families. He has directed numerous studies and published widely in professional journals on the topics of family and physician care for people with Alzheimer's disease and other dementia. He received a Fulbright Distinguished Scholar Award in 2007 to lecture and conduct comparative research in England on the organization and financing of care for people with dementia and their families in England and the United States. Dr. Fortinsky received his PhD in Sociology from Brown University.

Dementia Care With Black and Latino Families

A Social Work Problem-Solving Approach

Delia J. González Sanders, PhD, LCSW
Richard H. Fortinsky, PhD

SPRINGER / PUBLISHING COMPANY
NEW YORK

Springer Publishing Company, LLC
11 West 42nd Street
New York, NY 10036
www.springerpub.com

Acquisitions Editor: Sheri W. Sussman
Composition: Newgen Imaging

ISBN: 978-0-8261-0677-3
eBook ISBN: 978-0-8261-0678-0

11 12 13/ 5 4 3 2 1

The author and the publisher of this Work have made every effort to use sources believed to be reliable to provide information that is accurate and compatible with the standards generally accepted at the time of publication. The author and publisher shall not be liable for any special, consequential, or exemplary damages resulting, in whole or in part, from the readers' use of, or reliance on, the information contained in this book. The publisher has no responsibility for the persistence or accuracy of URLs for external or third-party Internet Web sites referred to in this publication and does not guarantee that any content on such Web sites is, or will remain, accurate or appropriate.

Library of Congress Cataloging-in-Publication Data
Sanders, Delia Gonzalez.
  Dementia care with Black and Latino families : a social work problem-solving approach / Delia Gonzalez Sanders, Richard H. Fortinsky.
    p. cm.
  Includes bibliographical references and index.
  ISBN 978-0-8261-0677-3 (alk. paper)
  1. Caregivers—Family relationships. 2. Dementia—Patients—Care—Social aspects. 3. Older African Americans—Care. 4. Older Hispanic Americans—Care. I. Fortinsky, Richard H. (Richard Harold), 1953-
II. Title.
  RA645.3.S26 2011
  362.196'83008996073—dc23   2011042086

Special discounts on bulk quantities of our books are available to corporations, professional associations, pharmaceutical companies, health care organizations, and other qualifying groups.
If you are interested in a custom book, including chapters from more than one of our titles, we can provide that service as well.
For details, please contact:
Special Sales Department, Springer Publishing Company, LLC
11 West 42nd Street, 15th Floor, New York, NY 10036–8002
Phone: 877-687-7476 or 212-431-4370; Fax: 212-941-7842
Email: sales@springerpub.com

Printed in the United States of America by Gasch Printing

To my husband Bill, whose enduring love, kindness, and generosity enabled me to let go of tasks in order to focus on writing. To my beloved children, Melanie, Richard and Lauren, and grandsons Ricky and John; to my dad Dario, a medic in the army in WWII who cared for many; to my mother Frances for her unwavering love, reflecting the ideal caregiver model of faith, hope, and love by simultaneously caring for us, my beloved grandfather "papa Jose" afflicted with dementia and cancer, and grandmother Maria Theódora "mama Lola," afflicted with Alzheimer's disease; to my sister Dolores for her love, humor, and shared family experiences; and to my mother-in-law and father-in-law Eleanore and Bill, for loving me.

In loving memory of members of our family unknown and known who had Alzheimer's disease or other forms of dementia, including my brother Joe, uncle Joe, aunt Hope, cousin Maria "cucita," and those who currently have dementia, aunt Mary Lou and cousin Jeanne, and to our courageous family caregivers who diligently adhere to our unique familismo cultural values by providing loving home care for our dear family members.

This work is dedicated to all dementia victims and caregivers, especially to those who participated in clinical programs and/or all research projects leading to the completion of this project. Their kind, enthusiastic contributions to efforts they knew would benefit future caregivers left me in awe at times in view of the challenges and responsibilities they faced daily. A todos les envió gracias y bendiciones de Dios con todo mi corazón.

Delia J. González Sanders

In loving memory of my mother Davida, who was a tireless caregiver and then experienced the dementia journey herself. With great admiration and respect for my father Charles, who unexpectedly found himself in the caregiving role.

To Patricia for her constant support, understanding, and good humor. To our wonderful children Kyle, Laura, and Celia, all continuous sources of inspiration and happiness.

Richard H. Fortinsky

Contents

Preface

The afflicted patient has been the primary focus of diseases that lead to one form or another of dementia. Because of the biogenic origin of diseases such as Alzheimer's, the treatment orientation has been medical with very little attention given to the social elements. Insofar as the dementia patient is the focal point, such an orientation is appropriate. Further, because of a common physiological and medical impact on the human brain among diverse social classes and ethnic groups, little research has been done to determine differences among various social groupings.

Stepping back just slightly, we can see that the secondary victims of dementia-related diseases are the caregivers. On the one hand are total care facilities that take over the life management of afflicted patients. Institutional necessities and medical directions have molded their protocols for keeping patients from harm and in a state of optimized life given the parameters of the disease and institutional resources. On the other hand, nonprofessional caregivers provide the majority of care for early stages of dementia-related diseases and in some cases, all stages. Generally, these are the family members of the victim. Because of the different family relational patterns among ethnic and cultural groupings, understanding the role of the caregiver in different social contexts is one of the most important skills that social workers need to master.

Based on original research by the authors as well as a wide array of published research, this book seeks to guide the professional social worker to successfully provide support for dementia caregivers. Importantly, the interventions target the unique challenges and opportunities found in Black and Latino families. Research-based self-efficacy and cognitive-behavioral problem-solving paradigms serve as foundational guidelines for the very practical issues social workers must help caregivers resolve. Detailed stepwise guides to assessment and intervention in an ethnic context provide alternatives to more blanket policies.

Included in this book are detailed forms, documents, and dementia care resources that social workers will need to use to both help them mold an appropriate strategy and relieve them of having to uncover all of the materials that are required for a successful outcome. Several supporting case studies in the chapters help the reader quickly contextualize the materials to real-world situations. Together with the empirical research, grounded theory, and appropriate tools, this work seeks to bring together compact yet comprehensive tools for dealing with a growing issue as the population ages and the demographics shift to a more diverse and complex mix.

Acknowledgments

I thank God for the love, grace, wisdom, and guidance to complete this work. I also thank my many beloved familismo members, friends, and colleagues whose humor, unwavering love, spiritual support, and prayers fostered diligence, resilience, and inner strength deep within me.

This book could not have been written without the contributions of many people. I am grateful for the support of Dean Sakofs in the School of Education and Professional Studies and SEPS-GC at Central Connecticut State University for the research reassigned time award that partially supported writing this book. I am also grateful for the kindness and patience of colleagues in the Social Work Department, Dr. Cathy Baratta, Dr. Pat Hensley, Cathy Gentile Doyle, LCSW, and Vinnie Testa.

A special thanks to Dr. J. Camille Hall, LCSW, University of Tennessee; Eboni Lanier Jones, LCSW, Duke University; Marcia McKenzie, MEd, Manager, Western MA Regional Office, Alzheimer's Association, Massachusetts Chapter; Dean Dr. Carolyn Jacobs and Dr. Joyce Everett, Smith College School for Social Work; Dr. Lourdes Mattei, Hampshire College; Elsie Dones, dementia outreach worker, Springfield, MA; and Diane K. Fisher, MSW, Alison Kleppinger, MS, Lisa Kenyon-Pesce, MPH, Carmen Dozal, Nellie Castro, Migdalia Gonzalez, Nelson Jimmo, Dr. Elizabeth Rodriguez-Keyes, LCSW, Dr. Julie Robison, Elia Castro, MA, and Astrid, Sandra, and Kelly Ruiz.

To Sheri Sussman, my editor, thank you for the crucial guidance, support, and encouragement without which this book would have been impossible.

I acknowledge the staff at both the Institute for the Hispanic Family in Hartford and the Alzheimer's Association Connecticut Chapter, for permission to develop and pilot social work, master's, and PhD student internship programs that provided critical insight into the clinical needs of ethnic caregivers, dementia-afflicted relatives, and extended families that contributed partially to the foundation for the research and social work problem-solving intervention for ethnic caregivers in this project. We acknowledge the work of Amaryllis Stevens, MSW, care consultant in the problem-solving approach for the Center on Aging, University of Connecticut Health Center, the Alzheimer's Association, and the Donaghue Foundation grant. Thank you all.

DJGS

I gratefully acknowledge the following sources of research support that enabled us to gain knowledge and insights that contributed substantially to the content of this book.

- Alzheimer's Association (Grant No. IIRG-06–26993)
- The Donaghue Medical Research Foundation (Grant No. DF02–063)

We also respectfully appreciate the willingness of all the family caregivers who participated in these studies to share their experiences with us. I also gratefully acknowledge the Physicians Health Services Chair in Geriatrics and Gerontology, which partially supported the time and effort spent to write portions of this book.

Finally, I am fortunate to work with a highly talented and dedicated team of research professionals at the UConn Center on Aging, and to all of them I extend my most sincere thanks and appreciation.

RHF

Introduction

America's population is becoming increasingly older and more ethnically diverse, and these demographic trends are projected to continue at least until the middle of the 21st century. Age-associated medical conditions such as Alzheimer's disease and other forms of dementia, characterized by progressive memory loss and cognitive decline, will occupy increasing time of health and social service providers. As dementia-related symptoms progress, family members assume greater care and decision-making responsibilities for their relatives with dementia. Published studies have found both similarities and differences among family caregivers of relatives with dementia from different ethnic and racial groups in terms of their experiences with health and social services, and in terms of their beliefs about the causes and consequences of dementia. Social workers must be prepared to encounter families from diverse racial and ethnic backgrounds grappling with the daily challenges of living with dementia. The two largest racial and ethnic groups in the United States, both currently and projected well into the future, are Blacks and Latinos.

SYSTEMS THEORY

Social workers are educated and trained to apply systems and person-in-environment perspectives in undergraduate generalist social work courses. Encouraged to continue learning throughout graduate studies and beyond in practice settings, social workers engage in life-long learning because each practice experience requires new knowledge, assessment, and critical thinking in order for them to evaluate the caregiver, afflicted family members, and family systems within the care context. In social work practice, a general systems approach consists of categories of systems, informal and formal.

What makes using systems theory interesting and effective when working with ethnic caregivers is the way in which the theory lends itself to enlist the assistance of a variety of informal and formal systems to help in the caregiving task and the methods employed to assess the system functioning. Generally speaking, Black and Latino help-seeking and help-receiving actions are almost always initiated by the dementia caregiver, or from the family kin or fictive system members as opposed to the dementia-afflicted family member. Having a framework that social workers can employ to ensure that resources from both informal and formal sectors are tapped into effectively and efficiently and that is also a system that is a "good fit" in understanding the kinship and fictive kin mutual aid network in Black and Latino familismo enable social workers to employ core concepts, skills, and tasks in practice to provide essential help for the caregiver and afflicted family member.

Three paradigms of systems theory help to inform our understanding of dementia family caregiving for Black and Latino caregivers. The first is systems theory developed by Pincus and Minahan (1973), which provides a resource system lens by which social workers can create a framework to assess the various systems that impact caregivers and afflicted family members.

The second systems paradigm comes from Keith's (1995) and Piercy's (1998) perception of the concept of wholeness relevant to the care process. The concept of wholeness identifies each part or role as a discrete contributing member within the network system while serving as an interconnected part of the whole system. This discrete role part can only function effectively when linked with the other interconnected parts, hence the wholeness concept (Keith, 1995; Piercy, 1998). Therefore, these system perspectives provide a framework to understand how each individual role self-delineates and yet links within the system process of familismo and the system process of kin networks as individuals apply their unique role skills in an effort to untie key care functions to the multidimensionality of the overall caregiving systems needs.

The third model discovered and introduced in this text is the concept of a symbiotic model of system care essential to understanding the nature of the caregiver role in social work practice with Alzheimer's disease and other irreversible dementia disease process cases. When a family member develops an irreversible dementia illness and is introduced to the family system social context of another family member, the individual assumes new roles: a caregiver role and a care receiver role. With the onset of new roles, another dimension of relationship within the social context system is formed, and thus a framework is established to allow for the dynamic growth and formation of a symbiotic relationship between the caregiver and the care receiver. Hence there is an underlying symbiotic assumption within this care model. The symbiotic systems model is used to describe the representation of the reality experienced by the caregiver and care receiver within the nature of this new relationship.

The symbiotic helping relationship with time gives way to the caregiver's memory serving as an external memory for the afflicted family member that is losing his or her own memory and brain function. Similar to a physically handicapped individual needing an external apparatus such as crutches in order to walk, the dementia-afflicted family member requires the use of an external brain and memory from caregiver(s) in order to function. As such this is a crucial symbiotic relationship between at least two individuals, the caregiver (s) and the care recipient.

Social workers need to understand the symbiotic system model as crucial dynamic interaction within the social context of the Black and Latino family caregiver. This text seeks to understand the caregiver and afflicted family member through the elements of this perspective that are interacting with each other and within a social context in one dimension. But in a parallel process we also view the independent needs of each individual within his or her own unique social context. Hence, as the afflicted family member becomes more demented, vulnerable, and disengaged from the informal and formal systems of care in the social context, the symbiotic relationship strengthens and becomes the link between the informal and formal systems of care in the social context of the caregiver and the care recipient. The practical social work implications of this perspective take into consideration that within this symbiotic model of care, essential tensions and real-life conflicts emerge between the caregiver and the care recipient, and with their conjoint yet separate respective social context, they seek to confront the increasing demands of the progressive dementia illness. Schwartz (1961) formulated a practice theory with a survival assumption that helps to illustrate this survival tendency.

A relationship between the individual and his nurturing group which we would describe as "symbiotic"—each needing the other for its own life and growth, and each reaching out to the other with all the strength it can command at a given moment. (pp. 146–147)

COGNITIVE-BEHAVIORAL THEORY

Although there are many other theories and practices that social workers may find helpful in working with Black and Latinos, the recommended practice by the authors of this text is the cognitive-behavioral problem-solving approach. Cognitive-behavioral theory is known to identify specific target symptoms, traits, and other behaviors, and to modify certain maladaptive ways of thinking, feeling, and behaving in the caregiver. The cognitive-behavioral intervention used in this section is adapted from two models (Ellis, 1962; Wilkinson, 2002). These cognitive-affective and behavioral models posit that a person's thinking, mood, and behavior are largely determined by the beliefs they have about themselves, their circumstances, and the world, and are usually based on absolutist thinking rather than on rational interpretations and factual evidence. Ellis (1962) identifies three words that are cues to "irrational or erroneous" interpretations of events. These words are "should, ought, and must" (Ellis, 1962, p. 63).

Cognitive-behavioral therapy can help family caregivers of dementia patients as they face real-life problems related to the course of the illness. Caregivers may report understandable pessimistic and anxious thoughts and feelings related to the problems caused by the disease process of the patient with dementia (Wilkinson, 2002). Also, some caregivers of dementia family members often experience erroneous thoughts regarding their ability to understand and provide assistance for the dementia family member's behavior symptoms, motivations, and emotional disturbance. Cognitive-behavioral techniques can be combined with disease care educational information on the nature of dementia as a means of assisting the caregiver to understand the dementia disease process (Gallagher-Thompson et al., 1992; James, 1999; Marriott, Donaldson, Tarrier, & Burns, 2000; Wilkinson, 2002).

In this text, cognitive-behavioral theory is used to provide a framework for social workers and other health care practitioners working with caregivers of a dementia-afflicted relative to understand some of the maladaptive cognitive affective and behavioral processes they may experience as they care for their family member and help caregivers to learn a more adaptive cognitive process. By teaching this specific cognitive process of thinking about themselves and the problems in ways that will help them change irrational beliefs, attitudes, opinions, or philosophies, the social worker can work to help them change their feelings and their coping behaviors. Often caregivers lump their own affective and situational concerns together with those affective and situational concerns of the afflicted family member, making it difficult for caregivers to perceive themselves as able to cope. This is especially true if the caregiver lives with or is in close proximity to the afflicted family member (González Sanders, 2006).

The social work practice approach introduced in this text has been examined in research and is considered evidence-based practice by the authors. It provides the necessary components to assist caregivers to tap into and employ problem-solving skills necessary to resolve the day-to-day problems as they emerge in the dementia caregiving context. This perspective assesses the origin of problems facing ethnic caregivers providing care for dementia-afflicted family members using a culturally competent perspective assessing whether the caregiver, the afflicted family member, and the kinship families possess the capabilities to problem-solve while respecting cultural values, beliefs, and family functioning characteristics.

Rather than focusing on the portrayal of Black and Latino caregiving families as pathological and perpetrators of the caregiving and social problems they face, the authors depict ethnic caregiving families as capable of adaptive and resilient actions in the face of caregiving adversities. This does not mean that social workers ignore the reality of adverse life conditions and circumstances that affect portions of the Black and Latino populations. Rather, social workers use ethical and culturally competent skills to assist Black and Latino caregivers face problematic situations that create risks to their well-being by helping them identify and tap into cultural values, strengths, and resources that counterbalance problems, assist them to engage kin and familismo networks to explore what constitutes protective factors, and function and problem solve effectively. The major purpose of this book is to provide practical guidance for the social work professional working with Black and Latino families living with the daily challenges of Alzheimer's disease and other dementia, based on sound theoretical framework, and based on the clinical and research experiences of the authors.

Chapters begin with a case study to help the reader link chapter content with social work practice considerations. The first chapter opens with an illustrative presentation and discussion of the rapidly growing racial and ethnic diversity of America's older population, with special focus on demographic- and health-related trends. Chapter 1 also summarizes population and family caregiving trends influencing dementia care in the United States as well as demographic trends and research interventions. Chapter 2 provides an essential overview of the epidemiology and clinical course of Alzheimer's disease and other common forms of dementia, with special focus on forms of dementia found to be more common among Blacks and Latinos. This chapter closes with an introduction to interpretations and meanings of dementia in Black and Latino cultural heritages, a central theme threaded throughout the rest of the book. Chapter 3 continues building concepts and theories under-lying family care and role responsibilities in Black and Latino cultures to help social work professionals gain a better understanding of ethnic family caregiving.

Chapters 4 through 8 form the heart of the book as a guide to ethnic family dementia care for social work professionals. Chapter 4 summa-rizes challenges faced daily in Black and Latino communities, ranging from immigration to language barriers to financial resource constraints to experiences of discrimination. The social work professional code of ethics is reviewed in this chapter as well. Chapter 5 presents social work roles relevant to this target population, and Chapter 6 catalogues assessment tools found useful in the authors' work with ethnic family caregivers of relatives with dementia. Chapters 7 and 8 pull together the concepts and tools by detailing how best to organize problems con-fronted by ethnic family caregivers into four domains highly relevant to dementia care, and how to implement interventions within each of these four working domains.

The book closes with two chapters linking recommended social work practice strategies from earlier chapters with broader social and eco-nomic challenges affecting the lives of ethnic family caregivers and the social work profession itself. Chapter 9 provides financing and service trends and outlooks on public health policy developments, particularly Medicare and Medicaid, that might affect how social work professionals can receive payment for their services with the target population of this book. It also provides future trends toward dementia care diagnosis and community-based service. Chapter 10 briefly reviews available informa-tion and health care technology to enhance social work communication with and advocacy for ethnic family caregivers.

REFERENCES

Ellis, A. (1962). *Reason and emotion in psychotherapy*. Secaucus, NJ: Lyle Stuart.

Keith, C. (1995). Family caregiving systems: Models, resources and values. *Journal of Marriage and the Family, 57*, 179–190.

Gallagher-Thompson, D., Rose, J., Florsheim, M., Jacome, P., DelMaestro, S., Peters, L., et al. (1992). *Controlling your frustration: A class for caregivers*. Palo Alto Health Care System.

González Sanders, D. J. (2006). *Familismo and resilience in Latino family caregivers of demen-tia afflicted relatives: An ethno-cultural cross-sectional study*. Unpublished research doc-toral dissertation. Northampton, MA: Smith College School for Social Work.

James, I. A. (1999). Using a cognitive rationale to conceptualize anxiety in people with dementia. *Behavioral and Cognitive Psychotherapy, 27*, 345–351.

Marriott, A., Donaldson, C., Tarrier, N., & Burns, A. (2000). Effectiveness of cognitive-behavioral family intervention in reducing the burden of care in carers of patients with Alzheimer's disease. *British Journal of Psychiatry, 176*, 557–562.

Piercy, K. W. (1998). Theorizing about family caregiving: The role of responsibility. *Journal of Marriage and the Family, 60*, 109–118.

Pincus, A., & Minahan, A. (1973). *Social work practice: Model and method.* Itasca, IL: F. E. Peacock.

Schwartz, W. (1961). The social worker in the group. In The National Association of Social Workers, *New perspectives on services to groups: Theory, organization, practice* (pp. 7–34). New York: National Association of Social Workers.

Wilkinson, P. (2002). Cognitive behavior therapy. In J. Hepple, J. Pearce, & P. Wilkinson (Eds.), *Psychological therapies with older people: Developing treatments for effective practice* (pp. 45–75). New York: Taylor & Francis.

I

Setting the Context for Understanding Ethnic Dementia Care

1

Population and Family Caregiving Trends Influencing Dementia Care

CASE EXAMPLE

I can't do this again. I'm too tired and my health is not good but I'm the only one left. If I don't care for her who will? Everyone else is gone, dead, my sisters, my brothers. There's no one else but me now. I just can't sleep anymore and I can't rest. I have to do it all. I have to take care of myself, too, you know. I have diabetes and high blood pressure. She lives with me now cause she can't take care of herself anymore. The worse she [sister] gets, the more trouble I have with my blood pressure and my diabetes. I don't go to church or anywhere. The doctor said I need help, so I am here. I am done.

Tina, a 67-year-old African American, is the primary caregiver for her sister Ruth, age 79, afflicted with Alzheimer's disease. This is Tina's fifth dementia caregiver role in the family. She is the youngest female in this large family of 10 siblings. Four older female siblings and her mother all died from what she now knows is not old age but Alzheimer's disease. The four older male siblings have died from complications related to other diseases. Tina is providing care for Ruth, the older sister who cared for their mother until the mother passed away. Tina has never married and does not have any children. Ruth has two adult children living across the country who have never been told about the disease afflicting their mother.

CHAPTER OVERVIEW

This chapter provides an introduction to several important overarching population, policy, and research trends that influence how care is provided by Black and Latino family members to their relatives with dementia living in the community. Because the hallmark symptoms of dementia—impairment of memory and other cognitive capacities—most often affect individuals after age 65, this chapter opens with an illustrative presentation and discussion of the rapid growth of America's older population as well as the increasing racial and ethnic diversity within the older population. The chapter then summarizes demographic, socioeconomic, and health-related trends in the Black and Latino older populations compared with those of older Whites. A synopsis of the demographic and socioeconomic characteristics of America's Black and Latino populations in total is then provided; this will demonstrate the broader structural characteristics of these racial and ethnic groups within which families provide care to older relatives with Alzheimer's disease and other dementia. As we shall see, Blacks and Latinos differ from each other and from Whites in several important social and economic respects that could ultimately affect the capacity of families to, provide such care. The chapter closes by turning to the topic of dementia caregiving, summarizing research on the prevalence and consequences of caring for a relative with dementia in ethnically diverse families, and on efforts by researchers and community-based partners to develop effective programs to help family members caring for relatives with dementia. Special emphasis is placed on research-guided family caregiver support programs that have included Black and/or Latino family caregivers as participants.

POPULATION TRENDS

Growth of the Older Population in the 20th and 21st Centuries

Results from the 2010 U.S. Census reveal that the number of Americans age 65 and older grew from 35 million in the year 2000 to 40.3 million in 2010, an increase of 15% compared with an increase in size of less than 10% for the total U.S. population during the first decade of the 21st century. Within the older U.S. population, it is the "oldest old" group, or those aged 85 and older, that grew the fastest between 2000 and 2010— nearly 5.5 million Americans were age 85 and older in 2010, an increase of nearly 30% compared with 4.2 million Americans in this age group in the year 2000 (Howden & Meyer, 2011).

These growth trends during the 2000–2010 decade represent a continuation of the steady growth of the older American population throughout the 20th century, but they pale in comparison to projected growth figures over the next several decades. As Figure 1.1 illustrates, after 2010, the size of the American population age 65 and older will grow even faster than previous decades, reaching a projected 72.1 million in 2030, and 88.5 million in 2050. The projected growth of the oldest old population is even more striking, reaching almost 9 million by 2030, and then more than doubling in 20 years to 19 million by 2050. The growth rates of the oldest old population are particularly significant for dementia care considerations in the near future because, as will be discussed in Chapter 2, the oldest old population has the highest prevalence of dementia.

What are the major reasons for the aging of America's population? First, in the early and middle parts of the 20th century, advances in public health such as clean water, sanitation systems, and development of vaccines greatly reduced infant and childhood mortality from causes related to communicable and infectious diseases. At a population level, greatly reduced infant and childhood mortality

FIGURE 1.1 Growth of the U.S. Older Population, Selected Years, 1900–2050

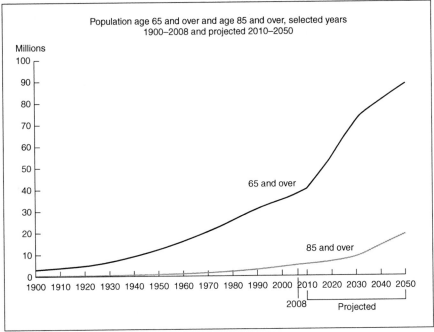

dramatically increased the average life expectancy of Americans born during the 20th century, such that babies born in 1900 could expect to live an average of only 47 years, whereas babies born in 2000 could expect to live an average of 74 years. Second, the latter half of the 20th century witnessed substantial advances in medical, pharmaceutical, and engineering sciences, yielding new knowledge about how to prevent and treat chronic diseases, new surgical techniques to prolong life, and new imaging techniques to detect signs of disease even before the appearance of symptoms. These scientific advances have led to increased life expectancies at later ages; between 1960 and 2006, the number of additional years that a person aged 65 could expect to live on average rose from 14.4 years to 18.5 years (Federal Interagency Forum, 2010).

Looking ahead, the major reason for the projected growth of America's older population at an even faster rate in the first half of the 21st century is the aging of the baby-boomer birth cohort. So-called "baby boomers" were born during a 19-year period of unusually high birth rates that began in 1946, after millions of U.S. men and women returned home from serving in World War II, and ended in 1964, after which birth rates dropped precipitously. More than 76 million baby boomers were born, and the first of these celebrated their 65th birthdays in January 2011 (Jacobsen, Mather, Lee, & Kent, 2011); they will continue to join the ranks of America's older population until the year 2029, swelling the older population as illustrated in Figure 1.1. As baby boomers begin to make their collective influence felt in America's older population, it will be important to realize that they experienced a higher level of educational attainment as a group than their predecessors, and that they grew up in an era where consumer preferences and choices in the health care arena became much more evident than ever before. Therefore, as older adults, baby boomers can be expected to demand greater amounts of information from, and bring more information to, encounters with health and social service professionals for all types of symptoms and health problems common to later life, including memory problems. Indeed, many baby boomers' adult children already provide care to parents with dementia; this issue will be discussed later in this chapter.

Growth of Racial and Ethnic Older Populations

The other major population trend influencing dementia care in the 21st century is the growing racial and ethnic diversity of the older U.S. population. Among respondents to the U.S. Census who identify as Black

TABLE 1.1   Percent Distribution of the Population Age 65 and Older by Race/Ethnicity, 2009, 2030, and 2050

	2009	2030	2050
White alone, non-Hispanic	80.1	71.2	58.5
Black alone, non-Hispanic	8.3	9.6	11.2
Hispanic	7.0	12.0	19.8
Asian alone, non-Hispanic	3.4	5.3	6.4
Other	1.2	1.7	2.1

From Jacobsen, L. A., Mather, M., Lee, M., & Kent, M. (2011). America's aging population. *Population Bulletin* 66, No. 1, Table 2.

or African American, the population age 65 and older is projected to more than triple in size between 2008 and 2050, from 3.3 million to 10.6 million. Among Census respondents who identify as Hispanic or Latino ethnicity, growth of the older population will be much more dramatic, rising from 2.7 million in 2008 to 19.8 million in 2050—a greater than sevenfold increase in size! Although not a topic in this book, it is also noteworthy that the older Asian population will experience a more than sixfold increase in size, growing to 7.5 million by 2050 (Federal Interagency Forum, 2010).

Table 1.1 provides a summary of expected changes in the racial and ethnic distribution of America's older population by displaying these figures as percentages. As the table shows, while non-Hispanic Whites made up 80% of the total U.S. population aged 65 and older in 2009, this percentage will drop to 58.5% by 2050. In sharp contrast, Hispanics made up only 7% of the U.S. older population in 2009; this percentage will increase to 12% by 2030 (surpassing the Black percentage), and to nearly 20% by 2050. These population trends make it clear that professionals working with older adults over the next several decades will be increasingly likely to encounter in their practices clients and families from diverse racial and ethnic backgrounds.

A final consideration of racial and ethnic diversity, from a generational perspective of the U.S. population, is that the baby-boomer birth cohort does not contain as large a proportion of racial and ethnic groups other than Whites as do younger age cohorts. Box 1.1 illustrates and explains this phenomenon from the viewpoint of potential generational differences in desired social programs and, by extension, public policies, due to a greater proportion of Blacks, Hispanics, and other groups of color in younger generations. This generational difference also is likely to result in a younger health and social service workforce that is more racially and ethnically diverse than the older adult population receiving services.

BOX 1.1 The New Generation Gap

BY MARK MATHER

During the last several decades, baby boomers, most of whom are non-Hispanic White, have dominated the U.S. population and labor force. But as they reach old age, they are being replaced by a younger cohort that is much more likely to be Hispanic, Asian, or multi-racial.[1] For example, between 2009 and 2030, the proportion of non-Hispanic White children is projected to drop by 9 percentage points, while the proportion of Latino children is projected to increase by 9 percentage points, to 31 percent. The rapid increase in diversity among younger cohorts may be creating a new kind of generation gap. Although historically the generation gap has been defined by different cultural tastes in music, fashion, or technology, this new demographic divide may have broader implications for social programs and spending for youth. Will America's majority-White older population support initiatives for a racially mixed youth population?

In 1980, the racial and ethnic divisions between age groups were fairly small (see the figure below). People in their 60s had a racial/ethnic profile similar to those in their 40s and 50s, who in turn looked similar to those in their 20s and 30s. The difference between age groups in the share who were minorities did not exceed 5 percentage points in successive generations.

By 2009, however, these generational differences had increased substantially. Those in their 40s and 50s—members of the baby-boom generation—are stuck between very different generations: parents and grandparents, most of whom are U.S.-born Whites, and U.S. children and grandchildren, who are increasingly Hispanic or Asian. Although non-Hispanic Black children are still a sizeable group (14 percent of all children in 2009), their numbers are growing at a much slower pace than the numbers of children in Hispanic and Asian families.

U.S. Census Bureau projections indicate that this racial/ethnic divergence between generations may be a temporary phenomenon. Over the next 25 years, the racial/ethnic differences between age cohorts are projected to

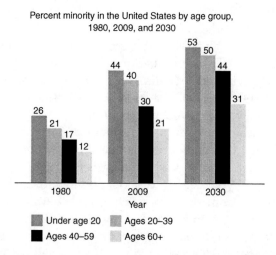

Percent minority in the United States by age group, 1980, 2009, and 2030

Under age 20 ▨ Ages 20–39
Ages 40–59 ■ Ages 60+

Note: Minorities include all racial and ethnic groups except non-Hispanic Whites.
From PRB analysis of data from U.S. Census Bureau, 1980 census, 2009 Population Estimates, National Population Projections, 2006.

(continued)

BOX 1.1   The New Generation Gap *Continued*

---

shrink somewhat as the number of minorities in older age groups increases. However, in 2030, roughly 69 percent of the population age 60 and older is still projected to be non-Hispanic White, distinguishing that age group from the younger generation.

Reference

1 Mark Mather, "The New Generation Gap" (2007), accessed at www.prb.org/Articles/2007/NewGenerationGap/aspx, on Jan. 13, 2011.

From Jacobsen, L. A., Mather, M., Lee, M., & Kent, M. (2011). America's aging population. *Population Bulletin* 66, No. 1, Box 1.

Characteristics of Older White, Black, and Latino Populations

How do older Blacks and Latinos compare to each other, and to older Whites, in terms of living arrangements, educational attainment, income, and health status? Similarities and differences in these characteristics across racial and ethnic groups offer clinically important clues to professionals about social, economic, and preexisting health-related circumstances faced by older adults from different racial and ethnic groups when they and their families seek treatment for memory and other cognitive problems.

Living Arrangements

Living arrangements, according to the U.S. Census definition, refer to persons (relatives or nonrelatives) who reside together in the same household. In the context of this book, living arrangements represent the immediate availability of family members, and patterns of living arrangements observed across racial and ethnic groups reflect the potential capacity of older adults to harness family members within their own household for support and ongoing care in the face of disabling conditions such as dementia. Figure 1.2 illustrates how older men and women from non-Hispanic White, Black, Hispanic, and Asian population groups compare in terms of their living arrangements. Results for older men are on the left-hand side of this figure, and results for women are on the right-hand side. Each bar represents a different population group as labeled, and the shadings in each bar refer to specific living arrangements as noted above the bars (e.g., lives with spouse, lives alone).

For all racial and ethnic groups, living arrangements of older adults reflect gender differences in marital status. Older men are more likely

FIGURE 1.2   Living Arrangements by Gender, Race, and Hispanic Origin, 2008

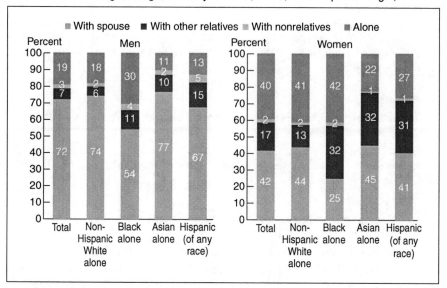

to be married, and therefore to live with spouses, than are older women because women have longer life expectancy and married older women are therefore more likely to outlive their spouses. Figure 1.2 clearly shows these gender differences in living arrangements. For all groups combined, 72% of older men but only 42% of older women lived with spouses in 2008; in contrast, only 19% of older men lived alone compared with 40% of older women. Regardless of racial and ethnic group, older women are more likely to live alone and less likely to live with a spouse.

Inspecting Figure 1.2 more carefully, it is evident that older Blacks show a unique pattern of living arrangements compared to older Whites and Hispanics. Thirty percent of older Black men live alone, which is much greater than for Whites (18%) or Hispanics (13%), whereas only 54% of older Black men live with a spouse compared to about 70% of older White and Hispanic men. Among older women, only 25% of older Black women live with a spouse, compared to 40%–45% for all other groups of older women. The reason for these substantial group differences is that Blacks are less likely to ever marry; therefore, they are less likely to have a spouse in older age regardless of gender-based differences in life expectancy. Census figures published elsewhere show that in 2009, 42% of Blacks aged 18 or older were "never married," compared with only 24% of Whites and 32% of Hispanics (U.S. Census Bureau, 2011).

Another important pattern of living arrangements found in Figure 1.2 is that Black and Hispanic men and women were more than twice as likely to live with other relatives compared to White men and women. The magnitude of differences is especially apparent among older women, where only 13% of older White women lived with other relatives, compared with 32% of older Black women and 31% of older Hispanic women. These figures suggest that older Blacks and Hispanics without spouses have a potentially stronger support system within their own households for emotional and physical support when living with chronic diseases such as Alzheimer's and other types of dementia. Of course, census figures can only reflect the availability of other family members within a household; determining the willingness and capability of these available family members to provide ongoing care and support to older relatives is directly related to the expertise of the professional. The clinically oriented chapters of this book are meant precisely to help treatment professionals achieve this expertise.

Educational Attainment

Attainment of higher levels of formal education is widely considered a common pathway toward higher income, better standard of living, and better health (Federal Interagency Forum, 2010). In the context of dementia care, level of educational attainment is also a key barometer of how well adults are likely to understand health-related information when they or their families seek treatment associated with memory-related concerns or already-diagnosed dementia. The topic of health literacy is gaining wider attention in the public health and medical sciences as a long-overlooked barrier to high-quality health care, and educational attainment is strongly related to health literacy for adults of any age and of any racial or ethnic background.

Older Americans today are more highly educated than ever before in U.S. history. In 1965, the year Medicare, Medicaid, and the Older Americans Act were all passed into law, only 24% of the U.S. older population had graduated from high school, and only 5% had at least a bachelor's degree. By 2008, these figures for the older population rose sharply to 77% with a high school education and 21% with at least an undergraduate college education (Federal Interagency Forum, 2010). All indications are that educational attainment levels will continue to rise for U.S. older adults as baby boomers join the ranks of the older population.

Despite this remarkable increase in educational attainment for older Americans over the past several decades, persistent differences

FIGURE 1.3 Educational Attainment of the U.S. Older Population, by Race and Hispanic Origin, 2008

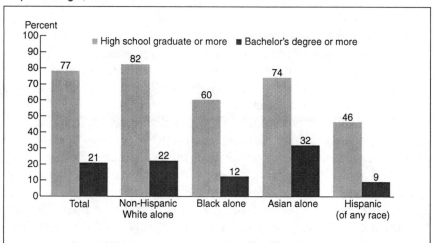

in educational attainment remain among racial and ethnic groups. As Figure 1.3 illustrates, in 2008 older Whites were much more likely to graduate from high school (82%) than were older Blacks (60%) or older Hispanics (46%). Older Whites (22%) were nearly twice as likely as Blacks (12%) and more than twice as likely as Hispanics (9%) to have a bachelor's degree or more education. These racial and ethnic disparities in educational attainment among older Americans may not be surprising given similar educational disparities in the younger population. However, for purposes of this book, it is important for the professional to determine the health literacy of older clients with the awareness that communication styles must be tailored to the level of understanding about dementia-related issues shown by Black and Latino individuals.

Income and Poverty Status

Racial and ethnic differences found in educational attainment carry over into differential income levels and poverty rates among older Whites, Blacks, and Hispanics. The Census Bureau publishes data on reported income for households headed by persons aged 65 and older (older households) and compares income levels across racial and ethnic groups. In 2008, the median income (an average based on the 50th percentile of all reported values) for all older households in the United States was $44,188. Older households headed by Whites had a median income of $46,720, which was considerably higher than $35,025 for Blacks and $33,418 for Hispanics. Poverty rates reported by the census showed even more striking group differences: 20% of Black older adults and 19.3% of Hispanic older adults were considered living at poverty level, compared to 7.6% for older White adults (U.S. Administration on Aging, 2009a, 2009b). These figures suggest that Black and Latino older clients may be less likely to have discretionary income for paid support services that are often purchased to supplement family care of older relatives with dementia. As discussed in Chapter 10, Medicaid insurance is intended for individuals of any age with lower income, and for older adults who are eligible for Medicaid and at risk for nursing home admission, there are home- and community-based services available in every state to help keep such disabled individuals at home.

Health and Disability Status

This section briefly compares and contrasts older Whites, Blacks, and Latinos on several global measures of health and disability as a way to provide population health profiles for Blacks and Latinos within which dementia may exist. Chapter 2 will discuss in detail racial and ethnic group similarities and differences in risk for and prevalence of Alzheimer's disease and other causes of dementia.

Chronic Health Conditions

On the basis of data from the 2007–2008 National Health Interview Survey, the most common chronic health conditions reported in the age 65 and older U.S. population are hypertension (56% of all older adults), arthritis (49.5%), heart disease (32%), any cancer (22.5%), and diabetes (19%). Older women were more likely to report arthritis and hypertension than older men, whereas older men reported higher levels of heart disease and cancer. Older Blacks were more likely than older Whites to report hypertension (71% vs. 54%) and diabetes (30% vs. 16%), whereas older Hispanics were also more likely to report diabetes than older Whites (27% for Hispanics). Not all disparities were in the direction of greater chronic condition prevalence for Blacks or Hispanics; older Whites were approximately twice as likely as both Blacks and Hispanics to report cancer (24%, 13%, and 12%, respectively), and older Hispanics were less likely to report arthritis (42%) than older Whites or Blacks (51% and 52%).

Self-Rated Health Status

Figure 1.4 summarizes results from the 2006–2008 National Health Interview Survey when older respondents were asked to rate their health as excellent, very good, good, fair, or poor. This is a widely used single-item measure of global self-rated health in national health

FIGURE 1.4 Respondent-Reported Good to Excellent Health Among the Population Age 65 and Older by Age Group, Race, and Hispanic Origin, 2006–2008

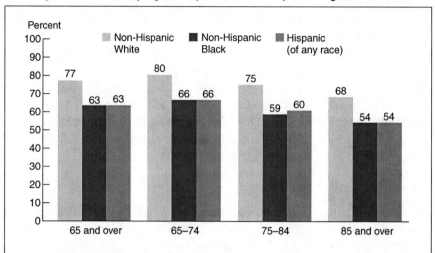

surveys and has been shown to be an independent predictor of mortality (DeSalvo, Bloser, Reynolds, He, & Muntner, 2006). In Figure 1.4, the combined percentages of respondents reporting their health as excellent, very good, or good are shown for different older age groups, and within each age group, responses are compared among Whites, Blacks, and Hispanics.

Results in Figure 1.4 indicate that, regardless of age group, Whites were more likely to report their health as excellent, very good, or good than Blacks and Hispanics. Overall, 77% of Whites and 63% of Blacks and Hispanics reported their health in this positive light. Percentages reporting positive health decreased with each succeeding older age group for all racial and ethnic groups, but the ethnic and racial differentials remained in favor of Whites within each age group.

Disability Status
Disability is measured most commonly by asking individuals if they have difficulty or need assistance performing personal care activities of daily living (ADL), such as bathing, dressing, and using the toilet, or instrumental activities of daily living (IADL), such as using the telephone, meal preparation, housework, shopping, and managing money. Another way to measure disability is to ask about difficulty performing physical functions, or to observe a person performing a physical function, such as stooping, reaching over one's head, lifting a weight, or grasping small objects. These types of questions have been asked in a variety of national surveys over the past few decades, allowing

researchers and policy makers the opportunity to determine whether and how disability rates in the middle-aged and older U.S. populations are changing over time.

For the older U.S. population as a whole, evidence from national surveys indicates that slightly smaller proportions report difficulty or inability to perform ADLs in more recent surveys than in surveys conducted longer ago (Federal Interagency Forum, 2010; Kramarow, Lubitz, Lentzner, & Gorina, 2007; Seeman, Merkin, Crimmins, & Karlamanglia, 2010). For example, results from the Medicare Current Beneficiary Survey (MCBS) show that the percentage of persons aged 65 and older reporting limitations in any ADL performance declined from 29.2% in 1992 to 25.5% in 2007 (Federal Interagency Forum, 2010). Limitations in IADL performance from the MCBS did not show any decline, but rather remained quite steady over this time period. More detailed analyses from the National Health and Nutrition Examination Surveys (NHANES), comparing disability trends between 1988–1994 and 1999–2004 in different age groups of the older population, suggest that the most significant declines in disability have occurred among Americans in their 80s and older, particularly in disability measures of mobility and functional limitations (ADL and IADL levels remained steady; Seeman et al., 2010).

Evidence is mixed regarding racial and ethnic group differences in disability rates in the older population. Data from the Hispanic Established Population for Epidemiologic Studies of the Elderly in the 1990s, as well as from the 2000 U.S. Census disability module, indicate a persistent pattern whereby older Hispanics reported more ADL disability than non-Hispanic Whites (Markides, Eschbach, Ray, & Peek, 2007). Results from the 2007 MCBS show that, among men aged 65 and older, 25.6% of Blacks reported an inability to perform physical functions such as stooping and reaching over their heads, compared with 20% of Hispanics and 19% of Whites. No racial and ethnic differences were found in such disability among older women, although disability rates were considerably higher among women than among men across all three racial and ethnic groups (33%–35%; Federal Interagency Forum, 2010). In a recent national study of Americans aged 65 and older based on data from the Health and Retirement Survey, Dunlop and colleagues examined racial and ethnic differences in the development of disability over 6 years (1998–2004) in persons who were disability free at the start of the study period. They found that Blacks and Hispanics who were interviewed in Spanish were more likely to develop disability than were Whites or Hispanics interviewed in English; these group differences were reduced after adjusting results for socioeconomic status of study participants, but Blacks and Spanish-language Hispanics were still more likely to develop disabilities (Dunlop, Song, Manheim, Deviglus, & Chang, 2007). Given this wide array of conflicting findings, more study with data from more recent time periods is required to help us more clearly understand the extent to which Blacks, Hispanics, and Whites compare on multiple levels of disability in later life.

Finally, there are troubling signs that disability rates in the middle-aged U.S. population are rising in recent years. In a recent study based on data from the National Health Interview Survey, significant increases between 1997 and 2007 were found in adults aged 50 to 64 in the proportion reporting needing help with ADL and several physical functions, particularly those activities and functions related to mobility limitations. Respondents in this survey were asked about health problems contributing to these disabilities, and back or neck problems, diabetes, and depression or other emotional problems showed the greatest increases as causes of disabilities between 1997 and 2007 (Martin, Freedman, Schoeni, & Andreski, 2010). While this study did not examine racial and ethnic differences, these findings are quite sobering because this is the age group that today represents the leading edge of baby boomers entering the ranks of the 65 and older U.S. population. Another study based on NHANES survey data found significant increases in disability among respondents aged 60 to 69 years between 1988–1994 and 1999–2004; Blacks in this age group reported greater disability increases over time than did Whites or Hispanics (Seeman et al., 2010). Taken together, these studies indicate that future cohorts of older adults may carry a higher disability burden than today's older population, and also that any racial and ethnic group health disparities found in earlier adulthood could yield greater and clearer health and disability-related differences among Whites, Blacks, and Hispanics in older age. These future trends could directly affect dementia care over the next several decades because, as Chapter 2 discusses, the risk for different types of dementia in later life has been associated with poorer health status earlier in life.

Demographic, Social, and Economic Trends in the Black and Latino Populations

This section highlights the diversity of nationalities that make up America's Black and Latino populations, as well as related social and economic trends in these populations, to raise awareness of the characteristics and circumstances of individuals and families that might provide care to older Black and Latino relatives with dementia.

U.S. Black Population

Composition and Geographic Location in the United States

Results from the 2010 U.S. Census reveal that nearly 38.9 million persons reported their race as "Black or African American" on the Census form, representing 12.6% of the total U.S. population in 2010 (Humes, Jones, & Ramirez, 2011). The size of the Black population grew by 12.3% between 2000 and 2010, slightly more than the growth of the total U.S. population in that period (9.7%).

The vast majority of Blacks in the U.S. population were born in the United States (nearly 94%). Among foreign-born Blacks, 59% were born in the Caribbean region, 24% in African countries, and 13% from Central and South America (Institute of Medicine, 2009).

While Blacks live in every state of the United States, more than 40% of all U.S. Blacks live in just six states—New York, Florida, Georgia, Texas, California, and Illinois. In 2004, states with the largest proportion of Blacks were Mississippi (37%), Louisiana (33%), South Carolina, Georgia, and Maryland (29% each); in the District of Columbia, 58% of the population was Black in 2004 (U.S. Census Bureau, 2007).

Social and Economic Characteristics

Trends in marital status in the total adult Black population are highly consistent with those found in the older population. More than 40% (43%) of Blacks aged 15 and older report never being married, a figure nearly twice the proportion of Whites never married (24%); marriage rates for Blacks and Whites are 34% and 57%, respectively (U.S. Census Bureau, 2007). One important implication of these marital status trends for family dementia care is that Black adult children who provide care to a parent with dementia are themselves less likely to have a spouse available for emotional support or to perform other family-related responsibilities while they care for their parent, than are White adult children who care for parents with dementia.

Finally, educational attainment and financial security disparities persist between adult Blacks and Whites in the United States. Disparities are found at the extremes of formal educational attainment. In 2009, in the population aged 25 and older, Blacks were less likely than Whites to finish high school (18% vs. 10% did not graduate high school) or to graduate from college (18% vs. 31% graduated from college; Pew Hispanic Center, 2011a). Similar proportions of Whites and Blacks were high school graduates and had some college. Financial security can be determined in a number of ways; here, we compare median household income and poverty rates. In 2009, the median income for U.S. households headed by Blacks was $33,500, compared to $55,000 for households headed by Whites. Poverty rates reflect these household income differences; 26% of Blacks lived at or below the federal poverty level compared to 10% of Whites (Pew Hispanic Center, 2011a).

U.S. Latino Population

Composition and Geographic Location in the United States
Results from the 2010 U.S. Census reveal that nearly 50.5 million persons reported their ethnic origin as "Hispanic, Latino, or Spanish" on the Census form, representing 16.3% of the total U.S. population in 2010 (Humes et al., 2011). The size of the Latino population grew by a remarkable 43% between 2000 and 2010, a growth rate matched only by those reporting their race as "Asian," which grew by the same amount over the decade to a total of 14.7 million.

Within the Hispanic U.S. population, there are many nationalities. By far the largest is Mexican; 31.8 million persons in the 2010 Census reported their origin as Mexican, representing nearly two-thirds (64%) of all Hispanics in the United States. The other larger nationality groups in the Hispanic population according to the 2010 Census include Puerto Rican (4.6 million), Cuban (1.8 million), Salvadoran (1.6 million), and Dominican (1.4 million). All of these groups grew in size by a substantial amount between 2000 and 2010, ranging from 36% for Puerto Ricans to 152% for Salvadorans (Ennis, Rios-Vargas, & Albert, 2011). These population trends strongly suggest that the 21st century will continue to witness a rapid growth and a broadening ethnic diversity in the U.S. Hispanic population, which will be reflected in the families who seek professional help for relatives with dementia.

Although Hispanics lived in all states, their geographic distribution by state was actually quite concentrated. California (28% of all Hispanics lived there) and Texas (19%) together accounted for nearly half of all Hispanics in the 2010 Census, followed by Florida (8.4%), New York (6.8%), and Illinois (4%). Different Hispanic nationality groups were concentrated in different states: Mexicans primarily in California, Texas, Arizona, and Illinois; Puerto Ricans in New York, Florida, New Jersey, and Pennsylvania; and Cubans overwhelmingly in Florida (Ennis et al., 2011). Put another way, Mexicans were most concentrated in the West and Southwest, Puerto Ricans in the Northeast and Florida, and Cubans in Florida.

Other key characteristics related to population composition of Hispanics are age and nativity status. In 2009, the median age of Hispanics was 27 years, compared to 36 years for the total U.S. population. While Mexicans and Puerto Ricans have a median age similar to all Hispanics combined (25 and 28, respectively), Cubans are a much older population, with an average age of 40. These three largest nationality groups within the U.S. Hispanic population also show variations in nativity status, which refers to whether they were born in or outside of the United States. More than one-third of Mexicans in 2009 were foreign born (36%), compared to 59% of Cubans. Puerto Ricans differ from other Hispanic nationalities in terms of nativity status because people born in Puerto Rico are considered native born and are U.S. citizens by birth. About two-thirds of Puerto Ricans in the United States in 2009 were born in the United States, and one-third were born in Puerto Rico (Pew Hispanic Center, 2011b, 2011c, 2011d).

This special citizenship status for Puerto Ricans has potentially important implications for family care of an older relative with dementia because both family caregivers and persons with dementia can travel freely from the U.S. mainland to Puerto Rico without immigration concerns. In the authors' experience working with families of Puerto Rican heritage, adult children or other relatives of persons with dementia often share caregiving responsibilities between the U.S. mainland and the island of Puerto Rico, often by transporting their older relative from one location to another twice a year. Although convenient for caregivers, disorientation associated with moving from one environment to another can be challenging for the person with dementia. For Hispanic families from other countries, immigration- and citizenship-related concerns can often overshadow dementia caregiving issues. Later chapters in this book discuss these nativity- and citizenship-related issues from a clinical perspective along with implications for professional work with Hispanic families.

Social and Economic Characteristics
Nearly two-thirds (63%) of Hispanics in the United States in 2009 reported speaking English proficiently. English proficiency varies widely among the largest Hispanic nationality groups: Puerto Ricans (81%) are most likely to speak English proficiently, compared to 63% of Mexicans and 58% of Cubans (Pew Hispanic Center, 2011b, 2011c, 2011d). The importance of verbal communication between professionals and families in dementia care cannot be overstated; therefore, professionals must be prepared to provide language translation services for Hispanic families and persons with dementia during professional visits to discuss dementia-related issues when English is not spoken proficiently.

Trends in marital status for the Hispanic population ages 18 and older indicate that they are less likely than Whites to be currently married, and more likely than Whites to be never married. Current marriage rates also vary by Hispanic nationality: 47% of Mexicans, 37% of Puerto Ricans, and 49% of Cubans were currently married in 2009; this compares to 56% of Whites (Pew Hispanic Center, 2011a, 2011b, 2011c, 2011d).

Disparities in educational attainment between U.S. Hispanics and Whites aged 25 and older are quite striking, with foreign-born Hispanics showing much less educational attainment than their native-born counterparts. Based on 2009 figures, fully 39% of all Hispanics did not complete high school, including 52% of foreign-born Hispanics and 22% of native-born Hispanics (compared to 10% of Whites). Thirteen percent of Hispanics graduated college, including 17% of native-born Hispanics, compared to 31% of Whites and 18% of Blacks (Pew Hispanic Center, 2011a). Within the Hispanic population, Mexicans have lower levels and Puerto Ricans and Cubans have higher levels of education than the Hispanic population as a whole (Pew Hispanic Center, 2011a, 2011b, 2011c). These formal educational disparities amplify the language barriers noted earlier, further raising the likelihood that health literacy among Hispanics may relatively low.

Finally, measures of financial security reveal that the median household income for Hispanics in 2009 was $40,000 compared to $55,000 for Whites and $33,500 for Blacks. Foreign-born Hispanic households had lower median incomes than native-born Hispanic households, but not by a large margin, and both exceeded that for Black households ($37,200 and $44,000, for foreign-born and native-born, respectively). Poverty rates for native- and foreign-born Hispanics were nearly identical at 23%, compared to 10% for Whites and 25% for Blacks (Pew Hispanic Center, 2011a). Mexicans and Puerto Ricans had poverty rates similar to the total Hispanic population (24%), while Cubans were less likely to live below the poverty level (15%; Pew Hispanic Center, 2011b, 2011c, 2011d).

FAMILY CAREGIVING FOR OLDER ADULTS

Prevalence, Circumstances, and Consequences in Ethnically Diverse Families

This section addresses the questions: Who are the individuals in America's families providing care to relatives with physical and mental health problems? What kinds of and how much care do families provide, and how does caregiving affect their own health and well-being? What types of interventions to help to family caregivers have been designed and tested? What do we know about these caregiving issues in Black and Latino families? Wherever possible, findings related to caregiving for individuals with Alzheimer's disease and other dementia are highlighted.

Family Caregiving Prevalence and Circumstances

The most recent national family caregiver survey with available results was conducted in 2009; this survey oversampled Black and Hispanic family members caring for relatives aged 18 or older with acute or chronic illnesses and disabilities, and also offered a Spanish-language version of the telephone interview. The total sample size in this survey was 1,480 and the racial and ethnic composition was 72% White, 13% Black, and 12% Hispanic (National Alliance for Caregiving [NAC] & AARP, 2009). A second, independent survey was conducted in 2008 of exclusively Hispanic family caregivers; English- or Spanish-language interviews were offered in this national telephone survey (Evercare & NAC, 2008). Together these two national surveys provide a current portrait of family caregivers in the United States with detailed information about Black and Hispanic caregivers. The Alzheimer's Association, a national advocacy organization that supports research to learn more about Alzheimer's disease and services to support family caregivers, recently published results of analyses conducted on responses from caregivers in the NAC and AARP survey who reported that they cared for a relative 50 years or older, or who reported caring for a relative with Alzheimer's disease or other dementia (Alzheimer's Association, 2011).

Caregiving within American households is quite common. In 2009, there were an estimated 36.5 million U.S. households in which caregiving took place for adults (someone "provided unpaid care to a relative or friend 18 years or older to help them take care of themselves") or for children with special needs (someone provided "unpaid care to any child under the age of 18 because of a medical, behavioral, or other condition or disability"). This translates into 31.2% of all U.S. households where caregiving took place in 2009. The highest prevalence of caregiving occurred in Hispanic households (36%), followed by Black (33%) and White (30%) households. Most caregiving was in the adult category, including 28 million households where adult-only caregiving occurred, plus 6.3 million where both adult and child caregiving occurred. In the vast majority of households (86%), unpaid care was provided to family members; friends received care in 11% of households (NAC & AARP, 2009).

Care recipients were most likely to be aged 75 or older (44% of all care recipients), and this is also the age group where Alzheimer's disease is most likely to occur compared to younger age groups. Compared to a similar survey conducted in 2004, the proportion of care recipients aged 75 and older rose in 2009, from 43% to 51% of all adult care recipients. An additional 28% of all care recipients were aged 50 to 74 years; therefore, of all individuals receiving unpaid care, 72% were aged 50 or older (NAC & AARP, 2009).

Given the topic of this book, it is important to point out that Alzheimer's disease or mental confusion was mentioned as a care recipient health problem by 22% of all caregivers, including 25% of Whites, 16% of Hispanics, and 14% of Blacks in the 2009 NAC and AARP study. A wide variety of other health problems were reported among care recipients, but in the 50-years-and-older care recipient group, the most frequently mentioned "main problem requiring care" was a tie between "Alzheimer's, dementia, and forgetfulness" and "old age" (15% each; NAC & AARP, 2009). Among caregivers in this study with relatives aged 60 or older, 32% said that Alzheimer's disease or other dementia was either the main problem or a secondary problem they cared for. Based on these latter results, the national Alzheimer's Association estimated that 10.9 million Americans provide unpaid care for a family member with Alzheimer's disease or other dementia in 2009 (Alzheimer's Association, 2010).

Comparisons between caregivers of persons with Alzheimer's disease and caregivers of other older adults in this study reveal that dementia caregivers are more likely to provide hands-on assistance with all personal care ADL. As Figure 1.5 illustrates, more than 30% of dementia caregivers provided help with every ADL shown, including 54% who helped with getting in and out of bed. Dementia caregivers were nearly twice as likely as caregivers to older adults without dementia to manage incontinence and diapers (31% vs. 16%) and more than twice as likely to help with feeding (31% vs. 14%). Additional tasks done by dementia caregivers more often included advocating for their care recipient with government agencies and service providers, and arranging and supervising paid caregivers from community agencies. Dementia caregivers also reported providing care for a longer period of time than their counterparts who provide care to older adults for other medical conditions (Alzheimer's Association, 2011).

Racial and ethnic group comparisons of caregiving circumstances reveal important differences that reflect differences in the larger populations discussed earlier in this chapter. Although the proportion of caregivers who were female was similar across all three groups (66%–70%), Black and Hispanic caregivers were considerably younger than Whites. The average age for all caregivers was 48 years (51 years for dementia caregivers); corresponding average ages for each racial and ethnic group were 42 for Hispanics, 44 for Blacks, and 50 for Whites. Black and Hispanic caregivers were much more likely to report caring for an unmarried person than were Whites, due in part to lower marriage rates among Blacks and Hispanics throughout the life course. The living arrangements of Black and Hispanic care recipients demonstrated the greater role of extended families in within-household caregiving circumstances than among Whites; the proportion of households where the care recipient lives with family members *other than* spouses or adult children was only 8% for Whites, compared to 31% for Blacks and 25% for Hispanics. Moreover, among family caregivers who live in

FIGURE 1.5 Proportion of Caregivers of People With Alzheimer's or Other Dementia Versus Caregivers of Other Older People Who Provide Help With Specific Activities of Daily Living, United States, 2009

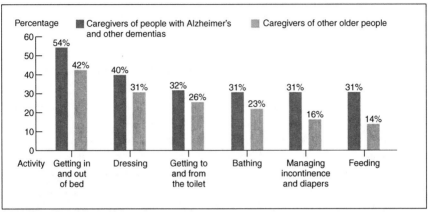

From Alzheimer's Association, 2011, p. 27.

a different household than the care recipient, more than 70% of Blacks and Hispanics reported visiting more than once a week, compared to 56% of Whites. Blacks and Hispanics reported spending more time each week providing care than Whites (25 hours, 27 hours, and 18 hours on average, respectively; NAC & AARP, 2009); this finding of greater involvement by Hispanic caregivers also was found in an independent national study (Evercare & NAC, 2008). Taken together, these findings portray Blacks and Hispanics as more highly engaged than Whites with nonspouse caregiving within households, and more involved in the care of family members who do not live in the same household.

Looking more specifically at caregivers to adults aged 50 and above in this national study, Black and Hispanic caregivers were in lower income categories than were Whites, Blacks were more likely than any other group to provide assistance with three or more ADL, and Hispanics were more likely than any other group to be a primary caregiver (Alzheimer's Association, 2011). These racial and ethnic group differences in caregiving circumstances mirror those found in numerous, more geographically limited, studies of family caregivers to older adults (Pinquart & Sorenson, 2005).

Health-Related Consequences of Caregiving

Widely known among clinical professionals and researchers is that caring for a family member with any physical or mental health problem over an extended period of time leads to negative psychological and physical health consequences for family caregivers. In the gerontological literature, the stress and coping process model has been the predominant framework used to better understand caregiving consequences, and dementia caregivers are by far the most frequently studied among all caregivers to older adults (Fortinsky, 2001; Pearlin et al., 1990; Sorenson & Pinquart, 2005). Therefore, the vast majority of knowledge about health-related consequences of family caregiving to older adults with disabilities derives from the literature on dementia care.

Family members responsible for managing dementia symptoms, which can include memory loss, impaired judgment, repetitive questioning, wandering, agitation, and incontinence, are themselves highly susceptible to health-related declines. Because the trajectory and accumulation of these symptoms vary widely among individuals, there is a tremendous amount of uncertainty among family caregivers about when to seek help to determine a diagnosis, and to discuss prognosis and treatment options (Fortinsky, 2008). The most frequently observed psychological health consequences associated with dementia caregiving are burden, depression and other mood disorders, and self-rated health; positive psychological consequences of caregiving are less studied, and include self-efficacy, uplifts, and spirituality (Dilworth-Anderson, Williams, & Gibson, 2002; Sorenson & Pinquart, 2005; Tremont, Davis, Bishop, & Fortinsky, 2008). Physical and physiological health consequences include increased respiratory and cardiovascular symptoms, increased stress-related hormones, and reduced immune function (Alzheimer's Association, 2011; Vitaliano, Zhang, & Scanlan, 2003). Spouses caring for loved ones with dementia have been found to have higher mortality rates than noncaregiving spouses (Schulz & Beach, 1999), and a recent literature review lends partial support to the hypothesis that caregiving can lead spouses to develop cognitive impairment or dementia due to the accumulation of numerous other psychological and physical health problems (Vitaliano, Murphy, Young, Echeverria, & Borson, 2011).

Racial and ethnic group differences have been observed in caregiving consequences among family caregivers generally, and for dementia caregivers specifically. Hispanic caregivers are more likely to report that their health is "fair" or "poor" (27%) than Black or White caregivers (15%). Black caregivers (21%) are less likely than Hispanics (35%) or Whites (32%) to rate their caregiving experience as "highly stressful," despite a greater likelihood of providing personal care as noted earlier (NAC & AARP, 2009). Black caregivers are also less likely to report burden and depressive symptoms, and Hispanic caregivers more likely to report depressive symptoms than White caregivers. These findings are more remarkable because Black and Hispanic caregivers tend to report more physical health problems than White caregivers (Pinquart & Sorenson, 2005). In terms of positive consequences, Black caregivers also are more likely than other racial and ethnic groups to appraise their caregiving situation in positive ways such as gaining more spiritual strength from the experience, and Black and Hispanic caregivers are more likely than Whites to perceive more uplifts from caregiving (Dilworth-Anderson et al., 2002; Pinquart & Sorenson, 2005). Hispanic caregivers are more likely than non-Hispanics to feel fulfilled in their caregiving role, and to report that their social life outside caregiving remains satisfactory (Evercare & NAC, 2008).

These findings portray a complex set of caregiving consequences, but there is little doubt that substantial proportions of family caregivers experience negative health-related consequences of their caregiving roles. Dementia caregiving offers additional stressors due to the symptoms associated with the dementia disease process (detailed in Chapter 2). Finally, Blacks and Latinos appear to derive more negative and also more positive consequences of caregiving than Whites.

Research on Interventions to Help Dementia Family Caregivers

A large amount of research has been conducted since the 1980s to test ways to help family caregivers of older relatives with dementia provide more effective care and preserve their own health and well-being. Several types of interventions have been designed and tested: (1) *psychoeducational* interventions are individualized or group programs led by professionals with specialized training that provide information about the Alzheimer's disease or other dementia disease process, skill-building approaches to more effectively respond to dementia symptoms, and supportive resources and services in the local community; (2) *supportive* interventions are group programs that focus on building peer-support among group participants by creating a comfortable setting to discuss successes and challenges of caregiving, and are led by either peers or professionals; (3) *psychotherapy* interventions are individualized programs guided by trained therapy professionals and offer more structured problem solving, emotion management, and time management skill training; and (4) *multicomponent* interventions that combine two or more of the other approaches, often with a technology component, and are led by skilled professionals (Alzheimer's Association, 2011; Sorenson, Pinquart, & Duberstein, 2002).

Many family caregiver interventions have been found to demonstrate small- to medium-sized positive effects on a wide range of psychological and physical health outcomes, while a smaller number have demonstrated reduced hospitalizations and nursing home admissions of care receivers when their caregivers receive the intervention. Psychoeducational and multicomponent interventions have been particularly effective when they are individually tailored to caregiver needs and offered for longer duration, usually 6 months or more (Belle et al., 2006; Gitlin et al., 2003; Gitlin, Winter, Dennis, Hodgson, & Hauck, 2010; Mittelman, Haley, Clay, & Roth, 2006; Mittelman, Roth, Coon, & Haley, 2004; Nichols et al., 2008; Nichols, Martindale-Adams, Burns, Graney, & Zuber, 2011; Teri, McCurry, Logsdon, & Gibbons, 2005). Supportive programs also have been found to be effective (Hepburn, Tornatore, Center, & Ostwald, 2001; Ostwald, Hepburn, Caron, Burns, & Mantell, 1999). Variations on these types of family caregiver interventions have been tested and found effective, including psychoeducational interventions with both caregivers and their relatives with dementia, or dyads (Whitlatch, Judge, Zarit, & Femia, 2006), telephone-delivered interventions with caregivers (Tremont et al., 2008), and interventions that link primary care practitioners with social workers and/or nurses to provide multicomponent interventions with family caregivers (Bass, Clark, Looman, McCarthy, & Eckert, 2003; Callahan et al., 2006; Fortinsky, Kulldorff, Kleppinger, & Kenyon-Pesce, 2009; Fortinsky, Unson, & Garcia, 2002; Vickrey et al., 2006).

Of all these interventions found to be successful as research projects, the one that featured a racially and ethnically diverse group of caregivers and reported on intervention effects on Black, Hispanic, and White caregivers was known as REACH II. This multicomponent intervention, carried out as a randomized, controlled trial, involved baseline caregiver risk appraisal to determine risk for depression, burden, neglecting self-care and healthy behaviors, social support unavailability, and poor response to their relatives' problem behaviors. The 6-month intervention was offered in English or Spanish; intervention components included didactic instruction, role playing, problem solving, stress management techniques, and telephone support groups with other study participants. Compared with minimal support (i.e., the control group), intervention participation led to greater improvements in depression, burden, social support, self-care, and response to problem behaviors in care recipients, for Hispanic, White, and Black spouse (but not other Black) caregivers (Belle et al., 2006).

Despite promising research results in many of these family caregiver intervention studies, to date few of these tested programs have been translated into permanent service programs available to family caregivers on a widespread basis. The most noteworthy exception to this trend is that the U.S. Administration on Aging has encouraged individual states to begin adapting selected interventions from this research project inventory into local communities. These family caregiver support program initiatives by the Administration on Aging are explained in more detail in Chapter 9. On a concluding note, much more remains to be learned about how family caregivers from different racial and ethnic groups will accept the types of interventions tested in research environments. In particular, more work is needed to determine how best to tailor family caregiving interventions to conform to the social and cultural contexts within which different racial and ethnic group families provide care to their older relatives with dementia. Social work professionals are well-positioned to help build on the successes and limitations of existing interventions designed to help dementia family caregivers.

REFERENCES

Alzheimer's Association. (2010). *2010 Alzheimer's disease facts and figures.* Chicago, IL: Author.

Alzheimer's Association. (2011). *2011 Alzheimer's disease facts and figures.* Chicago, IL: Author.

Bass, D. M., Clark, P. A., Looman, W. J., McCarthy, C. A., & Eckert, S. (2003). The Cleveland Alzheimer's managed care demonstration: Outcomes after 12 months of implementation. *The Gerontologist, 43,* 73–85.

Belle S. H., Burgio, L., Burns, R., Coon, D., Czaja, S., Gallagher-Thompson, D., et al. (2006). Enhancing the quality of life of dementia caregivers from different ethnic or racial groups. A randomized, controlled trial. *Annals of Internal Medicine, 145,* 727–738.

Callahan, C. M., Boustani, M. A., Unverzagt, F. W., Austrom, M. G., Damush, T. M., Perkins, A. J., et al. (2006). Effectiveness of collaborative care for older adults with Alzheimer disease in primary care: A randomized controlled trial. *Journal of the American Medical Association, 295,* 2148–2157.

DeSalvo, K. B., Bloser, N., Reynolds, K., He, J., & Muntner, P. (2006). Mortality prediction with a single general self-rated health question. *Journal of General Internal Medicine, 21,* 267–275.

Dilworth-Anderson, P., Williams, I. C., & Gibson, B. E. (2002). Issues of race, ethnicity, and culture in caregiving research: A 20-year review (1980–2000). *The Gerontologist, 42,* 237–272.

Dunlop, D. D., Song, J., Manheim, L. M., Deviglus, M. L., & Chang, R. W. (2007). Racial/ethnic differences in the development of disability among older adults. *American Journal of Public Health, 97,* 2209–2215.

Ennis, S. R., Rios-Vargas, M., & Albert, M. G. (2011). *The Hispanic population 2010: 2010 census briefs.* Report No. C2010BR-04. Washington, DC: U.S. Census Bureau, U.S. Department of Commerce.

Evercare and the National Alliance for Caregiving. (2008). *Hispanic family caregiving in the U.S.* Received February 17, 2011, from http://www.caregiving.org/data/Hispanic_Caregiver_Study_web_ENG_FINAL_11_04_08.pdf

Federal Interagency Forum on Aging-Related Statistics. (2010). *Older Americans 2010: Key indicators of well-being. Federal interagency forum on aging-related statistics.* Washington, DC: U.S. Government Printing Office.

Fortinsky, R. H. (2001). Health care triads and dementia care: Integrative framework and future directions. *Aging & Mental Health, 5*(Suppl. 1), S35–S48.

Fortinsky, R. H. (2008). Diagnosis and early support. In M. Downs & B. Bowers (Eds.), *Excellence in dementia care: Principles and practices* (pp. 267–284). Maidenhead, UK: Open University Press/McGraw-Hill.

Fortinsky, R. H., Kulldorff, M., Kleppinger, A., & Kenyon-Pesce, L. (2009). Dementia care consultation for family caregivers: Collaborative model linking an Alzheimer's Association chapter with primary care physicians. *Aging & Mental Health, 13,* 162–170.

Fortinsky, R. H., Unson, C., & Garcia, R. I. (2002). Helping family caregivers by linking primary care physicians with community-based dementia care services: The Alzheimer's Service Coordination Program. *Dementia: The International Journal of Social Research and Practice, 1,* 227–240.

Gitlin, L. N., Belle, S. H., Burgio, L. D., Czaja, S. J., Mahoney, D., Gallagher-Thompson, D., et al. (2003). Effect of multicomponent interventions on caregiver burden and depression: The REACH multisite initiative at 6-month follow-up. *Psychology of Aging, 18,* 361–374.

Gitlin, L. N., Winter, L., Dennis, M. P., Hodgson, N., & Hauck, W. W. (2010). A biobehavioral home-based intervention and the well-being of patients with dementia and their caregivers: The COPE randomized trial. *Journal of the American Medical Association, 304,* 983–991.

Hepburn, K. W., Tornatore, J., Center, B., & Ostwald, S. W. (2001). Dementia family caregiver training: Affecting beliefs about caregiving and caregiver outcomes. *Journal of the American Geriatrics Society, 49,* 450–457.

Howden, L. M., & Meyer, J. A. (2011). *Age and sex composition 2010: 2010 Census Briefs.* Report No. C2010BR-03. Washington, DC: U.S. Census Bureau, U.S. Department of Commerce.

Humes, K. R., Jones, N. A., & Ramirez, R. R. (2011). *Overview of race and Hispanic origin: 2010. 2010 Census Briefs.* Report No. C2010BR-02. Washington, DC: U.S. Census Bureau, U.S. Department of Commerce.

Institute of Medicine (IOM). (2009). *Race, ethnicity, and language data: Standardization for health care quality improvement.* Washington, DC: The National Academies Press.

Jacobsen, L. A., Mather, M., Lee, M., & Kent, M. (2011). America's aging population. *Population Bulletin 66,* no. 1, Table 2.

Kramarow, E., Lubitz, J., Lentzner, H., & Gorina, Y. (2007). Trends in the health of older Americans. *Health Affairs, 26,* 1417–1425.

Markides, K. S., Eschbach, K., Ray, L. A., & Peek, M. K. (2007). Census disability rates among older people by race/ethnicity and type of Hispanic origin. In J. L. Angel & K. E. Whitfield (Eds.), *The health of aging Hispanics: The Mexican-origin population* (pp. 26–39). New York: Springer Publications.

Martin, L. G., Freedman, V. A., Schoeni, R. F., & Andreski, P. M. (2010). Trends in disability and related chronic conditions among people ages fifty to sixty-four. *Health Affairs, 29,* 725–731.

Mittelman, M. S., Haley, W. E., Clay, O. J., & Roth, D. L. (2006). Improving caregiver wellness delays nursing home placement of patients with Alzheimer's disease. *Neurology, 67,* 1592–1599.

Mittelman, M. S., Roth, D. L., Coon, D. W., & Haley, W. E. (2004). Sustained benefits of supportive intervention for depressive symptoms in caregivers of patients with Alzheimer's disease. *American Journal of Psychiatry, 161,* 850–856.

National Alliance for Caregiving & AARP. (2009). *Caregiving in the U.S. 2009.* Retrieved May 31, 2011, from http://www.caregiving.org/data/Caregiving_in_the_US_2009_full_report.pdf

Nichols, L. O., Chang, C., Lummus, A., Burns, R., Martindale-Adams, J., Graney, M. J., et al. (2008). The cost-effectiveness of a behavior intervention with caregivers of patients with Alzheimer's disease. *Journal of the American Geriatrics Society, 56,* 413–420.

Nichols, L. O., Martindale-Adams, J., Burns, R., Graney, M. J., & Zuber, J. (2011). Translation of a dementia caregiver support program in a health care system—REACH VA. *Archives of Internal Medicine, 171,* 353–359.

Ostwald, S. K., Hepburn, K. W., Caron, W., Burns, T., & Mantell, R. (1999). Reducing caregiver burden: A randomized psychoeducational intervention for caregivers of persons with dementia. *The Gerontologist, 39,* 299–309.

Pew Hispanic Center. (2011a). *Statistical portrait of Hispanics in the United States, 2009.* Washington, DC: Pew Research Center.

Pew Hispanic Center. (2011b). *Statistical profile: Hispanics of Mexican origin in the United States, 2009.* Washington, DC: Pew Research Center.

Pew Hispanic Center. (2011c). *Statistical profile: Hispanics of Puerto Rican origin in the United States, 2009.* Washington, DC: Pew Research Center.

Pew Hispanic Center. (2011d). *Statistical profile: Hispanics of Cuban origin in the United States, 2009.* Washington, DC: Pew Research Center.

Pinquart, M., & Sorenson, S. (2005). Ethnic differences in stressors, resources, and psychological outcomes of family caregiving: A meta-analysis. *The Gerontologist, 45,* 90–106.

Schulz, R., & Beach, S. R. (1999). Caregiving as a risk factor for mortality. *Journal of the American Medical Association, 282,* 2215–2219.

Seeman, T. E., Merkin, S. S., Crimmins, E. M., & Karlamanglia, A. S. (2010). Disability trends among older Americans: National Health and Nutrition Examination Surveys, 1988–1994 and 1999–2004. *American Journal of Public Health, 100,* 100–107.

Sorenson, S., Pinquart, M., & Duberstein, P. (2002). How effective are interventions with caregivers? An updated meta-analysis. *The Gerontologist, 42,* 356–372.

Teri, L., McCurry, S. M., Logsdon, R. G., & Gibbons, L. E. (2005). Training community consultants to help family members improve dementia care: A randomized controlled trial. *The Gerontologist, 45,* 802–811.

Tremont, G., Davis, J. D., Bishop, D. S., & Fortinsky, R. H. (2008). Telephone-delivered psychosocial intervention reduces burden in dementia caregivers. *Dementia: The International Journal of Social Research and Practice, 7,* 503–520.

U.S. Administration on Aging. (2009a). *A statistical profile of Black older Americans aged 65+.* Retrieved June 2, 2011, from http://www.aoa.gov/AoARoot/Aging_Statistics/minority_aging/Facts-on-Black-Elderly2009-plain_format.aspx

U.S. Administration on Aging. (2009b). *A statistical profile on Hispanic older Americans aged 65+.* Retrieved June 2, 2011, from http://www.aoa.gov/AoAroot/Aging_Statistics/minority_aging/Facts-on-Hispanic-Elderly-2008.aspx

U.S. Census Bureau. (2007). *The American community—Blacks: 2004.* Report ACS-04. Washington, DC: U.S. Department of Commerce.

U.S. Census Bureau. (2011). *The 2011 statistical abstract of the United States.* Table 56. Retrieved June 5, 2011, from http://www.census.gov/compendia/statab/2011/tables/11s0056.pdf

Vickrey, B. G., Mittman, B. S., Connor, K. I., Pearson, M. L., Della Penna, R. D., Ganiats, T. G., et al. (2006). The effect of a disease management intervention on quality and outcomes of dementia care: A randomized controlled trial. *Annals of Internal Medicine, 145,* 713–726.

Vitaliano, P. P., Murphy, M., Young, H. M., Echeverria, D., & Borson, S. (2011). Does caring for a spouse with dementia promote cognitive decline? A hypothesis and proposed mechanisms. *Journal of the American Geriatrics Society, 59,* 900–908.

Vitaliano, P. P., Zhang, J., & Scanlan, J. M. (2003). Is caregiving hazardous to one's physical health? A meta-analysis. *Psychological Bulletin, 129,* 946–972.
Whitlatch, C. J., Judge, K., Zarit, S. H., & Femia, E. (2006). Dyadic intervention for family caregivers and care receivers in early-stage dementia. *The Gerontologist, 46,* 688–694.

Online Access References With Websites

For marital status by race citation: U.S. Census Bureau. (2011). *The 2011 statistical abstract of the United States.* Table 56. Retrieved June 5, 2011, from http://www.census.gov/compendia/statab/2011/tables/11s0056.pdf

For Income and Poverty Status Data

U.S. Administration on Aging. (2009). *A statistical profile of black older Americans aged 65+.* Retrieved June 5, 2011, from http://www.aoa.gov/AoARoot/Aging_Statistics/minority_aging/Facts-on-Black-Elderly2009-plain_format.aspx
U.S. Administration on Aging. (2009). *A statistical profile on Hispanic older Americans aged 65+.* Retrieved June 5, 2011, from http://www.aoa.gov/AoAroot/Aging_Statistics/minority_aging/Facts-on-Hispanic-Elderly-2008.aspx

2

Alzheimer's Disease and Other Causes of Dementia

CASE EXAMPLE

In those days everyone thought it was old age. Now we know my grandfather had Alzheimer's disease, too. But nobody would have thought it was a disease. Only the family and close friends and neighbors knew he would leave the house at times and get lost in the neighborhood. Nobody talked about [it]. Everybody knows everyone so someone in the neighborhood would bring him home if they saw him out. Or we would go out to look for him if we discovered he was not home. But the night he was killed by the car we were asleep, no one knew he was out.

Mrs. N is a 48-year-old Puerto Rican single parent. She was born in Puerto Rico and moved to the United States after her first child was born. She cares for her mother aged 65, recently diagnosed with Alzheimer's disease (AD). She also cares for her 96-year-old grandmother who lives in the three-family home with Mrs. N and her family. Mrs. N has three children; two adult married daughters aged 27 and 25 and a son aged 14. All occupy the three-family home in a predominately Latino neighborhood embedded in an urban northeastern U.S. city. Mrs. N is unemployed and receives disability assistance for back injuries sustained as a result of being struck by a car as she walked in an inner-city crosswalk. She manages her own care as well as her mother's and grandmother's care.

According to Mrs. N, her maternal grandfather's memory loss started when he was in his 50s but she is not sure. Because everyone thought his memory loss, confusion, and wandering were due to old age, no one was very concerned. In his 60s, he wandered out of the house during the night and was hit by a car. His widow, now 96 years old, lives with Mrs. N and Mrs. N's mother recently diagnosed with AD.

CHAPTER OVERVIEW

This chapter provides an overview of the known etiology and clinical course of AD and other common forms of dementia, with special focus on forms of dementia found to be more common among Blacks and Latinos. A review of the new and revised diagnostic guidelines for AD, released in April 2011 by the National Institute on Aging and the Alzheimer's Association, is provided in this chapter as well. The discussion then turns to the epidemiology of dementia, with special focus on the relative risk for developing different types of dementia in the U.S. Black and Latino populations, based on the latest published evidence. This chapter closes with an introduction to interpretations and meanings of dementia in Black and Latino cultural heritages, a central theme threaded throughout the rest of the book.

LEARNING ABOUT DEMENTIA DISEASE

As a first step in learning about dementia, it is very important to distinguish the term "dementia" from "Alzheimer's disease," because often these terms are erroneously used interchangeably. Dementia refers to several diseases and conditions that result in damage to brain cells or to connections between brain cells. AD is the most common type of dementia, and the way it affects brain cells differs from the way the brain is affected by other types of dementia, such as vascular dementia (VD). Clinically, however, patients with any dementia disease, Alzheimer's or otherwise, often present with a similar set of symptoms, frequently making it difficult for physicians and other health and social care providers to determine which underlying disease process is at work in causing those symptoms.

A second important introductory point is that none of the dementia diseases are caused by aging. In fact, the majority of older Americans live out their lives without experiencing dementia. At a population level, the risk for developing dementia clearly increases with advancing age; the rate of occurrence of dementia among people in their 80s and 90s is much higher than among people in their 60s and 70s. This age association with dementia occurrence is because the longer people live, brain cell damage has a longer time to develop and lead to dementia symptoms. Simply put, *all types of dementia are diseases of the brain, just as all types of heart disease are diseases of the heart.* Therefore, when symptoms that might be hallmarks of a dementia disease appear in an individual, they should not be attributed to normal aging and ignored. Often these symptoms are caused by brain cell damage, and often they may be caused by diseases or conditions that are reversible or even curable with proper treatment; examples of treatable reversible causes of dementia are thyroid problems, depression, and certain vitamin deficiencies. However, dementia diseases are considered irreversible; there are very few pharmaceutical products available to effectively treat dementia symptoms, and to date there are no cures for any dementia disease.

The final preliminary point is that scientists studying AD and other types of dementia have learned a great deal in the past two decades about exactly how brain cells are damaged in people with these diseases, and more recently about how certain "biomarkers," which are measures of biological fluid or imaging findings, appear to be related to observed brain disease and its progression. However, the mysteries of the brain continue to challenge scientists, and much more must be learned about how the brain is affected by dementia diseases before more effective pharmaceutical therapies can be offered to individuals with dementia.

In this section, we summarize currently published scientific knowledge about common symptoms associated with different types of dementia, underlying causes of the different dementia diseases and symptoms, clinical practice and scientific diagnostic guidelines, and the prevalence of dementia in the Black, Latino, and White U.S. populations.

Clinical Symptoms Associated With Diagnosis of Dementia

Dementia, regardless of type or underlying cause, is characterized by memory loss and decline in other cognitive capacities. Proper diagnosis of symptoms is most commonly pursued by referring to the criteria for dementia included in the *Diagnostic and Statistical Manual of Mental Disorders, 4th Edition (DSM-IV)*. According to the *DSM-IV*, decline in memory is absolutely required; in addition, at least one of the following cognitive abilities must show signs of decline:

- Ability to generate coherent speech or understand spoken or written language

- Ability to recognize or identify objects, assuming intact sensory function
- Ability to execute motor activities, assuming intact motor abilities
- Ability to think abstractly, make sound judgments, and plan and carry out complex tasks

Importantly, the decline in memory and other cognitive ability must be severe enough to interfere with a person's ability to carry out daily activities (Alzheimer's Association, 2011; American Psychiatric Association [APA], 1994).

Numerous behavioral and psychological symptoms may also occur in persons with dementia as defined by core cognitive symptoms. In many family care situations, these behavioral and psychological symptoms often cause caregivers the most distress, and even though they tend to appear when the disease process has progressed to a significant degree, sometimes months or even years after memory loss occurs, many families delay seeking diagnostic assistance until these types of symptoms appear. Clinically significant behavioral and psychological symptoms are found in about one-third of people with dementia living in the community, and in up to 80% of people with dementia living in nursing facilities. A recent review article of these symptoms classified them into four clusters: *mood disorders,* such as apathy, anxiety, and depression; *psychoses,* such as delusions and hallucinations; *aberrant motor behaviors,* such as pacing and wandering; and *inappropriate behaviors,* such as agitation, disinhibition, and euphoria (Tampi et al., 2011).

Careful clinical assessment of these types of symptoms may benefit people with dementia and their families, because effective pharmaceutical treatments are available to address many of these symptoms. However, it is always necessary to monitor these medications for potential side effects and adverse interactions with other medications that may be prescribed for other medical conditions. From a social work perspective, family caregivers are more likely to seek advice and guidance about how to manage these behavioral and psychological symptoms without using medications, or about how to find support services in the community so that they might find brief respite from their caregiving responsibilities.

This cognitive, behavioral, and psychological symptom profile helps paint an introductory portrait, or composite sketch, of the clinical presentation of a person with dementia. Later chapters in this book present cases that reflect different combinations of symptoms found in Blacks and Latinos who may seek professional assistance from social workers.

Irreversible Dementia Types and Their Characteristics

What are the common types of irreversible dementia and how do they compare in terms of underlying causes and presenting symptoms? The four types of irreversible dementia covered here are AD, VD, dementia with Lewy bodies (DLB), and frontotemporal dementia (FD). Together these account for more than 90% of all causes of irreversible dementia. It is also important to note, however, that recent studies suggest the coexistence of brain cell abnormalities that are characteristic of more than one of these dementia types, most often AD plus another type. This so-called "mixed dementia" type appears to be growing in prevalence for two main reasons: more advanced diagnostic imaging technology that enables observation of brain activity in ever-sharper resolution and detail, and considerable overlap in several clinical symptoms associated with different dementia types. Other causes of irreversible dementia are secondary to other medical conditions where brain cell damage occurs as part of the disease process underlying those conditions. These dementia types include Parkinson's dementia, dementia secondary to Down's syndrome, dementia secondary to brain cancer, dementia secondary to HIV/AIDS, and dementia secondary to alcoholism or syphilis. Presuming that the underlying medical condition is stable or well controlled, the dementia-related symptoms found in these patients could be addressed as they would be for patients with other, more common, dementia types. Lastly, quite rare known causes of irreversible dementia, which will not be covered in this book, are Creutzfeldt-Jakob disease (a more rapidly fatal type of dementia) and normal pressure hydrocephalus (caused by fluid buildup in the brain). Students interested in these less common types of dementia are encouraged to conduct focused literature reviews and seek out scientific and clinical experts in their locales who specialize in these types of dementia.

Alzheimer's Disease

Recent estimates indicate that 5.4–5.5 million Americans presently live with AD. AD is universally acknowledged as the most common type of dementia, although estimates vary regarding its proportionate share of all dementia types. Lower-end estimates that suggest that AD accounts for 50%–56% of all dementia are based on brain autopsy studies and on clinical case series studies, while higher-end estimates of 60%–80% are based primarily on epidemiological studies of community-dwelling populations (Alzheimer's Association, 2011; Querfurth & LaFerla, 2010). Here it is important to point out that definitive proof that an individual has AD can be established only upon brain autopsy after death; AD can be diagnosed in live individuals only by a process of differential diagnosis in which all other potential causes of dementia are ruled out. As we shall see, however, recent scientific advances have made it possible to sharpen differential diagnoses, especially imaging techniques that allow inspection of the extent of brain cell damage.

Symptoms and Related Brain Cell Damage in AD

A brief case study illustrates how a person with an eventual diagnosis of AD might initially present in a clinical encounter:

> An 82-year-old woman presented with a 3–4 year history of progressive memory loss, which primarily affected her short-term memory. A widow, she increasingly relied on her daughter to remind her of appointments and some day-to-day activities. A long-time driver and resident of the local area, she had recent problems with driving alone, becoming confused about routes to familiar places. She could not manage her financial affairs as usual, and she could not always tell her daughter whether she had taken her hypertension medications on time.

How does AD damage brain cells to lead to this clinical presentation? Scientific evidence to date points to two major microscopic protein culprits that invade and damage brain cells, commonly referred to as *plaques* and *tangles*. According to the *amyloid hypothesis*, plaques refer to β-amyloid peptide proteins that unnaturally accumulate in the brain due to an imbalance between production and clearance. This excess of cell-toxic β-amyloid leads to cell damage and loss of neurons and brain white matter. The complementary *tau hypothesis* contends that accumulation of the tau protein leads to the formation of neurofibrillary tangles, and the number of these tangles is a pathologic marker of the severity of AD. Once the processes leading to this deleterious protein accumulation begin, there is no known way to reverse them. As deposits of plaques and tangles grow in size and number, brain cell damage accelerates and eventually cell death occurs. Observable symptoms in people with AD reflect the parts of the brain that are affected by plaques and tangles at any given time. Short-term memory loss, the hallmark symptom of cognitive change, is due to these pathologies occurring initially in the hippocampal region of the brain, where short-term memory function is controlled. Subsequent cognitive and other symptoms result from cell damage that spreads to other parts of the brain that control executive function (logical and sequential decision making), language and communication function, and motor function. Behavioral and psychological symptoms develop as parts of the brain controlling mood and sensory functions experience cell damage and death.

To raise public and professional awareness about AD, the Alzheimer's Association has disseminated widely a message about "10 warning signs of AD" (www.alz.org/10signs). The primary intent of the 10 warning signs campaign is to dispel the myth that these symptoms, or warning signs, are a typical part of aging. The 10 symptoms are practical and concise, ranging from "memory changes that disrupt daily life" to "misplacing things and losing the ability to retrace steps" to "decreased or poor judgment." Spanish language versions of this message are available at the website. Any clinical encounter with a person or family member concerned about memory problems, and who has had no or few previous professional encounters about this concern, should include a review of the 10 warning signs. If one or more symptoms appear to be present, referral to a physician would help facilitate a diagnosis as early as possible in the progression of the disease.

Because brain cell damage with AD is insidious, progressive, and quite constant, onset of clinical symptoms is gradual, and symptom progression is slow but steady. The pace of symptom development and the types of symptoms that appear (beyond memory loss) are highly individualized; the natural course of AD averages approximately 10 years, but there is considerable variation around that average (Muangpaisan, 2007; Querfurth & LaFerla, 2010).

Diagnostic Guidelines for AD

In 2011, for the first time since they were established in 1984, clinical diagnostic criteria for AD were revised by a panel of medical and scientific experts convened by the National Institute on Aging and the Alzheimer's Association. Accompanying these revised clinical diagnostic guidelines was a set of research guidelines for diagnosing AD at earlier stages, including preclinical stages. In all, the National Institute on Aging/Alzheimer's Association Diagnostic Guidelines for Alzheimer's Disease cover three stages of the disease: (1) preclinical; (2) mild cognitive impairment; and (3) AD.

A major reason for the development of these diagnostic guidelines was accumulating scientific evidence over the past quarter century based on autopsies that brain pathology characteristic of AD (plaques and tangles) occurred in persons who had never developed or exhibited clinical symptoms of dementia while alive. In studies with living subjects, substantial brain pathology was found in individuals with normal cognition or only minimal impairment. Therefore, mounting evidence suggests that brain changes may occur years before the first clinical symptoms of dementia appear or are observed. Moreover, broad consensus was reached among scientists and many clinicians that AD reflects the symptomatic phase of a disease process that begins with brain pathology but no symptoms (preclinical), and then evolves into minimal symptoms involving memory loss or decline only (mild cognitive impairment, or MCI), and then further advances to the AD stage where additional symptoms beyond memory loss appear. The three diagnostic guidelines released in April 2011 focus on these three stages of the disease process. Workgroups assigned to these guidelines were charged with focusing exclusively on the spectrum of AD; other irreversible and reversible types of dementia were considered only when linked to differential diagnosis of AD (Jack et al., 2011; McKhann, 2011).

The first new guideline pertains to the preclinical stages of AD and sets out a series of recommendations for research into how evidence of brain damage in people without observable symptoms might be studied to determine the risk for developing symptoms and then more advanced stages of AD. This preclinical guideline document was developed for research purposes only and is not intended for use by clinicians due to the absence of observable symptoms in patients at this disease stage. In essence, these guidelines call for research intended to measure levels of biomarkers from cerebrospinal fluid and to determine how these biomarker levels are associated with levels of plaques and tangles observed via advanced diagnostic imaging techniques such as magnetic resonance imaging (MRI) or positron-emission tomography (PET). A goal of this line of inquiry is to determine if biomarker levels can be refined to develop predictions of who will develop into more advanced stages of AD in the future (Sperling et al., 2011).

The second new diagnostic guideline focuses on mild cognitive impairment (MCI), a stage of dementia that was first characterized in the 1990s. MCI represents an intermediate stage of cognitive function between normal functioning and fulfilling diagnostic criteria for AD and possibly other types of dementia (McKhann, 2011; Petersen, 2011). Core clinical criteria for an MCI diagnosis include concern regarding a change in cognition by patients or clinicians; impairment in memory, attention, or visuospatial skills; and preservation of independence in conducting all activities of daily living. Cognitive testing is recommended in the MCI guideline for individuals with these clinical criteria; scores on these tests are typically 1–1.5 standard deviations below the average for age- and education-matched peers (Albert et al., 2011). Two types of MCI have been distinguished, depending upon whether memory impairment is present (amnestic MCI) or whether another cognitive function such as visuospatial skill is impaired (nonamnestic MCI;

Petersen, 2011). Longitudinal studies have shown that individuals with amnestic MCI had a much greater likelihood of subsequently developing clinical criteria for AD, whereas individuals with nonamnestic MCI appear to be at higher risk for developing other dementia types, such as DLB or FD. The most extensively studied technique for predicting progression from MCI to dementia is imaging using the MRI technique. The new MCI diagnostic guideline recommends that suspected patients undergo MRI testing in addition to cognitive status testing and also that they undergo a thorough workup to rule out other causes for cognitive impairment, such as vascular disease and depression (McKhann, 2011). Finally, this guideline recognizes the fruitful progress made in isolating biomarkers that might increase the likelihood that individuals with MCI may develop dementia, but cautions that it is premature to recommend routine testing for presence of biomarkers due to the lack of scientific certainty of the role of these biomarkers (Albert et al., 2011).

The final new diagnostic guideline concerns refinements to the original 1984 clinical practice guidelines for determining whether symptomatic individuals are likely to have AD. This guideline workgroup proposed new terminology for classifying individuals with dementia caused by AD: probable AD dementia; possible AD dementia; and probable or possible AD dementia with evidence of the AD brain pathology process described earlier in this chapter. Explicit clinical criteria were presented for each of these classification groups (McKhann et al., 2011). As with the new MCI guideline, the new AD guideline recommends the use of cognitive testing and imaging techniques as part of the diagnostic process, but stops short of recommending that testing for biomarkers be used in routine clinical practice.

In summary, publication of new diagnostic guidelines for AD represents a synthesis of accumulating scientific knowledge about brain pathology, associated biomarkers, and refined clinical understanding of different symptomatic presentations of individuals with memory and other cognitive impairment. However, these new diagnostic guidelines also reinforce the critical importance of sound clinical judgment and comprehensive history taking, both of which were central features of medical care long before the advent of advanced technology.

Before leaving this topic of diagnostic guidelines for AD, it must be emphasized that these new guidelines represent a tremendous opportunity for individuals from different racial and ethnic groups to learn about AD and other types of irreversible dementia. Although none of these guidelines specifically recommend that racially and ethnically diverse research subjects be recruited for preclinical, MCI, or AD diagnostic studies, it will be important for Blacks, Latinos, and individuals from other racial and ethnic groups to consider volunteering for such laboratory or clinical studies when these opportunities are offered in their communities. As we shall see later in this chapter, it appears that Blacks and Latinos are at higher risk for developing AD; diverse population participation in diagnostic studies as envisioned by these new guidelines will greatly contribute to our knowledge about whether and how brain damage due to the plaques and tangles characteristic of AD might occur differently in persons from different racial and ethnic groups.

Treatment for AD

No known treatment is available to stop the damage and deterioration of brain cells in AD. Presently, there are five drugs approved by the U.S. Food and Drug Administration to help temporarily slow cognitive decline; however, the effectiveness of all of these approved drugs is modest, with only about one-half of people finding benefit, and the effects rarely last beyond 12 months (Alzheimer's Association, 2011). Of course, many pharmacotherapies are in clinical testing phases at any time and, as with participation in diagnostic studies, racial and ethnic diversity among volunteers are needed for experimental treatment trials to determine how Blacks, Latinos, and members of other racial and ethnic groups with AD respond to drug treatment.

Vascular Dementia

VD is also known as multi-infarct or post-stroke dementia and is the second most common form of dementia, affecting approximately 15%–25% of all people with dementia. As the name suggests, VD is caused primarily by decreased blood flow to parts of the brain, often due to a single major or series of smaller occlusive strokes that block arteries. Decreased blood flow leads to a reduction in the oxygen and nutrients carried by the blood to the brain, causing the brain to function less than optimally. Clinical symptoms depend upon the parts of the brain affected by decreased blood flow. A brief case study illustrates the recent history of a person who would likely receive a diagnosis of VD:

> A 70-year-old man with hypertension, diabetes, and coronary artery disease developed sudden weakness on one side of his body (hemiparesis) and also difficulty articulating words (dysarthria) 6 months ago. Three months after that episode, his wife noticed that he could not name his only grandchild and that he could not remember to take his medications. He also could not operate the remote control device for

their television or cook meals as usual. Upon physical examination, he demonstrated overactive reflexes on his left side (hyperreflexia).

The episode 6 months prior to the clinical encounter was most likely a stroke and, as is the case with VD, the temporal association between this cerebrovascular event and the onset of dementia (memory loss, other cognitive decline in this case study) was within 3 months. Clinical differences between VD and AD include the following:

- History of atherosclerotic disease: Strokes, transient ischemic attacks, presence of atherosclerotic risk factors such as diabetes mellitus and hypertension very common in VD; considerably less common in AD
- Onset of symptoms: Sudden or gradual in VD; gradual in AD
- Symptom progression: Often stepwise progression in VD (worsening with recurrent strokes); slow, progressive decline in AD
- Memory: Mild impairment in early stage in VD; prominent in early phase of AD
- Executive function: Marked impairment early in VD; mild or no impairment early, but prominent in later phase of AD

Symptoms of both types of dementia often overlap, making it difficult for clinicians to determine a differential diagnosis solely on clinical presentation; however, a careful history often helps identify a precipitating event such as a stroke, or a sudden notice of cognitive decline in a previously cognitively intact individual (Alzheimer's Association, 2011; Muangpaisan, 2007).

The great preponderance of evidence from national epidemiological studies indicates that Blacks and Latinos are more likely than Whites to have a history of atherosclerotic disease in middle and later life. For example, hypertension is considerably more common in Blacks than Whites, and type 2 diabetes mellitus is more common among Blacks and Hispanics than Whites. Because both hypertension and diabetes mellitus are treatable conditions, more effective treatment of, and ultimately prevention of, these diseases could be especially beneficial to Blacks and Latinos in reducing the risk of VD (Alzheimer's Association, 2010).

Dementia With Lewy Bodies

Lewy bodies are abnormal deposits of the protein α-synuclein that form and accumulate inside nerve cells of the brain. Approximately 10%–15% of cases at autopsy show characteristic signs of Lewy bodies. Criteria for a diagnosis of DLB are highly specific, particularly visual hallucinations, rigid gait, repeated falls, fainting spells, and transient loss of consciousness. Patients presenting with these symptoms, or with a history of these symptoms, are likely to receive a diagnosis of DLB, such as in the following case study.

> A 70-year-old man with a 6-month history of cognitive impairment and visual hallucination presented following repeated falls at home over the past week. His wife reported that his thinking, speaking, and routine activity performance had slowed considerably over the past few months. Physical examination showed that he had bilateral rigidity, parkinsonian gait, and masked face (decreased facial expressions).

Clinical differences between DLB and AD include the following:

- Fluctuation of cognitive function: Prominent, may fluctuate daily in DLB; little daily fluctuation in AD
- Parkinsonism: More common in DLB; less common in AD
- Psychiatric symptoms: More likely to occur early in the disease course with DLB; less likely with AD
- Verbal memory: Better in DLB; worse in AD
- Type of memory impairment: Semantic memory in DLB; episodic memory in AD
- Executive function: Poor early in the disease course in DLB; less severe in the early phase in AD
- Attention, visuospatial function, constructional abilities: More impairment with DLB; less impairment with AD
- Visual hallucinations: Common from the early phase in DLB; less prominent in AD

The biggest diagnostic challenge with DLB is distinguishing this dementia type from dementia secondary to Parkinson's disease. Generally, if the onset of dementia is within 12 months of parkinsonism's onset, it is likely DLB. Postural instability and masked face is more common in DLB, whereas tremors are more common with parkinsonism (Alzheimer's Association, 2011; Muangpaisan, 2007).

Frontotemporal Dementia

This rarer type of irreversible dementia affects the frontal lobe of the brain, where nerve cells are infiltrated by abnormal amounts of the protein tau. Pick's disease is the most common form of FD. This type of dementia tends to appear in younger adults than all other types of irreversible dementia, and in about one-half of all cases there is a family history of dementia in a first-degree relative.

A 50-year-old woman presents with marked behavioral changes over the past 2 years. She had poor personal hygiene and refused to bathe, which was uncharacteristic behavior. She also experienced weight gain of 20 pounds in 5 months. Her concentration at work declined noticeably and she was accused of stealing office supplies, again uncharacteristic behavior. Memory loss was only minimal.

Clinical differences between FD and AD include the following:

- Age at onset: Rarely 75 years or older with FD, onset increases markedly with age in AD
- Socially inappropriate behaviors: Common early in the course of FD; appear later in the disease course in AD in some individuals
- Memory impairment: Less prominent in the early phases of FD; nearly universal in the early stages of AD
- Mood: Marked irritability, lack of guilt, and withdrawal from the early phases of FD; sadness and guilt more common in AD
- Appetite, dietary change: Increased appetite, weight gain with FD; anorexia and weight loss more common in AD (Alzheimer's Association, 2011; Muangpaisan, 2007)

Challenges associated with FD include working with families who are often stunned by the relatively sudden change in personality of a loved one and confronting the fear expressed by first-degree relatives regarding their own risks of developing FD at a relatively early age. Support groups for FD are growing in popularity, so affected individuals and families should be referred to local support groups and encouraged to seek additional assistance from specialists, as this is considered less of a geriatric form of dementia than a psychiatric condition due to the behavioral symptoms that appear in the early stages of the disease process.

Reversible Causes of Dementia

When individuals present with memory loss or decline, reversible causes should be considered and excluded first, before moving to a consideration of the irreversible causes discussed earlier. Among the most common reversible causes are adverse effects of medications, delirium, depression, thyroid disorders, and certain vitamin deficiencies.

Medications

Many older adults take numerous prescription medications as well as over-the-counter medications for multiple, chronic, medical conditions and acute illnesses. Adverse drug events, which refer to a range of dosing and chemical interaction mistakes made by patients and prescribers, have been linked to numerous preventable and costly problems, including confusion, depression, falls, constipation, and hip fractures (Fick et al., 2003). Another problem related to taking multiple medications is nonadherence, or not taking drugs at prescribed times or intervals, which has been estimated at between 21% and 55% among older adults. Poor medication adherence is estimated to be a factor in more than 25% of emergency room visits (Strickler, Lin, Rauh, & Neafsey, 2008). Older adults experiencing adverse drug events or nonadherence often present clinically with symptoms mirroring cognitive declines synonymous with dementia. When these types of adverse effects of medications are suspected, such individuals should be referred to a physician for a complete medication review. Most often medication regimens can be reduced or refined to minimize risks for adverse interactions and nonadherence, and dementia-like symptoms usually clear after the refined regimen is established and followed properly. For older adults with low levels of health literacy or for whom English is not their primary language, as discussed in Chapter 1, extra care should be taken to ensure that medication regimens are clearly understood.

Delirium

Delirium refers to the acute effect of physical illness on brain function; most often acute illnesses causing delirium are found elsewhere in the body. Delirium often masks as dementia because the acute confusional state characteristic of delirium can mimic dementia symptoms, especially memory loss, disorientation, and impaired judgment. Acute onset and disorganized thinking with inability to maintain and shift attention are hallmark symptoms of delirium. However, provided the causative acute illness (e.g., infection) or environmental factor (e.g., hospitalization) can be identified and treated promptly, delirium is largely or completely reversible (Ham, 2002).

Depression is the most common mood disorder in older adults, affecting between 5% and 20% of older adults living in the community. Many older adults with clinical levels of depression present with memory loss or decline as well as poor concentration and decision-making capacity, which could easily be mistaken for dementia symptoms.

Careful clinical evaluations should be conducted, including social history, to rule out depression as a potentially reversible cause of dementia symptoms. Treatments for depression in older adults are as effective as for younger adults (Lammers, 2002).

Thyroid Disorders

Thyroid disorders refer to either overactive (hyperthyroidism) or underactive (hypothyroidism) thyroids, which could lead to cognitive symptoms that look similar to dementia symptoms. Patients presenting with dementia-like symptoms should always have thyroid measurements taken to ensure that these disorders are not the culprit, because they are easily treatable and any observed dementia symptoms should resolve (McKhann et al., 2011).

Vitamin Deficiencies

The most commonly found vitamin deficiencies that result in acute cognitive decline are vitamin B12 and folate deficiencies. When patients present with symptoms that appear to be synonymous with memory loss or decline and disorientation, clinicians should check vitamin B12 and folate levels using standard laboratory tests. If these serum levels are found to be abnormal and then treated in a timely fashion, dementia-like symptoms should be alleviated (McKhann et al., 2011).

EPIDEMIOLOGY OF DEMENTIA AND IMPLICATIONS FOR BLACKS AND LATINOS

Prevalence of AD and Other Dementia in the U.S. Population

Prevalence refers to the number of people with a disease at a defined point of time or time period. Prevalence can be thought of as a snapshot of the population with the disease at the time the picture is taken. In 2011, an estimated 5.4 million Americans of all ages had AD, including about 200,000 individuals younger than the age of 65. This population prevalence for the 65 and older population indicates that about 13% of all Americans in that age group have AD (Alzheimer's Association, 2011). Using the estimate that AD represents 60% of all types of irreversible dementia, a total of 9 million Americans are now living with some type of dementia.

　　Considering the projected rapid growth of the older population as discussed in Chapter 1, it is not surprising that projections for the prevalence of dementia over the next several decades call for a substantial increase in

FIGURE 2.1   Projected Number of Americans Aged 65 and Older With Alzheimer's Disease

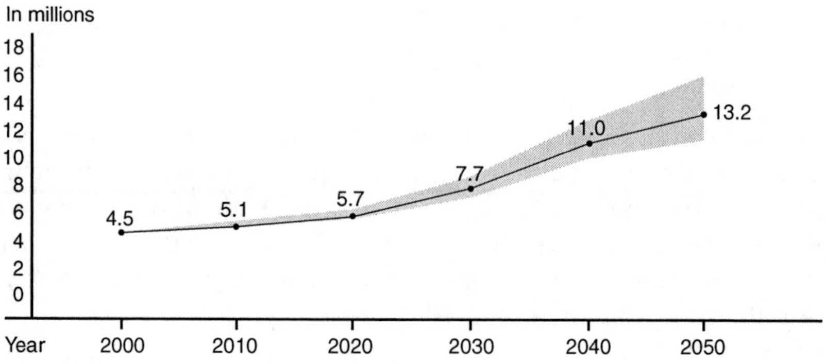

*Numbers indicate middle estimates per decade. Shaded area indicates low and high estimates per decade.

From Alzheimer's Association (2011, p. 17), data from Hebert et al., 2003.

the number of Americans living with AD. Figure 2.1 illustrates this projected growth in prevalence of AD in the population aged 65 and older; nearly 8 million by the year 2030, and more than 13 million by 2050. This figure does not include other types of dementia, but the trend is clear.

Dementia Prevalence by Gender and Age Group

More women than men have AD and other dementias, but this difference is due primarily to the fact that women have longer average life expectancies than men. To determine if there are true gender differences in the risk of developing dementia, numerous studies have examined the development of new cases of dementia (incidence) and compared men and women in terms of incidence rates over time. No significant differences by gender have been found, so at this time scientific consensus supports the conclusion that women are not more likely than men to develop AD or other types of dementia (Alzheimer's Association, 2011).

Age is the single biggest predictor of the likelihood of developing dementia but not, as noted earlier in this chapter, because aging causes dementia; rather, because living longer offers greater opportunity for brain cell damage to occur due to the numerous causes of dementia. Estimated population prevalence figures by age group indicate that of all Americans living with AD, 4% are younger than 65, 6% are between 65 and 74 years old, 45% are aged 75–84, and the remaining 45% are aged 85 or older. These figures make it clear that living beyond 75 years old substantially increases the risk of developing AD. Nevertheless, even in the 85 and older population, the "oldest old" discussed in Chapter 1, less than half the population (43%) have AD (Alzheimer's Association, 2011).

The relatively small group of Americans younger than age 65 living with dementia is referred to as a group with *younger-onset* or *early-onset* dementia (Alzheimer's Association, 2006). Very little is known about the early-onset population, including whether there are racial and ethnic group differences in susceptibility. However, it is likely that individuals with hypertension, other cardiovascular diseases, and diabetes in early and middle adulthood run a greater risk of developing VD at an earlier age than individuals without these diseases, especially if these chronic conditions are not well-controlled or treated. Considering that Blacks and Latinos have a higher prevalence of these diseases than Whites, as noted earlier in this chapter, it is possible that early-onset VD may be more likely in Black and Latino individuals. The only known study comparing age at dementia-symptom onset across any racial or ethnic groups was conducted with White and Latino subjects at five specialized medical centers across the country; this study found that Hispanics had an average age of symptom onset nearly 7 years earlier than Whites (Clark et al., 2005).

Dementia Prevalence and Comparative Risk for Blacks and Latinos

Before providing known trends in the comparative prevalence of dementia among Blacks, Latinos, and Whites, it is important to note that much more research is required to yield definitive results. The major reason for the lack of scientific data on prevalence and risk across racial and ethnic groups is because few studies have enrolled sufficient numbers of Blacks or Latinos in large enough geographic areas to support conclusive results. Another reason is the substantial expense involved in conducting comprehensive diagnostic testing for the presence of AD or other dementia according to the latest published guidelines in large enough study samples to yield conclusive findings.

Among existing studies with large enough samples and scientifically adequate methods for measuring cognitive decline or a diagnosis of AD, three were identified by an Expert Panel convened by the Alzheimer's Association to review evidence on race, ethnicity, and prevalence of dementia. The first study examined Whites and Blacks only and is known as the Aging, Demographic, and Memory Study (ADAMS), which compared persons in these racial groups aged 71 and older on measures from a standardized diagnostic evaluation to estimate dementia prevalence. The ADAMS study found that, in nationally representative samples, Blacks aged 71 and older were almost twice as likely as Whites to have AD or other dementia (21.3% vs. 11.2%, respectively; Potter et al., 2009).

The second selected study by the expert panel is the Health and Retirement Study (HRS), which in 2006 drew a nationally representative sample of more than 16,000 adults aged 55 and older and also included sufficient numbers of Latinos as well as Blacks. Survey respondents self-identified as White race, African American race, or Hispanic regardless of race. Measures of cognitive performance included tests to measure memory, working memory, and speed of mental processing; more details of the survey methods are available (Alzheimer's Association, 2010, pp. 63–64). Figure 2.2 illustrates the proportion of White, African American, and Hispanic HRS respondents in different age groups with cognitive impairment.

Results in Figure 2.2 indicate in a striking fashion that, across all age groupings, African Americans and Hispanics had higher prevalence of cognitive impairment than Whites. In the 55–64 age groups, which could be viewed as an early-onset group, although proportions with cognitive impairment are very low, African Americans were four times as likely as Whites and Hispanics were almost three times as likely as Whites to have cognitive impairment. In the oldest old age group, more than half of African Americans and nearly half of Hispanics had cognitive impairment, compared to just over one-quarter of Whites. These

FIGURE 2.2   Rates of Cognitive Impairment by Race and Ethnicity, United States, 2006

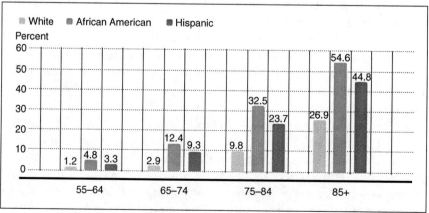

From Alzheimer's Association (2010, p. 50); data from the Health and Retirement Study, 2006.

results clearly allow the conclusion that, based on the measurement methods used, the prevalence of dementia is higher among Blacks and Latinos than among Whites. An important limitation of the HRS is its reliance on cognitive impairment tests that require mathematical skills, which may partially represent racial and ethnic differences in formal education that are known to exist in the adult and older adult populations (see Chapter 1), rather than true differences in cognitive status. Nevertheless, the Black versus White differences found in the older age groups in HRS are highly consistent with findings from the ADAMS study, which used more stringent diagnostic assessment methods.

The final study selected by the expert panel was the sole investigation that met the panel's most stringent criteria: comparison of Whites, Blacks, and Latinos across older age groups; use of population-based sampling methods to maximize the representativeness of the samples; and use of a standardized diagnostic evaluation to determine presence of AD and other dementia. This study was not national but was conducted in New York City, and is known as the WHICAP study—Washington Heights-Inwood Columbia Aging Project. Figure 2.3 shows WHICAP results comparing the prevalence of AD and other types of dementia in the three racial and ethnic groups within older age groups.

Results from the WHICAP mirror trends found in the HRS: In every age group shown, Blacks and Latinos had a higher prevalence than Whites of AD and other dementias. Differences in the two studies are found in comparing Blacks and Hispanics aged 75 and older; in WHICAP, Hispanics had a higher prevalence than Blacks, whereas in HRS, Blacks had a higher prevalence than Hispanics.

FIGURE 2.3 Rates of Cognitive Impairment by Race and Ethnicity, Washington Heights-Inwood Columbia Aging Project (WHICAP), 2006

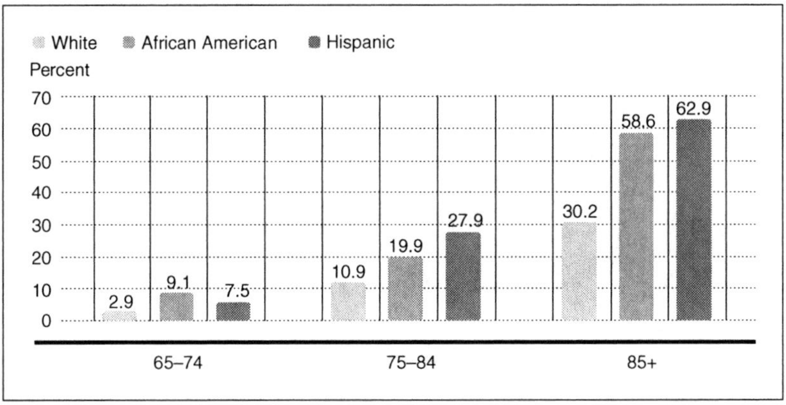

From Alzheimer's Association (2010, p. 52).

Taken together, results from these studies indicate that Blacks in older age groups have about twice the risk of Whites, and Hispanics about a 50% greater risk than Whites, of having cognitive impairment or diagnostic testing results consistent with AD or other dementia. Explanations for these results draw heated debates among scientists and clinicians yet they remain elusive, and it is likely that combinations of measured and unmeasured genetic, health-related, socioeconomic, and cultural factors play roles in observed apparent racial and ethnic group disparities in risk for developing some type of irreversible dementia in middle and later life.

Seeking Explanations: Risk Factors for Dementia and Implications for Blacks and Latinos

Racial and ethnic group differences in the prevalence of cardiovascular disease and educational attainment have already been discussed as partial explanations for observed differences among Whites, Blacks, and Latinos in dementia risk. While it is quite clear that VD differences across groups would be most directly affected by cardiovascular disease differences, the link between cardiovascular disease and AD is less well known. As Figure 2.4 shows, dementia and cardiovascular diseases coexist in many older adults, particularly hypertension, coronary artery

FIGURE 2.4 Prevalence of Coexisting Medical Conditions Among Medicare Beneficiaries With Alzheimer's Disease and Other Types of Dementia

Coexisting Condition	Percentage with Alzheimer's or Other Dementia and the Coexisting Condition
Hypertension	60%
Coronary heart disease	26%
Stroke — late effects	25%
Diabetes	23%
Osteoporosis	18%
Congestive heart failure	16%
Chronic obstructive pulmonary disease	15%
Cancer	13%
Parkinson's disease	8%

From Alzheimer's Association (2011, p. 38); data from Alzheimer's Association, characteristics, costs and health service use for Medicare beneficiaries with a dementia diagnosis: Report 1: *Medicare Current Beneficiary Survey, 2009.*

disease, stroke, and diabetes. More detailed studies are required to distinguish the effects of cardiovascular and metabolic diseases on AD from the effects of these diseases on VD.

Biological explanations, particularly for AD, focus primarily on the potential contributions of genetics and family history to risk, progression, and underlying brain damage mechanisms. Mutations in the apolipoprotein E gene, or *APOE* gene, have been found to play a significant role in the clinical presentation of AD. Studies are inconclusive, however, regarding whether racial differences exist in the contribution of the *APOE* gene to the development of AD (Chin, Negash, & Hamilton, 2011). To adequately unravel the uncertainties about roles played by race and ethnicity in risk for dementia, several steps are necessary. Because biomarkers are not influenced by socioeconomic or cultural factors, one step is for scientists and clinicians to develop partnerships to conduct biomarker studies using assay and imaging techniques, following the recommendations in the recently released preclinical diagnostic guideline for AD, with racially and ethnically diverse subjects (Chin et al., 2011; Sperling et al., 2011). A second step is to refine cognitive testing measures to be more sensitive to educational differences in capacity to complete numeric tasks, as well as to cultural differences in understandings of test items used in these measures (Chin et al., 2011). Finally, much greater emphasis must be placed on encouraging Blacks and Latinos to seek medical care or help from other health care and social care professionals as soon as possible if any of the 10 warning signs of dementia is detected by individuals or their families. Cultural and language barriers between Black and Latino individuals and health professionals must be overcome so that widely cited health disparities in other medical conditions due to differential access to care and to treatment-seeking behavior do not become the norm in the area of dementia care.

ETHNIC CONSTRUCTIONS, INTERPRETATIONS, AND MEANINGS OF DEMENTIA

According to Sontag (1977), in premodern times disease has been linked by societies and cultures to the beliefs and the particular meaning given for behavior before and after disease onset (Sontag, 1977). She notes, "For the Greeks, disease could be gratuitous or it could be deserved (for a personal fault, a collective transgression, or a crime of one's ancestors)" (Sontag, 1977, p. 43). Later, Christianity "imposed more moralized notions of disease, as of everything else, a closer fit between disease and 'victim' gradually evolved" (Sontag, 1977, p. 43). With the belief of victim came the need to place blame on self, leading to judgment and punishment by self and others (Sontag, 1977, p. 43). In the book *Illness as Metaphor* (1977), Sontag chronicles ways in which diseases were socially constructed as having evolved as a "common figure for social disorder," were "enriched with meaning" and given "feelings about evil" and then "projected onto the world" (p. 58). For example, "The medieval experience of the plague was firmly tied to notions of moral pollution, and people invariably looked for a scapegoat external to the stricken community. (Massacres of Jews in unprecedented numbers took place everywhere in plague-stricken Europe of 1347–1348, then stopped as soon as the plague receded.) With modern diseases, the scapegoat is not so easily separated from the patient" (Sontag, 1977, p. 71). The less known about the disease in terms of cause, treatment or cure, and the more mysterious the disease, the more proclivity toward assigning the attribute of evil to the disease, "like any extreme situation, dreaded illnesses bring out both people's worst and best" (Sontag, 1977, p. 71).

For some cultures, the same is still true today when seeking the meaning of dementia arriving in one's family. Often, the disease is viewed as attached to mental illness, which in some cultures may imply living in spiritual, moral, or physical violations of grace and thus incurring punishment. The dementia-afflicted person viewed as senile suggests to others that the person is abnormal, "crazy," or "not in their right mind" and should be feared and avoided. "The notion that the disease can be explained only by a variety of causes is precisely characteristic of thinking about diseases whose causation is *not* understood. And it is diseases thought to be multi-determined (that is, mysterious) that have the widest possibilities as metaphors for what is felt to be socially or morally wrong" (Sontag, 1977, p. 61). Her point is that illness is *not* a metaphor and that the most truthful way of regarding illness—and the healthiest way of being ill—is to resist such metaphoric thinking (Sontag, 1977). In some cultures, metaphoric thinking and myths associated to the origin and cause of the dementing diseases remain active cultural constructions.

The implication is that it is crucial for social workers to identify and understand the meaning Black and Latino caregivers and dementia-afflicted relatives and families give to the dementing illness. Exploring the values, standards, and assumptions culturally diverse families hold toward the dementing illness helps to open the path to a truthful, healthy way of working to solve issues related to the illness and manage emerging symptoms.

Ethnic social constructionist theory helps social workers establish social epistemologies and paradigms that assist in understanding the experiences and meanings diverse cultures in the United States give to AD and other related dementia, and their cultural help-seeking and help-accepting behaviors. This is especially true when social workers seek to learn about ethnic caregivers and afflicted family members in need of dementia care assistance. Practitioners aware of the different experiences, meanings, and understandings encountered by Black and Latino populations in the social environment reduce the tendency to distort the cultural assessment process and provide a more appropriate paradigm of care.

Critical thinking and reflection of the multicultural world enables social workers to become more cognizant of diverse others and become social theorist by seeking to "rediscover inhabitants of the globalizing world" (Lemert, 1999, p. 17). "We have no choice but to speak of our world, such as they are—and when we do, we become social theorist of a very practical and necessary sort" (Lemert, 1999, p. 17). In adding the perspective of social theorist to the social work assessment process, social workers enhance professional understanding of diverse clients and widen the vision of care by assessing client cultures as clients describe the experiences and meaning they give to their social environment.

Research points to new understanding of ethnic/racial differences in ideas about the cause and treatment of afflicted persons and the role of caregivers and culture (Hinton, Franz, Yeo, & Levkoff, 2005). As more and more studies begin to shed light on the role of folk beliefs, and the combination of folk and biomedical care that contribute to Black and Latino caregiving patterns, a paradigm shift needs to be made by social workers and other health care practitioners.

The social work profession differs from other helping professions by its conceptualization of individuals as parts of families, communities, cultures, and societies. It is this professional distinction that compels social workers to view the whole person and the focus on the importance of considering how issues of culture might influence African American and Black kinship care and Latino familismo care of family members suffering from Alzheimer's dementia. Understanding social and cultural differences in terms of how a disease process is experienced in diverse cultures serves as a fundamental framework for understanding the key factors experienced by African American, Black, and Latino caregivers of Alzheimer's dementia family members.

The social work practitioners' own self-examination of how they perceive diverse cultures, in terms of how cultures define and re-define themselves in a multicultural environment, enables social worker prac- titioners to be more aware of transference countertransference issues. Consequently, social work professionals may be better able to determine the best course of treatment and the meaning of the consequences of the treatment in terms of those who define themselves as being different from the dominant culture in the United States.

UNDERSTANDING THE ETHNIC FRAMEWORK

Lewis (2004) points out, "The notion that culture and self are dynamic processes, constantly being defined and re-defined as we continue to evolve in the world around us" (p. 276). Doka (2004) also notes the importance of the role of culture in the dementia caregiving experience: "Culture not only influences the perception of the disease, it frames the caregiving experience. Culture defines who is responsible and how those responsibilities are to be fulfilled" (p. 61). In the Latino cul- ture, a major shock ("susto") or trauma may be perceived as the cause of the disease. A 59-year-old Puerto Rican woman said her mother's Alzheimer's disease was caused by the death of her son: "She also had a son that was killed. I think that from there to here is when she prob- ably began to lose her memory because that was something really big" (Hinton et al., 2005, p. 1407).

The experiences of self in the social and cultural environment of Black and Latino caregivers present unique factors that affect the experience of caregiving. Salient factors include socioeconomic sta- tus, familial interdependence, fear of stigma regarding disease, lan- guage, immigration status, racism, and acculturation, to name a few (Sotomayor & Randolph, 1988), and are the important variables that illuminate and shape the Latino caregiving experience (Rivera & Marlo, 1999; Valle, 1998).

Some research suggests that members of the African American cul- ture consider "worriation" or stress "spells" to be a phenomenon occur- ring in normal life and not necessarily symptoms of dementia (Gaines, 2000). Hinton et al.'s (2005) research examined explanations dementia; the authors note, "A 72-year-old African-American man attributed his wife's Alzheimer's to her worries about her children who were 'mess- ing around out there in the streets, that dope and stuff.' He said, 'I don't think she could take it,' and hoped one day she would 'snap out of it'" (p. 1407). In addition, Whaley (2002) notes "the construct of 'cultural mis- trust,' i.e., Blacks' mistrust of Whites in various interracial situations, is a proxy for what has been described by some as cultural paranoia"

(p. 57). According to research by Whaley (2002), "cultural bias is responsible for errors in the psychiatric diagnosis of African Americans" (p. 57). For social workers, the first step to ensure an accurate diagnosis is to be sensitive to identifying areas of possible cultural biases that may cause inaccurate diagnosis and care. Lifestyle, education, and socioeconomic level are most likely to be the key determinants of disease explanations attributed to biomedical models as opposed to folk models.

CAREGIVER SELF-PERCEPTION

Family caregivers also may experience problems related to how they view themselves, and how they are viewed and expected to function by society, service providers, and policy makers. As previously noted, the vast majority of caregiving occurs within the family and the informal sector and, as indicated in some of the literature, ongoing long-term care has remained a family responsibility (Buchanan, 1984; Moody, 2002). "Responsibility for care of the aged by adult children—is treated ambiguously as a matter of law, custom and ethics" (Callahan, 1985; Moody, 2002, p. 61; Post, 1989; Schorr, 1980). Laws in half of the states could force adult children to give financial support to elder parents in need (Garrett, 1980; Lammers & Klingman, 1986). However, these laws are not usually enforced due to the diverse and conflicting attitudes regarding family caregiving responsibilities (Seltzer & Troll, 1982).

Societal, cultural, and gender role tends to determine the division of labor and influences who has primary responsibility for care of the parent with dementia disease (Crompton, 2001; Walker, 1983). The societal expectation is that females should provide the free labor involved in caring (Thorne, 1982; Walker, 1983, 1991). The political universal term "family" care or "family" caregiver is really understood as being the female adult child, that is, the potential care provider who, when the need arises, will step up to the plate and make financial, emotional, and physical sacrifices and assume the caregiving role (Green & Coleman, 1995; Schulz, O'Brien, Bookwala, & Gleissner, 1995). Supported by the ambivalence or lack of current policy and the cultural and societal expectations cast upon them, females tend to sacrifice their own careers and or educational opportunities to assume the caregiving role (Mutshler, 1994).

A mi me llaman del Welfare y me quieren mandar a trabajar, pero yo no lo puedo dejar solo porque la única persona que lo puede comprender soy yo, y como lo voy a dejar solo, ¿que se me vaya a andar, se me pierda? (Parra & Guarnaccia, 1998, p. 441)

English translation:

> The welfare call me and—they—want me to go to work, but I can't leave him alone because I am the only one that can understand him, and how I am going to leave him alone, what if he goes wandering, gets lost? (Parra & Guarnaccia, 1998, p. 441)

Hence, family caregivers frequently must assume one or more of the following roles: a free resource assumed available to provide care; a co-worker with the afflicted family member; a co-client with the need of assistance to support care of the afflicted member; the expert in the knowledge of the unique situation with the afflicted family member; and the "proxy voice" for the person with dementia (Clarke, 1999, p. 194; Keady, 1997; Nolan, Grant, & Keady, 1996; Twigg, 1989; Wuest, Ericson, & Stern, 1994). The pressures that family caregivers' experience and their plight highlight three specific areas of concern: "the magnitude of family caregiving, the genderization of family caregiving, and the professional involvement" in the family caregiving process (Clark, 1999, p. 194).

The fact that females generally live longer than males means that the caregiver of an Alzheimer's afflicted parent, spouse, partner, or family member will most likely be a female. Adult sons, male spouses, partners, and family members also provide care when necessary but they may not perceive this work to be a "usual" part of their gender role and may act differently as caregivers (Kramer, 1997a, b; Morgan & Eckert, 2000). While not all children or grandchildren are likely to be caregivers, adult children and grandchildren often acknowledge a responsibility or need to return care that parents or grandparents have provided them in the past—"Parents deserve some return for sacrifices they have made for their children"—and also voice a "need to preserve [the] family name and family dignity, protecting the family from outsiders" and a "willingness to provide financial assistance to parents" (Luna et al., 1996, p. 7).

Whether it is a spouse, an adult child, or some other relative or extended family member, caregivers are presumed to be knowledgeable about the needs and wants of the family member receiving their care. Fueled by the strong bond to nuclear family, extended family and fictive kin often sacrifice their own needs in order to make decisions in favor of the cultural core values of the family and group (Gutierrez & Lewis, 1999).

REFERENCES

Albert, M. S., DeKosky, S. T., Dickson, D., Dubois, B., Feldman, H. H., Fox, N. C., et al. (2011). The diagnosis of mild cognitive impairment due to Alzheimer's disease:

Recommendations from the National Institute on Aging and Alzheimer's Association workgroup. *Alzheimer's & Dementia, 7,* 270–279.

Alzheimer's Association. (2006). *Early onset dementia: A national challenge, a future crisis.* Chicago, IL: Author.

Alzheimer's Association. (2010). *2010 Alzheimer's disease facts and figures.* Chicago, IL: Author.

Alzheimer's Association. (2011). *2011 Alzheimer's disease facts and figures.* Chicago, IL: Author.

American Psychiatric Association. (1994). *Diagnostic and statistical manual of mental disorders (DSM-IV)* (4th ed.). Washington, DC: Author.

Buchanan, R. J. (1984). Medicaid: Family responsibility and long term care. *Journal of Long Term Care Administration, 12*(3), 19–25.

Callahan, D. (1985). What do children owe elderly parents? *Hastings Center Report, 15*(2), 32–33.

Chin, A. L., Negash, S., & Hamilton, R. (2011). Diversity and disparity in dementia: The impact of ethnoracial differences in Alzheimer's disease. *Alzheimer's Disease & Associated Disorders, 25*(3), 187–195.

Clark, C. M., DeCarli, C., Mungas, D., Chui, H., Higdon, R., Nunez, J., et al. (2005). Earlier onset of Alzheimer's disease symptoms in Latino individuals compared with Anglo individuals. *Archives of Neurology, 62,* 774–778.

Clarke, C. (1999). Commentary. *International Journal of Geriatric Psychiatry, 14,* 183–196.

Crompton, R. (2001). Gender restructuring employment, and caring. *Social Politics: International Studies in Gender, State, and Society, 8*(3), 266–291.

Doka, K. J. (Ed.). (2004). *Living with grief Alzheimer's disease.* Washington, DC: Hospice Foundation of America.

Fick, D. M., Cooper, J. W., Wade, W. E., Waller, J. L., Maclean, J. R., & Beers, M. H. (2003). Updating the Beers criteria for potentially inappropriate medication use in older adults. *Archives of Internal Medicine, 163,* 2716–2724.

Gaines, A. D. (2000). Alzheimer's disease in the context of Black (Southern) culture. *Journal of Gerontology: Social Sciences, 6,* 33–38.

Garrett, W. (1980). Filial responsibility laws. *Journal of Family Law, 18,* 793–818.

Green, V., & Coleman, P. D. (1995). Direct services for family caregivers. In R. A. Kane & J. D. Penrod (Eds.), *Family caregiving in an aging society: Policy perspectives* (pp. 46–63). Thousand Oaks, CA: Sage.

Gutierrez, L. M., & Lewis, E. A. (1999). *Empowering women of color.* New York: Columbia University Press.

Ham, R. J. (2002). Dementias and delirium. In R. J. Ham, P. D. Sloane, & G. A. Warshaw (Eds.), *Primary care geriatrics: A case-based approach* (4th ed., pp. 245–308). St. Louis, MO: Mosby.

Hinton, L., Franz, C. E., Yeo, G., & Levkoff, S. E. (2005). Conceptions of dementia in a multiethnic sample of family caregivers. *Journal of the American Geriatrics Society, 53,* 1405–1410.

Jack, C. R., Albert, M. S., Knopman, D. S., McKhann, G. M., Sperling, R. A., Carrillo, M. C., et al. (2011). Introduction to the recommendations from the National Institute on Aging and the Alzheimer's Association workgroup on diagnostic guidelines for Alzheimer's disease. *Alzheimer's & Dementia, 7*(3), 257–262.

Keady, J. (1997). Maintaining involvement: A meta concept to describe the dynamics of dementia. In M. Marshall (Ed.), *State of the art in dementia care.* London, England: Center for Policy on Aging.

Kramer, B. J. (1997a). Gain in the caregiving experience: Where are we? What next? *The Gerontologist, 37,* 218–232.

Kramer, B. J. (1997b). Differential predictors of strain and gain among husbands caring for wives with dementia. *The Gerontologist, 37,* 239–249.

Lammers, J. E. (2002). Depression. In R. J. Ham, P. D. Sloane, & G. A. Warshaw (Eds.), *Primary care geriatrics: A case-based approach* (4th ed., pp. 309–322). St. Louis, MO: Mosby.

Lammers, W., & Klingman, D. (1986). Family responsibility laws and state politics: Empirical patterns and policy implications. *Journal of Applied Gerontology, 5,* 5–25.

Lemert, C. (1999). (Ed.). *Social theory: The multicultural and classic readings.* Boulder, CO: Westview Press.

Lewis, G. (2004). What ever happened to culturalism: From Horney to Lacan. Scientific Meeting of Association for the Advancement of Psychoanalysis. February 13, 1997. Presenter: Mario Rendon. *The American Journal of Psychoanalysis, 64*(2), 276–277.

Luna, I., Torres de Ardon, E., Lim, Y. M., Cromwell, S. L., Phillips, L. R., & Russell, C. K. (1996). The relevance of familism in cross-cultural studies of family caregiving. *Western Journal of Nursing Research, 18*(3), 267–283.

McKhann, G. M. (2011). Changing concepts of Alzheimer's disease. *Journal of the American Medical Association, 305,* 2458–2459.

McKhann, G. M., Knopman, D. S., Cherkow, H., Hyman, B. T., Jack, C. R., Kawas, C. H., et al. (2011). The diagnosis of dementia due to Alzheimer's disease: Recommendations from the National Institute on Aging and Alzheimer's Association workgroup. *Alzheimer's & Dementia, 7*(3), 263–269.

Moody, H. R. (2002). *Aging, concepts and controversies* (4th ed.). Thousand Oaks, CA: Pine Forge Press.

Morgan, L. A., & Eckert, J. K. (2000). Burdens and boundaries. In E. W. Markson & L. A. Hollis-Sawyer (Eds.), *Intersections of aging readings in social gerontology* (pp. 392–400). Los Angeles, CA: Roxbury Publishing.

Muangpaisan, W. (2007). Clinical differences among four common dementia syndromes. *Geriatrics and Aging, 10,* 425–429.

Mutshler, P. (1994). From executive suite to production line: How employees in different occupations manage elder care responsibilities. *Research on Aging, 16,* 7–26.

Nolan, M., Grant, G., & Keady, J. (1996). *Understanding family care.* Buckingham, England: Open University Press.

Parra, P. A., & Guarnaccia, P. (1998). Ethnicity, culture, and resiliency in caregivers of a seriously mentally ill family member. In H. McCubbin, E. A., Thompson, A. I. Thompson, & J. E. Fromer (Eds.), *Resiliency in Native American and immigrant families* (pp. 431–450). Thousand Oaks, CA: Sage.

Petersen, R. C. (2011). Mild cognitive impairment. *New England Journal of Medicine, 364,* 2227–2234.

Post, S. (1989). Filial morality in an aging society. *Journal of Religion & Aging, 5,* 15–30.

Potter, G. C., Plasman, B. L., Burke, J. R., Kabeto, M. U., Langa, K. M., Llewellyn, D. J., et al. (2009). Cognitive performance and informant reports in the diagnosis of cognitive impairment and dementia in African-Americans and whites. *Alzheimer's & Dementia, 5,* 445–453.

Querfurth, H. W., & LaFerla, F. M. (2010). Mechanisms of disease: Alzheimer's disease. *New England Journal of Medicine, 362,* 329–344.

Rivera, P., & Marlo, H. (1999). Practitioner report: Cultural, interpersonal and psychodynamic factors in caregiving: Towards a greater understanding of treatment noncompliance. *Clinical Psychology and Psychotherapy, 6,* 63–68.

Schorr, A. L. (1980). *Thy father and they mother—A second look at filial responsibility and family policy* (Social Security Administration No. 13–11953). Washington, DC: Government Printing Office.

Schulz, R., O'Brien, A., Bookwala, T., & Fleissner, K. (1995). Psychiatric and physical morbidity effects of dementia caregiving: Prevalence, correlates, and causes. *The Gerontologist, 35,* 771–791.

Seltzer, M., & Troll, L. (1982). Conflicting public attitudes toward filial responsibility. *Generations, 7*(2), 26–27, 40.

Sontag, S. (1977). *Illness as metaphor.* New York: Farrar, Straus and Giroux.

Sotomayor, M., & Randolph, S. (1988). A preliminary review of caregiving issues among Hispanic elderly. In M. Sotomayor & H. Curiel (Eds.), *Hispanic elderly: A cultural signature* (pp. 137–160). Edinburgh, TX: Pan American University Press.

Sperling, R. A., Aisen, P. S., Beckett, L. A., Bennett, D. A., Craft, S., Fagan, A. M., et al. (2011). Toward defining the preclinical stages of Alzheimer's disease: Recommendations from the National Institute on Aging and Alzheimer's Association workgroup. *Alzheimer's & Dementia, 7*(3), 280–292.

Strickler, Z., Lin, C., Rauh, C., & Neafsey, P. (2008). Educating older adults to avoid harmful self-medication. *Journal of Communication in Healthcare, 1*, 110–128.

Tampi, R. R., Williamson, D., Muralee, S., Mittal, V., McEnemey, N., Thomas, J., et al. (2011). Behavioral and psychological symptoms of dementia: Part I—epidemiology, neurobiology, heritability, and evaluation. *Clinical Geriatrics, 19*, 41–46.

Thorne, B. (1982). Feminist rethinking of the family: An overview. In B. Thorne & M. Yalom (Eds.), *Rethinking the family: Some feminist questions* (pp. 1–24). White Plains, NY: Longman.

Twigg, J. (1989). Models of carers: How do social care agencies conceptualize their relationship with informal carers? *Journal of Social Policy, 18*, 53–66.

Walker, A. (1983). Care for elderly people: A conflict between women and the state. In J. Finch & D. Groves (Eds.), *A labor of love: Women, work and caring* (pp. 106–128). Boston, MA: Routledge.

Walker, A. (1991). The relationship between the family and the state in the care of older people. *Canadian Journal of Aging, 10*, 94–112.

Whaley, A. L. (2002). Psychometric analysis of the Cultural Mistrust Inventory with a Black psychiatric inpatient sample. *Journal of Clinical Psychology, 58*(4), 383–396.

Wuest, J., Ericson, P., & Stern, P. (1994). Becoming strangers: The changing family caregiving relationship in Alzheimer's disease. *Journal of Advanced Nursing, 20*, 437–443.

Valle, R. (1998). *Caregiving across cultures*. New York: Taylor & Francis.

3

Concepts and Theories to Understand Caregiving for Ethnic Caregivers

CASE EXAMPLE

My husband is supposed to be caring for his stepfather who has Alzheimer's disease but it is always me who does it all. I don't know why he just doesn't take care of things. He just won't talk about it. It's like he doesn't believe it. He keeps saying it's just old age. And then there's his stepsister, she calls and bothers him all the time about this or that. They are always arguing about who is paying for this and that and who is taking the father or the mother to the doctor or for appointments. I'll tell you who does it, me that's who. His stepsister has fought him for years. She takes care of his mother and has control over her money. I try to talk to my husband to tell him he has to talk to his stepsister to tell her to send money when she brings the mother here but he won't, so it's me doing it all and I'm tired now. I have to take care of my husband, and everyone else. Because when his stepsister has to go somewhere or has to work, she works part-time sometimes, and can't take care of his mother, she brings her to me and I do it all. I told her to put her in a day care but they won't take her anymore. She starts to fight or to cry and behaves bad so they won't take her. She does that here now when she comes here. Then I have both of them going at it. Something has to be done. I can't keep doing it all. My husband just sits there. He won't talk and he won't do nothing. It's like he don't believe they are sick or something. He won't tell anyone, it's just me doing all the talking but no one listens. She [stepsister] won't talk to me anymore because she knows what I think. It helps when I go to the Black church but then I come home and here we are again. That's where I heard about Alzheimer's when someone came to talk to us all. But my husband won't believe it. Just old age he says. I have to make him see what's happening. I need help.

In the case example, there are long-standing interwoven attachments among parents, kin, and fictive kin that cross nuclear family boundaries. Although these patterns existed for a considerable length of time and taxed family members' patience, they were never considered serious conflicts. However, once the aging parents began developing memory loss symptoms and were subsequently diagnosed with Alzheimer's disease, relationship conflicts escalated to problematic levels. Both adult child and stepchild caregivers and their spouses wanted to do what was best for their respective parent and stepparent but were unable to communicate sufficiently to problem solve. If attachments early in life fostered adaptive patterns of interaction with others, communication patterns that have become dysfunctional over the years can be regained with the assistance of a social worker. If the attachment experience was negative, communication or learning of communication skills will help, but will likely involve more time and clinical expertise from the social worker. In the latter case, the social worker should focus primarily on the meanings the caregivers assign to behaviors demonstrated by others in the care situation in order to identify misunderstandings. Once misunderstandings have been identified, the next step is to help the caregiver make a paradigm shift to correct thinking, feeling, and behaving in order to apply a more adaptive and healthy problem-solving interaction that fosters appropriate care solutions for the caregiver and afflicted family member(s).

ATTACHMENT THEORY AND ETHNIC CULTURAL VALUES

It is impossible to understand the roots and strengths of embedded cultural values and norms of Black and Latino family caregivers without a brief history into the research of attachment theory as it relates to the formation of kinship, familismo patterns of interaction, and ways the patterns function today in ethnic families. Therefore, the concepts and theories are briefly described in this section. Often, social workers seeking engagement with family caregivers require reaching out beyond the family caregiver to other family members. By reviewing the theoretical framework from which the nature of kinship and familismo can best be learned and understood, social workers also gain insight on how to handle a wide variety of problems and concerns in ethnic families. Ideally, social workers should act as supporters and facilitators assisting caregivers to identify the attributes that characterize resilience, such as family cohesion, flexibility, open communication, affirming patterns of interaction and problem solving, strengths, and resources they find helpful as they care for their dementia-afflicted family member. The division of labor and designated roles and responsibilities that help families maintain equilibrium when facing stressful and demanding care tasks also provide essential family system interaction information to assist social workers and caregivers to problem solve effectively. Social workers are required to search for both historical and current scientific evidence as the basis for making practice decisions. Hence, social workers today should utilize research to provide practical knowledge that both social workers and caregivers need to solve problems they confront.

Attachment is considered an important development milestone for all human beings. The classical attachment theoretical perspective combined with the broader attachment context found in the ecological, psychological, and social cultural context of attachment provides the full spectrum of the family and social support network, and is helpful in understanding the development of interdependent, collective, relational social support patterns found in Black kinship and Latino familismo. The contextual ecological attachment model bridges the ecological perspective and classical attachment theory into the culture-specific context of mother–infant attachment with multiple caregivers, which facilitates the examination of Black and Latino family relational exchanges that begin between Black mother and child and Latino mother and child. These relational exchanges between mother and child help develop internal working models in the context of social support networks that are found in the cultural perspective of Black and Latino child rearing within kinship familismo networks, and continue throughout the life span.

Research on cross-cultural, universal, and contextual patterns of attachment began with Mary Ainsworth's work in Uganda in 1954–1955 when she first operationalized Bowlby's conceptualization of attachment theory (Ainsworth, 1967, 1977). It is in this study that Ainsworth began to create the attachment classification system (Van IJzendoorn & Sagi, 1999, p. 713). The Uganda study revealed that the decisive factor for development of secure infant caregiver attachment was the continuity and quality of mother–infant interactions and that multiple caregivers did not interfere with the development of a secure attachment between infant and primary caregiver (Weisner & Galimore, 1977). This outcome speaks to the applicability of the mother–infant dyad, the Bowlby (1969, 1982) and Ainsworth, Blehar, Waters, and Wall (1978) attachment theories in terms of suitablility for use with "globally adaptive behavioral propensities that are realized in a specific way, depending on the cultural niche in which children have to survive" (Hinde & Stevenson-Hinde, 1990, 1991; Van IJzendoorn & Sagi, 1999, p. 714).

In a descriptive study of the Hausa of Nigeria by Marvin, VanDevender, Iwanaga, LeVine, and Le Vine (1977), examining attachment and exploratory behaviors of 18 infants, the researchers found that when not sleeping, "the Hausa infants were almost always in close physical contact or in the near proximity of one or more adult caregivers. All infants displayed attachment behavior to more than one caregiver, and on the average they appeared to be attached to three or four different figures, including their father" (p. 118).

According to Van IJzendoorn and Sagi (1999), subsequent, cross-cultural contextual research examining various cross-cultural patterns of attachment in cultural sites in China, Japan, Israel, Holland, and Africa found that the "universal validity of attachment theory could be confirmed using attachment-related constructs" (p. 715). In other words, the mother–infant dyad plus multiple caregiving networks and caregiving support systems attachment constructs applied in the social environment specific to a particular culture (Van IJzendoorn & Sagi, 1999). These early cross-cultural contextual studies provided new understanding about attachment processes across cultures and the strength of secure attachment outcomes related to the presence of multiple infant caregivers and support care networks in addition to the primary caregiver.

Falicov (1988), examining Latino attachment studies, confirms the importance of culture in mother–infant attachment and added more culture-specific behavior stating "While secure attachment is valued across cultures it is not culture-free" (p. 216). Other variables that may add to the different caregiver–infant dyad interaction behavior in cross-cultural attachment may be differences in educational achievement and socioeconomic status. The implication is that the infant–mother attachment formation may be a different experience for Black infants who have a kin network of care than for most White American infants (Van IJzendoorn, Bakermans-Kranenburg, & Sagi-Schwartz, 2006), and may be a different infant–mother attachment formation for Latinos as well (p. 122). Jackson (1993) "considered multiple caregiving as instantiated in African American families as distinctive and without parallel in the cross-cultural literature on attachment. Childcare for African American children is generally conducted within a relatively large social network of friends and acquaintances of the family" (Van IJzendoorn et al., 2006, p. 122). Jackson (1993) further notes that, many times, multiple adult caregivers have a responsibility for infant care, providing an array of family member attachment figures.

AFRICAN AMERICAN AND BLACK KINSHIP CARE

What is kinship care and how did this practice arise in the African American and Black culture? As noted in the attachment literature concerning African American and Black families, multiple caregivers and extended family members have historically functioned to provide informal social support to family members. The following section briefly summarizes the historical factors leading to the emergence of kinship networks in the heterogeneous African American and Black culture.

Historical Intergeneration Cultural Values and the Development of Kinship Care

Dilworth-Anderson (1992) notes that traditionally Black communities define family relationally. This means that family membership for many Black families consists by the nature of the relationship between persons not just blood relatives. Family boundaries are viewed in many cases as permeable and flexible in Black families (Dilworth-Anderson, 1992). Family members not related by blood are considered "fictive kin" and can be considered just as important in Black families as those related by blood (Dilworth-Anderson, 1992, p. 29). Traditionally, the African roots of African Americans and Blacks identify a collective society of origin described as a "nation" or "tribe," or "clan" family and household (Dixon, 2007, p. 2).

Nations or tribes, which consisted of several clans, range from a thousand to millions of people distinguished by a unique history where they traced their origins to God, first ancestors, or a national leader, and a common culture, distinguished by a distinctive language, geographical area, and social, political, and economic organization. The clan, which is distinguished by a totem, consists of many families and a family consists of children, parents, grandparents, aunts, uncles, brothers, and sisters who may have their own children and immediate relatives, and those who have died, and the unborn. Finally, the household or "family at night," the smallest unit, consists of parents, children, and sometimes grandparents (Dixon, 2007, p. 2).

Dixon notes the importance of spirituality in traditional African societies that viewed individuals as connected through the spirit during life and after death into immortality (Dixon, p. 2). The cultural value of collective life fostered connectedness in all development states of the individual within his or her cultural life and continued beyond the individual's passing. Mbiti (1990) states: "Because of the goal of achieving immorality, kinship, then, is one of the strongest forces in traditional

African societies. Kinship controls the thinking and behavior of the individual, governs all social relationships, and underlies the guiding principle common among African people: I am because we are, we are therefore I am" (p. 104).

Hence, social workers working with Blacks and Latinos need to understand the strength of kinship. The implication is "everyone is expected to share in the care of children and the aged" (Dixon, 2007, p. 3). Although many efforts were made to destroy the significance and meaning of their early African heritage when Africans arrived in the New World, there are recorded instances where the family history and kinship ties along with cultural beliefs and spirituality were resurrected and recorded from stories told by captives.

An analysis of African and Black history again and again points to the reconfiguration of the family kinship and fictive kin paradigm within the culture as the social and physical environment changed for the Black person. This critical cultural value woven within the Black culture family system has been a means of survival to many, enabling them to survive horrific hardships on life's historical journey. Dilworth-Anderson (1992) notes, "History therefore teaches us that shared meanings and symbols of extended familism in the Black community emerged, in part, in the face of slavery, oppression, and racism" (p. 29).

Kinship Care Today

Today, research reveals that the kinship and fictive kin network support system continues to function in the United States at a different level as compared to the survival context during the historical issues related to slavery and the pre-civil rights era (Dilworth-Anderson, 1992). The kinship network continues to provide aid in multiple ways such as sharing housing, food, or other resources, especially when members are in need. This is especially true when families of multiple generations find the needy to be children and the elderly.

The kinship and fictive kin network is a source of strength and support by sharing homes, time, energy, transportation, economic, and other practical resources. Black families generally first seek services within the kin network of mutual aid rather than seeking formal resources and services. Unemployment and economic challenges have always been a concern for many African American and Black families especially in single parent households where poverty among female heads of household is often severe (Dilworth-Anderson, 1992). For these more vulnerable members, the kinship networks often serve as survival assistance. "Poor black women, many of whom are unskilled, with low levels of education, and with more children to take care of as compared to white females, look to their extended family for support, especially to (given the history of their roles in the family) grandparents" (p. 30). This mutual aid system of care fosters within the system a desire for family members to return care to older adults who, in the past, may have often been the source of assistance to younger families.

Elderly parents are cared for and supported, in part because younger family members feel obligated to give back to the older generation that cared for them (Dilworth-Anderson & Goodwin, 2005, p. 211). Due to increasing need within younger generations and declining resources, some emerging research is beginning to reveal changes in the composition and strength of the kin network in African American families (Dilworth-Anderson & Goodwin, 2005; Jarrett & Burton, 1999; McDonald & Amstrong, 2001; Roschelle, 1997).

Influence of Kinship Care in Dementia Caregiving

In dementia care, however, it seems the kin network continues to be the primary structure and source of care. Because of the permeable and flexible close kin, distant kin, and even fictive kin being a part of the family, kinship and fictive kin network caregivers in African American and Black families are able to tap into the strengths of multiple caregiver members in various family systems for dementia care assistance. In fact, research findings show that kin caregivers to dependent older African Americans consist of an array of family members, such as adult children, spouses, nieces, nephews, in-laws, and grandchildren (Haley et al., 1995; Young & Kahana, 1995).

Non-kin or fictive kin consisting of close friends and neighbors also assist in providing care to the elderly. Who becomes the primary caregiver is driven by the quality of the relationship with the care recipient (Montgomery & Williams, 2001). Dilworth-Anderson and Goodwin (2005) note that as families and friends rally around the afflicted care recipient, they form structures of care consisting of a primary caregiver and various levels of both kin and fictive kin or "secondary" and "tertiary" care networks that serve to not only maintain and sustain the dementia-afflicted family member, but also may complement care by diversifying assistance and performing specialized tasks (p. 212). In research conducted in 1999, Dilworth-Anderson and colleagues examined responsibilities and duties of care and found four overlapping levels or structures of care: "(1) PST structure (primary, secondary, and tertiary), (2) PS structure (primary and secondary), (3) PT structure (primary and tertiary), and (4) PO structure (primary only)" (Dilworth-Anderson & Goodwin, 2005, pp. 212–213). The primary only caregiver perceived as the main authority or "head" had the most responsibility and decision-making authority and performed the largest number of caregiving tasks, whereas the secondary caregiver provided a similar number of tasks but with less responsibility for major decisions (Dilworth-Anderson & Goodwin, 2005, pp. 212–213). The tertiary level within the care network appeared to have more specialized care duties without any authority or responsibility for major decision making (Dilworth-Anderson & Goodwin, 2005, p. 212).

Case Example

I feel overwhelmed, helpless, stressed, trapped, and unable to balance all situations in my life. I feel like I have failed her [daughter]. I can't do anything to help my daddy get well, and I don't know what to do about my brother. We just don't put our daddy in a home. That just isn't right for us. We take care of our own.

Mrs. R, a female African American adult-child caregiver, aged 43, shares primary caregiving responsibilities with her mother, aged 72, for her late-stage Alzheimer's-afflicted father aged 70. Mrs. R, her husband, and their three children live on the second floor of a three-family home. Her mother and ailing father occupy the first floor, and the caregiver's younger brother and sister (recently separated from her husband) and her two children live on the third floor. The afflicted father was in final stage of the disease, "stage 7" (www.Alz.org 2010). He was no longer able to respond to family or others in the environment and had difficulty eating and had lost the ability to walk or sit without assistance. Her mother and the family wanted to keep him at home. Most of his days were spent sleeping.

Mrs. R works part-time and is enrolled in one college course during the day and shares the care of her father when not at work or school. Her mother had been diagnosed with arthritis, high blood pressure, and hearing loss. The caregiver's husband aged 43 works as a salesman in used car lot. The children ages 7, 9, and 13 are in school during the day. The oldest daughter is experiencing stress and grief over her grandfather's illness and is repeating a grade.

In addition, Mrs. R is extremely concerned about her younger brother (aged 39) occupying the third floor with the sister (aged 41) and her children (aged 10 and 12), because he has a history of chronic severe asthma. He was divorced 6 years ago and lived alone in a nearby apartment until her sister's husband moved out of the three-family home a year ago. When Mrs. R's brother-in-law moved out, the younger brother moved in to provide additional care to his parents. Because everyone worries about this younger brother due to a severe asthma attack 2 years ago that almost killed him, moving into the family home seemed like the best solution at the time.

In problem solving, the social worker and caregiver initially focused on caregiver self-care and on family member dementia care problems. To begin to ease the caregiver's stress level and to enable the afflicted family member to remain at home, the caregiver decided to accept assistance from home health aides, respite care, visiting nurses, and occupational and physical therapists. The caregiver was engaged in individual and family therapy to assist with the identified disease and family system issues. Family members decided to participate in the family counseling as well.

As noted in this case example, the kinship network is visible both in the care of the aging parents as well as of the most vulnerable. According to the literature, in most families kinship care is a vital system within the culture. "This system of care may include a structure of caregiving where several caregivers are present who are close, distant, and even fictive kin, and they most likely live in close proximity to one another. An informal social support system with the help of some formal support probably exists to provide a major foundation for those who provide care to older dependent family members" (Dilworth-Anderson, 1997, p. 33).

Kinship bonds in Jamaican families are also quite extended and often include grandparents living in the home (Miller, 2002). Aunts and uncles may assume the roles of caring for aging siblings and aging parents (Miller, 2002). In addition, nieces may assume the caregiving role for an aging or infirmed aunt or uncle and may return to Jamaica if necessary to fulfill the care responsibilities (Miller, 2002).

LATINO FAMILISMO

Historical Intergenerational Cultural Value Development of Familismo

In order for social workers to understand the nature, meaning, and strength of the concept of familismo in the Latino culture, one needs to examine the roots of Latino family bonding found in research. In a cross-cultural study by Harwood, Miller, and Irizarry (1995) comparing Latino mothers with Caucasian mothers, they found that Latino mothers had a much more sociocentric set of developmental goals for their infants and toddlers focusing on their ability to engage in appropriate intimate and non-intimate relatedness—"*buen educado*" or "proper demeanor"—as compared to the Caucasian mothers who emphasized more "self-maximization" (Falicov, 1998, p. 216). The cultural contextual "proper demeanor" consisted of an "ethical quality that connotes a person of moral goodness who readily fulfills obligations to family, friends, neighbors and co-workers" (Falicov, 1998, p. 216). The Latino emphasis on the cultural concept of "proper demeanor" suggests the use of ethnocentric cultural norms in the mother–infant dyad to shape the cultural attachment behavior toward the formation of familismo. This may suggest that the Latino cultural root of the family bond and relatedness and, thus, social support in familismo could be perceived as stemming from "proper demeanor" developed within Latino mother–infant attachment and caregiving interactions. It implies that the concept of "proper demeanor" attitude and behavior is what maintains the intergenerational and multigenerational child and caregiver relational bond and social support system found in familismo. Family members are often told, "In good times or in bad, *la Família* [the family] comes first" (Cuellar, 1990).

Familismo Today

In 1990, Cuellar wrote the following statement that is still relevant today.

> Many geriatric care provides carry out their treatment plans based on a model of independent aging individuals who function alone, and who decide for themselves what is best. In contrast, clinical experiences among Hispanic elderly suggest that geriatric care providers must be ready to incorporate family members in the decision making process, and consider what is best for the family as a whole, not just the aging individual involved. Hispanic cultures and kinship patterns provide strong support for needy elders, and geriatric health providers should learn how these can influence the organization and delivery of services. Therefore, geriatric care providers should consider the elderly's sensitivity to family economic and social conditions in preparing a treatment plan for Hispanic elderly, and involve their significant others in the process from the beginning. (Cuellar, 1990, p. 32)

Influence of Familismo in Dementia Caregiving

Researchers today continue to note the importance of familismo in the Latino dementia caregiver literature (Gallagher-Thompson, Talamantes, Ramirez, & Valverde, 1996; González Sanders, 2006; Valle, 1998). The Latino caregiver study conducted by González Sanders (2006) sampling 60 Latino caregivers from Connecticut and Massachusetts found familismo to be the most significant cultural value influencing Latino caregivers of dementia-afflicted relatives. This finding is similar to previous study findings by Gallagher-Thompson et al. (2003), which also found familismo to be a major value shared in Latino cultures and "regarded as the most important institution for Latinos regardless of the country of origin, length of residence in the United States, or social class...referring not only to the importance of family over the individual, but also to the unity and role division" (p. 48).

Case Example

I'm here not because I have a problem. I don't think I have a problem, but my sisters and my kids think I have a problem. I know I don't [laughs]. They said I promised my son I would come today. I think everyone just worries too much. I think if everyone would just mind their own business everything would be fine. Yes, I get a little forgetful and sometimes confused but doesn't everyone? We're just getting old. I think caring for my mother is more important. She's old and sick. I'm not old and I'm not sick. I'm sure how old she is now but she can't walk anymore. My sisters take care of her. I miss my daddy. He died a long time ago. I was his favorite. I don't remember how. I think that is why my sisters are mad at me. They have always been jealous. That's why they take things from my house. They are always stealing things from me. Is it time to go now?

Mrs. A, aged 48, is diagnosed with younger-onset Alzheimer's disease. She has been a single parent for 10 years after her husband left her and returned to El Salvador. Her son, aged 24, moved out of the house 3 years ago, works and attends college. Her daughter, aged 14, lives with her and attends middle school. Mrs. A is the youngest of four sisters. The oldest sister died 10 years ago from cancer. The remaining two sisters aged 52 and 54 have never married and live together with their mother aged 84 ever since their father died in 1973 in a car accident. They also provide care for Mrs. A and for their niece, although Mrs. A resists their efforts.

While the older sisters admit to having a long history of sibling conflict, their concern at this time is Mrs. A's increasing memory loss, confusion, and overall at-risk behavior. She forgets to pay bills. They have had to move four times within the past 3 years due to unpaid rent. The utilities are frequently turned off due to nonpayment. When the sisters visit there is little to no food in the house, and the day-to-day chores are not done. On several occasions doors were found unlocked after dark allowing anyone to enter the house. This is a risk because of the high-crime neighborhood environment. Mrs. A tells the sisters she does not cook and prefer to eat out. The younger daughter indicates that often there isn't enough money to eat out.

Driving safety has become a major concern. Mrs. A often gets confused and forgetful when driving. Her adult son reported she has been in 10 minor accidents in 2 years. Once her car is repaired she resumes driving. The car itself is unsafe and needs servicing, but all are concerned about Mrs. A's due to the increasing memory symptoms.

The 14-year-old daughter is experiencing role reversal. She is the parent in the house and is responsible for ensuring her mother pays bills, makes and keeps medical appointments, and gets to and from places safely. As a result, school attendance and academic standing have declined. Mrs. A either has not established rules for her adolescent daughter or does not remember to enforce the rules.

With Mrs. A's signed authorization, the social worker engaged the family members in the problem-solving process. In multiple family meetings, the social worker used knowledge of familismo to successfully engage family members in multiple care and support roles including helping Mrs. A manage her house; obtaining legal services and advice; and providing parenting support for her daughter through the Connecticut Department of Children and Families by requesting a family with service needs assistance; and obtaining medical and in-home assistance care management. In addition, the older sisters and extended family network established a long-term problem-solving plan to provide ongoing assistance. Mrs. A's resistance to family assistance lessened as memory loss increased.

ETHNIC CULTURAL VALUES AND NORMS

There are several cultural values and norms that social workers working with Latinos need to know and understand in order to provide culturally competent assistance. The Latino mother–infant attachment experience is an important factor in the development of the cultural contextual value of trust or *confianza* in the Latino infant and of socialization. Latino *confianza* is also essential in the subsequent development of attachment bonds and of healthy social relationships in the Latino familismo network (Valle, 1998). The notion of trust or *confianza* is not simply confidence; it possesses at least two meanings for Latinos. First, it means that strangers have established the proper rapport giving the Latino notice that the individual has followed the explicit and implicit cultural expectations for the interaction at hand, which is relatedness (Valle, 1998). Second, *confianza* means a particular level of mutual trust has been reached leading to security and bonding in the relationship (Valle, 1998). Understanding the development of *confianza* is an integral part in understanding the concept of *familismo* (Valle, 1998).

Carlson and Harwood (2003), studying attachment in Caucasian and Puerto Rican mother–infant dyads, found evidence to support the attachment behaviors illustrated by the Caucasian mother–infant pairs that tended to emphasize self-confidence and independence with a focus on autonomy, while the Puerto Rican mother–infant dyads tended to emphasize more interdependence and relatedness attachment patterns appropriate with Latino familismo interdependence cultural value (Carlson & Harwood, 2003).

Marín and Marín (1991), in research with Latinos, identify what they refer to as a "cultural script," which is the cultural value of "simpática" (used interchangeably with "simpático") that also refers to relatedness and bonding in social behavior directly related to interdependence and collective cultural functioning of familismo (p. 12). The use of the term "cultural script" suggests it may be shaped by an early, mother–infant and multiple caregivers exchange network through day-to-day interactions, as Bowlby (1969) and Ainsworth et al. (1978) theorized in their attachment studies. "Simpática" emphasizes dignity and respect toward others and strives to achieve harmony in interpersonal relationships through a level of conformity (Marín & Marín, 1991, p. 12).

Various Latino studies reveal "simpática," the Latino relatedness with others, is demonstrated through Latinos' empathy, and smooth, congenial, and pleasant social exchanges known as "plática" or "small talk" (Marín & Marín, 1991, p. 13; Kagan, Knight, & Martinez-Romero, 1982; Kagan & Madsen, 1971; Triandis, Marín, & Betancourt, 1984). It is also demonstrated through Latino-positive agreeable attitudes and behavior that de-emphasizes negative, disagreeable, and conflictual attitudes and behaviors, and seeks to avoid conflict with others (Marín & Marín, 1991, p. 13; Kagan, Knight, & Martinez-Romero, 1982; Kagan & Madsen, 1971; Triandis, Marín, & Betancourt, 1984).

These cultural values are all especially important for social workers to understand especially if the caregiver has not made progress in problem-solving efforts that require him or her to self-advocate, advocate for their afflicted family member, or use confrontational skills with service providers to obtain needed care services. Latinos functioning from cultural value may have difficulty in help-seeking or help-receiving problem-solving actions and may require social work assistance to obtain needed services. The foundation of social work practice with Latinos should have knowledge, appreciation, and sensitivity to cultural values in order to provide strategies to promote effective problem-solving assistance to dementia caregivers. In ethnic families, cultural values determine roles and drive division of labor assignments.

Division of Labor

Interest in ethnic child attachment patterns, role differentiation, and specialized care task assignments within the family, and the emerging networks of care are becoming more important as the ethnic aging population increases. Despite the diversity of ethnic subgroups represented in the Black and Latino populations, children and elderly are highly valued and generally it is the females in the family who play key roles in nurturing and maintaining the emotional and economic well-being of family networks (Dilworth-Anderson & Goodwin, 2005; Sotomayor, 1993). As concern about the care of the afflicted family member consumes the family, it is the family that makes a paradigm shift in order to position itself to function as a system of care. The case example of Mrs. A illustrates this point. What happens when a single mother with a 14-year-old daughter is diagnosed with younger-onset Alzheimer's disease? How are the tasks assigned? How are decisions made regarding division of labor and role responsibilities?

Role Responsibilities

Contemporary Black and Latino families are a reflection of generations of change in the landscape of American society. For both cultures, the heterogeneity of the populations in terms of subgroup, education, socioeconomic level, class, neighborhood, schools, available health, employment, day care, geographic region, and family structure provides varying assumptions and evolving realities of trends regarding contemporary family roles. For the most part, roles within the family emerge through the socialization process and patterns of care within each environment.

The macroeconomic and social forces influence the evolution of the mul-tilayered contextual process of the environment and determine the des-ignated roles of kinship and familismo family members. It is important for social workers to remember that for ethnic families, the kinship role designations and decision-making delegation processes not only work, but tend to work very well to support and sustain the added level of shared care required for the dementia caregiver. Another reason is that the kinship and familismo care networks not only appear to survive after years of application, but also seem to thrive when put to the test by caregivers when problem-solving multiple care challenges.

On the other hand, family roles are a concern when the roles cause dysfunction and impede the problem-solving efforts, although on the surface ethnic family member role functioning in kinship networks and familismo may appear to be overly enmeshed. However, social workers need to remember the historical development of attachment and social-ization and the meaning ethnic families have given the affiliation with one another. In most cases, the interactions between family members are serving a purpose unique and necessary to the particular family that is important to their problem solving, resilience, and coping. It is only when roles fail, block help, or prevent social work problem-solving that intervention is necessary. If this seems to be the situation, the first step for the social worker is to ask the caregiver if he or she needs help or would like help to assist family members. Social workers should never assume their intervention is welcome or required. Again, remembering the historical development of family attachment and socialization should be the first point of reference for the social worker. Some caregivers may prefer to try to work things out themselves with family members before inviting the social worker to help. The social worker should respect the caregiver's and family's desire to first try and work things out. If add-itional assessments and caregiver communications reveal more help is needed, by all means the social worker should offer to help.

For example, social workers may need to assist the caregiver when the care responsibilities begin to cause stress and perhaps impact care-giver care functions in a way that is weakening existing bonds, or to change affiliations between caregiver and members leading to feelings of alienated. When these alienations begin to create obstacles to care by blocking caregiver problem-solving efforts, social work help is needed. While some dissatisfaction and/or conflict is often a normal part of fam-ily interactions, in cases of extreme maladaptive functioning, the social worker needs to help the family achieve adaptive functioning. Examples of extreme maladaptive functioning include when family members completely disengage from the family because of the afflicted family member's memory loss issues, or when members from either overly rigid or overly permeable alliances foster maladaptive and problematic coalitions perhaps with the dementia-afflicted family member used as a pawn in their struggles. If the caregiver is unable to make care decisions for the afflicted family member due to differences of opinion, or distortive perceptions by members designated to be the decision makers, the social worker can be asked to intervene to correct misinformation and help members make an informed decision.

The role of the social worker can encompass various overlapping skill levels with ethnic populations. For example, the social work role can include the work of consultants, providing necessary disease, care information, and symptom management guidelines to the caregiver, the afflicted family member, and the family. Another social work role is that of coordinator to monitor and guide the problem-solving process as the caregiver applies the process to a wide variety of problems. In this role, the social worker maintains regular contact with the caregiver. The role of the social worker in some cases can be expanded to include the role of case manager, completing the assessment, planning the problem-solving intervention, guiding and monitoring progress, serving as the link with available resources, and maintaining regular and scheduled contact with the caregiver and family to ensure that the day-to-day problem-solving actions are helping the caregiver, the afflicted family member, and the family, as well as to ensure that care resources are available on an ongoing basis. It is not uncommon for the social worker to move into and out of roles as the caregiver, care recipient, and family care needs changes. The role of crisis intervener is also a social worker role that can be required in the family if a life or safety issue arises in the problem-solving intervention process. Unless the social worker is called upon to assist in a crisis situation and needs to take an active role, the social worker should guard against the desire to take over too much responsibility, thereby nullifying the problem-solving self-efficacy and mastery actions the caregiver is learning to apply. Such action could result in a reduction of caregiver self-confidence and problem-solving resiliency.

Family Members and Day-to-Day Care Decision Makers

When assessing the day-to-day caregiving responsibilities, social workers have to consider the unique and ever-changing family structure and context of the ethnic family. The social worker relies a great deal on the caregiver's input during the problem assessment and problem-solving planning to provide the contextual process of the environment.

Understanding the vicissitudes of the caregiver's life can help the social worker assess the caregiver's ability to implement the problem-solving plan of action. The family structure provides essential information about the caregiver's physical, economic, and emotional resources. Many caregivers find caring for a dementia-afflicted relative very demanding physically, economically, and emotionally, no matter how culturally attuned they are to providing care. While caregivers may find reward in the knowledge that they are fulfilling their obligations and cultural responsibilities, this does not change the fact that the depletion of physical, economic, and emotional resources can impede the caregivers' abilities to resolve problems. Therefore, understanding the evolving structure of ethnic families helps social workers better understand the plight of ethnic caregivers and the kinship family.

The evolving structure of ethnic minority families is partly due to the increase of families maintained by females with no spouse or partner (McLoyd, Hill, & Dodge, 2005). According to Duncan and Brooks-Gunn (1997), only 48% of all African American families were married-couple families, compared with 82% of non-Hispanic White families (McLoyd et al., 2005, p. 5). Close to half or 43% of the African American families were reportedly maintained by females without a spouse or partner, and 9% of families by males with no spouse or partner (McLoyd et al., 2005, p. 5). "In 2002, under 40% of Black children in the United States lived with both biological parents" (U.S. Bureau of the Census, 2003e).

What seem to be consistent are the prevalence of extended family households among African Americans (McLoyd et al., 2005) and the wider range of kinship care networks (Tucker & James, 2005). The reconfiguration and expansion of family roles are important responsibilities as people live longer and need care by family members and as marriages dissolve. These kinship or fictive kin members are family or close to family members who are potentially available to provide assistance by performing family functions or care responsibilities (Tucker & James, 2005). For example, it could be "a 'beloved aunt' who is usually [a] single and child-free woman [who] often has a particularly close and influential role in young peoples' lives. Similarly, male role models for many young men are their mothers' brothers, rather than their biological fathers" (Tucker & James, 2005, pp. 98–99).

According to McLoyd et al. (2005), many families report children with grandparents present (75%) and "grandparents are assumed to be providing assistance if they are the householders, whereas they are believed to be receiving assistance when they are living in their child's or someone else's household" (p. 6). While most two-parent households today have conjoint sharing of the economic responsibilities for the family, there is more variation in family forms in general (Tucker & James, 2005). With females sharing economic responsibilities came the need to reconstruct the maternal and paternal gender role expectations. Although historically working outside of the home has not been a "choice" but rather a norm for the African American female experience, today the need to contribute to the family sustenance is even more critical and common (U.S. Bureau of the Census, 2000). Key to understanding role development is to understand the underlying thoughts regarding how decisions are made, that is, knowing the ways in which the vicissitudes of African Americans' cultural conceptualizations of the role of mothers (and fathers), cultural models of optimal parenting, and ethno theories of children's development (McLoyd et al., 2005, p. 31). Because much of the research on African American families has focused on urban low-income populations, little is known about middle-class African American families or African American families from diverse socioeconomic backgrounds (McLoyd et al., 2005, p. 34). Hence, only limited information is known regarding how African American cultural values and roles relate to family processes (McLoyd et al., 2005, p. 34). While social workers need to be aware of the dearth of extant information regarding ethnic caregiver families, they should continue their efforts to seek out information about ethnic population in order to fully understand the psychosocial aspects of care ethnic families are faced with on a day-to-day basis.

Lesbian, Gay, Bisexual, and Transgendered Ethnic Caregivers

Social justice is the most important goal and value of the social work profession. Therefore, the purpose in this section is to understand the Lesbian, Gay, Bisexual, and Transgendered (LGBT) Black and Latino ethnic family caregiver functions, roles, and strengths. Social workers can help LGBT caregivers learn to apply the problem-solving process. To provide competent problem-solving services for LGBT family caregivers, it is important for social workers to understand the needs of LGBT caregivers and provide the information, resources, and care support that is appropriate for this separate culture. Equally important is for social workers to understand the long history of discrimination that has hampered self-disclosure and ways the sociocultural context impacts LGBT caregivers, creating barriers to service utilization. Coon (2003) cites Baron and Cramer (2000) in the following quote regarding diversity.

> The caregiving experience of LGBT in our society crosses both cohort and cultural boundaries, ranging from younger caregivers caring for former partners, neighbors, friends, who facilitated their coming-out

processes who have now grown older to older LGBT caregivers caring for long-time partners or friends. LGBT individuals also take on the role of providing care for their parents or other older biological family members. LGBT caregivers represent a diverse group in terms of ethnicity, race, language, national origin, and physical challenges. Many of these caregivers, depending upon their level of outness (the extent to which a person is willing to reveal their sexual orientation or gender identity to others), will be more or less reticent with agencies not known for serving the LGBT community. This may be particularly true for the older members of the community who faced many years of discrimination and intolerance, which may now be compounded by experiences of ageism, sexism, racism, or discrimination based on disabilities (Baron & Cramer, 2000). (Coon, 2003, p. 6)

This section begins by providing a definition of LGBT utilized in the literature and applied in this text. It will discuss identified LGBT family roles and briefly outline the "coming out" process discussed in the literature. It will also discuss the familial relationship with extended family members and other LGBT networks and communities, and ways in which this support network functions to provide caregiver support similarly to the kinship and fictive kin and familismo networks found in the Black and Latino families.

In general, "sexual orientation" refers to emotional and sexual attraction to others of a particular sex. Despite being commonly defined in the United States as being synonymous with sexual behavior (Herek, 1986), sexual orientation is no longer considered by human sexuality experts as a dichotomy between homosexuality and heterosexuality (Dworkin, 2000; Fox, 1996; Markowitz, 1995). Rather, sexual orientation can be conceptualized as: (a) a continuum from exclusively heterosexual to exclusively homosexual; (b) multidimensional, encompassing behavior, affiliation, feelings and desires, and spiritual components (Alquijay, 1997; Coleman, 1987); and (c) developed along a temporal dimension from one's past through the present and into thoughts about the future (Kimmel, 1978; Klein, Sepekoff, & Wolf, 1986; Money, 1988). Transgender individuals can self-identify as heterosexual, homosexual, or bisexual, but in addition, they express a strong sense of incongruity between their gender identity and their birth sex. As a result, transgender individuals can experience discrimination based not only on their sexual orientation but also their gender identities (Coon, 2003, p. 7).

LGBT caregivers are diverse in terms of sexual orientation, gender identity, age, ethnicity, race, culture, geographic location, education, income, family relationships, health, and physical abilities. Social workers working with LGBT caregivers need clarity of their conceptual understanding in order to provide the culturally sensitive approach necessary to assist LGBT dementia caregivers caring for their afflicted family member. According to Fredriksen-Goldsen and Hooyman (2007), in order to "advance caregiving research, the constructs of sexual orientation and gender identity need to be more clearly articulated and understood" (p. 131). Coon (2003) provides the following explanation regarding the difficulty of determining the true number of LBGT caregivers: "The number is hard to capture due to respondent fear of stigma associated with LGBT self-identification, as well as complexities surrounding the personal and professional definitions of 'lesbian,' 'gay,' 'bisexual,' and 'transgender' " (p. 7). One important point made by Coon (2003) is that in some cases the constructs are largely self-determined.

As such it is important for social workers to understand that the various constructs within the LGBT definition are dynamic and unique to the individual caregiver. Therefore, a culturally sensitive approach is not only to allow the LGBT caregiver to determine if and when the individual wants to disclose his or her sexual identity, but also to allow the caregiver to self-define the identity. This will prevent the social worker from quickly compounding issues with his or her own bias and prejudgments, and trying to fit the LGBT caregiver into the erroneous preconceived box of dualistic thinking identity construction that has been society's norm. By allowing the caregiver to take the lead, the social worker will not only meet the caregiver client where the client is, but also allow the caregiver to take responsibility in the treatment decision-making process in terms of targeting the issues on which to work.

Some LGBT family caregivers may not have the support of families of origin and may not want to include the family for a variety of reasons. Instead, they may rely on the LGBT community of relationships to provide social support networks. The caregiver will decide if, how, and when work is approached to target problems in the community of relationships within the social network.

Other LGBT caregivers may be similar to heterosexuals and have LGBT nuclear families, extended families of origin, and extended family members, as well as intimate or close friends and groups of close friends of partners (Fredricksen-Foldsen & Hoy-Ellis, 2007). What is also important is to dispel the myths that all LGBT individuals do not have families and that all ethnic LGBT caregivers do have supportive family networks. Some ethnic LGBT caregivers may or may not have nuclear, extended families and friends, or community care networks from previous partner relationships. Also, like heterosexuals, apart from the nuclear family, family of origin, and extended family networks, ethnic LGBT caregivers may or may not receive assistance from a variety of ethnic relationships, community groups, neighbors, and informal groups. To clarify: "In the general caregiving literature, kinship ties have been found to be related to the extent and pattern of care received" (Fredricksen-Goldsen & Hoy-Ellis, 2007, p. 6).

Although there is considerable research in the caregiving literature focusing on HIV/AIDs caregivers (Fredriksen, 1999; Wrubel & Folkman, 1997), there is a paucity of research regarding dementia caregiving experiences of "closeted" or "out" LGBT family members caring for dementia-afflicted family members, and even less research on "closeted" or "out" ethnic (LGBT) family caregivers. There are many aspects of the plight of social justice issues for LGBT caregivers in the literature: "LGBT caregivers and care recipients have been found to be less likely to benefit from formal services, both because of providers' insensitivity and prejudice as well as their own reluctance to utilize formal services" (Fredricksen-Foldsen & Hoy-Ellis, 2007, p. 6).

In general, the LGBT caregiving literature consistently identifies various kinds of prejudice—subtle or blatant—expressed by professionals or embedded in the formal service settings (Coon, 2003). Contemporary homophobia continues to impact the LGBT identity process of self-acceptance and the family and society's reaction to disclosure of sexual orientation.

Raphael and Meyer (2000) describe research by Warshow (1991) studying "closeted" middle-aged lesbians and found that closeted daughters were typically perceived by their families as single women who were expected to care for their aging mothers, and some "willingly assumed the role of caretaker" to the point of moving out of the home shared with their partner and moving in with their mother (Raphael & Meyer, 2000, pp. 140–141). Some of the other caregivers in the same study "moved the mother in with them and moved their lover either to another room or out of the house entirely until the mother died and the women could resume their lives as before" (Raphael & Meyer, 2000, p. 141).

The authors note the emerging "pattern of mothers increasingly relying on their daughters and turning to their daughters for caretaking in later life" (Raphael & Meyer, 2000, p. 141). What is implied here is when caring for a dementia-afflicted parent, the loss of memory in the parent may serve as a buffer and a protection, and may lessen the stress and crisis experienced in the disclosure process in the family of origin. Also implied is that in some cases the memory loss may allow for the development of a new dynamic in the afflicted member and the family of origin that serves as a buffer and protection. It is described by Raphael and Meyer (2000) as a "bittersweet" experience when the declining memory in the afflicted parent protects the afflicted parent from the stress and concern about the lesbian identity of the adult daughter and the impact the identity may have on the family (p. 142). Therefore, for some LGBT family caregivers, a "new constellation of nurturing relationships" develops grounded primarily in empathy and compassion and centered on the afflicted parent in need (Raphael & Meyer, 2000, p. 142).

Hoffman's (1994) film documentary about a midlife lesbian daughter's caregiving relationship with her Alzheimer's-afflicted mother provides some insight into ways in which the tragedy of memory loss enables the disease-afflicted mother, the lesbian daughter, and her partner, along with some other members from both families of origin and extended family, to develop care relationships "based solely on her (afflicted mother's) perception how people relate to her and care for her rather than on the knowledge of who they are and how they are related" (Hoffman, 1994; Raphael & Meyer, 2000, p. 142). While Hoffman documents a true story, more research is needed to examine and fully understand this dynamic within LGBT family systems. It would be helpful to know if the process could serve as a healing factor in the relationships within the families of origin and extended family networks, and whether LGBT family origin and extended family caregiving patterns may reduce caregiver stress and/or enhance care resilience in families.

Because very little is known about dementia caregiving among midlife and older lesbians, gay men, and the transgendered, more research is needed to explore the dynamics that exist within the LGBT Black and Latino caregiving families, extended families, and networks of care. Studying this population of caregivers whose experiences are likely to depart from the available heterosexual paradigm of care may increase and diversify our perceptions regarding how to best frame care services for LGBT caregivers in order to serve this population in an effective, efficient, and culturally sensitive manner.

The following case example illustrates one unique story and issues that emerged in a Latina caregiver experience as she sought social work problem-solving assistance for herself and her dementia-afflicted mother. This caregiver overcame many challenges in order to risk contacting a social worker to ask for assistance. These vulnerable caregivers often remain hidden and/or go unnoticed in dementia caregiving.

Case Example

I don't know what to do anymore. I feel like giving up. The last time I was so lonely and afraid like this I thought of killing myself. [crying] I was 17 but a friend talked me out of it. My L [partner] left me again. This is the third time in 5 years she said I am not honest because I hide her from my family. I love her but I don't know how to make things right. My dad has Alzheimer's disease. I take care of him since my mother died in a car accident 10 years ago. My mother knew I was lesbian but no one else in the family knows except for my older brother Luis. Mother told me not to say anything. My older brother knows because he is gay. But he moved to San Francisco 14 years ago because he didn't want the family to know. Latino families expect the girls to marry boys and boys to marry girls, [have] kids and take care of everyone. Everyone said daddy spoiled me. Everyone now in the family expects me to take care of my dad.

My other two younger sisters are married with kids. The youngest is divorced and has a baby. They work, too. Not the little one with the baby. They help when they can but I can't tell them about me. I'm afraid to be rejected. They think I'm an old maid...it hurts when I think of my life and now my dad's illness. I brought him to live with me. L [partner] was helping me take care of my dad. She works nights and is home during the day. I work at the dollar store parttime. L would go with us to the doctor because she speaks English. I don't speak very well but I do understand what they say.

My dad got sick after my mother died. He started to forget more and more. The family thought he would get over it with time because it was a "susto" [trauma shock] but he is not better and it has been 10 years. He needs to be watched all the time now because he goes outside to walk. One day he just walked away and I asked the neighbors to help me find him. We found him three blocks away in his pants, slippers and pajama top. He didn't remember his name or where he lived. Another neighbor recognized him and called me. Since then I don't leave him alone or let him go outside. I hurt on the inside. I miss my partner. Who will help with my dad now? I am very sad. Some days I just want to give up.

The social work problem-solving process for this caregiver began with crisis intervention due to the possible risk for self-harm. This 44-year-old lesbian adult child caregiver agreed to an immediate psychiatric evaluation to assess imminent risk for safety due to the suicide ideation. Once the risk for self-harm was eliminated, she returned to the dementia problem-solving intervention. She also decided to begin individual relationship and family therapy to work to resolve the issues with her partner and the long-standing lesbian "closet issues" with a plan to facilitate the "coming out" process if she so desired.

The caregiver had her father assessed by a bilingual geriatric psychiatrist to ensure that the appropriate diagnosis and care plan was in place for him. The caregiver agreed to receive caregiver support through culturally sensitive and language-appropriate respite assistance, a home health aide, and case manager to help with her father's dementia care symptoms. She registered her father in the MedicAlert and Safe Return emergency response systems for wandering and medical emergencies. Once the safety issues for herself, and the wandering issue and dementia assessment for her father with dementia were addressed and appropriate in-home care provided, the caregiver engaged in therapy.

She began long-term work addressing the depression symptoms, the issues related to the ruptured relationship with her lesbian partner, her long-standing lesbian identity and coming out issues with her family, the need for them to help more with the care of her father, the unresolved grief caused by the death of her mother, and her older brother's move to California.

One final note regarding the case example provided above: Dilworth-Anderson (2002) and Hinton and Levkoff (1999) have reported that cultural values and beliefs about the dementia disease determine not only who gives the care and why, but also whether caregivers will seek help outside the family system (p. S61). The authors note that some Black and Latino caregivers discuss the dementing illness in the context of somehow being linked to trauma, tragic loss, or other traumatic life-changing event that occurred in the afflicted member's life (Dilworth-Anderson, 2002; Hinton & Levkoff, 1999). Many LGBT ethnic caregivers, depending upon the degree of disclosure within the family, tend to experience more pressure that prohibits them as caregivers from seeking help outside of the family if there is a perceived risk of having to disclose or "come out," or disclose a trauma, tragic loss, or other traumatic or life-changing event.

Positive Aspects of Caregiving

Black and Latino caregivers for the most part express a sense of reward and of blessings, and embrace the opportunity to return care to the afflicted family member who once provided care for them. More recently, especially within the social work literature, greater attention has been placed on the strengths perspective, "…particularly as it relates to the positive aspects of caregiving for individuals with Alzheimer's disease" (Sanders, 2005, p. 58). This emerging body of literature on the idea of positive outcomes in caregiving suggests the need to further examine family caregivers of dementia relatives afflicted with Alzheimer's disease and related dementia in search of strengths, resources, and positive problem-solving outcomes. Studies have shown that positive outcomes from the caregiving role are fairly common. According to Sanders (2005) "between 55% and 90% of caregivers of older adults experience positive outcomes associated with caregiving" (p. 58). Moreover, caregivers who felt specific gains from their caregiving experiences were more likely to minimize the occurrence of negative risk factors resulting in less burden, improved health and relationships, and greater social supports (Cohen, Gold, Shulmana, & Zucchero, 1994). Hence, we see the need for social workers to understand the importance of the problem-solving process to further enhance caregiver strengths and positive aspects of care and how these strengths are tied to spirituality, resilience strength, and coping.

Positive caregiving for Latinos may be tied to the meaning given to the cultural construct. The nature and meaning for the Latino caregiver experience is centered on culturally defined values and perceptions requiring family members to adhere to socialized beliefs regarding responsibilities to family and family relationships, family relatedness, and family well-being (Cox & Monk, 1993; Harwood et al., 2000; John, Resendiz, & De Vargas, 1997). The nature of Latino caregiving is embedded within one's role in the family and demonstrated by the fulfillment of one's duty toward other family members, especially the ill elderly, regardless of the personal cost or consequences (Cox & Monk, 1993; Harwood et al., 2000; John et al., 1997). The meaning to the caregiver is found in the desired fulfillment of Latino family responsibilities and obligations to provide care (Cox & Monk, 1993; Harwood et al., 2000; John et al., 1997). For some Latinos, the meaning of the caregiving experience is associated with "desire, gladness, pleasure, and privilege" to be caring for their family member (John et al., 1997, p. 156). The needs of the Latino family caregiver are, in many instances, tightly woven within the needs of the family member with Alzheimer's disease and related dementia.

Spirituality and Ethnic Coping

What makes spirituality important to social workers? Interwoven within the cultural and racial frameworks are specific spiritual beliefs that have roots in historical events that have influenced the evolution of diverse cultures since life's inception. "It has been said that religion is for those who live in fear of going to hell, whereas spirituality is for those who have been there" (Jacobs, 2007). Understanding the ways in which specific spiritual beliefs help foster strength, resilience, and coping in the lives of clients is a significant key to understanding what may work for clients. This book embraces the concept of cultural competence, which dictates that social workers should have knowledge of culture-specific values, traditions, health beliefs, and spiritual beliefs, as well as the professional and interpersonal skills to provide service and care to all populations.

This is not to say that in order to be effective, the social worker should be personally spiritual and should actively preach or evangelize. Rather, what is meant here is that social workers that choose to ignore the spiritual dimension of clients are working from a deficit perspective, especially when working to assist individuals from diverse, ethnic cultures.

Strength and Coping

The literature indicates that in the Black community the church has played a major role, serving as a support system for many African American elders (Olsen, 2001). In general, spirituality is viewed as contributing to "feelings of well-being" in the African American community (Olsen, 2001, p. 9). In a study by Picot (1995a) the African American Alzheimer's disease caregivers who were sampled more frequently voiced the thought "God will bless me" than other rewards as positive aspects of caregiving (Roff et al., 2004). In another study using the same sample, Picot (1995b) found African Americans used "a palliative coping strategy, which relies on prayer and faith in God" (Rolf et al., 2004, p. 185). Mahoney, Cloutterbuck, Neary, and Zhan (2005), studying African American, Chinese, and Latino family dementia caregivers, found that African Americans went to their ministers for sources of support and advice. "Spirituality is essential to understanding many cultures as it provides values and beliefs that provide particular patterns, guides, interpretations, and ways of making meaning out of life's circumstances" (Jacobs, 2007, p. 193). In a study by Jones-Cannon and Davis (2005), researchers found "spirituality was a protective buffer and a resource factor that helped caregivers defend against stressors" (p. 122). Religion and spirituality were the predominating themes in the focus group's findings (Jones-Cannon & Davis, 2005, p. 122). The researchers examining coping among African American daughters described the importance of spirituality in coping with the demands of caregiving and ways in which spirituality seemed to help caregivers place the caregiving role in perspective for adaptive coping. Several participants noted, "To know that you can go to prayer and whatever you feel you're lacking or need more of you know that God is going to open the door and pour those blessings out and give you that little bit of patience [and] tolerance and that strength to continue to endure whatever it is that you're going through. Prayer and other folks,...being able to share with people who...are familiar with those kinds of experiences...and certainly prayer and studying the Word of God because it certainly gives you strength" (p. 122).

Latino caregivers tend to have the "most geographically diverse origins, as they come from North America, South and Central America, the Caribbean, and Spain" (Mahoney et al., 2005, p. 784). Researchers have pointed out the need to critically consider the subgroup and within-group diversity among Latinos (Aranda & Knight, 1997; Connell & Gibson, 1997; Delgado & Tennstedt, 1997; Gallagher-Thompson, 2000; Mahoney et al., 2005; Morano & Bravo, 2002). Often, research of Latino caregivers find participants are not born in the United States but have migrated from countries of origin (Aranda et al., 2003; Roff et al., 2004; Valle, 1998) or may have been born in the United States but maintained spiritual and cultural traditions from their homeland or have developed a combination of spiritual and cultural traditions from the country of origin and the United States. Hence, the Latino spiritual belief system may emanate from a wide range of origins, customs, and traditions, making it impossible to discuss in detail or in general in this section due to the vastness of the topic. However, what is clear is that, similar to the Black culture, spirituality has played an important role in the lives of Latinos throughout history. Social workers need to be aware of the vicissitudes of cultural origin and the meaning of spirituality within the self-identify for the caregiver and the afflicted family member as it emerges in the assessment and treatment process in terms of positive aspects of caregiving and caregiver strengths.

Spirituality may be a key factor for some Latino families and caregivers in terms of their understanding of dementia symptoms and the care process, and may delay or prevent caregivers from seeking help for their relatives (Cuellar, 1990; Olson, 2001; Valle, 1998). It may also be a source of adaptation and coping. Therefore, it is essential for social workers to recognize the unique cultural context of care and the spiritual motives driving the caregiver's actions. By momentarily suspending their professional medical knowledge and technical understanding of the disease process, the social worker opens the door to culturally sensitive discourse enabling the social worker to learn about the unique cultural construct of the disease and the spiritual beliefs surrounding the caregiver's understanding and coping mechanisms. Once the caregiver communicates his or her perspective, care must be taken by the social worker (a) to avoid overwhelming the caregiver with medical and highly technical interpretations about the dementia illness in the afflicted family member, and (b) to avoid devaluing the spiritual definition or meaning given to the dementia caregiving context.

Because there is a plethora of definitions of religion and spirituality in the literature (Cornett, 1998; Doka, 1993; Hugen, 1998; Kilpatrick & Holland, 1990), there are differing frameworks to consider. According to

Constable (1990), "For some, spirituality may or may not include belief in a *monotheistic* God" (Jacob, 2007, p. 191). Jacob (2007) offers the following definition of spirituality:

> It is one's personalized experience and identity pertaining to a sense of worth, meaning, vitality, and connectedness to others and to the universe. It incorporates faith—one's pattern of response to uncertainty inherent in life where the limits of material and human effectiveness are exceeded. It pertains to one's relationship with ultimate sources of inspiration, energy, and motivation; it pertains to an object of worship and reverence, and it pertains to the natural human tendency toward health and growth. (p. 191)

Canda and Furman (1999) define religion and spirituality as follows:

> Spirituality relates to a universal and fundamental aspect of what it is to be human—to search for a sense of meaning, purpose and moral frameworks for relating with self, others and the ultimate reality. In this sense, spirituality may express through religious forms, or it may be independent of them. Religion is an institutionally patterned system of beliefs, behaviors and experiences, oriented toward spiritual concerns, and shared by a community and transmitted over time in traditions. (p. 37)

For many Hispanic or Latinos, spirituality is a belief system that is strongly embedded within the folk medicine culture and that influences many cultural values and health and caregiving traditions for older adults (Cuellar, 1990). The central belief is identified in the concept known as "espiritismo" (Cuellar, 1990, p. 23). "Espiritismo consists of the belief that the world is of both good and evil spiritual beings that may affect human health and well-being in both negative and positive ways" (Cuellar, 1990, p. 23). The concept is expressed differently within Latino subgroups and often within generations in the subgroup. There is a dearth of knowledge in the literature about the origins of espiritismo (Cuellar, 1990) and how it is expressed in relation to dementia care. More research is needed to understand the meaning given to dementia in Latino folk medicine. Cuellar (1990) documents the following from a variety of sources.

> Nonetheless, we have some idealized descriptions of the Hispanic folk healing systems and how they vary from one group to the next (Casper & Phillipus, 1975; Delgado, 1978, 1980; Hamburger, 1978; Sandoval, 1975; Scott, 1974; Tamez, 1978). For example, Puerto Rican espiritismo is described as a Euro-American religious cult based on

an ethical code—which is concerned with communicating with spirits, and purifying the soul through moral behaviors, and contrasted with Cuban Santeria which is described as a combination of African beliefs and Catholic practices.

Taken as a whole, the Hispanic folk healing systems include various complex and sophisticated systems that utilize a variety of healers and techniques. Among Mexicans, the system is known as "curanderismo," among Cubans as "santeria," and Puerto Ricans as "espiritismo." Across the systems there are a variety of health care generalists and specialists: "curanderos" (general practitioners of Mexican folk healing), "yerbistas" (herbalists), "santeros" (Cuban faith healers), "espiritistas" (Puerto Rican faith healers), "farmaceticos" (pharmacists), and "santiguadores" (internists/chiropractors). The basic difference between santeros and espirititistas is that santeros do not take a moral position, as do espiritistas. (Cuellar, 1990, pp. 23–24)

Regardless of how the caregiver defines religion and spirituality, the social worker needs to be aware of the various expressions of folk medicine spirituality in both the Black and Latino cultures. Understanding the meaning in which folk medicine spirituality is experienced and lived within the culture, the individual, the family, and the caregiving environment is essential in order to be able to help clients bridge the gap between folk medicine and the recommended medical treatment and care by physicians.

Various studies examining cultural values and aspects of organized religion or spirituality in ethnic populations have found that for some Black (African American) and Latino caregivers, spirituality is directly associated with reports of positive aspects of Alzheimer's caregiving (Dilworth-Anderson & Gibson, 2002; Roff et al., 2004). Understanding the meaning of spirituality for Black and Latino caregivers is, in many cases, the door to understanding the center of the caregiving experience and the meaning it holds for the caregiver and family, and often leads to identifying coping strategies, resilience, and strengths.

REFERENCES

Ainsworth, M. D. S. (1967). *Infancy in Uganda: Infant care and the growth of love*. Baltimore, MD: John Hopkins University Press.

Ainsworth, M. D. S. (1977). Infant development and mother-infant interaction among Ganda and American families. In P. H. Leiderman, S. R. Tulkin, & A. H. Rosenfeld (Eds.), *Culture and infancy* (pp. 119–150). New York: Academic Press.

Ainsworth, M. D. S., Blehar, M. C., Waters, E., & Wall, S. (1978). *Patterns of attachment: A psychological study of the strange situation*. Hillsdale, NJ: Erlbaum.

Alquijay, M. A. (1997). The relationships among self-stem, acculturation and lesbian identity formation in Latina lesbians. In B. Greene (Ed.), *Ethnic and cultural diversity among lesbians and gay men* (pp. 249–265). Newbury Park, CA: Sage.

Aranda, M. P., & Knight, B. G. (1997). The influence of ethnicity and culture on the caregiver stress and coping process: A sociocultural review and analysis. *The Gerontologist, 37*(3), 342–354.

Baron, A., & Cramer, D. (2000). Potential counseling concerns of aging lesbian, gay, and bisexual clients. In R. M. Perez, K. A. DeBord, & K. J. Bieschke (Eds.), *Handbook of counseling and psychotherapy with lesbian, gay and bisexual clients* (pp. 207–224). Washington, DC: American Psychological Association.

Bowlby, J. (1969). *Attachment and loss volume I attachment.* New York: Basic Books.

Bowlby, J. (1982). Attachment and loss: Retrospect and prospect. *The American Journal of Orthopsychiatry, 52*(4), 664–678.

Carlson, V. J., & Harwood, R. L. (2003). Attachment, culture, and the caregiving system: The cultural patterning of everyday experiences among Anglo and Puerto Rican mother-infant pairs. *Infant Mental Health Journal, 24*(1), 53–73.

Casper, E. E., & Phillipus, M. J. (1975). Fifteen cases of embrujada: Combining medication and suggestions in treatment. *Hospital & Community Psychiatry, 26,* 271–274.

Coleman, E. (1987). Assessment of sexual orientation. *Journal of Homosexuality, 14*(1–2), 9–24.

Coon, D. W. (2003). *Lesbian, gay, bisexual, and transgender (LGBT) issues and family caregiving.* San Francisco, CA: Family Caregiver Alliance National Center on Caregiving.

Cox, C., & Monk, A. (1993). Hispanic culture and family care of Alzheimer's patients. *Health & Social Work, 18*(2), 92–100.

Cuellar, J (1990). *Aging and health: Hispanic American elders.* SGEC Working Paper Series Number 5, Ethnogeriatric Reviews. Stanford, CA: Stanford Geriatric Education Center Division of Family & Community Medicine.

Delgado, M., & Tennstedt, S. (1997). Puerto Rican sons as primary caregivers of elderly parents. *Social Work, 42*(2), 125–134.

Dilworth-Anderson, P. (1992). Extended kin networks in black families. *Generations, 16*(3), 29–32.

Dilworth-Anderson, P., & Burton, L. (1999). Critical issues in understanding family support and older minorities. In T. P. Miles (Ed.), *Full-color aging: Facts, goals, and recommendations for America's diverse elders* (pp. 93–105). Washington, DC: The Gerontological Society of America.

Dilworth-Anderson, P., & Goodwin, P. Y. (2005). A model of extended family support care of the elderly in African American families. In V. C. McLoyd, N. E. Hill, & K. A. Dodge (Eds.), *African American family life ecological and cultural diversity* (pp. 211–223). New York: The Guilford Press.

Dixon, P. (2007). *African American relationships, marriages, and families.* New York: Routledge Taylor & Francis.

Dworkin, S. H. (2000). Individual therapy with lesbian, gay, and bisexual clients. In R. M. Perez, K. A. DeBord, & K. J. Bieschke (Eds.), *Handbook of counseling and psychotherapy with lesbian, gay and bisexual clients* (pp. 157–181). Washington, DC: American Psychological Association.

Falicov, C. (Ed.). (1988). *Family transitions: Continuity and change over the life cycle.* New York: The Guilford Press.

Falicov, C. (1998). *Latino families in therapy: A guide to multicultural.* New York: Guilford Press.

Fox, R. (1996). Bisexuality in perspective: A review of theory and research. In B. Firestein (Ed.), *Bisexuality: The psychology and politics of an invisible minority* (pp. 263–291). Thousand Oaks, CA: Sage.

Fredriksen, K. I. (1999). Family caregiving responsibilities among lesbians and gay men. *Social Work, 44*(2), 142–155.

Fredriksen-Goldsen, K. I., & Hoy-Ellis, C. P. (2007). Caregiving with pride: An introduction. *Journal of Gay & Lesbian Social Services, 18*(3/4), 1–13.

Fredriksen-Goldsen, K. I., & Hooyman, N. R. (2007). Caregiving research, services, and policies in historically marginalized communities: Where do we go from here? *Journal of Gay & Lesbian Social Services, 18*(3/4), 129–145.

Gallagher-Thompson, D., Hargrave, R., Hinton, L., Árean, P., Iwamasa, G., & Zeiss, M., L. (2003). Interventions for a multicultural society. In D. W. Coon, D. Gallagher-Thompson, & L. W. Thompson (Eds.), *Innovative interventions to reduce dementia caregiver distress a clinical guide* (pp. 50–73). New York: Springer Publishing.

Hamburger, S. (1978). Profile of curanderos: A study of Mexican folk practitioners. *The International Journal of Social Psychiatry, 24*(1), 19–25.

Harwood, D. G., Barker, W. W., Ownby, R. L., Bravo, M., Aguero, H., & Duara, R. (2000). Predictors of positive and negative appraisal among Cuban American caregivers of Alzheimer's disease patients. *International Journal of Geriatric Psychiatry, 15*(6), 481–487.

Harwood, R. L., Miller, J. G., & Irizarry, N. L. (1995). *Culture and attachment: Perceptions of the child in context.* New York: Guilford Press.

Herek, G. (1986). On heterosexual masculinity: Some psychological consequences of the social construction of gender and sexuality. *American Behavioral Scientist, 29,* 563–577.

Hinde, R. A., & Stevenson-Hinde, J. (1991). Perspectives on attachment. In C. M. Parkes, J. Stevenson-Hinde, & P. Marris (Eds.), *Attachment across the life cycle* (pp. 52–65). London: Routledge/Tavistock.

Hoffman, D. (Producer & director). (1994). *Complaints of a dutiful daughter* [Film]. (Available from Women Make Movies, A D/D Production, New York, NY.)

Jacobs, C. (2007). Spiritual development. In J. G. Lesser & D. S. Pope (Eds.), *Human behavior and the social environment theory and practice* (pp. 188–203). New York: Pearson Education Inc.

Jarrett, R. L., & Burton, L. M. (1999). Dynamic dimensions of family structure in low-income African American families: Emergent themes in qualitative research. *Journal of Comparative Family Studies, 30,* 177–187.

John, R., Resendiz, R., & De Vargas, L. W. (1997). Beyond familism? Familism as explicit motive for eldercare among Mexican American caregivers. *Journal of Cross-Cultural Gerontology, 12*(2), 145–162.

Jones-Cannon, S., & Davis, B. L. (2005). Coping among African-American daughters caring for aging parents. *The ABNF Journal: Official Journal of the Association of Black Nursing Faculty in Higher Education, Inc, 16*(6), 118–123.

Kagan, S., Knight, G. P., & Martinez-Romero, S. (1982). Culture and the development of conflict resolution style. *Journal of Cross-Cultural Psychology, 13,* 43–59.

Kagan, S., & Madsen, M. (1971). Cooperation and competition of Mexican, Mexican American and Anglo American children of two ages under four instructional sets. *Developmental Psychology, 5,* 32–39.

Kimmel, D. C. (1978). Adult development and aging: A gay perspective. *Journal of Social Issues, 43,* 113–120.

Klein, F., Sepekoff, B., & Wolf, T. J. (1985). Sexual orientation: A multi-variable dynamic process. *Journal of Homosexuality, 11*(1–2), 35–49.

Mahoney, D. F., Cloutterbuck, J., Neary, S., & Zhan, L. (2005). African American, Chinese, and Latino family caregivers' impressions of the onset and diagnosis of dementia: Cross-cultural similarities and differences. *The Gerontologist, 45*(6), 783–792.

Marín, G., & Marín, B. (1991). *Research with Hispanic populations.* Newbury Park, CA: Sage.

Mbiti, J. S. (1990). *African religions and philosophy.* Oxford: Heinemann.

McDonald, K., & Amstrong, E. (2001). De-romanticizing Black intergenerational support: The questionable expectation of welfare reform. *Journal of Marriage and the Family, 63,* 213–233.

McLoyd, V. C., Hill, N. E., & Dodge, K. A. (Eds.). (2005). *African American family life: Ecological and cultural diversity.* New York: The Guilford Press.

Miller, R. J., Randolph, S. M., Kaufman, C., Dargan, V. W., & Banks, D. H. (2000). Non-family caregivers of the African-American elderly: Research needs and issues. *African American Research Perspectives, 6,* 69–81.

Money, J. (1988). *Gay, straight, and in-between: The sexology of erotic orientation.* New York: Oxford University Press.

Montgomery, R. J., & Williams, K. N. (2001). Implications of differential impacts of care-giving for future research on Alzheimer care. *Aging & Mental Health, 5*(Suppl. 1), S23–S34.

Olson, L. K. (2001). *Age through ethnic lenses: Caring for the elderly in a multicultural society.* New York: Rowman & Littlefield Publishers, Inc.

Rivera, P., & Marlo, H. (1999). Practitioner report: Cultural, interpersonal and psychody-namic factors in caregiving towards a greater understanding of treatment noncompli-ance. *Clinical Psychology and Psychotherapy, 6,* 63–68.

Roff, L. L., Burgio, L. D., Gitlin, L., Nichols, L., Chaplin, W., & Hardin, J. M. (2004). Positive aspects of Alzheimer's caregiving: The role of race. *The Journals of Gerontology. Series B, Psychological Sciences and Social Sciences, 59*(4), P185–P190.

Sandoval, M. C. (1975). Santeria: Agrocuban concepts of disease and its treatment in Miami. *Journal of Operational Psychiatry, 8,* 52–63.

Scott, C. S. (1974). Health and healing practices among five ethnic groups in Miami, Florida. *Public Health Reports, 89*(6), 524–532.

Tamez, E. G. (1978). Curanderismo: Folk Mexican-American health care system. *Journal of Psychiatric Nursing and Mental Health Services, 16*(12), 34–39.

Triandis, H. C., Marín, G., Betancourt, H., Lisanski, J., & Chang, B. (1982). *Dimensions of familism among Hispanic and mainstream Navy recruits.* Technical Report No. 14, Department of Psychology, University of Illinois, Champaign, IL.

Tucker, M. B., & James, A. D. (2005). New families, new functions post modern African American families in context. In V. C. McLoyd, N. E. Hill, & K. A. Dodge (Eds.), *African American family life: Ecological and cultural diversity* (pp. 86–110). New York: Guilford Press

Valle, R. (1998). *Caregiving across cultures.* New York: Taylor & Francis.

Van IJzendoorn, M. H., Bakermans-Kranenburg, M. J., & Sagi-Schwartz, A. (2006). In K. H. Rubin & O. B. Chung (Eds.), *Parenting beliefs, behaviors, and parent-child relations: A cross-cultural perspective* (pp. 107–140). New York: Taylor & Francis.

Van IJzendoorn, M. H., Sagi, A., & Lambermon, M. W. E. (1992). The multiple caretaker paradox: Data from Holland and Israel. In R. C. Pianta (Ed.), *New directions for child development: No. 57. Beyond the parent: The role of other adults in children's lives* (pp. 5–24). San Francisco, CA: Jossey-Bass.

Weisner, T. S., & Gallimore, R. (1977). My brother's keeper: Child and sibling caretaking. *Current Anthropology, 18,* 169–190.

Wrubel, J., & Folkman, S. (1997). What informal caregivers actually do: The caregiving skills of partners of men with AIDS. *Care, 9,* 691–706.

II

Social Work Process: Tools and Applications for Ethnic Populations

4

Social Work and the Social World of Culturally Diverse Caregivers

Culture is a body of learned beliefs, traditions, principles, and guides for behavior that are commonly shared among members of a particular group. Culture serves as a road map for both perceiving and interacting with the world. (Locke, 1992, p. 10)

CASE EXAMPLE

Sometimes I feel like I can't make it. I just get tired. But I am not giving up. In my culture we take care of our family no matter what. We care for each other to the end. Either I die or she dies so it's not that I don't want to care for my wife. We've been married for almost 40 years. But, I don't know who she is anymore. Everything has changed. We don't have any money, we lost our house and we now live in a small house with my (oldest) son (age 37). But he just lost his job and his wife left him and returned to Mexico. He hasn't been the same since his brother was killed in Iraq. He is looking for a job. I was an attorney but had to quit my job 5 years ago because my wife's memory worsened. There have been many losses [in the] past 5 years including losing my youngest son 4 years ago (age 29) in Iraq. We don't know what is happening to our family. If it hadn't been for the members of the family, I would have given up a long time ago. We have stayed close together and help each other no matter what. It's funny to see us all together because we are all mixed. I miss my son. I don't think my wife knows he's gone. It is better that way. I try and try to talk with her but she just looks at me. She is getting more scared and angry. I don't know why. I can't leave her alone for a minute. One night she was in the kitchen. I thought she was asleep. I heard noises and ran into the kitchen. I found her talking to herself in the kitchen. I don't sleep at night when she is awake. I'm afraid of what she will do.

This biracial (Black and Latino) male spouse caregiver aged 69 has been caring for his Mexican wife (aged 75) with Alzheimer's disease for 10 years. He has several medical issues, including obesity, high blood pressure, arthritis, and asthma. When his arthritis flares up, he uses a walker. He needs to have knee replacement surgery but has put it off in order to care for his wife. Their son was killed fighting in Iraq 4 years ago, leaving a Mexican national wife and two children (caregiver's grandchildren) who were born in the United States. Since the death of his son, his widowed daughter-in-law and the two children have moved in with them and help care for his wife. All of the family rallies around the caregiver and the dementia-afflicted spouse. Since then, family members have been visiting on a regular basis and provide some day-to-day help. He has four brothers and three sisters. His wife immigrated illegally and never became a naturalized citizen. She has extended family in Mexico that she has not seen since the memory symptoms increased 8 years ago. The family is worried that both the caregiver's wife and his daughter-in-law might be deported to Mexico. The United States federal immigration issues seem hostile to Mexicans. This is discouraging extended family members from travelling to the United States.

OVERCOMING ISSUES AND CHALLENGES

Many ethnically diverse family caregivers including Latinos often experience additional problems as they provide care for their afflicted family member (Cuéllar, 1990; Olson, 2001; Valle, 1998; Yeo & Gallagher-Thompson, 1996). Some of these problems include caregiver conflicts as they attempt to balance care of the family member between cultural values, norms, and traditions and adhering to differing dominant Western culture expectations regarding how care should be provided in the United States. Another set of problems could originate from this strong collective perspective in the Black or Latino family. "African American families serve to insulate and lessen the negative and often deleterious consequences that accompany racial group status" (Coard & Sellers, 2005, p. 265). In this case, the caregiver and the person with dementia may be perceived by the family, not as individual persons, as Western culture dictates, but part of interconnected families, kin networks, groups, and whole communities. As a result, the caregiver may experience a sense of stress and/or restriction related to seeking care support outside of the family cultural traditions.

Other problems could be due to differences in the caregiver's ability to understand technical terms, to understand and communicate in the English language, and to conceptualize the disease diagnosis and treatment from the perspective of the medical community. Additional problems could be related to institutional barriers due to lack of familiarity with resources or lack of knowledge about where or how to obtain services. The use of language or cultural dystonic screening and management tools for dementia may be inadequate in ethnic populations. The current literature notes the presence of cultural bias in cognitive tests and overall health literacy among ethnic elders as also problematic depending upon the level of education and acculturation (Cuéllar, 1990; Olson, 2001; Valle, 1998; Yeo & Gallagher-Thompson, 1996). Spirituality may be a key factor for some Latino families and caregivers in terms of their understanding of dementia symptoms and may delay or prevent caregivers from seeking help for their relatives (Cuéllar, 1990; Olson, 2001; Valle, 1998). In addition, help-seeking behaviors may be influenced by level of acculturation and/or fear of deportation (Cuéllar, 1990; Olson, 2001; Valle, 1998). The degree to which family caregivers have experienced racism, discrimination, and a sense of powerlessness will influence their help-seeking behaviors outside of the family, the kin network, and the Latino cultural framework (Cuéllar, 1990; Olson, 2001; Valle, 1998). Caregiver's lack of awareness of community or health resources and/or lack of transportation add to the caregiver's problems (Cuéllar, 1990; Olson, 2001; Valle, 1998). Transporting a dementia-afflicted family member demonstrating inappropriate or unsafe behavior on public transportation may place everyone at risk. The problems for culturally diverse caregivers and dementia-afflicted family members fluctuate depending upon their socioeconomic status, educational level, and knowledge of dementia (Cuéllar, 1990; Olson, 2001; Valle, 1998).

UNDERSTANDING THE SOCIAL WORK ROLE WITH ETHNIC CAREGIVERS

Helping family caregivers identify, understand, and resolve problems for themselves, their dementia-afflicted relatives, and the family can present many challenges. The goal of this social work problem-solving model is to provide social workers and caregivers with a simple, clear model of problem solving to reduce the stress and to help caregivers, patients, and families focus on the target problem in a way that helps facilitate the resolution of the problem. Engaging the caregiver in every step of the process is key to establishing a working relationship. Writing about Jamaican families Brice-Baker (1996) indicates, "The Jamaican family finds it difficult to admit that there is a problem it cannot handle"

(p. 93). When professional help is required, the Jamaican family generally adheres to the advice of professionals (i.e., teachers and doctors) and will do all that is required to follow recommendations (Brice-Baker, 1996). Social workers regard the caregiver as the expert in their life situation and also as the expert in identifying the particular target problem to work. The variety of problems presented by the caregiver may include any or all of the following plus others: (1) caregiver's physical, mental, and emotional health issues; (2) insufficient knowledge regarding the disease; (3) assistance in knowing how to manage Alzheimer's symptoms; and (4) maladaptive coping patterns related to the disease symptoms presented by the dementia-afflicted family member. In addition, the caregiver may experience feelings of grief and loss related to changes in his or her own life dreams, career goals, or life aspirations, or from having to withdraw from their social relationships and activities and interests. The increased dependency by the dementia-afflicted relative on the caregiver often results in the caregiver feeling resentment, anger, frustration, and a sense of hopelessness and helplessness. Jamaicans have a strong work ethic and take the adage "time is money" very seriously (Brice-Baker, 1996, p. 94). "Difficulties arise due to lack of understanding of the condition when family members place blame for the symptoms on the person with dementia" (Adamson, 2001, p. 395). The feelings experienced by the caregiver, while normal, can negatively impact the caregiver's inability to understand and manage the dementia symptoms emerging in the afflicted family member. The efficient provision of appropriate, clear, and understandable information regarding memory loss from the disease is most essential for the caregiver. Social workers working with this population should be well-informed about the condition of dementia and be able to communicate to family members an awareness of the condition as well as what can be done to assist the caregiver in the care of their family member. Social workers should also be aware of the available resources. "Appropriate implementation of services is important, not only as the first step in providing practical support for the person with dementia and their families but also, as we have seen for some family members, having a definite diagnosis of dementia can bring a sense of relief in uncovering a legitimate reason for symptoms" (Adamson, 2001, p. 395).

For most ethnic minorities, a family member's transition from home care to day care, respite, or alternative out-of-home care can be a traumatic experience. Social workers can help caregivers make sense of the care information and can provide examples and illustrations that may help the caregiver better understand the information and begin to consider making the paradigm shift from providing full care to sharing care of the family member with qualified professionals. By building a collaborative relationship with the caregiver, the social worker helps ease the transition and decrease the resistance to services outside of the family. A problem-solving plan is one of the tools the social worker employs to help the caregiver think about and identify the most appropriate problem to target for work, while maintaining important family care and adherence to cultural values.

Caregiver grief related to anticipated loss is a reality faced by family caregivers as they provide day-to-day care and treatment of their relatives afflicted with this life-threatening illness. Caregivers are faced with the grim reality of the growing number of symptoms rendering the person with dementia more dependent day by day. The caregiver's stress and worry increases and often the caregiver has no one with which to discuss these tormenting thoughts and feelings and is often forced to internalize intense feelings of distress, anger, helplessness, and loss. Each phase of the disease brings new and unique circumstances and problems. As the illness progresses, caregivers are often faced with the daunting task of making end-of-life decisions. End-of-life planning is an extremely difficult time for all. The social worker can provide support as caregivers anticipate their family member's imminent death and face multiple difficult decisions.

Throughout the caregiver's journey of care, the social worker and caregiver build a therapeutic relationship in which the social worker serves multiple roles with the caregiver. One role is that of being an active interdisciplinary team member who, when the situation dictates, engages other members of the medical care team involved with the caregiver and patient. Together, the team works to provide enhanced communication and uniformity in care, tapping into the skill strengths and resources of each member of the interdisciplinary team. The social worker's assessment includes clinical, social, and environmental perspectives, evaluating the caregiver and afflicted family members' needs in multiple levels of life functioning that other professionals working solely from the medical perspective may not assess at the time of consultation. With the caregiver and the patient's permission, social workers generally involve the primary care physician and other professionals involved in care to work as a team, functioning together to support and educate the caregiver, the afflicted family member, and the family on treatment options and resources. They also work to encourage the caregiver, patient, and family to keep the physician and other health care providers informed of care concerns and symptom changes.

Cultural Sensitivity and Cultural Competence

In this multiple-level intervention process, the social worker, the afflicted family member, and the caregiver function together as long as the dementia-afflicted member is able to remain fully involved and participate in the care decisions. As the disease progresses and the afflicted family member becomes more frail and vulnerable and is unable to help make appropriate care decisions, a gradual shift occurs leading the caregiver to assume more responsibility for care. During this time, the social worker makes a matrix change in order to allow the work of caring for the afflicted family member to progress while the responsibility for care shifts more in the direction of the caregiver who is now assuming more caregiving responsibilities and care decisions. In some Black and Latino families, other members of the family may become involved to help balance responsibilities or to ensure the authoritative power for care is delegated appropriately and respected by everyone involved in care.

Often in Black and Latino families, extended family members may be part of the team providing care from the beginning, with a division of labor established in order to share the caregiving tasks with the primary caregiver and others involved in the care work. In addition, certain members may be designated specific roles as the family resources change or as the care needs change. The ongoing social work role is to assess the changing dynamics of the family system and to identify the members' designated roles in a culturally sensitive manner. This will help determine how to utilize the available resources to assist the primary caregiver in meeting the changing care needs of the afflicted family member. The following case example provides an illustration of just such a shift in authority and care responsibilities.

In one Latino family, the male spouse, aged 79, was the primary caregiver of his dementia-afflicted wife aged 81 until he was diagnosed with cancer of the esophagus and required care. The middle-aged adult daughter who had been primarily responsible for the activities of daily living, such as bathing, dressing, feeding, and toileting her dementia-afflicted mother, assumed all dementia care responsibilities and decisions for her mother, including communications with physicians and other care professionals. She also assumed the day-to-day care for her ailing father who remained at home between radiation and chemotherapy treatments.

As the care needs changed, an interesting familismo hierarchy care pattern emerged. When the ailing elderly male spouse became ill, the oldest adult son assumed the role of head of household, meaning he made the financial decisions and managed the household resources. Although he lived in another town and state about 45 minutes away with his own wife and five children, as the oldest adult son, he assumed the medical major care decisions for his cancer-stricken father and handled communication with the treating physicians and care team. Meanwhile, the adult daughter continued to manage the activities of daily living for both the dementia-afflicted mother and cancer-stricken father. She additionally handled the communication with her mother's physicians and care team. The increased responsibility caused the adult daughter to experience role engulfment and burn out. Within the extended family network some care responsibilities shifted as other members assumed various home and care responsibilities for the two afflicted elders; however, most of the work was done by the adult daughter. One change involved two elderly female siblings of the dementia-afflicted sister (primary caregiver's aging aunts) volunteering to take turns providing weekend care for their sister, enabling the adult daughter to attend church, and take some brief respite time.

Another change involved the granddaughter (the daughter of the primary caregiver; a divorced mother with two small children) assuming responsibility for transporting the Alzheimer's-afflicted grandmother to physicians, doing the marketing and shopping, and picking up prescriptions for both grandparents. The granddaughter arranged work hours to help care for her ailing grandparents and support her mother, the primary caregiver. The granddaughter lived about 30 minutes from her mother and grandparent's home. Because the ailing elders were unable to speak English fluently, the primary caregiver and adult son handled communication with medical professionals and staff.

Equalizing Power Differentials Among Ethnic Caregivers

The familismo pattern changed and responsibilities shifted again after the cancer-afflicted father died. The work of equalizing power within the traditional family network of familismo care began anew. With the intervention of the social worker, the older son stopped functioning as head of his parent's household and became a conjoint care decision maker with his sister (the adult daughter) who continued to care for their dementia-afflicted mother. The son was able to begin to reassume his role within his nuclear family, decrease his travel to his parent's home, and restore a sense of equilibrium to that system. This eased his stress level while maintaining the integrity of the family network. Another member of the familismo network began to assume more care responsibilities and moved into the family home, providing the necessary resources. The granddaughter moved into the surviving elder's family house so she could continue to help provide transportation and support her mother and dementia-afflicted grandmother. Thus, the granddaughter added to the existing role of a single working mother who was caring for two children an additional role of caring for her mother and grandmother in the family home. The granddaughter assumed the role of managing the household functioning, providing transportation for all, and providing emotional support for her mother while her mother handled the majority of the day-to-day caregiving functions for the dementia-afflicted member. Housekeeping, lawn, and garden work were delegated to other members of the extended family who hired individuals to help. The adult son was kept informed by the caregiver (his sister) of all treatment and physician recommendations and the status of his ailing mother. The primary caregiver was fully involved and participated in all of the care decisions; however, the major care decisions were always made between the adult daughter and son.

Although the kinship network or familismo family network of care embodies the core values and characteristics of the family within the Black and Latino groups, the kinship network or familismo network can also be a significant source of stress as family interactions are not always supportive, especially if there is a problem in role and responsibility distribution. Cultural competence, then, is not only the social worker's cultural respect and awareness of kinship or the familismo-based network of care that may exist, but also the ability to assess the family or individual(s) involved in the care to determine if this traditional family model is functional and has the strength and capacity to withstand the demands of caring for a dementia-afflicted family member (Gallegos, 1991). Once this assessment is made, the social worker can move ahead to propose the appropriate interventions.

Not all Black and Latino families have functional resources to tap into within the family network. In some if not most families, ruptures in interpersonal relationships influence a member's desire to assist. The role of the social worker is to distinguish the causal effects of the ruptures and how to help members learn to understand the process between members that are shaped by past beliefs, behavior, and reactions to behaviors that impede the care process for the dementia-afflicted family member. The social worker's ability to conduct relationship assessments and strengths in the family interaction network is critical to moving the care work forward. Working to restore healthy and adaptable family functioning is often key to the stability of family function and the capacity to change.

Once the need to change is determined, the social worker can begin the work of moving family members into a new pattern of behavior that will better adhere to the cultural value of caring for the elderly in need. This will help the family system to reorganize patterns of interactions to maintain reliability and predictability in serving useful functions of care and care support for their loved one. Sometimes relationships are ruptured because extended family members disagree about the care decisions and about seeking help from formal out-of-family resources.

Often each family member has his or her own opinion and sense of knowing related to an understanding of cultural values, and about how and upon whom to depend or trust within and outside the family when seeking help from more formal resources. "In addition to familism a configuration of other cultural variables influence help seeking and the use of social services" (Gutiérrez & Lewis, 1999, p. 173; Rogler et al., 1983). "These include *confianza*, the value of trust in self and others; *personalism*, a concern for personal dignity, together with a person-oriented approach to social relations and a distaste for impersonal relationship (Queralt, 1984; Rogler et al., 1983); and *verguenza* and *orgullo*, a sense of shame and strong pride" (Gutiérrez & Lewis, 1999, p. 173).

The function of the social worker is to be aware of these values and their origin within the cultural socialization process of the family members and to work to reinforce interactions within the culturally-based, close social relationships. The social worker also serves as a bridge between the impersonal public health resource and the family, thus lessening the distaste for impersonal formal relationships. In the capacity of a bridge builder, the social worker functions as a power base that draws the energy from the informal kinship and familismo networks and the formal resource networks forming a new model of power that fosters effective and increasing power within both networks, leading to change.

Because of another, often misunderstood cultural value known as *fatalism*, Latinas may view themselves as unable to control or modify issues within the environment. *Fatalism* is "the belief that events are determined by forces outside one's control" (Gutiérrez & Lewis,

1999, p. 173). It is an especially important cultural value for the social worker to understand and work to reframe this for the Latino caregiver. The cultural skill involves helping the caregivers learn that they can master some events and modify problems within the environment. The social worker begins by engaging the caregivers in a problem-solving process by which the caregivers learn to resolve their own problems according to the particular role each has; this shows respect for the cultural values and the hierarchy of power and authority while strengthening the caregivers' own abilities to resolve the problems. When the roles change as they did in the example above, the social worker needs to provide the support according to each caregiver's new role, and the shifting needs required by the afflicted family member and the new role, authority, and responsibilities of those involved. The social worker's care plan is then altered to meet the needs of each afflicted elder.

In the traditional Jamaican family, a paternalist social order with extended members has been pervasive in social relationships (Miller, 2002). However, the family members most likely to provide care for the aging matriarch or ill elders are generally the female members. "Grandparents frequently live in the home of one of their children, and it is not uncommon for a child to remain in his or her parents' home long past the age of eighteen. Some never leave home and remain to head the household of aging parents" (Miller, 2002, p. 26). The close-knit network of family members are considered "the most important group a person belongs to" (www.kwintessential.co.uk/resources/global-etiquette/jamaica.html 2010). Similar to the African American and Latino family, the Jamaican family culture is a network of familial relationships with which an individual has spent most of his or her that provides emotional, economic, and social support. The kinship network generally consists of aunts, uncles, cousins, and grandparents, and other members. In time of need, most Jamaicans prefer to seek assistance or "partner" with family members and/or close friends than from formal institutions (www.kwintessential.co.uk/resources/global-etiquette/jamaica.html 2010).

There is no doubt that in the cultural family, intergenerational and multigenerational functioning connections are key factors in both the ethnic caregiver and the ethnic person making the dementia treatment decisions (Dilworth-Anderson et al., 2001; Olsen, 2001; Pierce, 2002; Sanchez, 2001; Valle, 1998). The family value of familismo for Latinos and the kinship ties for African Americans and Blacks help provide insight into the family value-based socialization patterns and into the unique problem-solving process that fosters the family caregiver's ability to function effectively and to adapt to change in the face of chronic, progressive illness. To move the problem-solving process to the next step of social work assistance, it is necessary to link the cultural information to frameworks of family care fostering empowerment, problem solving, and mastery.

In the literature, Spark and Brody (1970) are credited with applying the potential for family interaction to influence problems and the adaptation to aging. Applying the Spark and Brody (1970) perspective to family therapy models that are generally considered to be systemic in nature helps the social worker to focus work from the individual to the interactions of various members of the family associated within the family. This helps the social worker apply therapeutic approaches that might promote healthier functioning for the caregiver, afflicted family member, and those connected with their lives. As mentioned in the previous chapter, John Bowlby identified a need for the therapeutic approach to shift work from the individual to inclusion of the family (Bowlby, 1949). Pierce (2002) provided a circular process perspective describing the interactions that occur within families as members engage with one another. In this text, a similar yet different family circular illustration is employed in a new and diverse way to provide a concept map titled Ethnic Theoretical Perspective Concept Map: Cognitive Behavioral, Problem-Solving, and Self-Efficacy Process (Figure 4.1). This concept map helps visualize and track the interconnectedness of the ethnic minority caregiver with the familismo, kin, and fictive kin networks, and with the ethnic community and other informal and formal resource services within the context of the problem-solving caring network. The concept map illustrates each step of the six-step cognitive behavioral problem-solving process that social workers employ as a means of learning, understanding, applying, and teaching this new problem-solving process to caregivers of dementia-afflicted family members.

Every detail of the process will be discussed in subsequent sections of this text in order to help social workers learn and effectively apply the process with clients. In addition, the theoretical perspectives leading to the development of the ethnic theoretical perspective will be discussed. The cognitive behavioral process has been found successful in research and clinical social work practice with ethnic family caregivers caring for relatives with dementia by both authors of this text, thereby making this new process social work evidence-based practice.

FIGURE 4.1 Ethnic Theoretical Perspective Concept Map: Cognitive Behavioral, Problem-Solving, and Self-Efficacy Process

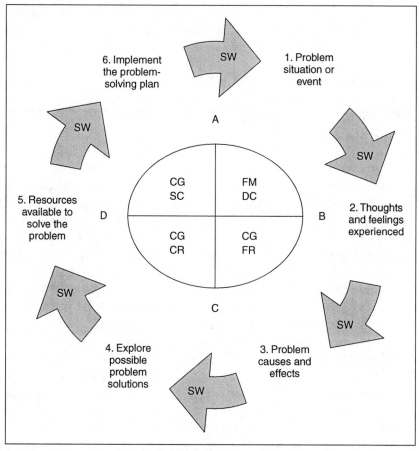

Intervention focus is on four domains of care: (A) CGSC—caregiver self-care; (B) FMDC—family member dementia care; (C) CGFR—caregiver family resource; and (D) CGCR—caregiver community resource.

SW-Arrow flow represents role of the social work (SW) relationship as the constant factor in the caregiver (CG) problem-solving process.

1. Social worker helps caregiver identify the problem situation or event.
2. Social worker helps caregiver to clarify the thoughts and feelings about the problem.
3. Social worker helps caregiver identify causes and effects of the problem on caregiver and dementia-afflicted relative.
4. Social worker and Black or Latino caregiver jointly explore ways to problem solve.
5. Social worker and Black or Latino caregiver jointly identify familismo, kin or fictive kin, and other informal or formal resources available.
6. Social worker and Black and Latino caregiver jointly set a date to implement the problem-solving plan. Caregiver puts problem-solving plan into action; consults the identified family members, and/or informal or formal resources advocating for self and relative for help to problem solve.

The Black or Latino caregiver experiences role relief and resilience. Reciprocity and norms regarding familismo/kinship responsibility and cultural values for the care of the relative with dementia are maintained with the problem successfully resolved. The Black or Latino caregiver experiences empowerment, resilience, and self-efficacy.

This social work paradigm of care is important for several reasons. First is the notion that kinship and familismo natural support systems may assist in easing the stress of the care burden for the caregiver and family by providing a protective and supportive network of care. The kinship network of care is presumed to understand the context of life for the afflicted member; however, the network often lacks the knowledge, skills, and resources required to assist in the problem-solving process (Dilworth-Anderson & Gibson; Gallagher-Thompson et al., 2000; Yeo et al., 1996). Dilworth-Anderson and Gibson (2002) note the following.

> For minority caregivers of elders with Alzheimer['s] or a related demen-tia, lower education, lack of access to information or resources, cer-tain religious beliefs, and the cultural value of caring for one's "own" can foster providing care to dependent elders in isolation. Caregivers, therefore, may seek or be aware of few resources outside the family or tribe to help care for demented elders or to provide direct support to them, which increases reliance on information rather than formal support. (p. S57)

For social workers, the underlying assumption of empowerment prac-tice with clients and caregivers of ethnic backgrounds is that the clients are generally disempowered through their membership in historically devalued and oppressed groups (Parsons, 2002). This notion of disem-powerment generally has roots in the clients' past experiences with the systems, policies, and services that have rendered them unable to achieve their desired goals or to acquire the services needed to care for themselves and family members. With repeated failed efforts, the cli-ent often internalizes failure, and a learned hopelessness and alienation from formal services takes place (Parsons, 2002). Parsons (2002) further notes, "Accepting shortcomings as a reflection of oneself results in self-blame and ensures perpetuation of the sense of powerlessness" (p. 397). Caregivers presenting with problems or symptoms that include "isola-tion, depression, alienation, feeling hopeless, and learned helplessness and a need for community connections" (Parsons, 2002, p. 392) are often viewed as experiencing disempowerment and require specific strate-gies that include an empowerment intervention.

The second reason the illustrated paradigm is important is that, in order to empower the caregiver in the management and care of the afflicted family member, it is essential to emphasize the importance of the social worker, the caregiver, and the family network as care mem-bers sharing in leadership and power functions of care. To assist the care members, the social worker draws upon the diverse skills of the profes-sional trained with specific education, helping expertise, and knowledge about resources to help the caregiver. The caregiver draws upon the role of the identified care person in the family who has the designated power to make the care decisions conjointly with the afflicted family member and who is the expert in terms of knowledge of the care context. As noted previously, often the family network designates roles to members and draws upon the various members' skills and the resources available within the network to help support the care work decisions. Viewing empowerment as a process, Parsons (2002) states the following.

> Empowerment may be defined as a process through which people become strong enough to participate within, share in the control of, and influence events and institutions affecting their lives; in part, empowerment necessitates that people gain particular skills, knowledge, and sufficient power to influence their lives and the lives of those they care about (Torre, 1985). The process of empowerment is ongoing and involves changes in three dimensions of one's self: personal, interpersonal, and sociopolitical participation. (p. 397)

As with all other models of social work interventions, social workers working to empower caregivers adhere to principles that guide practice in the empowerment process and begin with a collaborative strength-based assessment between caregiver and social worker that focuses on the three dimensions: "personal, interpersonal, and sociopolitical participation" (Pearson, 2002). The goal is to listen to facilitate the caregiver's expression of problems and to incorporate the caregiver's perceptions into the care plan. Once the assessment is complete, the work moves forward with a partnership effort between the social worker and caregiver, which will be helpful in the continued development of shared power, thus raising empowerment of the caregiver. By fostering an environment of safety through trust and support, the social worker helps to amplify the caregiver's voice in the decision-making process (Parsons, 2002). If this is successfully achieved by the social worker, the caregiver will feel safe and will more readily engage in interaction with the social worker, telling his or her care story knowing it will be heard and will be included in the mutual decisions made to target and solve the problems selected for work. Hence, the relationship between social workers and caregivers are collaborative with shared power (Parsons, 2002). The process lends itself to "building interdependence, creating hope, and achieving collective action" (Parsons, 2002, p. 397). Parsons (1994, 1998, 1999, 2002) and Chamberlin (1997) identified outcomes involving changes in the three dimensions of one's self (Parsons, 2002, p. 397).

Toseland and Rivas (2009) identify the social workers' leadership power and influence as evidence of their ability not only to lead the problem-solving process but also to help empower members of the group with which they are working. While Tosland and Rivas (2009) are speaking specifically about social work group work, the same framework is applicable in the context of work with caregivers and family kinship group networks. Toseland and Rivas (2009) distinguish the "social worker power as *'attributed power'* ... which comes from the perception among group members or others outside the group of the worker's ability to lead and *'actual power'* which refers to the worker's resources for changing conditions inside and outside the group. Actual power depends on the sources of a worker's influence" (pp. 93–94).

Working to empower ethnic family caregivers that are caring for a dementia-afflicted family member begins with engagement in the partnership process with the social worker. The engagement process is a skill that the social worker uses in building the relationship with the caregiver. To use the skill, the social worker must be able to recognize the "actual power" and the "attributed power" and use both to assist the caregiver. With the recognition of power, the social worker can move the work forward to accomplish the treatment goals through the translation of power to the caregiver, the afflicted family member, and the care network. Social justice, the core value that drives the social work profession, should lead the social worker to exercise the power judiciously and according to the professional standards set by the National Association of Social Workers (1996). It can be said that Black and Latino "cultures are structured around hierarchies, which require individuals to give proper respect to those with more power so for more open communication to take place in the helping relationship, a reduction of the power imbalance may be necessary" (Gutiérrez & Lewis, 1999, p. 181; Miller, 2002; Mizio, 1981).

Within the power base of Black and Latino cultures, certain individuals with more power may be looked to for information in order to give meaning to a disease process and in order to identify the direction the family network will take to provide care. It can be viewed as an informal sanction or delegation of power authorizing the identified caregiver. Often, diverse cultures give definition and meaning to Alzheimer's disease and other related irreversible dementias based on cultural norms, values, and beliefs (Dilworth-Anderson & Gibson, 2002). Accepting the caregivers' definition and the meaning the dementing disease holds for them may be a key factor in helping to equalize power and build trust and confidence in the social work and caregiver relationship. In addition, it may help caregivers to feel understood, accepted, and confident in their ability to communicate the caregiving concern appropriately, when they may otherwise feel uncomfortable seeking help outside the family.

This does not mean that the social worker is then precluded from exploring erroneous definitions, meanings, or understandings. As mentioned earlier in the chapter, social workers regard the caregiver as the expert in his or her life situation and also as the expert in identifying the particular target problem for work. But the social worker is still able to contribute to the focus for work and will be able to assist the caregiver to better understand the disease process by sensitively confronting erroneous understandings related to the disease process. But it can only happen when the caregiver experiences a sense of self-confidence and confidence in the social worker. This effort may begin to help balance power by facilitating the transfer of some of the power and control in the working relationship from the social worker to the client.

Applying Parson's (2002) perspective, the social worker's working relationship with a dementia caregiver is generally viewed as a partnership; however, included in this working relationship with the caregiver is the added care relationship with the afflicted family member. Social workers working with a dementia caregiver need to think critically about occasions in which mutual decisions of assistance for the caregiver will also include the afflicted family member. Actions of trust and support in the engagement and treatment process are inherently with the afflicted family member in primary strategy planning and assessment of care to reduce the afflicted family member's sense of powerlessness. The social work empowerment process that includes the caregiver and the afflicted family member will be discussed more in Chapter 6.

Sandwich-Generation Ethnic Caregivers and Implications for Care

According to the literature, it can be said that several stressful experiences seem to cluster at midlife for some families as the family cycle reaches a point where adults have to take on additional roles other than what is generally required in the nuclear family. These additional roles may be viewed as creating additional stress and conflict as parents learn to cope with the demands of raising children, a rebellious teenager, or working outside of the home. When parents also find themselves called upon to take care of an aging parent or a dementia-impaired in-law or parent, integrating the additional role can be difficult. Generally, families utilize grandparents as resources to help support the parenting role. In Black and Latino families, the grandparent generation is seen as a source of amplified family structure with collaborative family decision and resource input. However, when dementia afflicts one or more of the grandparents, there is a shift in the family system equilibrium as parents experience pressure to meet the needs of their disease-afflicted older parent or family member. The shift from resource provider within the kinship or the familismo network to a contributor of pressure to the family caregiver may lead to caregiver role ambiguity or caregiver role strain. In social work, the term "sandwich generation" is used to describe the role strain experience of adults who are pressed on one side as they try to balance the simultaneous roles of caring for children, a home, and employment, and pressed on the other side as they care for an aging-dependent dementia-afflicted parent or family member (Rossi, 1980; Stassen Berger, 1983, p. 482).

There are factors suggesting that the sandwich generation's experience of role strain is one of the negative consequences experienced by Blacks and Latinos in dementia caregiving (Dilworth-Anderson & Goodwin, 2005; González Sanders, 2006). Role strain is defined as difficulty in meeting role demands (Williams, Dilworth-Anderson, & Goodwin, 2003). Research indicates that in both the Black and Latino cultures, the dementia caregiver is typically a middle-aged female family member who simultaneously is providing care to the afflicted family member, in addition to fulfilling the role of spouse/partner, parent, and employee (Dilworth-Anderson & Goodwin, 2005; González Sanders, 2006). Latino caregivers may face a number of socioeconomic and institutional barriers when seeking to access and utilize health care services and community-based care for themselves and their afflicted family members. Moreover, other demographic characteristics of ethnic caregivers further demonstrate the dual pressures of caregivers from the sandwich generation who are rearing children and caring for elderly frail family members, which may place them at greater risk of experiencing detrimental health and mental health problems (González Sanders, 2006). In addition, caregivers who share the household with the dementia-afflicted family member are more likely to have difficulty meeting the multiple role demands and tend to experience high levels of role strain (Dilworth-Anderson & Goodwin, 2005; González Sanders, 2006). A member of the sandwich generation caring for a dementia-afflicted parent is more susceptible to increased emotional stress, poorer physical health, and perceived less self-efficacy and problem solving (Dilworth-Anderson & Goodwin, 2005; González Sanders, 2006). In some cases, families whose strong cultural values drive the caregiving process due to a sense of duty and obligation may experience role engulfment (Dilworth-Anderson & Goodwin, 2005; Skaff & Pearlin, 1992).

An example of role strain on the sandwich generation is illustrated in the following Jamaican American family whose father, aged 48, was diagnosed with younger-onset Alzheimer's disease.

The father, a respected audiologist in private practice, experienced memory lapses that forced him to transfer his practice to his partner. The primary caregiver was his wife. She had worked as an interpreter but quit her job to care for her husband. They had two sons and a daughter. The daughter and youngest son were away in college. The oldest son was married and had three children, now adolescents. Both parents worked outside of the home and cared for the children.

The youngest son left college to return home to work and to help provide for his parents. The daughter who was finishing college was encouraged to remain at school and finish but was forced to find a job to help support herself. The spousal caregiver quickly found out that many accounting mistakes were made by the Alzheimer's-afflicted father in the years when memory symptoms first began. To keep from losing their home, the caregiver was forced to sell their home, sell some of their furniture, and move into a rental home. The stress of the multiple losses led the spousal caregiver to experience depression. Never a stay-at-home mother, the spousal caregiver felt overwhelmed by all of the changes, loss of incomes, the overwhelming expenses, and the medical needs of the afflicted family member, and began to experience severe depression. This forced the older son and daughter-in-law into a sandwich generation position, requiring them to assume the bulk of the caregiving responsibilities for both the dementia-afflicted family member and the spouse diagnosed with severe depression in addition to their own family needs.

The ethnocultural family genogram, or cultural gram discussed in Chapter 6, provides an illustration of the ethnic minority caregiver and patient with dementia within the family/kinship hierarchy context. Cultural mapping will also be discussed in detail in Chapter 6 in conjunction with the ethnocultural ecomap.

Ethnic minority family caregivers of dementia patients experience a unique subset of problems. A culturally relevant problem-solving framework is therefore essential for the problem-solving intervention approach to be more successful (Valle, 1998). "Cultural mapping through problem solving," suggested by Valle (1998, p. 131), provides an essential ethnic cultural framework for problem solving. This will help facilitate the ethnic minority family caregiver's engagement in the problem-solving process, will reinforce learning at the ethnic minority caregiver cultural pace, and will ensure that the caregiver will be able to maintain the problem-solving skill. In recommending the culturally appropriate problem-solving framework, Valle (1998) implies an understanding of the culturally diverse family caregiver's proclivity to experience difficulty accessing community service resource or health care for themselves and/or for the person with dementia due to lack of awareness of the community service or actual institutional barriers due to language and institutional discrimination and racism.

When we think about culture, we think about the many aspects included in the concept of culture. In linking the concept of culture to humanity, one must include the caregiver's self-identification, thoughts, behavior, beliefs, actions, traditions, symbols, language or other forms of communication, values, and the racial, ethnic and social group affiliations that give meaning to the particular culture. Also included are age, gender, spirituality, political affiliations, mental and cognitive abilities, education, health, and other physical meanings of life that the individual possesses. In the National Association of Social Workers Standards for Social Work Practice with Family Caregivers of Older Adults (2010) document, cultural competence has been explained as the following.

The process by which individuals and systems respond respectfully and effectively to people of all cultures, languages, classes, races, ethnic backgrounds, religions, and other diversity factors in a manner that recognizes, affirms, and values the worth of individuals, families, and communities and protects and preserves the dignity of each. (p. 10)

IMMIGRATION AND ACCULTURATION CONSTRAINTS TO CARE

Case Example

A 48-year-old male spousal caregiver whose primary language was Spanish stated, "I need help with my wife and my son. I don't know what to do anymore. My wife's memory is getting worse and my son does not get services anymore. He used to get school [assistance] but that stopped when he turned 18. We are living in the United States with expired visas. I can't get help without someone finding out we are here illegally and deporting us. We can't go back to Colombia. There are seven members of her family in Colombia with Alzheimer's disease. Just last month she was still driving and could run errands but last week she got lost two times between home and the food store, which is a few blocks away. She is more confused now. My son is severely mentally retarded and there is no help for him there. That is why we came here. Now he spends his days lying on

*the sofa. I have to leave him alone with my wife who was diagnosed with
Alzheimer's disease while I work at MacDonald's. I lock them both in the
house while I work so my wife will stay inside. Our daughter married two
years ago and they have a son age 1. They live across town close to their
work. It is too far for my wife to drive. My daughter visits and tries to help
us with food but she has a baby now. She can't help us much.*

Social workers generally have the training and practical knowledge to
serve minority caregivers who experience care issues related to language, immigration, and acculturation that are likely to present barriers
to care. The goal is to bridge the gap between the unmet need and actual
service use among caregivers. To be effective, social workers must be
aware of the regional variations in ethnic populations, immigration
patterns, and individual group acculturation outcomes and identity.
Murry (2000) notes the challenge found in characterizing a single type
of African American family due to the heterogeneity of Black family
life with regard to value systems, lifestyles, and social class structure.
Applying the sociocultural perspective, Dilworth-Anderson, Burton,
and Johnson (1993) indicate that the ecological circumstances within the
daily life of African Americans dictate the vicissitudes and diversity of
the individual Black life experience. Difference in the individual's adherence to value systems, cultural values, and ethnic distinctions is attributed to the salience of ethnic identity and the experiential frameworks
(Hill, McBride Murry, & Anderson, 2005). "Today African American
families live in increasingly diverse locations and regions" (Hill et al.,
2005, p. 26). But within these diverse locations, at more of a microlevel,
Blacks seem to share a "strong sense of community" (Hill et al., 2005, p.
27). "Community" according to Warren (1978) is "a shared geographic
and psychological space, indicating shared interests, social characteristics, and social interaction" (Hill et al., 2005, p. 27).

"With increased immigration, Black Americans draw national and
cultural affiliations from many countries around the world, in addition
to regional variations in historical and cultural practices and migration patterns within the United States. These variations may indeed
reflect ethnic differences within the African American population.
With increasing diversity among African Americans, within-group ethnic variation is sorely understudied and, thus, an emerging issue" (Hill
et al., 2005, pp. 23, 25). Also impacting the African American population
is the increasing diverse immigrant populations from various countries.
"Increased immigration to the United States is a significant sociocultural factor affecting African Americans. As of 2002, the nation's foreign-
born population totaled almost 12% (32.5 million; Schmidley, 2003), the

highest proportion since 1930 and roughly equal in size to the African American population" (Hill et al., 2005, pp. 23, 25).

While many African American, Black, and Latino caregivers tend to be citizens of United States, many are not. "Almost half of the nation's foreign born population is from Latin America (mainly Mexico, followed by Cuba, the Dominican Republic, and El Salvador), whereas one-fourth is from Asia (the Philippines, China, Vietnam, and India are top countries of origin) and about 20% is from Europe (U.S. Bureau of the Census, 2002)" (Hill et al., 2005, p. 25). The changing multiple sociocultural factors are important to consider when working with foreign-born caregivers of dementia-afflicted family members. This increase of immigrants may shift population infused into American society and increase competition for community resources, services, and employment. This suggests the importance of culturally competent training for social workers in order for them to provide informed care for immigrants of varying racial and ethnic backgrounds of cultural relatedness.

Migration Trauma and Caregiving

Some of the studies of acculturation in the literature intermix psychic, social, cultural, and behavioral factors including the importance of language in self-definition and cultural relatedness (Lewis, 2004; Pérez-Foster, 1996, 1999, 2001), and the immigrant's identity and social transformation process through the acculturation process as the person confronts the new host culture (Akhtar, 1995; Volkan, 1993). According to Akhtar (1993) and Volkan (1993), the person's age and developmental level during which the immigration takes place are essential as a means of understanding the adaptation process in both the individual's psychic and social arenas.

> Since moving from one location to another involves loss—loss of country, loss of friends and loss of previous identity—all dislocation experiences maybe examined in terms of the immigrant's or the refugee's ability to mourn and/or resist the mourning process. The extent to which the individual is able intrapsychically to accept his or her loss will determine the degree to which an adjustment is made to the new life. (Volkan, 1993, p. 65)

Migrating Latinos exposed to the dominant mainstream cultural patterns of the United States Anglo-American culture are thought to experience multiple levels of change. The change occurs in Latino values, norms, attitudes, beliefs, and behaviors and is subsequently labeled acculturation (Gordon, 1964). The cultural change takes place through cultural learning perceived to occur as new immigrants make repeated contact with new cultures, groups, or nations (Berry, 1980; Dohrenwend & Smith, 1962; Marín, Otero-Sabogal, & Pérez-Stable, 1987, p. 184).

Acculturation at the individual level has been identified by Graves (1967) as "psychological acculturation because it refers to changes in attitudes, behaviors, beliefs, values, and the like in individuals as a result of acculturation" (cited in Cuéllar et al., 1995, p. 278). For Martinez et al. "acculturation is a multidimensional construct that describes phenomena resulting from continuous contact between groups of individuals from different cultures and subsequent changes in the cultural patterns of one or both groups" (Martinez, DeGarmo, & Eddy, 2004, p. 132). Buekens et al. state that "acculturation" is the "process of cultural change in which one group or members of a group assimilate various cultural patterns from another. For example, in the United States, Latino immigrants become acculturated when they acquire the language and customs of the Anglo-American culture, and abandon certain traits of their Latin-American culture" (Buekens, Manson, & Delvaux, 2000, p. 2). In 1936 Redfield et al. defined the concept of acculturation (Redfield, Linton, & Herskovits, 1936). Subsequently Cuéllar et al., reaffirmed the earlier definition for research use as follows: "Acculturation comprehends those phenomena which result when groups of individuals having different cultures come into continuous first-hand contact, with subsequent changes in the original cultural patterns of either or both groups" (Cuéllar, Arnold, & Maldonado, 1995, p. 278; Redfield, Linton, & Herskovits, 1936). According to Cuéllar (1995, p. 278), this definition of acculturation is the preferred definition because of the wording "comprehends those phenomena which result," which Cuéllar reasons as "incorporating changes at both the macro (social/group) and micro (individual) levels." Cuéllar (1995, p. 279) views acculturation as an "interactive, developmental, multifactorial, multidirectional, and multidimensional process."

Identifying Resources for Care

Because immigration can result in sudden change from an "average expectable environment" to a strange and unpredictable one (Akhtar, 1993, p. 1052; Hartman, 1950; Pérez-Foster, 2001), the stages of the acculturation process affect other critical biopsychosocial variables such as an individual's mental health (Golding, Burnam, Timbers, Escobar, & Karno, 1985; Graves, 1967; Griffith, 1983; Hatcher & Hatcher, 1975; Padilla, 1980; Padilla et al., 1982; Szapocznik & Kurtines, 1980; Szapocznik, Scopetta, Kurtines,

& Aranalde, 1978), social support resources (Griffith & Villavicencio, 1985; Henderson, 1990; Henderson & Gutierrez-Mayka, 1992; Miranda, 1995, 2000; Lang, Munoz, Bernal, & Sorensen, 1982; Villa, 1998; Yeo & Gallagher-Thompson, 1996), political and social beliefs (Alva, 1985; Kranau, Green, & Valencia-Weber, 1982), physical health (Reed et al., 1982), and resilience (Pérez-Foster, 2001; Simic, 1985; Valle, 1989; Yeo & Gallagher-Thompson, 1996). The literature on the psychological outcome of immigration identifies a range of factors that may impact one's acculturation process (Akhtar; 1995; Pérez-Foster, 1996, 1999, 2001; Valle, 1998).

Akhtar (1995, pp. 1054–1056) outlines eight developmental, social, cultural, and ecological factors important to assess, as they may psychically impact an individual's identity formation caused by immigration and continue through the stages of the acculturation process. First, assess if the individual's immigration is temporary or permanent. Second, identify the degree of choice in the individual's leaving the home country. Third, determine whether it is possible for the person to return to the home country for visits. Fourth, assess the age of the person at the time of immigration. Fifth, identify the reason the person has left his or her country. Sixth, determine the extent to which the individual has reached intrapsychic ability for separateness. Seventh, assess how the new host country receives the individual (racism, prejudice, and discrimination or accepting, valuing), and eight, find the amount of cultural difference between the new host country and the country of origin (skin color, language). Pérez-Foster (2001) identifies four migration factors that can significantly effect acculturation and result in acculturation trauma: "1) premigration trauma, that is, events experienced just prior to migration that were a chief determinant of the relocation; 2) traumatic events experienced during transit to the new country; 3) continuing traumatogenic experiences during the process of asylum-seeking and resettlement; and 4) substandard living conditions in the host country due to unemployment, inadequate supports, and minority persecution" (Pérez-Foster, 2001, p. 155). She adds that the "sense of isolation and absence of familial support serves as yet another strike against the already stressed newcomer" (Pérez-Foster, 2001, p. 158). The migration experience is a stressful experience and affects each family member differently. "The migrant typically enters society at the lower levels of the social strata, and his/her primary group relationships are altered (i.e., separation of part or the total family)" (Parra & Guarnaccia, 1998, p. 434). In addition, the acculturation process can take considerable time. The acquisition of host country language, values, and behaviors can also be a source of stress (Parra & Guarnaccia, 1998; Rogler, Gurak, & Cooney, 1987).

Language Barriers and Isolation

With the increasing numbers of immigrants, the influences of culture, language, and historical backgrounds are often perceived as an "out-group" experience by the mainstream American population (McLoyd, Hill, & Dodge, 2005). This perception of "out of group" may be due to the combined in-group value of language, interdependence, and maintenance of boundaries, and the new host's majority group seeking to limit the new group's participation in the wider experience (McLoyd et al., 2005). Whatever the forces be, what is clear is that often the barriers erected tend to create increased isolation and gaps in care. When unacculturated, monolingual, or limited English proficiency migrants cope with stressors associated with illegal documentation and lower socioeconomic status (SES) in addition to isolation, the added burden of caregiving for a dementia-afflicted family member can be devastating. When these caregivers turn to community organizations or institutions for assistance, there is likely to be a large disparity between the needs of the caregiver, the afflicted family member, and the availability of bilingual, bicultural social workers and/or other service providers. "Language affects the bilingual client's ability to express thoughts, feelings, and emotions and the clinician's understanding and interpretation of the client's verbal and non verbal responses" (Malgady & Zayas, 2001, p. 41). Clinical social workers tend to be the front-line contact for clients belonging to the ethnic minority groups and are often called upon to provide culturally sensitive diagnostic and treatment services to these clients. Therefore, social workers need to be trained to provide culturally sensitive, competent, and diagnostically accurate care. "Given the attention to the consideration of cultural and linguistic diversity in the formulation of diagnostic criteria in the *DSM-IV* (for example, 'ethnic and cultural considerations,' p. xxxiv) and its glossary of 'culture bound syndromes,' there is a critical need now to understand the diagnostic process in the light of such considerations" (Malgady & Zayas, 2001, p. 40). Understanding the sociocultural context of African Americans from diverse backgrounds is a key factor in order for social workers to be ready to encounter the full spectrum of acculturation. Hill, McBride Murry, and Anderson (2005) argue that the key to identifying and applying the strengths perspective to African American families begins by identifying and defining universal concepts and family processes within African American individual's sociocultural contexts, including acculturation and communication patterns. Hill, McBride Murry, and Anderson (2005) cite the following contributions by several scholars.

Cauce (2002) identified acculturation (i.e., adaptation to a host culture), enculturation (i.e., learning abut one's own culture), and ethnic minority socialization (i.e., learning about the unique experiences of being in a "minority group") as three measureable ways to begin to assess culture. Used together, they can shed light on individual differences and within-group variations. Similarly, Gjerde (2004) called for understanding culture by beginning with individuals and determining what they have in common with other individuals. Rather than attempting to identify an "objective," "distant" culture that shapes individuals, one should determine how individuals shape and create cultures within families and communities. Identifying potentially universal concepts and family processes; determining how these concepts are manifested commonly and uniquely across cultures, while considering who is involved in the lives of families; and identifying the goals, values, and beliefs surrounding family activities, and the communication patterns, are other ways to understand cultural practices and cultural variation (Cooper, Jackson, Azmitia, & Lopez, 1998). (Hill, McBride Murry, & Anderson, 2005, p. 35)

The social worker must be ready to encounter the full spectrum of acculturation. Valle (1998) stresses the importance of the "intercultural engagement process" that takes into consideration vicissitudes of the culture within the fixed historical formulation of culture and the more fluid qualities of the emerging, unique sociocultural context manifested in the current reality of individual family life (p. 23). Valle's acculturation assessment model will be discussed in greater detail with case examples in Chapter 6. Along with acculturation, language has an impact on the caregiver's help-seeking and help-receiving behaviors and in the formation of the caregiver and social worker relationship.

Facilitating Communications With Health Care Providers

Communication between social worker and client can be challenging even in the best-case scenarios when the client and social worker are of the same culture and speak the same language. When there are differences in cultural backgrounds and language, the challenges increase dramatically. Most traditional social work therapeutic approaches rely heavily on communication. These approaches are generally highly verbal and utilize intellectualized methods and frameworks containing various forms of communication. In order for the caregiver to be engaged in the helping relationship with the social worker, the caregiver must feel part of the collaborative effort. To view themselves as linked into the collaborative effort, caregivers must feel sufficiently confident to trust that if they risk the effort to communicate, they will be understood. Therefore, the caregiver may need to have some sense of empowerment in order to trust their ability to communicate their private thoughts, feelings, experiences, and problems to the social worker. On the other hand, the social worker at this point must proceed with an important assumption—that the diagnostic assessment of any bilingual caregiver is no simple matter. It requires critical thinking in every aspect of communication and verbal and nonverbal language. The language used in communicating from the speaker's perspective may express their subjective experience in one way, while the listener's perspective may function to receive the communication in a different perspective. The role of the social worker is to be aware of the complex role of language and bilingualism in the caregiver's presentation, and of the clinical material in both latent and manifest content. There is growing research (Amahti-Mehler, Argentieri, & Canestri, 1993; Perez Foster, 1998a, 2001) on ways in which bilingual language affects the expression of symptoms and ways in which social workers and other clinicians can assess the presentation of the symptoms. Perez Foster (2001) writes the following regarding social work and other clinical assessment and bilingual language in the clinical environment.

> There is now a substantial multidisciplinary literature (Amahti-Mehler, Argentieri, & Canestri, 1993; Perez Foster, 1998a) on the ways in which bilingualism affects the expression of symptoms and their subsequent assessment by clinicians. For example, there is evidence of differences in the neurocognitive organization of language in the bilingual speaker's mind, such that significant segments of languages learned after the initial developmental language acquisition period appear to be stored in different areas of the cortex (Kim, Relkin, Lee, & Hirsch, 1997; Ojemann, 1991; Paradis, 1977). Potential ramifications are suggested for the functional access of experiential memory when stored in one language code, and retrieved through a different code (Marcos & Alpert, 1976; Perez Foster, 1992, 1996a, 1998a). (Perez Foster, 2001, p. 161)

A key issue for social workers working with migrant or immigrant caregivers is whether the immigrant can be appropriately understood and evaluated, and if so, can the assessments be done in both languages if the caregiver is bilingual. Another key factor is whether available bilingual staff should be called upon to assist in the assessment if the social worker is unable to complete the assessment. Finally, not having language proficiency places the caregiver in a vulnerable situation in which fear, trepidation, and frustration of not being understood can shift the power quickly in the clinical environment, creating circumstances where confusion, suspicion, and lack of engagement may occur, resulting in a culturally dystonic experience for both the caregiver and the social worker. The embarrassment and shame associated with not being able to make oneself understood can be interpreted culturally in a variety of ways. While this can have the same, albeit lesser, impact on the social worker, it is important that the social worker be aware of the proclivity of the caregiver to seek a way out of the embarrassing situation. It is important that the social worker guide the discussion toward a culturally sensitive resolution that fosters continued engagement by the caregiver in the helping relationship with the social worker.

If dual-language staff members and or dual-language assessments and evaluations are not available, and a moderate-to-poor English-speaking caregiver is being assessed, the social worker needs to be aware that there may be a risk of discrepancies in the assessment process. The psychosocial history, among other things, is information about the caregiver's personal development, the environments in which the developmental experiences took place, the people who play significant roles in those experiences, and the language and environmental cultural context unique to the individual, the family, and the afflicted family member. It is also what gives meaning to the caregiver's subjective developmental experience of the afflicted family member's emergence into Alzheimer's disease and the critical factors that led to the identification of dementia. The story generally also includes the associated links of the dementia symptoms causing the disorganization and deconstruction of the once independent healthy family member's life role in the family and the subsequent reconstruction of the family member's new role within the family context of a dementia-afflicted dependent family member in need of care. With the growing diversity of aging ethnic populations and the increasing diversity within each of the major ethnic subgroups, ensuring the appropriate language assistance for ethnic caregivers of dementia-afflicted relatives will be a challenge for social workers in the decades ahead. In helping dementia caregivers and their afflicted family members, the social worker must address the needs of both the afflicted family member and the caregiver, each of which may have different language barriers that require varying communication assistance. Training social workers to sharpen their cultural competence skill levels in order to support the cultural context is essential.

To address the needs in the Black and African American communities and to improve care outcomes, social work practice must also address the use of language in the cultural frame. While there are situations in which language barriers do exist due to immigration by non–English-speaking cultures, such as elderly from Africa, the Caribbean, Haiti, or Jamaica who may speak no or limited English or varying dialects, some literature points to "a difference in linguistic style" for Blacks (Stevenson, Winn, Walker-Barnes, & Coard, 2005, p. 319). Stevenson et al. (2005) add the following and cite Asante (1987) and Smitherman (1977).

> Most prominent are the use of rhythm, styling, lyrical balance, and melodious voice to convey meaning. Asante (1987) remarks that this linguistic style, termed "tonal semantics" by Smitherman (1977), is the hallmark of Black rhetorical expression. Words and phrases may have different, even opposite, connotations depending on the speaker's vocal tone and rhythm. For example, the word "bad' means "good" if said in a certain way. Ignorance of such linguistic nuances on the part of therapist can result in potentially serious misunderstandings about clients' intents and experiences. Traditional African American communication is further distinguished from typical American English by three additional culturally specific modes of discourse: call-response, signification and narrative sequencing (Smitherman, 1977). (Stevenson et al., 2005, p. 319)

The authors provide a description of each of the specific modes of discourse noted above and ways in which the linguistic style pervades aspects of everyday life.

> Call response "is the spontaneous verbal and nonverbal interaction between speaker and listener in which all of the speaker's statements ('calls') are punctuated by expressions ('responses') from the listener" (Smitherman, 1977, p. 104). Responses may be subtle (e.g., a slight head nod) or emphatic (e.g., a shout, banging on a table). Although most carefully preserved in the church, it also pervades aspects of everyday communication and emphasizes traditional West African values of group cohesiveness, cooperation, and the collective common good. (Stevenson et al., 2005, pp. 319–320)

Social workers seeking to be culturally competent need to recognize that the interchange between the listener (social worker) and communicator (client) is highly important in terms of communicating empowerment and a balance of power in the working relationship, in addition to empathy and understanding. For many Blacks, the former social worker-client therapeutic alliance may not function well. Some classical social work training requires the social worker to take the stance of the discerning, silent, nonverbal expert in order to allow the client to receive a mirror reflection and self-assess. This may not be effective or culturally sensitive. In fact, according to Stevenson et al.

(2005), the social worker may run the risk of disrespecting the caregiver communicating, "I am the expert and you are the 'crazy'" one (p. 320). What does seem to work well is a genuine interest in the information being communicated by the caregiver, listening above and beyond the animated, passionate display of emotion or emphasis on detail. The most effective connection is one that is interactive and engages in both nonverbal or verbal communication that transmits a signal to the caregiver that he or she is heard, understood, and the "expert source" of information about the caregiving situation and the disease process in the family member. The use of sarcasm or other methods tend to serve as openings for the use of humor or other interactions that lead to openings for new understanding.

Story telling is often employed by Blacks to communicate subjective details about real or hypothetical events. This method of story telling, also referred as narrative sequencing, helps clients recreate an emotional experience of an event. As the narrative unfolds, a variety of emotions may emerge that serve to illustrate important facts or details regarding the experience. It is important that social workers understand this form of communication and allow the narrative sequencing to occur. This is contrary to Western culture that would prefer individuals to "get to the point" or quickly report just the facts (Stevenson et al., 2005, p. 320). Social workers who are familiar with the linguistic styles and the use of various modes of discourse within the culture are less apt to attribute pathology where there is none, and will be more apt to tap into cultural resources and caregiver strengths that could help the caregiver, the afflicted family member, and the family. Understanding cultural language nuances may also prevent ruptures in the therapeutic alliance. Ruptures can occur when caregivers interpret the social worker's ignorance of the language as cultural disrespect or lack of sensitivity. Relationship barriers may lead to engagement avoidance and caregiver self-disclosure anxiety. Basic understanding of the language nuances may also help to prevent the caregiver's premature dropout from the social work and client relationship.

Caregiver who are immigrant newcomers or who have chosen to maintain the language of their home country as opposed to adopting the new host country's language of English present additional challenges to social workers when a family member develops dementia. These could be populations from Mexico, Puerto Rico, and other Latin American countries in addition to immigrants from Africa and the Caribbean. Variations of stress and trauma culturally constructed in narrative sequencing patterns in the home country language can create formidable challenges for social workers. For social workers with the shared language and culture, the therapeutic alliance and connection for work may lessen the complexity. The implication for the caregiver is "we share a common language and culture." Caregivers are more apt to experience a culture and language connection and a sense commonality and hope in this shared, culturally syntonic relationship.

When to Use Interpreters

However, for most social workers this is a complicated issue. The social work profession perceives the relationship itself as curative, and the foundation frame of the intervention process. In addition, a culturally competent social worker understands language to be a key point of cultural contact with clients and the essential pathway to establish the therapeutic alliance. The literature points to the need to address social service availability in Spanish as a civil rights issue because of its importance in the lives of Latinos (Delgado, 2007; Suleiman, 2003), which raises questions regarding if and when to use Spanish interpretation or translation services. Consideration should be given to the quality of service to be provided, and who will provide the service. Also important is what kind of training will the interpreters receive to provide Latinos and Blacks with the quality language services they deserve. Other literature notes dissatisfaction by Latinos and other groups of color with health care interactions, and indications that quality of health care was adversely affected because of language barriers. Also noted were cultural groups experiencing cultural bias, racism and discrimination due to language barriers (Johnson, Saha, Arbelaez, Beach, & Cooper, 2004; Morales, Cunningham, Brown, Liu, & Hays, 1999; Timmins, 2002). Delgado (2007) analyzing the relationship between Latino language proficiency and physician use reaffirmed the findings of Derose and Baker (2000).

> The magnitude of the association between English proficiency and number of physician visits was similar to that for having poor health, no health insurance, or no regular source of care. (Derose & Baker, 2000, p. 76).

Other studies found that Latinos are at a double disadvantage when seeking health care from English-speaking physicians because "Latinos tended to make fewer comments," and when comments are made, "they are more than likely ignored" (Rivadeneyra, Elderkin-Thompson, Silver, & Waitzkin, 2000). Still other studies found lack of adherence to treatment because of language barriers, and the use of translators was not always seen as a sufficient remedy (Murphy, Roberts, Hoffman, Molina,

& Lu, 2003). When considering the use of translators or interpreters, it is important for the social worker to consult with the caregiver to determine if the caregiver would like to use a translator or interpreter. Once that is established it is crucial for the social worker to again consult with the caregiver to determine if the caregiver prefers a family member or a staff member to step into that role. Granted there are times when the only option will be one or the other due to lack of family or staff availability, but it should not be assumed that a family member or a staff member is preferred. If the caregiver prefers a family member, the caregiver should be allowed to select the family member. It should not be assumed that the person who accompanied the caregiver should automatically move into that role. It may be a conflict of interest for a family member to be involved and may cause conflict, shame, or embarrassment to the caregiver or the family group. The same is true when considering a staff member as an interpreter. It is important for the social worker to consult the caregiver to determine if the staff member being considered to provide language assistance has the approval of the caregiver. In close-knit communities where cultures live, work, and socialize together, there could conceivably be a staff member who may be known to the caregiver socially and whose involvement in the treatment of his or her family may cause shame and embarrassment in the larger cultural community. Conversely, it could be very helpful to a caregiver to find a familiar person working as a staff member in the social service or health care agency who would be willing to provide language assistance. By deferring the decision to the caregiver, the social worker is not only building trust with the caregiver, but is also communicating respect by enabling the caregiver to maintain some control of the intervention process and fostering a client empowered role in the therapeutic alliance. Added to the complexity of delivering appropriate language and translation assistance to the caregiver, the social worker needs to consider the availability of suitable educational materials. This can be an expensive, lengthy, and complex issue due to the significant differences in educational backgrounds of the caregivers.

Educational Disparities

Educational disparities in Black and Latino caregivers in extant research populations find a variety of challenges in terms of limited knowledge about dementia as a disease process, limited access to resources for support, and increased learning challenges to manage the dementia disease symptoms as they emerge in the family member. In a study conducted by Ho, Weitzman, Chi, and Levkoff (2000) examining stress and service use by 117 minority caregivers living in the Boston area, 70.6% of African American and 68.9% of Latino caregivers reported having completed high school or less education.

Financial Constraints

Latino caregivers reported having a family income of under $20,000; African American family income "while low, was slightly higher" (Ho, Weitzman, Chi, & Levkoff, 2000, p. 75). In a subsequent study of 60 Latino caregivers by González Sanders (2006) conducted in Massachusetts and Connecticut, "more than half (62%) [of] Latino caregivers reported a 12th grade or lower educational attainment and only 38% indicated they worked either full-time or part-time" (p. 63). In the latter study "nearly 75% of the Latino caregiver respondents report an annual income below $29,999" (González Sanders, 2006, p. 63). African Americans and Latinos with educational and economic disparities can create additional stresses as family caregivers work to balance employment outside of the home and the caregiving role within the home. However, previous research (e.g., Macera et al., 1992; Picot, 1995a; Picot, Debanne, Namazi, & Wykle, 1997; Roff et al., 2004) that compared Caucasian and African American attitudes about caregiving found that education and income demographic characteristics of caregivers were related to caregiver attitudes and outcomes, with persons of lower education and SES reporting less burden and more positive attitudes toward caregiving, and African Americans experiencing less distress by care recipient disruptive behaviors (Haley et al., 1996; Miller, Campbell, Farran, Kaufman, & Davis, 1995). Two explanations could be that caregiving is seen as a more normative experience (Dilworth-Anderson & Anderson, 1994; Haley et al., 1996), or that a learned cultural pattern has helped African Americans live through many difficult life experiences (Farran et al., 1997; Roff et al., 2004).

Nonetheless, educational attainment and family income are important to consider in terms of caregiver needs assessments and biopsychosocial assessments. As mentioned previously, ethnic minority families, and specifically Blacks and Latinos, tend to include a larger number of persons in the caregiving constellation (Montgomery & Kosloski, 2000). Therefore disparities in formal education are likely to exist within these networks of care. Acculturation, familial roles, and differences in family structure contribute to caregiver expectations, as in the case of Latinos whose family caregiving resources tend to generally include spouses or adult children in the caregiving role, while the Black caregiver network may include family and close fictive kin networks of care resulting in varying educational attainment levels.

Social Worker as Resource for Caregiver

In view of the variables that may exist within the caregiving frameworks among Black and Latino caregivers, the social worker serves as the ideal resource for caregivers. Social workers working with caregivers can complete the required assessments and easily stress the need for more family-focused community and medical care, and serve as an advocate for the care of the afflicted family member and with the varying caregiver members of the family. Ideally, the social worker is involved with the care of the entire family, knowledgeable in the coordination of a wide range of medical, social, and practical services. Social workers typically have the training and practical knowledge to serve as the link between systems. They can help to identify and open pathways to care.

Ethnic Family Community Resources

Social workers can coordinate services ranging from prenatal care of the primary caregiver to teen counseling for the child of the caregiver or afflicted family member. They can identify a support group, find elder care, locate violence prevention programs, and facilitate transportation access. According to Ho, Weitzman, Cui, and Levkoff (2000), "Social workers typically have the training and practical knowledge to serve in that capacity, and seem central to alleviating unmet service needs among minority and low-income caregivers of ADRD [Alzheimer's disease related dementia] elders" (p. 83).

UNDERSTANDING THE CAREGIVER EXPERIENCE OF DISCRIMINATION AND RACISM

Most assessment instruments used in social, behavioral, and mental health agencies may be based on middle-class, Western European/North American assumptions, values, and norms. "It may be particularly helpful for social workers to offer expanded assistance to minority caregivers in locating and accessing culturally-competent services" (Ho et al., 2000, p. 83). Understanding how these instruments are helpful for some populations and knowing that they may not be entirely appropriate for some Black and Latino cultural groups are essential parts of social work values and ethical training responsibilities as professionals.

PROFESSIONAL ETHICAL DILEMMAS AND THE NASW CODE OF ETHICS

The following is noted in the National Association of Social Workers Code of Ethics (1996).

Value: Dignity and worth of the person
Ethical Principle: Social workers respect the inherent dignity and worth of the person.
Social workers treat each person in a caring and respectful fashion, mindful of individual differences and cultural and ethnic diversity. Social workers promote clients' socially responsible self-determination. Social workers seek to enhance clients' capacity and opportunity to change and to address their own needs. Social workers are cognizant of their dual responsibility to clients and to the broader society. They seek to resolve conflicts between clients' interests and the broader society's ethical principles, and ethical standards of the profession. (p. 6)
4. Social workers' ethical responsibilities as professionals
4.02 Discrimination
Social workers should not practice, condone, facilitate, or collaborate with any form of discrimination on the basis of race, ethnicity, national origin, color, sex, sexual orientation, age, marital status, political belief, religion, or mental or physical disability. (pp. 22–23)

At least three pragmatic questions are at the center of the issue. How do social workers intervene with caregivers and families so that caregivers ultimately engage with the social worker in order to link to the social service or health care environment? How do social workers distill specific clinical guidelines for assessing the complex experiences of Black and Latino caregivers who may present for services alone or in the context of their family group? How do social workers obtain and assess important biopsychosocial information relevant to these varied heterogeneous ethnic groups following a needs-assessment approach, delineating the uniqueness of caregiver mental health, social-environmental issues, and the needs of a dementia-afflicted family member? Chapters 6, 7, and 8 of this book address these questions with information gained from research with Black and Latino caregivers and the clinical experiences of the authors.

REFERENCES

Adamson, J. (2001). Awareness and understanding of dementia in African/Caribbean and South Asian families. *Health and Social Care in the Community, 9*(6), 391–396.

Akhtar, S. (1995). A third individuation: Immigration, identity, and the psychoanalytic process. *Journal of the American Psychoanalytic Association, 43*(4), 1051–1884.

Alva, S. A. (1985). Political acculturation of Mexican American adolescents. *Hispanic Journal of Behavioral Sciences, 7*, 345–364.

Amahti-Mehler, J., Argentieri, S., & Camestri, J. (1993). *The Babel of the unconscious.* Madison, CT: International Universities Press.

Bandura, A. (1991). Self-efficacy mechanism in physiological activation and health-promoting behavior. In J. Madden IV (Ed.), *Neurobiology of learning, emotion and affect* (pp. 229–269). New York: Raven Press.

Bandura, A. (1977). Self-efficacy: Toward a unifying theory of behavior change. *Psychological Reports, 84*, 191–215.

Bass, D. M., Clark, P. A., Looman, W. J., McCarthy, C. A., & Eckert, S. (2003). The Cleveland Alzheimer's managed care demonstration: Outcomes after 12 months of implementation. *The Gerontologist, 43*, 73–85.

Berry, J. W. (1980). Acculturation as varieties of adaptation. In A. M. Padilla (Ed.), *Acculturation: Theory, models, and some new findings* (pp. 9–25). Boulder, CO: Westview Press.

Berry, J. W. (1998). Acculturation and health: Theory and research. In S. S. Kazarian & D. R. Evans (Eds.), *Cultural clinical psychology: Theory, research, and practice* (pp. 39–57). New York: Oxford University Press.

Berry, J. W., Kim, U., Power, S., Young, M., & Bujaki, E. (1989). Acculturation studies in plural societies. *Applied Psychology: An International Review, 38*(2), 185–206.

Bowlby, J. (1949). The study and reduction of group tensions in the family. *Human Relations, 2*, 123–128.

Brice-Baker, J. (1996). Jamaican families. In M. McGoldrick, J. Giordano, & J. K. Pearce (Eds.), *Ethnicity family therapy* (pp. 85–96). New York: Guilford Press.

Buekens, P., Manson, A., & Delvaux, T. (2000). Measuring acculturation among immigrants. *Archives of Public Health, 58*, 1–5.

Coard, S. I., & Sellers, R. M. (2005). African American families as a context for racial socialization. In V. C. McLoyd, N. E. Hill, & K. A. Dodge (Eds.), *African American family life: Ecological and cultural diversity* (pp. 264–284). New York: The Guilford Press.

Cooper, C. R., Jackson, J. F., Azmitia, M., & Lopez, E. M. (1998). Multiple selves, multiple worlds: Three useful strategies for research with ethnic minority youth on identity, relationships, and opportunity structures. In V. C. McLoyd & L. Steinberg (Eds.), *Studying minority adolescents: Conceptual, methodological, and theoretical issues* (pp. 111–125). Mahwah, NJ: Erlbaum.

Cuéllar, I., Arnold, B., & Maldonado, R. (1995). Acculturation rating scale for Mexican Americans-II: A revision of the original ARSMA scale. *Hispanic Journal of Behavioral Sciences, 17*(3), 275–304.

Cuéllar, J. (1990). Aging and health Hispanic American elders. Stanford Geriatric Education Center. *Number 5 Ethnogeriatric Reviews*, 246–263.

Delgado, M. (2007). *Social work with Latinos: A cultural assets paradigm.* New York: Oxford University Press.

Delgado, M., Jones, K., & Rohani, M. (2005). *Social work practice with refugee and immigrant youth in the United States.* Boston, MA: Allyn and Bacon.

Derose, K. P., & Baker, D. W. (2000). Limited English proficiency and Latinos' use of physician services. *Medical Care Research Review, 57*, 76–91.

Dilworth-Anderson, P. (2001). Family issues and the care of persons with Alzheimer's disease. *Aging & Mental Health, 5*(1), 49–51.

Dilworth-Anderson, P., & Anderson, N. B. (1994). Dementia caregiving in Blacks: A contextual approach for research. In E. Light, N. Niederhe, & B. Lebowitz (Eds.), *Stress effects on family Alzheimer's patients*. New York: Springer Publishing.

Dilworth-Anderson, P., & Goodwin, P. Y. (2005). A model of extended family support care of the elderly in African American families. In V. McLoyd, N. E. Hill, & K. A. Dodge (Eds.), *African American family life: Ecological and cultural diversity*. New York: Guilford Press.

Dohrenwend, B. P., & Smith, R. J. (1962). Toward a theory of acculturation. *Southwestern Journal of Anthropology, 18*, 30–39.

Dombrouski, J., & McCahill, C. (2004). Practical ethics. Hable usted Español? *Hospital Health Network, 78*, 35.

French, J., & Raven, B. (1959). The basis of social power. In D. Cartwright (Ed.), *Studies in social power*. Ann Arbor, MI: Institute for Research, University of Michigan.

Fortinsky R. H., Kercher, K., & Burant, C. J. (2002). Measurement and correlates of family caregiver self-efficacy for managing dementia. *Aging & Mental Health, 6*, 153–160.

Fortinsky R. H., Unson C. G., & Garcia R. I. (2002). Helping family caregivers by linking primary care physicians with community-based dementia care services, *Dementia, 1*, 227–240.

Furstenberg, A. L., & Rounds, K. A. (1995). Self-efficacy as a target for social work intervention. *Families in Society: The Journal of Contemporary Human Services*, 587–595.

Gallegos, J. S. (1991). Culturally relevant services for Hispanic elderly. In M. Sotomayer (Ed.), *Empowering Hispanic families: A critical issue for the 90s* (pp. 173–190). Milwaukee, WI: Family Service America.

Golding, J. M., Burnam, M. A., Timbers, D. M., Escobar, J. I., & Karno, M. (1985). *Acculturation and distress: Social psychological mediators*. Paper presented at the convention of the American Psychological Association. Los Angeles, CA

González Sanders, D. J. (2006). *Familismo and resilience in Latino family caregivers of dementia afflicted relatives: An ethno cultural cross-sectional study*. Unpublished dissertation, Smith College School for Social Work, Northampton, MA.

Gordon, J. M. (1964). *Assimilation in American life: The role of race, religion and national origins*. New York: Oxford University.

Graves, T. (1967). Acculturation, access, and alcohol in a tri-ethnic community. *American Anthropologist, 69*, 396–421.

Griffith, J. (1983). Relationship between acculturation and psychological impairment in adult Mexican Americans. *Hispanic Journal of Behavioral Sciences, 5*, 431–459.

Griffith, J., & Villavicencio, S. (1985). Relationship among acculturation, sociodemographic characteristics and social supports in Mexican American adults. *Hispanic Journal of Behavioral Sciences, 7*, 75–92.

Gutiérrez, L. M., & Lewis, E. A. (1999). *Empowering women of color*. New York: Columbia University Press.

Haley, W. E., Roth, D., Coleton, M. I., Ford, G. R., West, C. A. C., Collins, R. P., et al. (1996). Appraisal, coping, and social support as mediators of well-being in Black and White family caregivers of patients with Alzheimer's disease. *Journal of Consulting and Clinical Psychology, 64*, 121–129.

Hartmann, H. (1950). Comments on the psychoanalytic theory of the ego. In *Essays on ego psychology* (pp. 113–141). New York: International University Press.

Hatcher, C., & Hatcher, D. (1975). Ethnic group suicide: An analysis of Mexican American and Anglo suicide rates in El Paso, Texas. *Crisis Intervention, 6*, 2–9.

Henderson, J. N., Gutierrez-Mayka, M. K., Garcia, J., & Boyd, S. (1993). A model for Alzheimer's disease support group development in African American and Hispanic Populations. *The Gerontologist, 23*, 409–414.

Hill, N. E., McBride Murry, V., & Anderson, V. D. (2005). Sociocultural contexts of African American families. In V. C. McLoyd, N. E. Hill, & K. A. Dodge (Eds.), *African American family life: Ecological and cultural diversity*. New York: The Guilford Press.

Ho, C. J., Weitzman, P. F., Cui, X., & Levkoff, S. E. (2000). Stress and service use among minority caregivers to elders with dementia. *Journal of Gerontological Social Work, 33*(1), 67–88.

Johnson, R. L., Saha, S., Arbelaez, J. J., Beach, M. C., & Cooper, L. A. (2004). Racial and ethnic differences in patient perceptions of bias and cultural competence in health care. *Journal of General Internal Medicine, 19,* 101–110.

Kim, K. H., Relkin, N. R., Lee, L. M., & Hirsch, J. (1997). Distinct cortical areas associated with the native and second languages. *Nature, 388,* 171–174.

Kranau, E. J., Green, V., & Valencia-Weber, G. (1982). Acculturation and the Hispanic woman: Attitudes toward women, sex-role attribution, sex-role behavior, and demographics. *Hispanic Journal of Behavioral Sciences, 4,* 21–40.

Lang, J. G., Munoz, R. F., Bernal, G., & Sorensen, J. L. (1982). Quality of life and psychological well-being in a bicultural Latino community. *Hispanic Journal of Behavioral Sciences, 4,* 433–450.

Lewis, G. (2004). What ever happened to culturalism: From Horney to Lacan. Scientific Meeting of Association for the Advancement of Psychoanalysis. February 13, 1997. Presenter: Mario Rendon. *The American Journal of Psychoanalysis, 64*(2), 276–277.

Locke, D. C. (1992). *Increasing multicultural understanding: A comprehensive world.* Newbury Park, CA: Sage.

Macera, C. A., Eaker, E. D., Goslar, P. W., Deandrade, S. J., Willaimson, J. S., Comman, C., et al. (1992). Ethnic difference in the burden of caregiving. *The American Journal of Alzheimer's Disease and Related Disorders & Research, 7,* 4–7.

Marcos, L. R., & Alpert, M. (1976). Strategies and risks in psychotherapy with bilingual patients. *American Journal of Psychiatry, 133,* 1275–1278.

Marín, B. V., Otero-Sabogal, R., & Pérez-Stable, E. (1987). Development of a short acculturation scale for Hispanics. *Hispanic Journal of Behavioral Sciences, 9*(2), 183–205.

Martinez, C. R., DeGarmo, D. S., & Eddy, J. M. (2004). Promoting academic success among Latino youths. *Hispanic Journal of Behavioral Sciences, 26*(2), 128–151.

McLoyd, V. C., Hill, N. E., & Dodge, K. A. (Eds.). (2005). Introduction ecological and cultural diversity in African American family life. In V. C. McLoyd, N. E. Hill, & K. A. Dodge (Eds.), *African American family life: Ecological and cultural diversity* (pp. 3–20). New York: The Guilford Press.

Miller, B., Campbell, R. T., Farran, C. J., Kaufman, J. E., & Davis, L. (1995). Race, control, mastery, and caregiver distress. *Journal of Gerontology: Social Sciences, 50*B, S374–S382.

Miller, D. (2002). *An introduction to Jamaican culture for rehabilitation service providers.* Buffalo, NY: Center for International Rehabilitation Research Information and Exchange, University of Buffalo.

Miranda, A. O. (1995). *Adlerian life styles and acculturation as predictors of the mental health of Hispanic adults.* Unpublished doctoral dissertation. Georgia State University, Atlanta.

Miranda, A. O., Estrada, D., & Firpo-Jimenez, M. (2000). Differences in family cohesión, adaptability, and environment among Latino families in dissimilar stages of acculturation. *The Family Journal: Counseling and Therapy for Couples and Families, 8*(4), 341–350.

Mizio, E. (1981). *Training for service delivery to minority clients.* New York: Family Service Association of America.

Montgomery, R. J. V., & Kosloski, K. D. (2000). Family caregiving: Change, continuity and diversity among caregivers. In M. D. Lawton & R. L. Rubenstein (Eds.), *Interventions in dementia care: Toward improving quality of life.* New York: Springer Publishing.

Morales, L. S., Cunningham, W. E., Brown, J. A., Liu, H., & Hays, R. D. (1999). Are Latinos less satisfied with communication by health care providers? *Journal of General Internal Medicine, 14,* 409–417.

Murphy, D. A., Roberts, K. J., Hoffman, D., Molina, A., & Lu, M. C. (2003). Barriers and successful strategies to antiretroviral adherence among HIV-infected monolingual Spanish-speaking patients. *AIDS Care, 15,* 217–230.

National Association of Social Workers. (1996). *National Association of Social Workers code of ethics*. Washington, DC: National Association of Social Workers.

National Association of Social Workers. (2010). *NASW standards for social work practice with family caregivers of older adults Draft for Public Comment*. Washington, DC: National Association of Social Workers.

Ojemann, G. A. (1991). Cortical organizational of language. *Journal of Neuroscience, 11*, 2281–2287.

Olson, L. K. (Ed.). (2001). *Age through ethnic lenses* (pp. 230–241). New York: Rowman & Littlefield Publishers, Inc.

Olson, L. K. (2001). Gender and Long-term care: Women as family caregivers, workers, and recipients. In L. K. Olson (Ed.), *Age through ethnic lenses* (pp. 230–241). New York: Rowman & Littlefield Publishers, Inc.

Padilla, A. M. (Ed.). (1980). *Acculturation: Theory, models and some new findings*. Boulder, CO: Westview.

Padilla, A. M., Olmedo, E. L., & Loya, F. (1982). Acculturation and MMPI performance of Chicano and Anglo collage students. *Hispanic Journal of Behavioral Sciences, 4*, 451–466.

Padilla, A. M., & Perez, W. (2003). Acculturation, social identity, and social cognition: A new perspective. *Hispanic Journal of Behavioral Sciences, 25*(1), 35–55.

Paradis, M. (1977). Bilingualism and aphasia. In H. Whitaker & H. Whitaker (Eds.), *Studies in neurolinguistics* (Vol. 3, pp. 65–121). New York: Academic Press.

Parra, P. A., & Guarnaccia, P. (1998). Ethnicity, culture, and resiliency in caregivers of a seriously mentally ill family member. In H. I. McCubbin, E. A. Thompson, A. I. Thompson, & J. E. Fromer (Eds.), *Resiliency in Native American and immigrant families* (pp. 431–450). Thousand Oaks, CA: Sage.

Pearce, J. (2002). Systemic therapy. In J. Hepple, J. Pearce, & P. Wilkinson (Eds.), *Psychological therapies with older people: Developing treatments for effective practice* (pp. 77–102). New York: Taylor & Francis.

Pearlin, L. I., Mullan, J. T., Semple, S. J., & Skaff, M. M. (1990). Caregiving and the stress process: An overview of concepts and their measures. *The Gerontologist, 30*(5), 583–594.

Pérez-Foster, R. M. (1992). Psychoanalysis and the bilingual patient: Some observations on the influence of language choice on the transference. *Psychoanalytic Psychology, 9*, 61–76.

Pérez-Foster, R. M. (1996a). The bilingual self duet in two voices. *Psychoanalytic Dialogues, 6*(1), 99–121.

Pérez-Foster, R. M. (1998a). *The power of language in the clinical process: Assessing and treating the bilingual person*. Northvale, NJ: Jason Aronson.

Pérez-Foster, R. M. (1999). Las Mujeres women speak to the word of the father. In R. C. Lesser & E. Schoenberg (Ed.), *That obscure subject of desire: Freud's female homosexual revisited* (pp. 130–140). New York: Routledge.

Pérez-Foster, R. M. (2001). When immigration is trauma: Guidelines for the individual and family clinician. *American Journal of Orthopsychiatry, 71*(2), 153–170.

Picot, S. J. (1995a). Choice and social exchange theory and the rewards of African American caregivers. *Journal of National Black Nurses' Association, 7*, 29–40.

Picot, S. J., Debanne, S. M., Namazi, K. H., & Wykle, M. L. (1997). Religiosity and perceived rewards of Black and White caregivers. *The Gerontologist, 37*, 89–101.

Redfield, R., Linton, R., & Herskovits, J. J. (1936). Memorandum for the study of acculturation. *American Anthropologist, 38*, 149–152.

Reed, D., McGee, D., Cohen, J., Yano, K., Syme, L. L., & Feinleib, M. (1982). Acculturation and coronary heart disease among Japanese men in Hawaii. *American Journal of Epidemiology, 115*, 894–905.

Rivadeneyra, R., Elderkin-Thompson, V., Silver, R. C., & Waitzkin, H. (2000). Patient centeredness in medical encounters requiring an interpreter. *American Journal of Medicine, 108*, 470–474.

Roff, L. L., Burgio, L. D., Gitlin, L., Nichols, L., Chaplin, W., & Hardin, M. (2004). Positive aspects of Alzheimer's caregiving: The role of race. *Journal of Gerontology: Psychological Sciences, 59B*(4), 185–P190.

Rogler, L., Cooney, R., Constantino, G., Early, B., Grossman, B., Gurak, D., et al. (1983). *A conceptual framework for mental health research on Hispanic populations.* New York: Hispanic Research Center.

Rogler, L. H., Gurak, D. T., & Cooney, R. S. (1987). The migration experience and mental health: Formulations relevant to Hispanic and other immigrants. In M. Gavira & J. D. Arana (Eds.), *Health and behavior: Research agenda for Hispanics.* Chicago, IL: University of Illinois at Chicago.

Rossi, A. S. (1980). Aging and parenthood in the middle years. In P. B. Baltes & O. G. Brim Jr. (Eds.), *Lifespan development and behavior.* Vol. III. New York: Academic Press.

Sánchez, C. D. (2001). Puerto Rican elderly. In L. K. Olson (Ed.), *Age through ethnic lenses: Caring for the elderly in a multicultural society* (pp. 86–94). New York: Rowman & Littlefield Publishers, Inc.

Schmidley, D. (2003). The foreign-born population in the United States: March 2002 (*Current Population Reports, Series P20–539*). Washington, DC: U.S. Bureau of the Census.

Simic, A. (1985). Ethnicity as a resource for the aged. *Journal of Applied Gerontology, 4,* 65–71.

Skaff, M. M., & Pearlin, L. I. (1992). Caregiving: Role engulfment and the loss of self. *The Gerontologist, 32,* 656–664.

Stassen Berger, K. (1983). *The developing person through the life span.* New York: Worth Publishers, Inc.

Stevenson, H. C., Winn, D. M., Walker-Barnes, C., & Coard, S. I. (2005). Style matters: Toward a culturally relevant framework for interventions with African American families. In V. C. McLoyd, N. E. Hill, & K. A. Dodge (Eds.), *African American family life: Ecological and cultural diversity* (pp. 311–334). New York: The Guilford Press.

Suleiman, L. P. (2003). Beyond cultural competence: Language access and Latino civil rights. *Child Welfare, 82,* 185–200.

Szapocnik, J., & Kurtines, W. (1980). Acculturation, biculturalism and adjustment among Cuban Americans. In A. Padilla (Ed.), *Acculturation: Theory, models and some new findings* (pp. 139–160). Boulder, CO: Westview Press.

Szapocnik, J., Scopetta, M. A., Kurtines, W., & Aranalde, M. A. (1978). Theory and measurement of acculturation. *Interamerican Journal of Psychology, 12,* 113–130.

Timmins, C. L. (2002). The impact of language barriers on the health care of Latinos in the United States: A review of the literature and guidelines for practice. *Journal of Midwifery and Women's Health, 47,* 80–96.

Toseland, R. W., & Rivas, R. F. (2009). *An introduction to group work practice* (6th ed.). New York: Pearson Education, Inc.

U.S. Department of Education, National Center for Education Statistics (2002). *The condition of education, 2002* (Based on U.S. Department of Commerce, Bureau of the Census, October Current Population Surveys, 1972–2000). Washington, DC: U.S. Government Printing Office.

Valle, R. (1998). *Caregiving across cultures: Working with dementing illness and ethnically diverse populations.* Washington, DC: Taylor & Francis Publishers.

Villa, V. (1998). Aging policy and experience of older minorities. In J. S. Steckenrider & T. M. Parrott (Eds.), *New directions in old-age policies* (pp. 211–233). Albany, NY: State University of New York Press.

Volkan, V. D. (1981). *Linking objects and linking phenomena: A study of the form, symptoms, metapsychology and therapy of complicated mourning.* New York: International University Press.

Yeo, G., & Gallagher-Thompson, D. (Eds.). (1996). *Ethnicity & the dementias.* Washington, DC: Taylor & Francis.

5

Social Work Roles and Expertise in Providing Services to Ethnic Caregivers

CASE EXAMPLE

*C*lara *is a monolingual, Spanish-speaking Puerto Rican daughter caring for her mother Doña Pancha diagnosed with Alzheimer's disease. The afflicted family member resided in Puerto Rico with her husband and adult son. She worked in the family home and country store selling the produce harvested by her husband and son from their family farm. However, Doña Pancha's increasing weight loss, confusion, and wandering episodes led Clara to send for her mother to have her evaluated in a Latino clinic associated with the hospital close to Clara's home in the United States. It was there that Clara and her mother first heard about Alzheimer's disease.*

Clara's father and older brother are farmers and live in a remote location in the mountains of Puerto Rico. The father and son live in the family home located in the mountains where they work the farmland and only make visits to their other family residence and country store in the lower terrain as necessary to deliver the harvested crops for sale in their store. They want Doña Pancha to return home and resume her life duties with them selling the harvest and maintaining the family residence in the lower terrain. They do not agree with or understand the diagnosis of Alzheimer's disease, nor do they accept the care plan or what has been said about their wife and mother. They view the dementia symptoms as a part of normal aging and believe Doña Pancha can learn to deal with the symptoms at home in her normal routine in Puerto Rico. There is growing conflict in the family regarding what is best for Doña Pancha. Clara believes her mother, who is in late mid-stage Alzheimer's disease, is no longer able to be responsible for the duties required by her father and brother—manage the store and the residence, live alone for long periods of time and care for herself. Her mother requires ongoing supervision to ensure she is safe, taking the required medications, eating regular meals and is completing other activities of daily living such as bathing and dressing appropriately. She also requires regular medical care.

In addition to caring for her ailing mother, Clara has her own nuclear family issues requiring time, skill, and energy. Clara's husband Manny, also Puerto Rican, has a long history of mental illness and is currently diagnosed with schizophrenia. Because he is often noncompliant with medications, Clara has to supervise his medications. Clara's son and daughter also have mental health issues. One is diagnosed with severe depression and the other is diagnosed with bipolar disorder. All members of Clara's family are in mental health treatment via individual and family counseling. This caregiver views her commitment to her family members as her obligation and her cultural role responsibility as the daughter in the family.

There are multiple challenges for the social worker working with Clara and her mother to help her father and brother resolve the dementia care issues. A key issue is role clarity for the worker. While it is important to help Clara by serving in a variety of roles that will help the extended family network, it is important for the social worker to maintain the boundaries that will enable Clara and her family to continue care with the providers already counseling her husband and children. The social worker can provide support and information as necessary to the counseling social workers involved with the nuclear family if Clara authorizes the disclosure. If Clara, her husband, and the social worker think it is appropriate, the social worker can assist the nuclear family to understand and cope with Doña Pancha's emerging Alzheimer's symptoms while she resides in Clara's home and while Clara continues in the primary caregiver role.

What is the nature of social work with Black and Latino caregivers? What do social workers do? Where and how do social workers intervene? For all of us, these are puzzling questions that are not easily answered. Given the demands, responsibilities, and challenges of social work, this can be a daunting experience. Yet everyday social workers are answering these questions for themselves and for their clients. To serve clients efficiently and ethically, social workers need to be knowledgeable, thoughtful, and competent. This sensitive work is conducted through the relationship with the client. This relationship does not just happen; it has to be purposeful and established with specific professional goals and values. It also has to be focused toward a particular goal that is mutually agreed upon with the client. Hence, empathy, understanding, and a freedom of communication are essential to develop a working relationship enabling the social worker and the client to work together toward a common purpose (Compton & Galaway, 1989).

Initially, students desiring to be social workers do so through professional education in the academy. It is often at this beginning stage that they observe professors and agency supervisors living the role of the profession. It is also in the academy that social work students first take on a variety of assignments in the classroom and in agencies that help them begin to learn to work in social services. This structured goal-oriented learning process is influenced by the historical evolution of social work and social work theory, practice, and skill development. It is here that the social work professional's identity begins to take shape. The history, mission, goals, ethics, and values of the profession are learned through hands-on experiences supervised jointly by faculty and agency-skilled social work professionals with experience working with a variety of individuals, families, and groups.

Social workers at the beginning or at the generalist level learn to work at four levels of intervention in the interaction between persons and the environment; this is known as the ecological approach (Barker, 1968; Bronfenbrenner, 1977). In applying Bronfenbrenner's (1977) ecological approach to Black and Latino family members in the role of dementia caregivers, the social worker assesses the interaction of the caregiver in the following four levels: (1) microlevel; (2) mesosystem level; (3) exosystem level; and (4) macrolevel. At the microsystem-level intervention, social workers work with caregivers and the environment in the immediate setting, such as interactions with other family members at home and how the size and design of the home affects this interaction, the family, and the dementia-afflicted family member in the home or in another setting. At the mesosystem level, the interventions involve work in the interrelationships among the various settings in which the caregiver is developing or seeking to develop relationships to create teams with organizations and the network of helping professional agencies. It would include the relationships among home, work, colleagues, or peer groups. For some caregivers it might include relationships in senior centers, volunteer work environments, hobbies, or church groups.

The exosystem would include "the major social structures that impinge" on the caregiver (Stassen Berger, 1983, p. 16). "Theses include formal and informal institutions of society, such as neighborhood, the mass media, agencies of the government, transportation facilities, and informal social networks" (Stassen Berger, 1983, p. 16). At the macrosystem-level intervention, social workers intervene at the community, institutional, and societal levels (Nichols, 2011). For caregivers, this might be "the overarching institutional patterns of the culture or subcultural such as the economic, social, educational, legal, and political systems, of which the micro-, meso-, and exosystems are concrete manifestations. The macrosystem is the source and carriers of the ideologies that affect everyone's development" (Stassen Berger, 1983, p. 16). One example for this might be how much value a particular culture places on elder care or family dementia care, as this will influence how elders or dementia-afflicted individuals are treated in the setting. The implication for social work is that the social worker needs to assess the caregiver interactions and to consider the overall context of the vicissitudes of the caregiver's life development, life experience, and current functioning, rather than simply looking at the caregiver as just having one issue or behavior in need of evaluation when considering an intervention plan.

At each of these levels of intervention, the social worker develops specific helping roles to be effective with the client in the particular levels selected by the social worker and client for work. In most interventions, the worker engages in an increasingly differentiated and complex set of roles for a substantial length of time. One role might be to help meet the needs of the caregiver within the family and work and/or the community environment in which the caregiver resides. Another role might be helping the caregiver secure and sustain housing or employment. Teaching caregivers to advocate for themselves and their family members in order to change the medical or community environment to be more responsive to the family's needs is another area of social work. This might mean helping caregivers to understand social policies such as those related to the Americans with Disabilities Act. Social workers at all levels—baccalaureate, master's, and doctorate—have different role responsibilities. Generalist-level social workers tend to focus on the broader and more general issues and problems impacting caregivers. Their work tends to be short term and focused on immediate needs or problems. Generalist social workers might serve in elderly-protective capacities, responding to elder abuse or neglect, might help families improve elder care capabilities or serve in nursing homes or elder day care centers. They may lead groups focused on teaching caregivers a new task or on enhancing caregivers' dementia knowledge or education. They might also work in nonprofit agencies or hospitals providing caregivers with links to medical institutions, community resources, transportation, or in-home case management services. At the master's and doctorate levels, social workers provide more direct clinical service that involves assessment of the person in the actual environment, in addition to assessments of the psychiatric categories that fit the *Diagnostic and Statistical Manual of Mental Disorders* (*DSM-IV-TR*) as well as other areas of social work practice.

> MSW and doctorate-level social workers provide clinical services. They also design, plan, evaluate, and administer human service programs in conjunction with other professional practitioners and corporate or union leadership. Often, too, they conduct research, write grants to obtain funding for new programs, and conduct community needs assessments. (Suppes & Cressy Wells, 2003, p. 300)

Social workers at the master's level and doctoral level also have advanced clinical practice skills to provide more in-depth and complex services to clients. While they assess the caregiver through the added clinical lens applying more in-depth psyche-focused work, they also keep the four-prong ecological approach in mind. This can be challenging to the social worker considering the demands of the many role requirements and dynamic circumstances the caregiver and the afflicted family member experience as they seek to meet the demands of the evolving disease process as well as many other life demands. Lack of role clarity and muddled goals for work may increase social work stress and burnout. Lloyd, King, and Chenoweth (2002) cited the conflict that can be experienced by social workers causing stress and burnout in the following statement.

> Role ambiguity was found to be an important source of dissatisfaction for social workers in research carried out by Balloch et al. (1998). They found that the most frequently mentioned sources of subjective stress included being exposed to conflicting demands, being expected to do things which were not part of the job, being unable to do things which should be part of the job, and being unclear about what was expected. Role ambiguity occurs when there is uncertainty about the scope of the job and about the expectations of others. Stress arising from unclear goals or objectives can ultimately lead to job dissatisfaction, lack of self-confidence, a lowered sense of self-esteem, low motivation to work, and intention to leave the job (Sutherland & Cooper, 1990). (Lloyd, King, & Chenoweth, 2002, pp. 258–259)

Because there is substantial diversity and complexity in social work roles, the potential for variability in stress levels does exist. However, learning predictors of stress and working to reduce role ambiguity when working with caregivers can help reduce the incidence. Identifying the nature of the required social work role with the client often requires sifting through multiple issues. The issues and problems for social workers identified in this text are largely focused on problems related to the needs of caregivers to dementia-afflicted family members. This field of practice includes a broad range of work from a frightened, stressed caregiver to problems of family violence due to behavior disregulation caused by the progressing dementia disease in the afflicted family member. There may also be a world of potential family problems that could be experienced by the family members of the afflicted relative and the caregiver who are part of the constellation within this system. Having clarity regarding who the actual client is and the problems targeted for work helps to reduce the stress. Having skills and expertise necessary in terms of the cultural expectations and resources may also decrease barriers that exist and reduce stress.

Essential to giving value to the joint relationship between social worker and caregiver and to moving the work with the caregiver forward is establishing role clarity, partializing problems and keeping the task simple. By focusing on the problem-solving work that is necessary, and possible during a specific time-frame caregiver stress and social worker stress and burn out may be lessened. This chapter will briefly discuss some of these varied social work roles. It will describe ways in which social workers assisting Black and Latino dementia caregivers can tap into the appropriate knowledge base to obtain assistance in providing care to the care-giving family members. It will help social workers define their job's domain, clarify their role, expertise, unique contribution to the care team, allowing them to serve as a respected member of the care team and with professionals in allied fields working with the caregiver, the afflicted family member, and the family. The increasing numbers of ethnic older adults diagnosed with Alzheimer's disease and other related irreversible dementia has added another dimension to social work with older adults to include social work focused on dementia care. Although there are no specific credentials for this practice work as yet, the hope is that this text will provide a contribution to that critically needed social work practice.

SOCIAL WORKER ENGAGEMENT PROCESS ROLE

Before looking at each role, we need to first view the social work engagement process. For most social workers, the initial stage in the engagement process with ethnic caregivers is seen as critical. Because of discrimination and other factors, ethnic elders are especially vulnerable to health disparities, poverty, and thus an increased need for social services (Suppes & Cressy Wells, 2003). The elements of diversity—age, gender, race or ethnicity, religious affiliation, social class, community location, and sexual orientation—interact with the elements of the social worker to add to the complexity of the work in the engagement process. The social worker often enters into uncharted waters with idealized professional values serving as guidelines for culturally competent work. Most Latino and Black caregivers may perceive themselves as living within at least three worlds. One world is the familiar cultural expectations with language, customs, and values well-known and understood. The second is the new cultural environment filled with uncertainty and unfamiliar customs, language, and laws. Then there is the new world of the dementia illness, usually an unknown area to most caregivers. It is in the midst of these multiple worlds that engagement takes place (Figure 5.1). It is also in this multiple-world experience that the work of sorting out the caregiver's needs and problems for work while respecting familial cultural values takes place for the social worker. The following illustration provides a visual way of understanding how these worlds might interface in the Black and Latino culture when caring for a relative with dementia.

It is in the engagement process that understanding and a freedom of communication and cooperation develop as the social worker and caregiver work toward the common goal. The social worker's interaction with the caregiver and vice versa form the framework considered to be the building blocks of the relationship bridge. This bridge is strengthened with each interaction that communicates respect and trust. The main bonding agent is trust on which rests the ability of each participant to relate and communicate openly and bring their area of knowledge

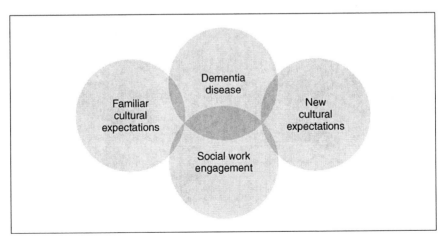

FIGURE 5.1   Black and Latino Family Caregiver Multiple Worlds Interface with Social Work Engagement

and expertise toward resolving the issue. According to Compton and Galaway (1989), the client system, or in this case the caregiver and the social worker, contribute from their areas of knowledge the necessary information to move the work forward.

The caregiver or client system provides information about "what brings them in contact with the social work practitioner" and "what they expect from this contact"; the social worker provides "a body of information about a variety of problems, resources that might be available" to help solve the problem, "certain methods and skills of helping, and an orderly way of proceeding (a pattern of thinking if you will) that move the client and worker toward a problem solution. This orderly way of proceeding increases the probability of appropriate selection and use of (1) what the client brings to the situation and (2) the practitioner's knowledge and information geared toward the goal of improving the client's ability to realize aspirations and values." (Compton & Galaway, 1989, pp. 370–371). Figure 5.2 illustrates how the working relationship forged between the social work and caregiver forms a working relationship bridge to engage in a problem-solving process.

Hence, the goal is to use the engagement process to establish the bridge forming a working relationship between the caregiver and the social worker. As the caregiver communicates what brings him or her

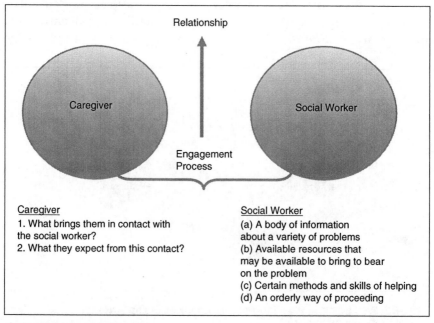

Relationship

Caregiver

Social Worker

Engagement
Process

Caregiver
1. What brings them in contact with
the social worker?
2. What they expect from this contact?

Social Worker
(a) A body of information
about a variety of problems
(b) Available resources that
may be available to bring to bear
on the problem
(c) Certain methods and skills of helping
(d) An orderly way of proceeding

FIGURE 5.2   The Social Worker and Caregiver Forge a Relationship through the Engagement Process

in contact with the social worker and clarifies what is expected from the social work contact, the social worker completes the required assessments then proceeds to marshal up the required knowledge and information geared toward the relationship expectation as communicated by the caregiver. With this information, the social worker is able to step into the appropriate professional helping role. Within the relationship for work, the social worker assumes the required role and joins the caregiver in the forward motion of identifying the caregiver's strengths and deficits while providing a supportive relationship and simultaneously employing items a to c illustrated in the figure. Following are brief descriptions of some of the professional helping roles a social worker might employ to help the caregiver.

Brokering Services

In this role, the social worker uses the skill of networking to identify resources that serve to link the caregiver and/or caregiver family to needed resources. A caregiver, for example, may need in-home respite care for the afflicted family member. The broker role also requires the social work skill of knowledge of available resources. Generally, social workers functioning in this role will be knowledgeable about the location and quality of the resources available and the eligibility requirements and fees required for the caregiver to obtain the resources. The social worker in the brokering role not only provides the contact information for the resources but also verifies that the resources were actually acquired and that the caregiver was able to utilize the services effectively to assist the need (Kirst-Ashman & Hull, 2002; Suppes & Wells, 2009). The culturally competent social worker assisting Black and Latino caregivers in this role recognizes that culture is an active part in the interaction between the social worker and the specific ethnicity of the caregiver and is also important in the interaction with the linked resource person at referral agency or institution. The caregiver's "ethnicity brings the added connotation of belonging to a specific cultural group with its unique language, customs, and attendant beliefs. In essence, ethnicity is the active expression of culture" (Valle, 1998, p. 10). When serving in the broker role, social workers also need to be cognizant that "cultural considerations play a definite role in how the caregiver and the family/significant other perceive the professional or provider" they are being referred to for assistance (Valle, 1998, p. 11). Because Black and Latino caregivers' help-seeking and help-receiving behaviors are also influenced by the underlying responses of the ethnic family, culture

(Valle, 1998) refers to practitioners working with caregivers of different ethnicities in this role as "cultural brokers" (p. 155). In the broker role described by Valle (1998), the social worker is focused on helping improve the transactions between caregivers and their environment and/or between needs and resources. He cites himself and others, including Birkel and Reppucci (1983) and Vega and Murphy (1990), in describing the role of cultural brokers.

> In the broadest context a cultural broker includes individuals who are able to bridge their own to another's culture. They are what Birkel and Reppucci (1983, p. 187) note as open networks that provide connections to other social systems. In this context, cultural brokers represent individuals who can establish working linkages between specifically targeted ethnically diverse populations and dementia-care practitioners and their parent organizations (Valle, 1981, 1998, p. 155; Valle & Bensussen, 1986; Vega & Murphy, 1990). (Valle, 1998)

Case Management or Care Management Services

Perhaps as early as the 1970s, social workers began to recognize the increased need to develop a method of managing the diverse service needs for clients with multiple issues. As clinical social work continued to emerge, the question of case management began to take center stage. The question seemed to be whether case management is part of the clinical work enabling the therapist to monitor the client's engagement with other supportive resources and services, or would case management be a separate role defined and established independently of the clinical social work role. It is believed that social work case management or care management services is an approach deriving from the critical need to link clients to complex services delivery systems successfully and monitor the clients' adaptive use. "The use of case managers and incorporation of case management principles by all caseworkers was thought to help coordinate and facilitate the provision of various services at the time they are most needed. Ideally, clients will not 'fall through the cracks' so easily as they often have in the past because they got lost in the complexity of modern-day bureaucracies and service delivery systems" (Woods & Hollis, 1990, p. 490). The move toward case management was further emphasized by the increasing federal programs requiring accountability of resources and clear evidence that the federal programs were actually assisting those they were designed to assist and that the provision of concrete services was helping people enhance and utilize their own coping capacities (Devore & Schlesinger, 1991). Case management functions included tasks focusing on the functions of assessment, linking, and monitoring services. The social worker in the case manager role either completes these functions on his or her own or works in an interdisciplinary team that engages in formal relationships with others who were assigned a particular task in the repertoire of techniques required to assist clients' multiple needs (Devore & Schlesinger, 1991). Case management as defined by Rubin (1986) clarifies the role further, stating it is "an approach to service delivery that attempts to ensure that clients with complex, multiple problems and disabilities receive all the services they need in a timely and appropriate fashion" (p. 212).

Today, depending upon the complexity or multiplicity of client problems, case management is a role that allows social workers to focus work in a variety of agencies and institutions. It may be a specialty role working to provide support to a foster family caring for an older adult, therefore working within the state agency in the foster care system. Or it may be part of mental health treatment for adults, or part of individual clinical social work with adults engaged in individual or family therapy. It can also be a specialty role working with caregivers and caregiver families tending an afflicted family member suffering from Alzheimer's disease and/or other multiple health and relational or social issues. Basically, the role of case manager blends roles previously discussed, in addition to the role of monitor or manager to ensure that each spoke of the sphere is fulfilling the required role to achieve maximum benefit for the client. Case management "has a goal of increasing access and ensuring that good quality care is provided" by all professionals involved in the overall care plan (Suppes & Wells, 2003, p. 12).

To ensure or manage the quality of care, individual social work counseling is a part of case management. In this way, the appropriate and effective planning, locating, securing, and monitoring of services can be done. Case management may be short- or long-term depending upon the needs of the caregiver. Case management is of special benefit for caregivers and dementia-afflicted family members who are faced with other multiple ill health, frailties, chronic, and progressive illness, and who, for whatever reason, are unable to obtain services on their own.

Advocacy

The role of advocacy can be considered similar to brokering; however, in this role the social worker is more assertive using professional and political power focused on networking activities to bring justice to the caregiver by acquiring the services or resources that they are entitled to but that the caregiver has either been unable to obtain on their own or has been unjustly denied services. This would be a social worker not necessarily found in community organizations among political leaders but rather what Valle (1998) labels "client-focused advocacy" (p. 158). In this role, the social worker would be oriented to caregiver service and resource distribution. For Black and Latino caregivers, the group members' history of victimization through racism or discrimination may call for a more aggressive and assertive skilled activity on the part of the social worker when interacting with agencies or institutions in search of services or resources for ethnic caregivers who have in the past been unjustly denied resources. The social worker would do this through the service and resource distribution networks rather than through political power and influence networks. "Moreover, they do not represent a social movement in the usual, more 'political' sense of the ideal, that is, they may know about the political processes in the ethnic community, but they do not function as the community's leaders" (Valle, 1998, p. 159).

Individual and Family Counseling

The social worker working with individual and family counseling is also often a case manager, as mentioned earlier. The Black and Latino caregiver's unique cultural history, life experience, circumstances, education, socioeconomic status, family interaction patterns, and individual temperament will form the response to dementia care responsibilities. Social workers providing individual and family counseling require an advanced master's degree in social work clinical education beyond the baccalaureate degree. In this role, the social worker provides caregivers with supportive counseling services that help provide a safe environment where caregivers can voice their concerns, vent feelings, and receive nonjudgmental empathic responses that often serve to ameliorate the day-to-day care stressors that arise. Although most caregivers do not require mental health therapy due to psychiatric illness, there are times when the caregiver experiences puzzling emerging dementia symptoms in the family member or when the equilibrium of his or her own life circumstances tilt and inner balance or family balance begins to slip as the dementia care needs place added strain on the family structure. In the following statements Stevenson, Winn, Walker-Barnes, and Coard (2005) stress the importance of culturally relevant approaches for African American clients.

To work effectively with African American families, clinicians must experience intense and meaningful engagement in and understanding of cultural context, legacies, and styles of these families. This includes developing awareness of the current and historical realities of discrimination and racism that impact the socioemotional functioning of African American families and contribute to their current mistrust of the majority culture and mental health professionals. (Stevenson, Winn, Walker-Barnes, & Coard, 2005, p. 326)

The assistance of a knowledgeable and sensitive social work professional who understands the overall pattern of relationships among individuals and subgroups within the family, and who has knowledge of the trajectory of the dementing disease can provide new strengths and skills to the caregiver. This is the first step in helping the caregiver formulate solutions or identify plans to resolve issues and restore inner-self and family equilibrium. Individual counseling also provides a safe place for caregivers to explore and confront their own emotional responses to the changes occurring in themselves, the afflicted family member, and their lives. It is in counseling that the immediate reactions of shock, fear, anger, and grief can be allowed to emerge, the changes explored and understood, and the reactions tolerated through adaptive coping. In addition, counselors can assist caregivers face the challenges by being available for consultation, providing guidance and support.

Grief Counseling

For many Black and Latino caregivers, the dementing disease and the grief process are culturally constructed (Doka, 2004). Although there are some common themes in caregiving, it is key for the social worker to understand the caregiver's individual and family cultural construction for both the disease and the grief process, and then together with the caregiver establish the appropriate grief counseling intervention that values the caregiver's and family's cultural construction. Grief often takes on multiple meanings for cultures; therefore, it is important for the professional to suspend his or her own personal meaning of grief in order to explore the meanings communicated by the caregiver and members of the family. According to Doka (2004) referencing Jackson (1971) and Lewis and Chavis-Ausberry (1996), African American families value survivorship.

Many African-American families who live under stressful conditions are accustomed to coping with crisis, uncertainties, and changes. There is a pride of survivorship. A person continues to be prized as long as he or she can function and relate even in the face of cognitive impairment. (Doka, 2004, p. 60)

Part of survivorship is coping adaptively. For most Black and Latino families, spirituality is a particularly strong force in coping with grief. "Therapists should also assess the role and meaning of clients' spiritual beliefs and practices and their utility in affecting clients' emotional well-being" (Stevenson et al., 2005, p. 326). Valle (1998) cautions the practitioner working with Latino caregivers against making assumptions regarding the meaning given to the cause and progression of Alzheimer's disease. For some Latinos, the cause and affect may not be based on the neurological aspects of the disabling disease. Rather, some Latinos, depending on their formal education, socioeconomic, and acculturation level, may be associating the memory and behavior changes in the afflicted family member to cultural or spiritual beliefs. Hence, Latino caregivers may be lead "to seek corresponding ethnocultural remedies" for the afflicted family member and for themselves (Valle, 1998, p. 27). Social workers need to be able to recognize the strength of the cultural beliefs regarding the disease and grief process in order to provide the caregiver with the understanding to make the paradigm shift from cultural beliefs to true, comprehensive diagnostic assessment and treatment for the afflicted family member.

Also important when working with ethnically diverse caregivers of Alzheimer's disease is for social workers to know that the grief process for many dementia-afflicted individuals, caregivers, and families often begins at the moment the diagnosis of Alzheimer's disease is made (Doka, 2004). "The persona of the individual is so changed that others experience the loss of that person as he or she previously existed" (Doka, 2000, p. 478). Because each individual travels a unique dementing disease journey, the changes brought about by the progressive disease has been described by some as complex and "an emotional roller-coaster" with the afflicted family member, caregiver, and family experiencing a mixture of feelings of loss associated with a "living-grief" (Doka, 2004, p. 159). "Anticipatory grief" and "anticipatory mourning" are useful concepts noted by Rando (1986, 2000) and cited by Doka (2004) to define the grief process as experienced by caregivers and families. And these are the concepts that the social worker in the grief counseling role will find essential when working with caregivers and family members of the dementia-afflicted individual. Therese A. Rando (2000) defines *anticipatory mourning* as "a reaction and response to all losses encountered in the past, present, or future of a life-threatening illness. These losses and the grief reactions they evoke are part of the daily experience of those who experience Alzheimer's disease or other dementias. Patients, families, and even professional caregivers can experience these losses" (Doka, 2004, p. 140).

The losses will increase over time as the disease progresses and more memory loss symptoms emerge. Many times, this grief is not openly acknowledged by the caregiver or the family for a variety of reasons—cultural beliefs being one. For the caregiver, the grief experience is enmeshed in multiple levels of history, life circumstances, identities, memory, and especially the caregiver's sense of self. Social workers providing grief counseling need to have knowledge of the disease process and the grief process, as well as the necessary skills related to what the cultural construction brings into the equation in order to work to resolve the disequilibrium experienced within the caregiver and the family system.

Adult Day Care Services

Adult day care centers are day programs tailored specifically for the Alzheimer's afflicted family member to provide respite for caregivers. They are generally supportive care but not necessarily day health or rehabilitation care programs. The adult day care programs are generally of two types, the "medical model" and the "social model" (Mittelman, Epstein, & Pierzchala, 2003). Day care programs generally consist of social work services, supervised recreational activity, a hot meal program, transportation, and occasionally may include health services. They are usually located in community agencies or other protective settings. The programs are utilized by caregivers who either desire to provide more recreational and group stimulus and activities for the afflicted family member, and/or for caregivers who need time away from the afflicted family member to run errands, take time away to rest, or to take care of necessary preparations for the family member in need. For many Black and Latino caregivers, accessing such services can be especially difficult because of language, economic, and transportation issues (Valle, 1998).

In addition, it may be considered very challenging for working caregivers in need of regular day care support if the adult day care is located outside of the community or if there are no other culturally similar participants at the day care. Caregivers may have concerns that the afflicted family member may be isolated from others or remain culturally invisible in the setting. Social workers seeking to link caregivers with culturally syntonic day care settings need to ask questions to ensure that the agencies can provide some degree of racial and ethnic concordance by providing a culturally comfortable environment caring for other individuals of the similar culture, that there is linguistic concordance with staff able to communicate in the language required to engage, assess, and maintain the safety of the afflicted family member and/or that an interpreter is readily available, and that there are culturally relevant activities. Social workers should help the caregiver obtain this information and should instruct the caregiver to ask some standard assessment questions regarding the day care facilities, as mentioned by Mittelman et al. (2003). The following check list and questions were obtained from the National Adult Day Services Association (2011, www.nadsa.org).

Site Visit Checklist:

- Did you feel welcome?
- Were the center services and activities properly explained?
- Were you given information regarding staffing, programming, and costs?
- Is the facility clean, pleasant and free of odor?
- Is the building and site wheelchair accessible?
- Is the furniture sturdy and comfortable?
- Are there loungers and chairs with arms for relaxation if appropriate?
- Is there a quiet place in the center?
- Did the staff and participants seem cheerful and comfortable?
- Are participants involved in planning activities?

Questions to ask when visiting a center:

- How many years has the center been in operation?
- Does the center have a license, certification and/or accreditation?
- What are the hours of operation?
- Are transportation services offered?
- What is the cost?
- Hourly or daily charge, other charges?
- What type of payments are accepted?
- Is financial assistance available?
- Is specialized care provided for conditions such as memory loss or TBI?
- What is the staff/participant ratio?
- What kind of training does staff receive?
- Do participants have access to services such as physical or occupational therapy?
- What type of activities are provided?
- Are meals and/or snacks provided?
- Dietary assistance?

National Adult Day Services Association, www.nadsa.org (2011)

Mittelman et al. (2003) also suggest that caregivers ask the day care center for references and encourage caregivers to speak to other caregivers who use the center to obtain their opinions about the day care center. Valle (1998) recommends that social workers and ethnic caregivers explore the quality of service provided to ethnic dementia-afflicted individuals in the day care center of interest to ensure that the ethnic population served is one of the target populations of the center, rather than being "an after thought, and be providing only a sort of 'second class' service to members" (Valle, 1998, p. 101).

Crisis Intervention Services

Crisis intervention requires many levels of cultural skill competence on the part of the social worker. Recognizing the need to act effectively and quickly using the appropriate care assessment skills to ensure caregiver and afflicted family member safety is critical. In some geographic locations, mobile crisis units are available to make emergency home visits and provide help in non-life-threatening situations. A social worker working with the family should be aware of the crisis intervention services available to help diverse caregivers in their area, and should provide the information to the caregiver before a crisis occurs to ensure that the caregiver is able to access crisis care quickly when needed. In addition, social workers should do all possible measures to maintain the rapport that has been established and follow all safety requirements for the caregiver and the afflicted family member. It is important to establish rapport in the language and manner compatible to the cultural group if at all possible.

According to Valle (1998), it "will greatly expedite the intercultural engagement process. Moreover, the ethnically diverse family members'/ significant other's feelings of crisis at the time rapport is built and help is extended may propel them to new perceptions of coping that would be introduced by the practitioner. There is always the possibility that the crisis could overwhelm the ethnic group members. Much will depend on the practitioner's as well as the bicultural-pair's dementia competence and cultural capabilities" (p. 76). Preplanning in the event of a future crisis is an important step in the initial assessment phase when the social worker and caregiver discuss the afflicted family member's status or when the diseased process is discussed. By engaging in this crisis preplanning phase together, the social worker and the caregiver can establish a plan with well-coordinated protocols in place to care for the afflicted family member but to also inform other family members as requiring notification and involvement. Some Black and Latino families designate certain kin or familism members to assume specific roles in the event of a crisis. It is important for the social worker to have advance knowledge of the particular expectation for the caregiver, the afflicted family member, and family in order to ensure that the culturally appropriate steps are taken in a crisis. It is important that clinical social workers receive training in crisis intervention frameworks in order to meet the needs of clients. Eaton and Roberts (2002) identify a seven-stage crisis intervention model. The seven stages provide a guide for social workers to follow when dealing with crisis and are listed as follows:

(1) Plan and Conduct a Crisis Assessment (Including Lethality Measures), (2) Establish Rapport and Rapidly Establish Relationship, (3) Identify Major Problems (Including the "Last Straw" or Crisis Precipitants), (4) Deal With Feelings and Emotions (Including Active Listening and Validation), (5) Generate and Explore Alternatives, (6) Develop and Formulate an Action Plan, (7) Follow-up Plan and Agreement. (Eaton & Roberts, 2002, p. 90)

It is critical that the social worker is skilled in crisis intervention to be able to assess whether the crisis requires immediate medical emergency hospital treatment or inpatient care for the caregiver or the afflicted family member. It is also essential to have an emergency preplan in place and that is kept up to date with the required authorized contact information. There are various methods of triage screening, including telephone crisis intervention, mobile crisis intervention, walk-in crisis intervention, and critical incident stress management (Eaton & Roberts, 2002). Social workers should be familiar with the various techniques required to provide a timely intervention.

Adult Foster Care Services

Adult foster care may be a cost-effective and more appropriate home care alternative for some older individuals needing assistance. Social workers play essential roles in assessing qualifications for individuals to enter adult foster care services and to ensure that foster care services are meeting clients' needs. Adult foster care for individuals over the age of 60 generally includes room, board, and basic supervision of self-care services in a family home. It is generally designed to assist adults who require frequent or regular assistance with activities of daily living, such as dressing, bathing, eating, brushing teeth, or combing hair but do not require nursing or on-site medical care services. Adult foster care for elders in most states is a service separate from the developmental disabilities department. State departments of social services provide eligible older adults' foster care assistance through adult foster care homes that are private pay or state, pay depending upon the assessment. The state generally uses the same process for older adult foster care assistance that is used for long-term care assistance under the state guidelines and provides case management services to monitor the services provided. States also have established criteria to determine which individuals are appropriate and not appropriate for state adult foster care assistance. States also have a medical review team that assesses applicants to determine if they are eligible for older adult foster care assistance. States differ in terms of service listings and criteria to determine eligibility and length and types of services provided. For example, the South Dakota Department of Social Services, Adult Services and Aging Adult Foster Care (2010) website lists the following criteria to determine whether older adults are appropriate or not appropriate for older adult foster care.

Individuals Appropriate for Adult Foster Care

- Oriented to time, person, and place and not a danger to themselves or others in the adult foster care home
- Unable to live independently
- Require minimal supervision and/or assistance in completing one or more of the following: dressing, personal hygiene, transportation, ambulation, nutrition, health supervision
- Capable of taking action for self-preservation in case of fire or storm with direction
- Usually has control of bowel and bladder, but may have stress incontinence and/or is capable of meeting their own needs when incontinent

Individuals Not Appropriate for Adult Foster Care

- Consistently not oriented to time, person, and place to such a degree that they pose a danger to themselves or others in the home
- Unable or unwilling to meet own personal hygiene needs under minimal supervision
- Has a communicable disease or infectious condition that poses a threat to the health or safety of other residents of the home
- Chronically disruptive and unable or unwilling to comply with adult foster care rules
- Behavior poses a threat to other residents
- Unable to self-medicate or medicate with the assistance of supervision or monitoring
- Require a complex, therapeutic diet

- Require any other type of care that can only be provided safely by or under the supervision of a licensed practical nurse or a registered nurse

Source: The South Dakota Department of Social Services Adult Services and Aging Adult Foster Care (2010) website: http://dss.sd.gov/elderlyservices/services/fostercare.asp

Many states also have specific licensure requirements for older adult foster care providers to prevent neglect, exploitation, and unsanitary conditions and to ensure a safe environment. Providers must meet the licensure requirements to receive reimbursement from state funds.

States also provide this service to elders under state statutes that protect people aged 60 or older from abuse, neglect, or exploitation. The state protective service department requires medical professionals, social workers, police officers, clergy, and nursing home staff to report any suspected issue of abuse, neglect, or exploitation to the protective services department. In addition, friends, neighbors, family members, and acquaintances are also required to report suspected cases to the social services department. In general, a detailed assessment is completed by a social service worker employed by the state social services agency. If the individual does qualify for adult foster care's 24-hour living arrangement with supervision, then the individual will be granted the service to ensure that he or she will receive appropriate care and protection from abuse, neglect, and exploitation. In this role, the social worker functions as a case manager within a state department of social services.

The social worker assesses the individual to determine care needs and develops a comprehensive plan to help address these needs regardless of income or assets. Social workers engage with clients on various levels to complete the required steps for thorough assessment and care. For example, there may be a social worker completing the initial investigation and the initial assessment. Once the initial step is complete, the individual may be referred to a case management social worker to monitor that treatment needs are met and that staff is working in a coordinated effort to ensure that the individual's health, safety, and well-being are attended to at each level of the social service care plan. If the elder has family, then the social worker meets with the caregiver and/or afflicted person and family to determine whether either person is in need of protective services and, if so, assesses the urgency to determine if crisis intervention and/or support services are required.

If the caregiver elder or afflicted individual did not have family and was unable to care for themselves or make care decisions, the social service worker would most likely refer the case for adjudication in order to petition the court to provide legal representation to facilitate the appointment of a conservator for the elder. The Public and Government Relations Office, Connecticut Department of Social Services, Publication No. 95–8 (2006), lists some of the services on page 2 of their publication. The list is included here.

The underlying goals behind the social worker's efforts are:

- Preserving the elderly person's right of self-determination
- Helping him or her remain in the preferred living situation whenever possible
- Preventing injury or bodily harm
- Safeguarding legal rights

In addition to supportive counseling, the plan may include arranging for and coordinating any of the following services:

- Adult companion
- Adult day care
- Homemaker, housekeeper, or choreperson
- Meals-on-Wheels
- Emergency response system
- Emergency placement, if appropriate

In extreme cases:

If an elderly person does not give consent to receive "necessary and reasonable services," and it is felt he or she lacks the capacity to give consent, the Department of Social Services, Protective Services Program may seek court authorization to provide those services.

In certain circumstances, the Department may petition the probate court for the appointment of a conservator whose role it is to make decisions on behalf of the client. If possible, a family member will assume that role or if none is available or capable, the Commissioner of the Department of Social Services will be named conservator.

Source: The Public and Government Relations Office, Connecticut Department of Social Services, Publication No. 95–8, p. 2 (2006).

Other states' departments of social services should have similar public documents guiding the protection, service, and care of elders. It is important for the social worker to be familiar with (a) the state requirements for social services department reporting, (b) the foster care procedures, and (c) the services provided in their state in order to adhere to state and federal laws governing the protection and care of elders and the elder foster care system procedures.

It is always important for the social worker to meet the client where the client resides during the engagement, assessment, and treatment process. It is also essential to allow the client to determine his or her level of cultural comfort when seeking an adult foster care placement. Therefore, when seeking foster care placements for Black and Latino older adults, if the client does not state a preference, it is important for the social worker to inquire if the client prefers to be placed in a culturally familiar adult foster home. While there are distinct requirements for the eligibility and licensing of foster care residences that are private for-pay and state supported for-pay, ethnic identity may be helpful in promoting and sustaining efficacious foster care placement outcomes for older adults.

Self-Help and Therapeutic Groups

Although there are many types of therapeutic groups, this section will focus on self-help and therapeutic groups. Self-help and therapeutic groups are two additional support services social workers can provide for caregivers. Both types are based on the purpose of the group and the motivation of the individuals in the group. They provide a safe place were individuals can openly discuss concerns, needs, and stressors. The utility of the groups has gained greater acceptance as a means of facilitating common benefits in small, face-to-face interactions with individuals who are facing or have faced similar situations (Reid, 2002). The social workers' role is to facilitate the group process by blending their professional styles and skills according to the need and the purpose of the group. Buffum and Madrid (1995) note the following as focus of self-help groups.

> The focus of self-help groups is not on insight into behavior or the reconstruction of personality, the traditional focuses of psychiatric practitioners. Instead, the focus is on controlling members' dysfunctional behavior, decreasing stress by giving advice and sharing coping strategies, and maintaining members' self-esteem and legitimacy in the face of societal pressure. (p. 499)

In addition, self-help groups focus on mutual support and socialization of members. According to Marram (1978), cited by Buffum and Madrid (1995), the socialization process includes at least a three-prong process: (1) helping members stay in contact with others, (2) providing perspectives and values of the group, and (3) helping members' perspective remain in accord with societal norms. In general, self-help groups are facilitated by participants in the group and are not led by a social worker. However, a social worker may be placed in the role of consultant in order to field questions before or after groups meet or may make an appearance in the group to help participants move the group function forward if it becomes necessary or to provide assistance with information or resources.

The therapeutic groups are designed for individuals with high levels of cognitive functioning and focus on thoughts, feelings, and behaviors. Yalom (1985) identified 11 therapeutic factors of the insight-oriented or process-oriented groups. These factors are obtained from Yalom's (1985) text and cited by Buffum and Madrid (1995) and listed next (p. 491).

Yalom's (1985) Therapeutic Factors for Group Therapy

1. Imparting of information

Information is presented through lecture or teaching aids, or information is shared among members

2. Instillation of hope

The therapist and group have the attitude that the client will get better and that the treatment modality is beneficial

3. Universality

Problems, thoughts, feelings are shared by other group members— no one is alone or isolated with one's own issues

4. Altruism

Each group member gives to another within the group; this process is therapeutic and increases the giver's self-esteem

5. Corrective recapitulation of the primary family group member

The members' responses are influenced by past family experiences. Members gain insight into their behavior when they learn that their reactions to others are similar to their reactions to their own family members

6. Development of socializing techniques

By accepting feedback about their interpersonal communication and behavior, members become more socially skillful in relationships

7. Imitative behavior

Growth is demonstrated when the client identifies with other members, imitating the healthy aspects of other members of the group

8. Interpersonal learning

Interpersonal learning results from feedback from others and insight into oneself. This learning is transferrable to other situations, enabling clients to assert themselves, trust others, test reality, give to others, and expect caring from others

9. Group cohesiveness

There is a feeling of connectedness among group members. Cohesiveness is demonstrated when positive as well as negative feedback can be given in an atmosphere of acceptance, without group disintegration

10. Catharsis

Clients express their deeply felt emotions

11. Existential factors

Clients realize that loneliness, death, and the meaning of existence are issues for all men and women; that there is a limit to how much control humans have over these issues; and that there is universal learning about human existence

Source: Yalom, I. (1985). *The theory and practice of group psychotherapy* (3rd ed.). New York: Basic Books.

Yalom's (1985) therapeutic factors can be applied to other types of groups such as education, activity, and task groups to name a few. Therapeutic support groups similar to therapeutic groups may also be initiated and facilitated by social workers and designed specifically to help members learn about and/or cope with an illness or the illness of a family member. Therapeutic groups are insight- and process-oriented groups led or facilitated by at least one clinical social worker and designed to benefit the members. Therapeutic groups may also be designed to be supportive therapeutic groups that help the group members to cope with the sources of stress in their lives and focus on existing strengths (LaSalle & LaSalle, 1991).

The clinical social worker in the role as facilitator perceives each member in the therapeutic group as a client and also views the entire group as the client in terms of the groups' functioning. For example, if a member of the group dies or develops a terminal disease and the members demonstrate maladaptive coping, denial, or ineffective grieving, the social worker would develop an intervention plan to help one, several, or all therapeutically. The social worker might also reassess members to determine if one or more require individual therapy to help them regain adaptive coping.

Social workers seeking to formulate groups with Black and Latino dementia caregivers must recognize that developing cultural awareness goes beyond just learning about another racial or ethnic group. It entails a willingness on the part of the social worker to explore personal attitudes regarding one's own ethnic roots, historical experiences with racial and ethnic groups and one's own belief systems. In addition, it is essential for social workers to examine ways in which their family of origin, community, and society have influenced their feelings about themselves, and their feelings toward Black and Latino racial groups. Further, social workers need to consider their attitudes and feelings regarding ethnic elders and consider the importance of sensitivity to differences between elders of the dominant group and elders of ethnic cultures. This is not to say that only social workers of the particular ethnic culture can run successful groups. Rather, it is just the opposite. Social workers have a profound influence in the group process. Therefore humility is a key factor when working with ethnic elder in groups. Humility conveys an attitude of vulnerability and a willingness to learn in the social worker, and places the ethnic elders in the role of expert with expert power and a sense of strength and accomplishment.

When considering group work, either self-help or therapeutic, social workers need to keep in mind that caregivers and family groups associated with dementia-afflicted elders differ due to socioeconomic, education, acculturation, generational, and linguistic factors. Some individuals may have strong ties to cultural beliefs and values, while other family members may be less connected. Social workers should consider tailoring groups to meet the needs of the population within their respective service area. Gallagher-Thompson, Talamantes, Ramirez, and Velarde (1996) cite Henderson, Gutierrez-Mayka, Garcia, and Boyd (1993) who observed successful Spanish-language support groups for Latino caregivers and note the elements of the group that they considered contributing to the success of the groups.

> They emphasized making the program user-friendly, in that it was developed with support from the community and filled a very pressing need. Also, services were offered in a flexible manner (in terms of number of meeting, location of the meeting, and the agenda to be followed), and practical problems that provided barriers to caregiver attendance were dealt with (such as transportation difficulties). (p. 145)

Gallagher-Thompson et al. (1996) indicated that the community was positive about the group; therefore, it was anticipated that the group would most likely continue as long as the bilingual and bicultural staff remained. Henderson and Gutierrez-Mayka (1992) also noted that the group content was tailored specifically to meet the needs of the groups. The groups were ethnically homogeneous and focused on ethnocultural themes, values, gender roles, and the stigma associated with the illness, which was perceived as "mental" as opposed to declining memory or neurodegenerative disease. This focus was different from the "typical" content in the usual Alzheimer's or dementia support groups available to nonethnic populations (Gallagher-Thompson et al., 1996, pp. 145–146).

Tailoring groups for Black and African American caregivers may also be effective. Dilworth-Anderson and Goodwin (2005) report that contrary to the extant literature indicating the resilience and high level of coping strengths in African American caregivers, the caregiving reality is very different. While there are many strengths to report, the demands of the progressive dementing illness on a family member and caregiver do have negative consequences on the caregiver, even with the cultural belief that providing care to family members in need is the right thing to do. Dilworth-Anderson and Goodwin (2005) cite Williams and Dilworth-Anderson (2002), indicating the African American and Black caregivers received support from the Black church or utilized formal support services that were linked in some way with the Black church. Dilworth-Anderson and Goodwin (2005) and Williams and Dilworth-Anderson (2002) recommend increased efforts to provide assistance to the Black churches providing support to caregivers. Social workers seeking to tailor services to African American and Black caregivers might find it helpful to explore the support being given through Black church groups in their respective geographic area and identify ways to provide a pathway to bridge caregiver support to the formal service communities. Because Black church communities are considered inside culture groups, facilitating the link from these communities would continue the premise of inside culture groups and reduce the risk of cultural dissonance.

For Jamaican families, two strong cultural values are work ethic and family cohesiveness. In help-seeking behavior, historically, the family and extended family resources have been an important resource for the Jamaican family. According to Brice-Baker (1996), "The Jamaican family finds it difficult to admit that there is a problem it cannot handle" (p. 93). In tailoring caregiver support groups for the Jamaican caregiver, the social worker might consider creating a group that would be unique to the needs of the caregiver and the specific family system with a content agenda that caregivers would find essential to their unique family situation They may also consider working with the family to schedule support groups at a time when the identified family members could attend. Brice-Baker (1996) also noted that "therapists working with these families will find their work rewarding because the individuals are truly motivated to help one another" (p. 95).

Respite Care

Respite care allows caregivers time of rest, relaxation, recreation, and self-care. It is temporary relief or a break from caregiving duties for the caregivers. Respite care can be formal or informal services at home or out of the home. Mittelman et al. (2003) identify three types of formal respite care services: "(1) home health aides, homemakers, and companions; (2) community activities and adult day programs; and (3) overnight respite care in a residential facility such as an assisted living residence or nursing home" (p. 256). Respite can be arranged as needed for either a few hours a day to a weekend for a 2-week vacation. Some caregivers use respite care when they have their own medical or care issues to resolve. While these programs do exist and are beneficial for many caregivers, Black and Latino caregivers generally prefer to utilize informal care through kin or fictive kin or familismo networks.

As noted in earlier chapters, due to the history of Black slavery, discrimination, and injustice, when the need arose for a supportive and protective care environment for the vulnerable, Black and African American caregivers and families tended to seek internal help from within the culture (Dilworth-Anderson & Marshall, 1996). They have historically depended upon the family kin networks or fictive kin for social support and respite care. Lincoln and Mamiya (1991) cited by Dilworth-Anderson and Marshall (1996) note "As a result, the family and church in the African-American community have provided the social support that was often lacking due to discrimination from enacted laws and accepted practices within American society" (p. 68). Dilworth-Anderson and Marshall (1996) state, "Within African-American families, support is primarily provided through relational networks that consist of consanguine relationships as well as non kin (Dilworth-Anderson, 1992; Taylor, 1986; Taylor & Chatters, 1991). Boundaries in African American families tend to be fluid and flexible, allowing for the acceptance of dependent generations into existing households" (p. 69). This is not to say that respite is always only sought within the culture. The implication for social workers is to explore the meaning of within culture versus outside of culture respite services with the caregiver rather than assuming the respite care preference.

For many Latinos, formal respite services conveyed as help for the caregiver may not be well-received or accepted by the caregiver as would be for most Blacks or African Americans. A social worker focusing on acquiring respite care for the caregiver as opposed to focusing on the afflicted family member might be considered by the caregiver and family as a violation of a cultural norm, and as insensitive, disrespectful, and insulting. Among most Latinos, and specifically Mexican Americans, the focus on self-respite care by the social worker may lead the caregiver to think that they are perceived by the social worker as weak or incapable or unwilling to fulfill the culturally assigned role, a perceived violation of cultural norm. Gallagher-Thompson et al. (1996) writes "Engaging in services to benefit yourself as a caregiver suggests that you are unwilling or incapable of accepting your role and responsibility. Family members may be outraged, as they perceive the caregiver as being selfish. The sense of obligación (obligation and reciprocity), particularly to aging parents, is very strong" (p. 144). For some Latinos who enthusiastically adhere to cultural norms and values, accepting respite from outsiders would be the equivalent of admitting that the care of the afflicted family member is a burden (Gallagher-Thompson et al., 1996). This tends to create sociocultural dissonance. According to Gallegos (1991), "Sociocultural dissonance refers to the discordant stress imposed upon the bicultural individual who is forced to choose between values of the minority culture and the dominant culture" (p. 186).

The culturally competent social worker will have to think very carefully about how to sensitively communicate the need to consider the use of formal respite services and how to assist the Latino caregiver in need of formal respite services to accept the service without feeling he or she is in violation of a cultural norm. One suggestion is for the social worker to tailor the formal respite assistance and communication in support of service utilization in a way that it is perceived as a value to the Latino elder, family, and community. In addition, it is important for the social worker to explore the service provider to verify that the formal respite services are dementia specific and culturally and linguistically appropriate for the caregiver and dementia-afflicted individual. To do less is to risk sociocultural dissonance.

Haitian families living in the Untied States have strong ties to their culture and community (Bibb & Casimir, 1996, p. 97). Like other ethnic groups Haitian groups have a history of struggles in their homeland, characterized by political unrest, poverty, revolution, and natural disasters. Similar to the African American and Jamaican cultures, slavery existed for decades until liberation was granted. Social workers creating groups for Haitian caregivers and their families might find tailoring support groups to include family members and content focusing on the family's needs most beneficial for all.

The twofold communication challenge for social workers may be in (a) locating translation services when the caregiver and family group members need language assistance, and (b) getting the members to agree to have a translator present with minimum risk to sociocultural dissonance. Many Haitians strongly believe their family problems and medical needs are private. Laguerre (2001) quoted the following Haitian elder, "One cannot speak directly to the physician. It is embarrassing to speak through a translator because sometimes it is private business; I would rather keep it between me and the physician" (p. 107).

Another challenge for social workers may be that many Haitians who have migrated to the United States still have families on the Haitian island that the caregiver may include as part of the group work content either by being physically present in the group or present as opinions or contributions brought by others arise. For some Haitian caregivers transnational aspects of care may include (a) keeping multiple family networks informed about the dementia care issues experienced by the elder in the United states, (b) dealing with conflicts originating from island family members' opinions regarding the care of the afflicted family member, and (c) learning adaptive ways of managing family relationships in the United States and in Haiti (Laguerre, 2001). Because of the socioeconomic issues experienced by Haitians, mobility may be limited, the family members in the United States and Haiti may rely more on the caregiver to provide care and keep everyone informed.

Transportation and Housing Assistance

Caregiver unawareness of community or health resources and/or lack of transportation add to caregiver problems (Cuéllar, 1990; Olson, 2001; Valle 1998). Transporting a dementia-afflicted family member demonstrating inappropriate or unsafe behavior on public transportation may place everyone at risk. For ethnic family caregivers of a low socioeconomic level, transportation for themselves and the afflicted family member can be challenging, especially if they have to depend upon public transportation and if the family member is incontinent.

One Latina caregiver told of an instance where she had to leave a store suddenly because her mother was incontinent. She was very embarrassed to have to take public transportation home but had no choice because she did not drive and other family members who had transportation were at work. In another case, a Latina spousal caregiver who worked to support herself and her dementia-afflicted husband conveyed two issues related to transportation. The first was her husband's refusal to stop driving even though he had twice mistakenly driven out of state because he became confused and forgot he was going to the supermarket just 5 minutes away from home. Both times, law enforcement assisted in his safe return home.

The second issue was the her fear of losing her job because of the increasing need to leave work to transport her husband to appointments due to medical issues related to memory loss and other physical impairments. The job not only provided income but also provided medical insurance for her and her husband.

So, while the research indicates that Black and Hispanic dementia afflicted family members are more likely to live with relatives including spouses (González Sanders, 2006; Yeo & Gallagher-Thompson, 1996), this does not necessarily mean that transportation is not an issue. Tran and Dhooper (1996) cited by Bossè (2000) listed the 10 most common social service needs of elderly Latinos over age 65 and "transportation" was listed as number one (p. 101). The other nine were, "use of senior center, food stamps, ability to eat at a senior center, home-delivered meals, homemaker services, routine telephone calls to check on one's health, use of a home health aid, visiting nurse service and use of church based services for the elderly" (Bossè, 2000, p. 101). Tran and Dhooper (1996) found that "Puerto Rican elderly had significantly greater needs than Cuban Americans on all ten of the measures and significantly more than Mexican Americans on three: transportation, routine telephone calls to check on health, and food stamps. Mexican American elderly also had significantly greater needs than Cuban Americans on all but one measure" (Bossè, 2000, p. 101). Bossè (2000), citing Yeatts, Crow, and Folts (1992), found the accessibility problems were resolved by the following; "locating service sites close to minority neighborhoods or establishing satellite centers close to such neighborhood...churches, schools, and other private or public halls, meals brought to one of these central locations and transportation problems resolved various arrangements with transit authorities or carpools" (p. 114). Tran and Melcer (2000) found that Cuban seniors living alone were more apt to use senior transportation to access services than Cuban seniors living with family members. Gallagher-Thompson et al. (1996) and Henderson et al. (1993) note the importance of providing assistance with "transportation difficulties" in order to enable caregivers to attend support group meetings (p. 145). Exploring transportation issues for Black and Latino caregivers will enable social workers to identify issues in advance and take the necessary steps to identify successful solutions.

Housing assistance comes in many forms for the ethnic caregiver and afflicted family member. For the most part, ethnic caregivers tend to reside with or in close proximity to the afflicted family member. González Sanders' (2006) study of 60 Latino caregivers in the northeastern United States reported caregiver proximity to the care recipient revealed that 45% of the Latino caregivers reported living in the same household with the care recipient, while 52% indicated they lived within walking distance or less than 30 minutes away. This study included participants from five Latino subgroups. The study data

TABLE 5.1   Living Arrangements

Own house apartment	30%
Family member house	35%
Senior apartments/disability apartment	30%
Nursing facility (other situation)	5%

From González Sanders, D. J. (2006) *Familismo and resilience in Latino family caregivers of dementia afflicted relatives: An ethno-cultural cross-sectional study* (p. 69). Unpublished doctoral dissertation, Smith College, Northampton, MA.

also yielded the following information regarding living arrangements (Table 5.1).

Dilworth-Anderson, Williams, and Williams (2001) write, "African Americans have a long history of sharing households and moving among them," but further note the importance of considering the within-group differences in urban versus suburban residence populations. They note that economically poor kinship care networks generally located in urban settings may be "homogeneously poor regardless of whether or not they share a household," and therefore "fewer resources are available to dependent older people" (Dilworth-Anderson et al., 2001, p. 99). A study of 330 elderly Black caregivers conducted by Williams and Dilworth-Anderson (2002) found that the majority of caregivers (89%) were middle-aged female family (kin) with a "mean age of 54.2" and the majority (58%) shared a house with the afflicted family member while "only 2% [of] care recipients lived more than 30 minutes away" (Dilworth-Anderson & Goodwin, 2005, p. 214).

The literature for Black and Latino caregivers in most subgroups indicates that ethnic elders tend to live in communities with like members of their ethnic group and consider out-of-home placement for their ill elderly only as a last resort, while Puerto Rican caregivers and elders may engage in more travel between the United States and the island, their desire to remain connected to the culture. Massey and Bitterman (1985), cited by Bossè (2000), provide evidence that "document segregation of Puerto Ricans due to their low socioeconomic status and black ancestry, which closes off white neighborhoods to them and leaves them on the fringe of the black ones. This segregation has the added effect of limiting access to agencies that serve whites and those that serve blacks" (p. 111). Social workers need to be cognizant of these issues in ethnic communities and explore ways to build the caregiving resource infrastructure in order to help reduce ethnic segregation and ethnic health and caregiving service disparities.

Social Services in Hospitals and Nursing Homes

Social service in hospitals is generally considered part of the services offered to individuals. Social workers provide important contribution to the care of older adults in hospital settings. Berman-Rossi (2001) states "diagnostic related group (DRG) treatment and managed-care discharge policies frame the organizational context in which social workers practice" (p. 739). According to Blumenfield (1982) cited by Berman-Rossi (2001) social workers provide direct practice by engaging in the following; "(1) helping patients and families cope with illness and hospitalization, (2) thinking through discharge options and arranging community supports, (3) educating the staff to the needs of older patients, and (4) providing support for others who work with these 'low status' clients" (p. 739). Some of the actions of social workers are listed by "diagnostic related group treatment and managed-care discharge policies frame the organizational context in which social workers practice" (Berman-Rossi, 2001, p. 737).

Some social workers work with hospitals to provide community medical orientation and education for preventive community outreach services. In this way social workers serve as the link between the institution and the community, facilitating the ability of the community's elderly to secure the needed and appropriate services (Laurie & Rich, 1984). Dementia-afflicted individuals may be hospitalized for a variety of reasons including pre-existing chronic health conditions and injuries requiring acute care. In late-stage Alzheimer's disease, the afflicted-family member may develop conditions that require repeated hospitalizations for medical interventions. Hospital emergency rooms are often the first to see the caregiver and dementia-afflicted individual.

Because ethnic minorities are also often health disparity populations, social workers provide an essential role beginning with assessment, providing for critical and ongoing care needs, and discharge planning. By engaging with the caregiver and afflicted-family member from the initial assessment, the social worker is able to contribute to the care by helping to orchestrate the various medical treatment services required by the afflicted family member in a way that the patient, caregiver, and family can understand. Often this involves arranging for an interpreter and acting as the contact person for the various family members, kin, and fictive kin networks who are intensively following the care of the family member. This is a critical service when the impaired individual with complicating medical issues requires nursing home placement and has to remain in the acute care hospital setting until long-term care can be arranged with medical facilities (Berman-Rossi, 2001).

Nursing home placement is the last resort for Black and Latino caregivers. The literature finds that 80%–90% of care for ethnic older family members is provided by family care or informal relative networks (Berman-Rossi, 2001). For that reason, social workers need to introduce this option to family caregivers with caution to avoid cultural dissonance. Most ethnic caregivers find the use of nursing home placement insulting and shameful. Du Bois, Yavno, and Stanford (2001), writing about care options for Mexican Americans, note "the available data suggest that only the most severely disabled Latinos are institutionalized" (p. 77). They also cite Wallace and Lew-Ting (1992) who found evidence that "older Mexican Americans have lower rates of nursing home utilization than both African Americans and non-Latino whites. In fact, they have lower rates of institutionalization than other Latino groups" (p. 77). According to González (2000) and Yeo (1993), African Americans' use of nursing homes is underrepresented, suggesting that informal relative-based care is more frequently preferred and utilized.

The social work role in the nursing home often begins during the assessment session before the elder is placed in the nursing facility (McInnis-Dittrich, 2002). It is at this time that the social worker first meets with the perspective resident and the family. The social worker may be responsible for assisting the caregiver with discharge planning and transition of the family member to the nursing home if the dementia-afflicted individual is recovering in a hospital from acute illness or surgery. Once in the nursing facility, the social worker role includes helping the elder to adjust to the new residence, the structured life, and daily routines.

There are many challenges for the new resident apart from the dementia diagnosis. There is the adjustment to loss of privacy and a shared room with an unfamiliar face and voice, and visitors who are present at different times of the day and night. This can be difficult even for individuals with dementia and may cause fear that will often require social work counseling intervention.

There are also the multiple losses for both the caregiver and for the family member with dementia. For the caregiver there may be the guilt, shame, and fear that one is abandoning the family member and is violating a major cultural value by not keeping that person at home. There may also be a sense of failure experienced by the caregiver for not being able to provide the needed care for the family member as expected by the family. For the dementia-afflicted family member, it is the loss of independence, home, family, familiar neighborhood, friends, and community environments.

There is also the loss of familiar sensory information such as sights, smells, noises, and activity unique to life at home. The social worker helps the caregiver and family through individual and family counseling. The social worker also provides the new resident with opportunity for counseling and is available for intervention if staff determines there is a need. Similar to the hospital setting, the social worker works with an interdisciplinary care team as the case manager coordinating the care plan, and orchestrates meetings and referrals to various professionals in order to provide consistency and quality in care. The social worker keeps the caregiver and family informed of the progress and communicates recommendations made by care team members to enhance treatment.

Finally, the social worker may also work with the caregiver and family to identify financial resources to help with the expenses involved in nursing home placement and care of the dementia-afflicted family member. The social worker provides assistance and support at each step of the preadmission, admission, and placement process by providing education, resources, and counseling. If the resident requires acute care during the placement at the nursing facility, the social worker takes the lead and assists the caregiver in arranging for the transfer to and from acute or rehabilitation care as treatment requires for the afflicted family member.

To provide continued emphasis on the importance of culturally competent social work, the National Association of Social Workers (2000) developed 10 standards for cultural competence in social work practice. The following standards are quoted from the National Association of Social Work (2007) Cultural Standards and Indicators for Cultural Competence in Social Work Practice.

Standard 1. Ethics and Values

Social workers shall function in accordance with the values, ethics, and standards of the profession, recognizing how personal and professional values may conflict with or accommodate the needs of diverse clients.

Standard 2. Self-Awareness

Social workers shall seek to develop an understanding of their own personal, cultural values and beliefs as one way of appreciating the importance of multicultural identities in the lives of people.

Standard 3. Cross-Cultural Knowledge

Social workers shall have and continue to develop specialized knowledge and understanding about the history, traditions, values, family systems, and artistic expressions of major client groups that they serve.

Standard 4. Cross-Cultural Skills

Social workers shall use appropriate methodological approaches, skills, and techniques that reflect the workers' understanding of the role of culture in the helping process.

Standard 5. Service Delivery

Social workers shall be knowledgeable about and be skillful in the use of services available in the community and broader society and be able to make appropriate referrals for their diverse clients.

Standard 6. Empowerment and Advocacy

Social workers shall be aware of the effect of social policies and programs on diverse client populations, advocating for and with clients wherever appropriate.

Standard 7. Diverse Workforce

Social workers shall support and advocate for recruitment, admissions and hiring, and retention efforts in social work programs and agencies that ensure diversity within the profession.

Standard 8. Professional Education

Social workers shall advocate for and participate in education and training programs that help advance cultural competence within the profession.

Standard 9. Language Diversity

Social workers shall seek to provide or advocate for the provision of information, referrals, and services in the language appropriate to the client, which may include use of interpreters.

Standard 10. Cross-Cultural Leadership

Social workers shall be able to communicate information about diverse client groups to other professionals.

Source: National Association of Social Workers (2007), pp. 4–5. Retrieved January 7, 2011, from www.socialworkers.org

The brochure containing the definitions of the concepts used, the interpretations, and the complete standards and indicators of cultural competence are available on the National Association of Social Workers website located at www.socialworkers.org

REFERENCES

Balloch, S., Pahl, J., & McLean, J. (1998). Working in the social services: Job satisfaction, stress and violence. *British Journal of Social Work, 28,* 329–350.

Barker, R. G. (1968). *Ecological psychology: Concepts and methods for studying the environment of human behavior.* Stanford, CA: Stanford University Press.

Berman-Rossi, T. (2001). Older persons in need of long-term care. In A. Gitterman (ed.), *Handbook of social work practice with vulnerable and resilient populations* (2nd ed.). New York: Columbia University Press.

Bibb, A., & Casimir, G. J. (1996). Haitian families. In M. McGoldrick, J. Giordano, & J. K. Pearce (Eds.), *Ethnicity family therapy* (pp. 97–105). New York: The Guilford Press.

Birkel, R. C., & Reppucci, N. D. (1983). Social networks, information-seeking, and utilization of services. *American Journal of Community Psychology, 11,* 185–205.

Bossè, R. (2000). Elderly Puerto Ricans. In S. Alemán, T. Fitzpatrick, V. T. Thanh, & E. W. González (Eds.), *Therapeutic interventions with ethnic elders: Health and social issues* (pp. 91–118). New York: Haworth Press, Inc.

Brice-Baker, J. (1996). Jamaican families. In M. McGoldrick, J. Giordano, & J. K. Pearce (Eds.), *Ethnicity family therapy* (pp. 85–96). New York: The Guilford Press.

Bronfenbrenner, U. (1977). Toward an experimental ecology of human development. *American Psychologist, 32,* 513–531.

Buffum, M., & Madrid, E. (1995). In D. Antai-Otong (Ed.), *Psychiatric nursing: Biological and behavioral concepts* (pp. 487–506). Philadelphia, PA: W. B. Saunders Company.

Compton, B. R., & Galaway, B. (1989). *Social work processes* (4th ed.). Belmont, CA: Wadsworth Publishing.

Cuéllar, J. (1990). *Aging and health: Hispanic American elders.* Stanford, CA: Stanford Geriatric Education Center.

Devore, W., & Schlesinger, E. G. (1991). *Ethnic-sensitive social work practice.* New York: Macmillan Publishing.

Dilworth-Anderson, P. (1992). Extended kin networks in black families. *Generations, 17,* 29–32.

Dilworth-Anderson, P., & Marshall, S. (1996). Social support in its cultural context. In G. R. Pierce, B. R. Sarason, & I. G. Sarason (Eds.). *Handbook of social support and the family* (pp. 67–79). New York: Plenum Press.

Dilworth-Anderson, P., Williams, I. C., & Williams, S. W. (2001). Elderly of African Descent. In L. K. Olson (Ed.), *Age through ethnic lenses: Caring for the elderly in a multicultural society* (pp. 95–102). New York: Rowman & Littlefield.

Doka, K. J. (2000). Mourning psychosocial loss: Anticipatory mourning in Alzheimer's, ALS, and irreversible coma. In T. A. Rando (Ed.), *Clinical dimensions of anticipatory mourning: Theory, and practice in working with the dying, their loved ones, and their caregivers* (pp. 477–492). Champaign, IL: Research Press.

Doka, K. J. (2004). *Living with grief Alzheimer's disease.* Washington, DC: Hospice Foundation of America.

Du Bois, B. C., Yavno, C. H., & Stanford, E. P. (2001). Care options for older Mexican Americans: Issues affecting health and long-term care services needed. In L. K. Olson (Ed.), *Age through ethnic lenses: Caring for the elderly in a multicultural society* (pp. 71–85). New York: Rowman & Littlefield.

Gallagher-Thompson, D., Talamantes, M., Ramirez, R., & Velarde, I. (1996). Service delivery issues and recommendations for working with Mexican American family caregivers. In G. Yeo & D. Gallagher-Thompson (Eds.), *Ethnicity and the dementias* (pp. 137–152). Washington, DC: Taylor & Francis.

Gallegos, J. S. (1991). Culturally relevant services for Hispanic elderly. In M. Sotomayer (Ed.), *Empowering Hispanic families: A critical issue for the 90s* (pp. 173–190). Milwaukee, WI: Family Service America.

González Sanders, D. J. (2006). *Familismo and resilience in Latino family caregivers of dementia afflicted relatives: An ethno-cultural cross-sectional study.* Unpublished doctoral dissertation, Smith College, Northampton, MA.

Henderson, J. N., & Gutierrez-Mayka, M. (1992). Ethnocultural themes in caregiving to Alzheimer's disease patients in Hispanic families. *Clinical Gerontologist, 11*(3/4), 59–74.

Henderson, J. N., Gutierrez-Mayka, M. K., Garcia, J., & Boyd, S. (1993). A model for Alzheimer's disease support group development in African American and Hispanic populations. *The Gerontologist, 23*, 409–414.

Jackson, J. (1971). Negro aged: Toward research in social gerontology. *The Gerontologist, 11*, 52–57.

Laguerre, M. S. (2001). Diasporic aging: Haitian Americans in New York City. In L. K. Olson (Ed.), *Age through ethnic lenses: Caring for the elderly in a multicultural society* (pp. 103–112). New York: Rowman & Littlefield.

LaSalle, P., & LaSalle, A. (1991). Small groups and their therapeutic force. In G. Stuart & S. Sundeen (Eds.), *Principles and practice of psychiatric nursing* (4th ed., pp. 809–826). St. Louis, MO: C. V. Mosby.

Lewis, I., & Chavis-Ausberry, J. (1996). African-American families: Management of demented elders. In G. Yeo & D. Gallagher-Thompson (Eds.), *Ethnicity and the dementias.* Washington, DC: Francis & Taylor.

Lincoln, C. E., & Mamiya, L. G. (1991). *The black church in the African American experience.* Durham, NC: Duke University Press.

Lloyd, L., King, R., & Chenoweth, L. (2002). Social work, stress and burnout: A review. *Journal of Mental Health, 11*(3) 255–265.

McInnis-Dittrich, K. (2002). *Social work with elders: A biopsychosocial approach to assessment and intervention.* Boston, MA: Allyn and Bacon.

Mittelman, M. S., Epstein, C., & Pierzchala, A. (2003). *Counseling the Alzheimer's caregiver: A resource for health care professionals.* Chicago, IL: American Medical Association.

National Adult Day Services Association. (2011). *National Adult Day Services Association Site Visit Checklist.* Retrieved from www.nadsa.org

National Association of Social Workers. (1994). *Social work with older people: Understanding diversity* (pp. 17–18). Washington, DC: National Association of Social Workers.

National Association of Social Workers. (2007). *Indicators for the achievement of the NASW standards for cultural competence in social work practice.* Washington, DC: National Association of Social Workers

National Association of Social Workers. (2011). *Social work in gerontology (SW-G) (BSW Level).* Washington, DC: National Association of Social Workers.

Nichols, Q. (2011) *Connecting core competencies: A workbook for social work students.* Upper Saddle River, NJ: Pearson Prentice Hall.

Olson, L. K. (Ed.). (2001). *Age through ethnic lenses: Caring for the elderly in a multicultural society.* New York: Rowman & Littlefield.

Rando, T. A. (1986). *Loss and anticipatory grief.* Lexington, MA: Lexington Books.

Rando, T. A. (2000). *Clinical dimensions of anticipatory mourning: Theory and practice in working with the dying, their loved ones and their caregivers.* Champaign, IL: Research Press.

Reid, K. E. (2002). Clinical social work with groups. In A. R. Roberts & G. J. Greene (Eds.), *Social workers' desk reference.* New York: Oxford University Press.

Rubin, A. (1986). Case management. In A. Minahan (Ed.), *Encyclopedia of social work* (18th ed., pp. 212–222). Silver Spring, MD: National Association of Social Workers.

Stassen Berger, K. (1983). *The developing person through the life span.* New York: Worth Publishers.

Stevenson, H. C., Winn, D. M., Walker-Barnes, C., & Coard, S. I. (2005). Style matters: Toward a culturally relevant framework for interventions with African American families. In V. C. McLoyd, N. E. Hill, & K. A. Dodge (Eds.), *African American family life: Ecological and cultural diversity* (pp. 311–334). New York: The Guilford Press.

Suppes, M. A., & Cressy Wells, C. (2003). *The social work experience: An introduction to social work and social welfare.* New York: McGraw-Hill Education.

Sutherland, V., & Cooper, C. (1990). *Understanding stress.* London: Chapman and Hall.

Taylor, R. J. (1986). Receipt of support from family among black Americans: Demographic and familial differences. *Journal of Marriage and the Family, 48,* 67–77.

Taylor, R. J., & Chatters, L. M. (1991). Extended family networks of older black adults. *Journal of Gerontology, 46,* S210–S217.

The Public and Government Relations Office. (2006). Connecticut Department of Social Services, Publication No. 95–8, p. 2.

The South Dakota Department of Social Services. (2010). *Adult services and aging adult foster care.* Retrieved from http://dss.sd.gov/elderlyservices/services/fostercare.asp

Tran, T. V., & Dhooper, S. S. (1996). Ethnic and gender differences in perceived needs for social services among three elder Hispanic groups. *Journal of Gerontological Social Work, 25*(3/4), 121–147.

Tran, T. V., & Melcer, J. (2000). Cuban-American elders. In S. Alemán, T. Fitzpatrick, V. T. Thanh, & E. W. González (Eds.), *Therapeutic interventions with ethnic elders: Health and social issues* (pp. 119–138). New York: Haworth Press, Inc.

Valle, R. (1998). *Caregiving across cultures: Working with dementing illness and ethnically diverse populations.* Washington, DC: Taylor & Francis.

Valle, R. (1981). Natural support systems minority groups and the late life dementias: Implications for service delivery, research and policy. In N. E. Miller & G. D. Cohen (Eds.), *Clinical aspects of Alzheimer's disease and senile dementia* (vol. 15, pp. 277–299). New York: Raven Press.

Valle, R., & Bensussen, G. (1986). Hispanic social networks, social support, and mental health. In W. M. Vega & M. R. Mirands (Eds.), *Stress and Hispanic mental health. Relating research to service delivery* (pp. 147–173). Washington, DC: U.S. Government Printing Office. DHHS Publication No. ADM 85–1410.

Vega, W. A., & Murphy, J. W. (1990). *Culture and the restructuring of community mental health.* New York: Greenwood Press.

Wallace, S. P., & Lew-Ting, C. W. (1992). Getting by at home: Community-based long-term care of Latinos. *Western Journal of Medicine, 157*(3) 337–344.

Williams, S. W., & Dilworth-Anderson, P. (2002). Systems of social support in families who care for dependent African American elders. *The Gerontologist, 42,* 224–236.

Yalom, I. (1985). *The theory and practice of group psychotherapy* (3rd ed.). New York: Basic Books.

Yeatts, D. E., Crow, T., & Folts, E. (1992). Service use among low-income elderly: Strategies for overcoming barriers. *The Gerontologist, 32*(1), 24–32.

Yeo, G. (1993). Ethnicity and nursing homes: Factors affecting use and successful components for culturally sensitive care. In C. Barresi & D. Stull (Eds.), *Ethnic elderly and long-term care.* New York: Springer Publishing.

Yeo, G., & Gallagher-Thompson, D. (Eds.). (1996). *Ethnicity and the dementias.* Washington, DC: Taylor & Francis.

6

Social Work Assessment Tools for Use With Ethnic Caregivers

*D*esde la familia se transmite un modo de ser y estar en el mundo, por las familias pasan los intercambios generacionales y los contenidos de la memoria. La familia es el espacio particular para resolver los más graves problemas de los adultos mayores, es el gran capital con el que cuenta la sociedad, pero también con el que cuenta cada uno de los miembros que pertenece a una familia. (Fajardo Ortíz, 2002, p. 27)

The family transmits a way of becoming and being in the world. Through the family pass the exchanges of generations and the contents of memory. The family is the particular space to resolve the most serious problems of the elderly. It is the highest authority that the society relies on, but it is also where each member relies on the family, and each is valued for belonging to the family. (Translation of quote from Fajardo Ortíz, 2002, p. 27)

The purpose of this chapter is to provide a framework to assess Black and Latino Alzheimer's disease caregivers in concert with the needs of the afflicted family member. Often caregivers and the afflicted family member function as a dyad with problems intertwined. In order to clarify the problems of each member of the dyad and appropriately separate problems for work, the social worker needs to complete an assessment using a series of essential tools. Once this is done, the caregiver and the social worker are better able to understand the presenting issue and jointly identify the target problem(s) for work to facilitate the establishment of an appropriate intervention plan.

As mentioned previously, building trust in the relationship is at the heart of social work care. Without trust, the working relationship will face many challenges moving forward. When done correctly, the assessment process can help begin to build a strong trust foundation in the relationship. By engaging in the process of defining the caregiving situation and clarifying the role(s) in the process, the social worker and the caregiver use a combination of coherent assessment tools and illustrations to define and understand their roles and how they function within the care situation with the afflicted family member. The full assessment also illustrates the functioning of the afflicted family member, the family, and culture in the care process and identifies problems for work. This chapter discusses the ethnic family caregiver assessment sheet, the ethnocultural genogram, and the ethnocultural ecomap.

CASE EXAMPLE

Juan, a monolingual Spanish-speaking adult son from El Salvador in Central America, was caring for his mother recently diagnosed with Alzheimer's disease. He and his mother were in the United States illegally and living "in hiding" with his Dominican girlfriend. His girlfriend, concerned about his mother's memory problems, took her to the neighborhood clinic for an assessment. Worried about the immigration status, he travelled to Rhode Island to visit a cousin to see if he could help Juan provide care for his mother or help him and his mother obtain naturalization or find a job close by in order to care for his mother. While visiting his cousin's friend's house he was arrested during a drug raid. After posting bail he returned to his home to await trial.

Worried that he could be rearrested and deported at anytime and concerned about his mother's increasing confusion and memory loss, he decided to take his mother to Florida and arrange for his mother to live with his older brother. Borrowing money from his girlfriend and other friends, he and his mother made the trip to Florida. A couple of days later he returned to his home state to await his court appearance and to contact the immigration office to see whether he could obtain help for his mother to remain in the United States in order to receive treatment and care for Alzheimer's disease.

Meanwhile his brother, who lived alone and worked long hours and weekends, soon found his mother needed more supervision than he could provide. Memory loss, increased confusion, and behavior disregulation forced Juan's brother to miss work in order to ensure her safety at home. His brother had no choice but to send his mother back to Juan. Juan and his girlfriend resumed caregiving responsibilities and explored ways to arrange for legal immigration status and to care for his mother. Before he could succeed at this, Juan was adjudicated in a federal court and was sentenced to 5 years in prison then deportation to the El Salvador after his release.

Juan's mother remained with the girlfriend who became the new caregiver. This was challenging for her because the girlfriend worked as a domestic and had to rely on friends and neighbors to help with care while she worked. Desperate to find a safe place for Juan's mother, she worked through her own family in the Dominican Republic to locate relatives for Juan's mother in El Salvador. It took time, money, and effort from many Latinos, but she eventually located extended family members who agreed to take care of her. She notified both brothers, and both agreed it was best to send her to the home country and place her in the care of family. Juan said he planned to resume care for his mother after he was deported and returned home. Juan's mother was sent to the Dominican Republic to be met by extended family members who would care for her and travel with her to El Salvador.

THE PURPOSEFUL USE OF TOOLS TO GRAPHICALLY ILLUSTRATE THE FUNCTIONING AND INTERACTION OF ETHNIC CAREGIVER, CARE RECIPIENT, AND THE FAMILY WITHIN THE SOCIAL ENVIRONMENT

The collaborative assessment process itself involves a relationship inter-action in which the social worker engages the caregiver in a journey to describe their self-constructed reality in the caregivng situation employing tangible and graphic representations. When done correctly the assessment helps the social worker to assist the caregiver in identify-ing essential information about the caregiver self, the care recipient, the caregiving situation, and the caregiver environment. The purpose of the assessment is to develop a coherent case formulation. During the assess-ment meeting, the caregiver's information, situation perspective, the meaning the caregiver ascribes to the situation, and the caregiver's feel-ings, thoughts, and emotions are the central focus. The caregiver's real-ity serves to generate significant pieces of information, some of which the caregiver may not have conceptualized before with a professional who can help. In combination, these factors enable the social worker to critically analyze the content, synthesize the factors, and apply elements of learned theory(s) in order to establish a hypothesis for the plan for care (Cournoyer, 2008).

The ethnic family caregiver assessment presented next was cre-ated and used successfully with African American, Black, and Latino caregivers by this author. Even though the assessment sheet seems to require a substantial amount of content, I can testify to its value and success in the treatment process. Often, ethnic caregivers seek help for the afflicted family member and overlook their own symptoms also in need of care. This is especially true of populations such as Blacks and Latinos who have been socialized to provide care for afflicted fam-ily members and older adults in need of care and to put aside their own needs. Using the following assessment, which includes both the needs of the caregiver and the care recipient, ensures that the needs of both members of the dyad will be assessed and targeted for care by the social worker. The role of race plays a significant role in the caregiving process and how the process unfolds in the family (Roff et al., 2004). Race also has identified explanations indicating that caregiving is seen more as a "normative experience" with caregiving satisfaction and mastery especially among African Americans (Dilworth-Anderson & Anderson, 1994). The assumption is, therefore, made that if the caregiving experience is seen as normative, then it is possible that the stress, depression, and anxiety experienced by ethnic caregivers can also been seen as normative. If that is true, the normative care experience, however difficult, may make it more challenging for ethnic caregivers to identify their own need for help and may instead seek help for family members in hope that by helping the family member (culturally acceptable) the caregiver too may receive help.

THE ETHNIC FAMILY CAREGIVER ASSESSMENT: CONFIDENTIAL ETHNIC FAMILY CAREGIVER ASSESSMENT

Evaluation Date _____Time:_____Referral Source

Name _____D.O.B. _____Age ____Gender_____

Address _____

_____

Telephone Number(s) _____

_____

Current living situation: Where_____ Type_____ How long _____

With whom _____

Status (M)___(P)___(S)___(D)___(W)___ Ethnicity/Racial Group _____

Religion _____Primary Language _____ Education _____

Folk healers botanicals shop used: No ____Yes ____ If Yes, Date: _____

Reason: _____

Folk remedies used: _____

_____

_____

Spiritual/cultural issues influencing treatment: _____

Activities/hobbies: _____

Caregiver strengths: _____

Employment _____Retired _____ SES _____

In case of emergency, contact: _____ Telephone _____

Presenting Problem Described by Caregiver:

_____

_____

_____

_____

_____

Protective services: Yes _____ No _____

History of Presenting Symptoms (include psychosocial stressors, past treatment):

_____

_____

_____

_____

_____

_____

_____

Physician/Family Service Providers/Agencies Currently Involved With Caregiver

Provider/Agency Name   Contact Person   Telephone No. (1)   Telephone No. (2)

Current Medication   Dosage   Start Date

Special needs or physical challenges:

_____

Date and reason for most recent medical exam:

_____

_____

Next scheduled medical exam: _____

Has the caregiver experienced the following symptoms?
(Social worker reads symptoms and caregiver rates the symptoms experienced on a scale from 1 to 10.)

<u>Most Severe</u>   <u>Moderate</u>   <u>Mild</u>   <u>Least Severe</u>

1	2	3	4	5	6	7	8	9	10

_____Anxiety

_____Panic attacks

_____Fear

_____Sadness

_____Crying episodes

_____Anger

_____Frustration

_____Suicidal thoughts

_____Worry

_____Feelings of desperation

_____Confusion

_____Memory lapses/changes

_____Unwanted, repeated or negative thoughts

_____Dizziness

_____Shortness of breath

_____Blurred vision

_____Stomach pains

_____Backaches

_____Headaches

_____Chest pains

_____Learning difficulty

_____Difficulty making decisions

_____Difficulty problem solving

What is the caregiver's perception of their quality of life?
(Social worker reads scale options and caregiver rates their current overall Quality of Life on a scale from 1 to 10.) (Circles one)

1	2	3	4	5	6	7	8	9	10
Terrible		Unbearable		Bearable		Fair			Wonderful

Other Current Symptoms

Disturbance of Sleep	Absent_____	Present_____
Falling asleep_____	Staying awake _____	Waking early_____
Nightmares _____	Night tremors _____	Sleep walking _____

Explain _____

Eating Disturbance	Absent_____	Present _____

Explain _____

Sexual Disturbance	Absent_____	Present_____

Explain_____

Current Suicidal Ideation   Absent_____ Present_____

Explain_____

History of Suicidal Ideation   Absent_____ Present_____

Explain_____

History of Suicidal Attempts_____

Substance Abuse   Absent_____ Present_____

Explain_____

History of substance abuse_____

Explain_____

Has the caregiver or family member with dementia (FMWD) experienced the following?

Caregiver_____ FMWD _____heart attack

Caregiver_____ FMWD _____stroke

Caregiver_____ FMWD _____high blood pressure

Caregiver_____ FMWD _____diabetes

Caregiver_____ FMWD _____cancer

Caregiver_____ FMWD _____epilepsy

Caregiver_____ FMWD _____hyperthyroid/hypothyroid

Caregiver_____ FMWD _____hypoglycemia

Caregiver_____ FMWD _____alcoholism/drug abuse/addiction

Caregiver_____ FMWD _____mental health issues

Caregiver_____ FMWD _____sexual abuse

Caregiver_____ FMWD _____emotional/physical/verbal abuse

Caregiver_____ FMWD _____family violence

Caregiver_____ FMWD _____death/loss

Caregiver_____ FMWD _____allergies/asthma

Caregiver_____ FMWD _____enuresis or encopresis

Social Work Clinical Observations and Impressions

Dress/Appearance   Appropriate_____ Meticulous _____Disheveled

Speech Rate   Unremarkable_____ Other_____

               Tone   Unremarkable_____ Other_____

               Spontaneous? _____ Amount? (%)_____

Behavior   General Activity Unremarkable _____Other

               Motor Activity   Unremarkable _____Other_____

               Compulsions   Unremarkable _____Other_____

Tics/Repetitive Behaviors   Unremarkable _____Other_____

Observed Affect Full__ Labile__ Constricted___ Flat____ Appropriate Y__N___

Explain_____

Thought Form   Goal-directed   Y_____ N_____ Explain_____

                      Relevant   Y_____ N_____ Explain _____

Thought Perception	Auditory hallucinations Y____N ____
	Visual hallucinations Y____N ____
Thought Content	Suicidal ideations Y____N ____
	Homicidal ideations Y____N ____
	Paranoid ideations Y____N____
	Preoccupations/obsessions Y____N____
Cognitive Function	

Orientation X3 (person, place, and time) Y____N____
Attention impairment   Y____N____
Concentration impairment Y____N____
Immediate recall/retention impairment
Y____N____
Recent memory impairment Y__N__ Method____
Remote memory Y____N___ Method____

Judgment	Good ____ Fair ____ Poor ____
Impulse Control	Good ____ Fair ____ Poor ____
Insight	Good ____ Fair ____ Poor ____

DSM-IV-TR **Diagnosis**

Axis I   _____*DSM-IV* Code_____
            _____*DSM-IV* Code_____
            _____*DSM-IV* Code_____
Axis II   _____*DSM-IV* Code_____
            _____*DSM-IV* Code_____
            _____*DSM-IV* Code_____
Axis III   _____*DSM-IV* Code_____
            _____*DSM-IV* Code_____
            _____*DSM-IV* Code_____
Axis IV   Psychosocial and Environmental Problems (check and describe)
Axis V   Global Assessment of Functioning Scale
          Estimated Score ____   Current _____   Previous year _____

Does caregiver need assistance/referral to following services?
Case management _____Care team for FMWD _____
Individual counseling _____ Family counseling _____
Grief counseling_____Group or support counseling_____
Housing _____Home care support _____
Hospice _____Language or interpreter _____
Educational information _____Employment assistance _____
Financial assistance _____Insurance _____
Immigration and naturalization _____ Legal services _____
Medical treatment _____Protective services _____
Transportation services _____

Other psychosocial and environmental services needed _____
Resources to care for FMWD: Yes_____ No_____
Is care team currently working with FMWD Yes_____ No_____
Other services needed to care for FMWD_____
Other social work recommendations for caregiver _____
Is caregiver referral to primary care physician required? Yes_____ No_____
If yes, explain _____
_____
_____
_____

Is FMWD referral to primary care physician required? Yes_____No_____
If yes, explain _____
_____
_____
_____

Social worker and caregiver jointly draw ethnocultural genogram.
Ethnocultural Genogram _____Family

Social worker and caregiver jointly draw ethnocultural ecomap.

Ethnocultural Ecomap _____ Family

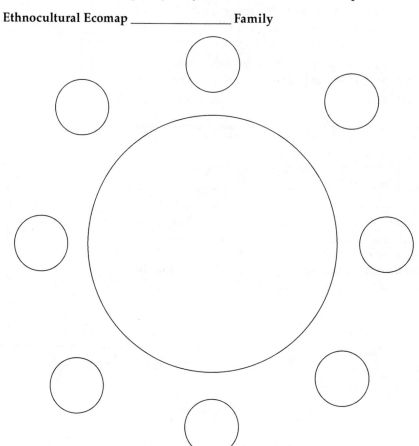

Caregiver's Roles & Relationships

With FMWD	Unremarkable _____	Other _____
Nuclear family	Unremarkable _____	Other _____
Step family	Unremarkable _____	Other _____
Parents	Unremarkable _____	Other _____
Siblings	Unremarkable _____	Other _____
Extended family	Unremarkable _____	Other _____
Friends	Unremarkable _____	Other _____
Other adults	Unremarkable _____	Other _____
Spiritual supports	Unremarkable _____	Other _____
Social clubs	Unremarkable _____	Other _____
Folk healers	Unremarkable _____	Other _____
Merchants	Unremarkable _____	Other _____
Botanicals	Unremarkable _____	Other _____

Barriers to Treatment

Language ___Vision ___Hearing ___Literacy ___ Other _____ None____

Other developmental history or trauma including racism or discrimination:

_____

_____

_____

_____

_____

_____

_____

_____

Social worker and caregiver discussed:

_____Evaluation summary

_____Caregiver desired treatment outcomes

_____How critical psychiatric issues are to be addressed

_____How medical issues are to be addressed

_____Problem-solving intervention process

_____How problem-solving plan will be established

_____How problem-solving plan will help in the care of family member

_____The domains of the problem-solving plan

_____The goals of problem-solving

_____The date and times of social worker and caregiver meetings

_____ Length of problem-solving intervention with social worker

_____Discharge plan after problem-solving process is learned

_____Termination and follow-up plan

Other caregiver or family member with dementia factors not discussed previously:

_____

_____

_____

_____

_____

Social Worker: _____Date _____

Signature of Assessing Social Worker and Professional Designation

© 2003, 2011djs

The Rationale, Purpose, and Description

Social workers are ethically required to use the appropriate assessment tools in order to effectively evaluate the needs of their clients. When working with diverse populations, the NASW Standards for Cultural Competence in Social Work Practice (2007), Standard 4. Cross-Cultural Skills states the following (p. 4): "Social workers shall use appropriate methodological approaches, skills, and techniques that reflect the workers' understanding of the role of culture in the helping process."

The Confidential Ethnic Family Caregiver Assessment (González Sanders, 2003) is divided into several sections to help capture the necessary pieces of information to critically analyze the needs of the ethnic caregiver, the family member with dementia, and the caregiving situation. Pages 1 and 2 collect demographic information, initial and historical problem information, and current service and medical providers, special needs, and medical and medication information.

It is essential to note that a section on folk beliefs and folk healing and botanicas has been included in the assessment. Folk beliefs and folk healing and "espiritismo" or use of "spiritualists" is an important source of cultural healing support for some families seeking help for chronic health and mental health problems (Schensul, Wetle, & Torres, 1993). The use of community "spiritual centers" or indigenous botanical (botanicas) stores selling herbal and other cultural remedies are not unique to either the Black or Latino culture and are highly valued in some of the cultures (Kilgannon, 2005; Schensul et al., 1993). While there are many definitions of folk medicine, Becerra and Iglehart (1995; cited in Delgado, 2007) define folk medicine as follows.

> The term "folk medicine" has a variety of definitions in its modern context. It can refer to: (1) specific practices of ethnic group members...(2) the use of medical practitioners outside the Western medical establishment; (3) "good" remedies—those drawn from earlier, superior traditions; or (4) "bad" remedies—those with which primitive societies treat themselves in lieu of trained medical care. (p. 152)

While some controversy exists on the part of some of the medical establishment, about folk beliefs, folk healings, espiritismo, and use of botanical stores by various cultures, it is essential for social workers to recognize that folk healing methods may be useful and add value for the individual being assessed (Delgado, 2007). Some Latinos do not hesitate to seek medical care from the formal health care system for physical symptoms and may also use folk healing methods informally and not disclose the use. For behavioral or mental health issues, some Latinos may delay seeking help from formal health care service providers, preferring to use information from informal networks consisting of family, local community merchants such as botanicas, the community-oriented Catholic churches, and spiritualists and folk healers (Schensul et al., 1993). These informal networks are perceived as culturally more feasible and accessible because they often include "24-hour service, material and psychological support, bilingual and bicultural communication, involvement of the family in resolution of the problem, and personal connections to other systems of service" (Schensul et al., 1993, p. 66).

A social worker seeking to be culturally competent needs to actively seek, listen to, and obtain information regarding any folk healing practices the caregiver carried out in the past or currently and the reasons folk healing was sought to understand the symptom that was the focus of care for either the caregiver or the family member with dementia. According to Schensul et al. (1993), "the approach to healing offered by spiritualists is holistic, is culturally appropriate for those who accept its premises, draws upon cultural symbols with deep personal and cultural meaning for therapeutic measures, and offers continuous and comprehensive emotional and social support" (p. 67). Therefore, if the ethnic caregiver senses negative judgment, avoidance, conflict, or rejection of folk healing practices on the part of the social worker, the caregiver may not engage with the social worker fully. Worse, the caregiver may withhold essential symptom information from the social worker necessary to complete an accurate assessment. Even worse still, the caregiver may completely disengage from the helping process in an effort to protect him- or herself from what might be considered inappropriate counter-cultural judgmental attitudes or to protect his or her valued relationship with the folk healer. In some cities some cultural folk healers and spiritualists have experienced resistance from some of the formal institutions. For self-protection, spiritualists have moved folk healing practices into their homes (Schensul et al., 1993).

However, it is equally important for the social worker to be careful not to overly validate folk practices either. If the practices seem benign the practices should just be acknowledged, noted, and respected as part of the culture. What is important to note is the symptom(s) for which the caregiver was seeking a remedy, either for self or for the afflicted family member. In some studies, the use of folk healing has been found to coincide with mainstream health care practices (Zapata & Shippee-Rice, 1999). However, if the remedies are causing, or could cause, harm, it is the responsibility of the social worker to provide professional guidance to stop the risk of harm to either the caregiver or the care recipient. When done in a culturally sensitive manner, the caregiver will be receptive to the social worker's request because, above all, the caregiver desires to do what is in his or her best interest, and the safety of his or her family member is a top priority. Otherwise, the social worker should consider the use of folk healing as a cultural strength and move forward in the assessment while remembering that the goal is to not only formulate a complete assessment, but also build a working relationship with the caregiver.

The assessment form collects information on the caregiver's physical and mental health needs, current symptoms, and the perception of quality of life. The form inquires about the caregiver and family member's historical and/or current physical, emotional, and medical issues and provides the social worker with a template to note first impressions and clinical observations of the caregiver. While some would argue that the diagnosis is incongruent with the strengths perspective, diagnosis here is used as an added perspective to help the social worker understand the context of reality experienced by the client in the past, prior to arriving for this meeting and assessment. In order to define the problem(s) situations, it is necessary to include the historical steps that have been taken in the past by the caregiver and to include the steps of diagnosis or judgments or assumptions made by other professionals. The goal is indeed to focus on the client strengths; however, identifying all aspects of the assessment and care journey, no matter the perspective, is equally important. For ethnic caregivers the assessment goal is to be inclusive of information, not exclusive. The social worker's clinical diagnosis of the caregiver and needed resources for the family member are recorded on the assessment form. The ethnocultural genogram and the ethnocultural ecomap are included in the assessment. Ideally these should be on separate pages to allow the social worker and caregiver to separate these pages from the preceding pages in order to collaborate in filling out the two documents. More information on these two assessment tools is provided in the Sections B and C.

The later portions of the assessment form allow the social worker to reframe the relationship information collected in the earlier portion regarding basic information about the caregiver's roles and relationships by reviewing various groups using generic information. This section helps to clarify roles identified in the ethnocultural genogram and systems identified in the ethnocultural ecomap. Often, when discussing this section with the social worker, caregivers identify patterns or are reminded of situations that they did not think about or recall during the preparation of the ethnocultural genogram and ecomap. This page also solicits information about past racism or discrimination to help the caregiver recognize that the social worker understands that in the caregiver's historic, socially constructed reality, he or she may have experienced trauma, racism, or discrimination. Basically this section gives the caregiver permission to discuss past hurts and experiences leading to barriers to care and that may influence future help-seeking or help-receiving behaviors. It also serves to validate the caregiver's experiences and empower the caregiver to verbalize any concerns regarding past or future care. It also communicates the fact that the social worker is willing and able to meet the caregiver, during which time the caregiver has the opportunity to discuss historical or unresolved issues experienced in the person-and-situation perspective of social environment.

A check-off list is included at the end of the form to prompt the social worker to review and summarize items discussed during the initial assessment. It also provides the caregiver with an overview of the process the social worker and caregiver will follow in the actual intervention and problem-solving plan, including future meeting dates and times. The ethnocultural genogram and the ethnocultural ecomap illustrations will be discussed in further detail later in this section.

Completing the Ethnic Family Caregiver Assessment Sheet

At first glance, the assessment sheet might seem daunting in terms of its length, content, and complexity. However, this document is to be used as an engagement tool and completed over the course of several meetings if necessary. The Eurocentric perspective might view this assessment as a document similar to a survey requiring immediate completion of each section with a question-and-answer back and forth interaction, similar to a tennis volley interaction. That is not the case here. When seeking to interact with Black or Latino caregivers, a culturally sensitive approach lends itself better to the process. Rather than viewing the completion of this document as a survey, the social worker should view the data-gathering process as an engagement process that both the social worker and the caregiver are learning to use. While it will be guided by the professional social worker, the process requires the expertise of the caregiver who is the expert reporter of the information. Hence, the social worker needs to perceive him- or herself in the role of joint learner with the caregiver, taking a journey into the culture and experience of the caregiver. The caregiver serves as the expert, leading the social worker into the journey of the story, which will include concerns, symptoms, care responsibilities, and historical and current experiences. By allowing the caregiver to set the pace in the assessment process, the social worker is empowering the caregiver and fostering a balanced power distribution in the interaction. This foundation will help create and sustain trust in the relationship.

However, it is important for the social worker to be very familiar with the sections and content of the assessment in order to guide the process. Prior to beginning the interaction, the social worker should advise the caregiver that the goal of the meeting is to complete the assessment and that, as they discuss the caregiver's concerns, the social worker will be taking notes that will help in the plan of care. In that way the caregiver will be aware that writing and note taking will occur and not distrust the social worker in the process. This frees the social worker to fill in the necessary information as the caregiver conveys his or her story.

The tone of the meeting should be relaxed yet professional. Too much familiarity communicated by the social worker during the first meeting may cause discomfort to the Black or Latino caregiver, who tends to view professionals as requiring respect. The plan of the social worker should be to meet in a private location and to engage the caregiver in a conversation to learn about his or her unique care story and to problem solve. In the African American or Black culture, this method of communication can be viewed as a way to build rapport and closeness. Dixon (2007) provides communication style information that social workers should keep in mind when working with Black and Latino caregivers, especially when working with female caregivers. According to Dixon (2007), privacy is valued by most African American and Black females. "Also, women generally do not like to engage in public conversation where they can be judged by others . . . communication styles stem from early socialization" (p. 200). According to Dixon (2007), in general Black women culturally use communication to build interdependence and to talk about their stories and problems and to problem solve. Black men, on the other hand, may use communication styles for other reasons, including "to hold center stage, which is achieved by exhibiting knowledge and skills, or verbally performing through storytelling, joking, imparting information, or lifting and transforming (as ministers and motivational speakers)" (p. 200). In addition, Black women and men differ in terms of how they process information under stress. John Gray (1992; cited in Dixon, 2007) "asserts that women generally cope with stress by talking about problems, while men cope with stress by going inward. A major reason men cope with stress inwardly is because of the importance of being competent. Because masculinity includes being competent, men feel compelled to be problem solvers" (p. 200).

Culturally competent social workers need to focus on what Dixon and Osiris (2002) consider to be the three essential qualities in communication in Black and African American cultures, to be "talking and listening with care (TLC)" (p. 203). They note that talking and listening with care consists of merging three components: (1) talking, (2) listening, and (3) caring, which builds "effective talking and listening with a caring attitude" (p. 203). Latinos also use "platica" (chat) as a means of building interdependence and closeness as well.

Like African Americans, Latinos and Latinas are also used to minimum public conversation and rapport building, and cope with stress in similar ways as their cultural counterparts. For Latinos, this culturally appropriate method of engaging in communication often begins with light discussion about the weather as trust is assessed in the interaction. If trust is sensed in the interaction with the social worker, then Latinos will be less compelled to delay in discussing the problem. If trust is not sensed, Latinos may delay longer but will eventually describe the problem. When trust is sensed in the interaction with the social worker, Latinas will more easily begin to share concerns and discuss thoughts and feelings while problems solving but will keep their guard up until they are fully satisfied that trust has been established.

To be culturally competent, social workers need to defer their own desire to move too quickly into the nuts and bolts of the assessment. Engaging Latino caregivers in pleasant conversation by communicating interest in them and their care story is more apt to lead to the formation of the rhythm and harmony of the communication in the interaction and help them negotiate the sections of the assessment. Similar to their Black and African American counterparts, a back-and-forth "volley" will seem awkward, stiff, impersonal, and intrusive when it is structured around the assessment. The social worker should engage communication and engagement around interest and concern for the caregiver in order to understand the needs of the afflicted family member. Social workers should know that if there is a pressing problem for either the Black or Latino caregiver, regardless of gender, it will be communicated in the first meeting, especially if it has to do with care recipient's needs or safety. This does not mean that the social worker should not ask questions related to the assessment content. The social worker should. In fact, as the caregiver communicates the story, many details that are relevant to a particular section of the assessment should be noted; that way the social worker can very easily and systematically guide the conversation into obtaining additional information for that section from the caregiver. Allowing the caregiver's and social worker's conversation and interaction rhythm to emerge and form naturally in the course of listening to the caregiver story will seem more natural, much less intrusive, and will tend to convey an attitude of caring and interest on the part of the social worker. This will move the work forward, enabling all to focus on communicating in the needs of the caregiver and the care recipient in a culturally competent assessment environment that is considered safe, trusting, and comfortable for the caregiver.

This assessment plus the two illustration assessments discussed next provide the caregiver and the social worker graphic data to help clarify and understand the *familismo* or kinship and fictive kin network as it currently functions in the ethnic family system. The roles assumed by the caregiver and other family members illustrated in both the ethnocultural genogram and in the ethnocultural ecomap identify the various relationships and systemic interaction patterns in the caregiver's psychosocial environment that may foster or hamper care. The social worker works jointly with the caregiver to explain all assessments and illustrations in order to help the caregiver understand the importance of providing complete information to help form an appropriate care plan. Second, the social worker and caregiver use the assessment and illustration content to help the caregiver fully understand the person-and-situation perspectives.

The content should be viewed as a whole and assessed in terms of the subjective experience of the caregiver. While every effort needs to be made to capture the information as accurately as possible, it is important to validate this with the caregiver as he or she provides the information. Also important is not to make the assessment the center of the interaction. It is essential that the social worker shows the caregiver the assessment and provide a general explanation of the sections and state the need to complete the assessment form in order to complete an accurate assessment and formulate a care plan to appropriately help the caregiver. It is also a good idea to advise the caregiver that at times the social worker will be writing and filling in responses as the caregiver provides information. But engaging the caregiver should be the center of the interaction, not the form. This is another reason the social worker should be very familiar with the assessment content. The social worker should focus on the needs of the caregiver, make eye content, present active-listening body language, and display the attitude of a learner, because it is the caregiver who is the expert and who knows the care situation better than anyone. Following is a completed Confidential Ethnic Family Caregiver Assessment Sheet for the case example described at the beginning of the chapter.

CONFIDENTIAL ETHNIC FAMILY CAREGIVER ASSESSMENT

Evaluation Date ___3/7/2011___ Time: 2:45 PM Referral Source: *Self*
Name __Juan_____ D.O.B. ___1968___ Age 43 Gender __M__
Address ___201 Main Street_
Hartford, CT
Telephone Number(s) __Home *xxx xxx-xxxx* Cell *xxx xxx-xxxx*_
Current living situation- Where: *apartment* Type: *3 family home* How long: *5 yrs*
With whom: *mother and girl friend*
Status (M)__(P)_X (S)__(D)__(W)__ Ethnicity/Racial Group: *Latino/El Salvador*
Religion: Baptist Primary Language: Spanish Education: *10 grade high school*
Folk healers botanicals shop used: No ___Yes X If Yes, Date: *2/22/2011*
Reason: *Caregiver and his mother had a cold and a cough*

Folk remedies used: *He and his mother use herb teas, cough medicine and chest rubbing oil from the Dominican Republic. He also uses a special soup that is made with specific spices that help with chest cold, cough, and congestion. His girlfriend helps prepare the remedies. His mother is confused so they have asked the folk healer to come to the house every week to pray with his mother. This was helping for a while but the folk healer moved to another town. His visits to the house are now less frequent due to the distance. The caregiver has not been able to identify another healer in the community.*

Spiritual/cultural issues influencing treatment: *Folk healer visits the house to pray*
Activities/Hobbies: *Caregiver likes carpentry and to work on cars*
Caregiver Strengths: *He can help friends and neighbors with carpentry*
Employment: *Drives taxi part time* Retired _____ SES *below 15K*
In case of emergency, contact: *Girlfriend/ GAna___* Telephone: *XXX XXX-XXXX*

Presenting Problem Described by Caregiver:
Caregiver stressed because his mother is leaving the house when he and his girl-friend are at work. A neighbor found his mother a block away without a coat on and confused. The neighbor took his mother to his house and called his wife who called the caregiver. He had to leave work to get his mother and take her home. Both he and his girl friend work nights. She works as a janitor cleaning businesses at night, and he drives the taxi for a friend who allows him to keep the tips. Now he and his girlfriend have to take turns staying at home because his mother's memory and con-fusion is getting worse. Caregiver needs to find someone to stay with his mother at night while he and his girl friend work. Two weeks ago the caregiver went to Rhode Island to see whether a cousin could help him find someone to care for his mother. While he was there the police raided the house, and he was arrested. His girlfriend had to borrow money to get him out of jail. Now he is more stressed because he has

to go to court and could be deported. He has no relatives in this state to take care of his mother. His girlfriend who is also undocumented and living in the United States and from the Dominican Republic cannot take care of her because she has to work. Caregiver cannot sleep and is feeling overwhelmed with the care responsibilities, stress, and worry about his what is going to happen to him and his mother if he is arrested and deported.

Protective services _____Yes _____No X

History of Presenting Symptoms (include psychosocial stressors, past treatment): *Caregiver stress has become worse since his mother started leaving the house. This is not the first time she has left the house without anyone knowing. She had done it 5 times now. Although he feels like he needs to get her to the doctor, he doesn't have the money.*

Physician/Family/Service Providers/Agencies Currently Involved With Caregiver

Provider/Agency Name   Contact Person   Telephone Number
   None
_____

_____

_____

_____

Current Medication   **Dosage**   **Start Date**
Apart from over-the-counter Advil, the caregiver and his mother are only using folk medicine from the botanica in the Dominican Republic neighborhood community

_____

Special needs or physical challenges:
The caregiver fell on the ice in January 2011 and landed on his back. He has a pain and trouble walking, especially in cold weather. He takes the Advil for pain

Date and reason for most recent medical exam:
Neither he nor his mother had physical exams since they arrived in the United States 5 years ago.

Next scheduled medical exam:
No exam scheduled for the caregiver or his mother at this time

Has the caregiver experienced the following symptoms?
(Social worker reads symptoms and caregiver rates the symptoms experienced on a scale from 1 to 10.)

Most Severe			Moderate		Mild		Least Severe		
1	2	3	4	5	6	7	8	9	10

<u>1</u> Anxiety

<u>3</u> Panic attacks

<u>3</u> Fear

<u>3</u> Sadness

<u>10</u> Crying episodes

<u>1</u> Anger

<u>1</u> Frustration

<u>10</u> Suicidal thoughts

<u>1</u> Worry

<u>1</u> Feelings of desperation

<u>6</u> Confusion

<u>10</u> Memory lapses/changes

<u>1</u> Unwanted, repeated, or negative thoughts

<u>6</u> Dizziness

<u>6</u> Shortness of breath

<u>10</u> Blurred vision

<u>1</u> Stomach pains

<u>1</u> Backaches

<u>1</u> Headaches

<u>1</u> Chest pains

<u>10</u> Learning difficulty

<u>3</u> Difficulty making decisions

<u>3</u> Difficulty problem solving

What is the caregiver's perception of his or her quality of life?

(Social worker reads scale options, and caregiver rates their current overall Quality of Life on a scale from 1 to 10.) (Circles one)

1	2	3	4	5	6	7	8	9	10
Terrible		Unbearable		Bearable		Fair		Wonderful	

X

Other Current Symptoms

Disturbance of sleep   Absent_____   Present <u>X</u>

Falling asleep <u>X</u> Staying awake <u>X</u>   Waking early <u>X</u>

Nightmares <u>X</u>   Night tremors _____ Sleep walking

Explain: *Caregiver awakens in the night after nightmare, but can't remember details of dream.*

Eating Disturbance   Absent_____   Present <u>X</u>

Explain: *Caregiver is too worried to eat. His stomach aches, and he loses his appetite*

Sexual Disturbance   Absent_____   Present X (sometimes)

Explain: *He stresses about his mother, he and his girlfriend fight, and no sex.*

Current Suicidal Ideation   Absent X   Present _____

Explain _____

History of Suicidal Ideation   Absent X   Present _____

Explain _____

History of Suicidal Attempts _____

Substance abuse Absent_____ Present _____

Explain _____

History of substance abuse _____

Explain _____

Has caregiver or family member with dementia (FMWD) experienced the following?

Caregiver_____ FMWD_____heart attack

Caregiver_____ FMWD _____stroke

Caregiver_____ FMWD _____high blood pressure

Caregiver_____ FMWD _____diabetes

Caregiver_____ FMWD _____cancer

Caregiver_____ FMWD _____epilepsy

Caregiver_____ FMWD _____hyperthyroid/hypothyroid

Caregiver_____ FMWD _____hypoglycemia

Caregiver_____ FMWD _____ alcoholism/drug abuse/addiction

Caregiver_____ FMWD _____mental health issues

Caregiver_____ FMWD _____sexual abuse

Caregiver_____ FMWD __X__emotional/physical/verbal abuse

Caregiver_____ FMWD __X__family violence

Caregiver_____ FMWD __X__death/loss

Caregiver__X__ FMWD __X__allergies/asthma

Caregiver_____ FMWD __X__enuresis or encopresis

Social Work Clinical Observations and Impressions

<u>Appearance</u>

<u>Dress/Appearance</u>		Appropriate X	Meticulous _____ Disheveled _____
<u>Speech</u>	Rate		Unremarkable X Other _____
	Tone		Unremarkable X Other _____
	Spontaneous? __X__		Amount? (%) <u>80%+</u>
<u>Behavior</u>	General Activity		Unremarkable X Other _____
	Motor Activity		Unremarkable X Other _____
	Compulsions		Unremarkable X Other _____
Tics/repetitive behaviors			Unremarkable X Other _____

Observed Affect—full_X_ labile__ constricted___ flat___ Appropriate Y X N ___

Explain _____

<u>Thought Form</u>	Goal-directed Y X	N_____	Explain _____
	Relevant Y X	N_____	Explain _____
<u>Thought Perception</u>	Auditory Hallucinations Y_____	N X	
	Visual Hallucinations	Y_____ N X	
<u>Thought Content</u>	Suicidal ideations	Y_____ N X	
	Homicidal ideations	Y_____ N X	
	Paranoid ideations	Y_____ N X	
	Preoccupations/Obsessions	Y_____ N X	
<u>Cognitive Function</u>			
	Orientation X3		
	(person, place & time) Y X	N ___	
	Attention impairment	Y_____ N X	
	Concentration impairment	Y_____ N X	
	Immediate recall/retention		
	impairment	Y_____ N X	
	Recent memory		
	impairment Y_____ N X	Method: lunch	
	Remote memory Y__ N X	Method: year born	
<u>Judgment</u>	Good X Fair _____	Poor _____	
<u>Impulse Control</u>	Good X Fair _____	Poor _____	
<u>Insight</u>	Good X Fair _____	Poor _____	

DSM-IV-TR Diagnosis

Axis I *DSM-IV-TR* Code *309.28 adjustment disorder with mixed anxiety and depressed mood & V62.2 occupational problem, V62.4 acculturation problem, V62.81 Relational Problem NOS*

Axis II <u>None</u>

Axis III *Chronic back pain, undiagnosed*

Axis IV Psychosocial and Environmental Problems (check and describe)
Caregiver is experiencing reactions to multiple psychosocial stressors. His biological mother diagnosed with Alzheimer's disease is presenting with multiple symptoms that require above-normal care and supervision by the caregiver. The caregiver works part time and is undocumented. This prevents him from providing appropriate care for himself and his mother. This creates additional stress and environmental difficulty in functioning. There is little familial support or social support available. The caregiver presents with a mild depressed mood, anxiety, insomnia, and difficulty concentrating, especially after family member with dementia exhibits memory loss symptoms,

confusion, or related problem. The recent legal issues have caused the caregiver more stress as the threat of arrest, imprisonment, and deportation exists. Overall, the caregiver is functioning pretty well and has meaningful relationships, part-time work, and is actively seeking assistance to solve care and treatment problems for FMWD.

Axis V   Global Assessment of Functioning Scale
            Estimated Score   Current _65_   Previous year _65_

Does caregiver need assistance/referral to following services?

Case Management _X_   Care team for FMWD _X_
Individual counseling _X_ Family counseling _X_
Grief counseling_____ Group or Support counseling _____
Housing _X_   Home care support _X_
Hospice _____ Language or Interpreter _X_
Educational information _X_   Employment assistance _X_
Financial assistance _X_   Insurance _X_
Immigration & Naturalization _X_ Legal Services _X_
Medical treatment _X_   Protective services _____
Transportation services _____
Other psychosocial and environmental services needed _____

Resources to care for FMWD: Yes _X_   No _____

Is care team currently working with FMWD? Yes_____   No _X_
Other services needed to care for FMWD—*Other family members or extended family resources to take over family member ailing with dementia.*

Other social work recommendations for caregiver—*To ensure afflicted family member is safe; the caregiver or a responsible person should provide supervision for family member with dementia at all times. Also secure locks should be installed in the home, and the FMWD should be registered with First-Alert and safe return ASAP.*

Is caregiver referral to primary care physician required? Yes _X_ No _____

If yes, explain—*Caregiver needs a physical examination to assess the back pain he states was caused by fall on ice and to rule out other medical issues.*

Is FMWD referral to primary care physician required? Yes _X_   No _____
If yes, explain:
Family member with dementia symptoms is caregiver's mother. She has not received a physical exam since they arrived in the United States 5 years ago. The caregiver is not sure of the date his mother received the last physical exam in his or her home country, that is, the Dominican Republic, prior to leaving the country. The caregiver describes his mother's memory loss and confusion as serious and does not think his mother is able to provide the date of her last physical exam.

THE ETHNOCULTURAL GENOGRAM

McGoldrick and Gerson (1985) were among the first few to write about genograms in family assessment. While this source is one of the first written on genograms, this information serves as a strong foundation for genograms. Their text entitled *Genograms in Family Assessment* (1985) continues to be used today as a reference for both novice and the experienced social workers. They were able to identify the rationale behind the construction of genograms as a means of providing a graphic view, mapping the complex family formation and tracking family generations, relationships, and roles. Social workers seeking in-depth training in creation of the genogram are strongly encouraged to review the text by McGoldrick and Gerson (1985). Because Alzheimer's disease and other related irreversible dementia could have been present in previous generations, it is helpful for both the caregiver and the social worker to map out the various disease paths traversed by the living and diseased family members. In addition, comorbidity of other diseases present in past generations of family members and those present at the time dementia emerged is helpful for the social worker to analyze and understand. This is especially true if there is a genetic predisposition to a particular disease. Recording the data requires the social worker to engage the caregiver in the process of diagramming representations of the family structure. In ethnic family, multiple generations are often living near or residing with the family caregiver. This often makes the process more doable for the caregiver.

The goal of this section is to build on McGoldrick and Gerson's (1985) framework by providing a simple ethnocultural aspect necessary to capture the *familismo* and kin network in ethnic families, in particular Black and Latino families. Because of the unique social interaction patterns found within Black and Latino families family networks, and fictive kin, the complex roles, especially when considering the role delegation that may occur in some families, make it not only helpful but necessary to have a graphic view of the systems as they interface within the structure of the wider family context. The ethnocultural genogram helps the caregiver and social worker to identify the family clusters and schisms. It serves to illustrate the family system structure and to identify sources of social support as well as sources of conflict, concern, and added stress for the caregiver and the afflicted family member.

There are many computer-generated genograms available today; it seems more efficient to utilize a computer-generated program for a variety of reasons, and what is recommended in this text is that social workers complete this in two steps, collaborating with the ethnic caregiver so that the social worker can sketch the diagram guided by information provided by the caregiver. This process helps both the caregiver and the social worker engage in a joint effort to complete the project.

The first step is to include this in the initial assessment when meeting face to face with the caregiver if this first session lends itself to this endeavor. This is because social workers are always encouraged to meet the client where he or she resides and if the client, in this case the caregiver, seems to have a more urgent need, then the social worker should defer to the caregiver's need at the time. Then, in the second meeting when the more urgent caregiver need has been addressed, the social worker and caregiver can work to complete the genogram content. Engaging the caregiver with the understanding that he or she is the expert who can provide essential family information is key to the success of this effort. It has been my experience that during the creation of the ethnocultural genogram, the process of engaging in this effort by both the social worker and the caregiver enhances the level of engagement between the caregiver and the social worker, moving the relationship to a deeper level of understanding, trust, and commitment. As the caregiver shares critical self and family historical and current relationship information with the social worker, bonding occurs. The required trust and engagement, which may take several meetings with the social worker to build without the ethnocultural genogram, seems to occur quite naturally during the creation of the ethnocultural genogram completed either in the initial or second meeting.

While family members can be a source of assistance and social support, family patterns of interaction between members can also be a source of stress. The inner patterns of family relationships can be discussed during this time in a very natural manner. Hence, obtaining sensitive information by using an illustration like the genogram can serve to lower caregiver psychic defenses and minimize cultural values regarding protecting the family system. Asking questions similar to the following help the social worker to identify family supportive groups or units within the larger family network that work best together, thus further identifying resources or strengths within the family system.

Who would you call upon to help you in the care of your family member?

Who do you believe would best support your care decisions?

Apart from you, who would your family member _____ allow to care for him or her?

Which member(s) is the most trusted in terms of care decisions?

Are there certain family members who work best together?

If so, can you identify those members in this diagram?

Is there a certain member in the family who has been delegated specific responsibility by the family?

While there are no negative questions noted above, the conversation should naturally proceed toward allowing the caregiver to identify members who are least (1) able to help, (2) apt to be supportive of care decisions, (3) trusted, or (4) able to work together. A response by the social worker might be, "I see, these members can help. But not these, is that correct?" "Is there a reason for them not being able to help?" If this does not come up in the process naturally, it is very appropriate to ask the questions at the end of the process. By asking the questions at the end, the social worker can voice a need to be thorough and have a clear understanding of what the caregiver experiences in the family interactions when caring for the loved one. The social worker can emphasize the importance of the caregiver's explaining his or her experiences and how the experiences influence the caregiver's story of care. By focusing the need for content back to the caregiver's experience, the social worker may be better able to uncover information that has not yet been offered and that is important to the care situation.

Family organization and structure identified in this process will also provide the elements important to the unique family illustrated. The family preference for collectivistic functioning and the different values connected to unique family arrangements and coping should be more evident in contrast to nuclear family functioning. The meaning of gender roles, generational hierarchies, styles of communication, and problem solving among family members should be explored by the social worker. The strength of blood and nonblood relationships should also be explored if it does not emerge in the process of creating the ethnocultural genogram. Identifying inadequate or unfavorable interactions and family stressors caused by unexpected or traumatic transitions or splintering family factions can help the social worker understand the impact of these interactions and situations on the family, perhaps weakening the family's and caregiver's ability to manage the self and the caregiver role effectively.

In addition, the family life cycle before and after the family member was diagnosed with dementia can be outlined in order to understand the family pattern structure change. While most families have some universal biological and developmental events, for ethnic caregiver families more diverse cultural patterns of care may be embedded within the family in terms of timing, stages, and transitions. These patterns are generally shaped by the unique meaning the disease has for the family, the nationality, religion, folk belief, socioeconomic status, education, and migration and acculturation level. This caregiver's subjective reality must always be in the social worker's mind when working with Black and Latino caregivers. Oval and rectangular boundaries can be drawn around the specific patterns identified and notations can be made either in the key or near the drawn ovals and rectangles, with brief notes stating the nature of the pattern and the reason it has been separated from the whole. The social worker can be creative in highlighting the patterns and identifying how to note them. The essential criterion is that both the social worker and the caregiver understand the reason for establishing the oval and rectangular boundaries and the meaning these have in contributing to the assessment and in establishing the problem-solving plan of care.

In the case study example, Juan's ethnocultural genogram would include three generations: (1) Juan and his partner, his brother, and his brother's family in Florida; (2) Juan's mother, father, and their sibling information, and extended family network; and (3) the next earlier generation, Juan's maternal and paternal grandparents and their *familismo* network. The social worker and Juan would work to identify the required details of the genogram as well as those family systemic networks that may serve as resources in support of care for his mother both in the United Sates and in the home country, the Dominican Republic (see Appendix A at the end of this chapter).

THE ETHNOCULTURAL ECOMAP

Stemming from ecology, the ecomap has been an important social work assessment tool for many years as a means of examining the relationship between people and their psychosocial environment (Germain, 1981). Auerswald (1968, 1990) was one of the first to recognize the importance of including the physical and social environment in the assessment of client functioning. Since then the ecological theory has evolved into being one of the cornerstones of social work practice informing the generalist and clinical level of work. Understanding the transactions between the client and the environmental forces increases the social worker's ability to understand the vicissitudes of the client's world and, in turn, identify the impact of forces of inequality and injustice, or the forces that serve to build on and strengthen the client's resources. Learning the caregiver's motivation to overcome the former or learning ways in which he or she tapped into confidence and competence for the latter is itself a strengths perspective. The use of the concept *ethnocultural ecomap* is a descriptive concept that seeks to build on the original ecomap perspective used in a generic way by social workers; for example, the Eurocentric work on Caucasian population conducted for many years (Hartman, 1978; Hartman & Laird, 1983). In this text, the ethnocultural ecomap provides a framework that is more culturally syntonic and inclusive of the caregiver's cultural reality context as it is experienced by Black and Latino caregivers. The assessment motive is basically the same as used in the past, which is to understand the caregiver within the context of the caregiving situation. What is different is the social worker's and caregiver's effort to capture the added dimensions of multicultural experiences that provides insight into multiple cultural contexts in which ethnic caregivers interact have not been captured before. Also captured is the cultural meaning that the systems may have for the ethnic caregiver's cognitive, emotional, behavioral, and interaction processes and nuances within the Black and Latino caregiving cultures. Although Blacks and Latinos in some cases share a similar subculture or ecological position, capturing the subtle differences is important. Finally, this assessment also captures the meaning this context has for the caregiver when the subculture and culture interaction is different.

For Black and Latino caregivers who often function in a diverse and multidimensional ecological situation, simply helping the caregivers to evaluate and give meaning to these multidimensional factors tends to affect their situation. The social worker employing the ethnocultural ecomap has the responsibility to identify and reflect back to the caregiver the unique experience conveyed by the caregiver in this ethnocultural ecomap assessment. For example, the caregiver might be an adult daughter. The daughter might have children in school and a spouse or partner. There might be various *familismo*, kin, or fictive kin that provide support and assistance in interacting with the various systems in the ecological context. Identifying these informal resources and systems in the ecomap is essential to understand the role of the family and extended family within the context of the environment. This systemic group is considered the information network of resources.

In addition, the caregiver may have to interact with various formal care professionals for the afflicted parent inside or outside of the culture and with multicultural individuals in various cultural contexts. The adult son might also have to interact with various formal systems involved with himself, the spouse or partner, and the children within the culture, and also interact with others in the general community, such as churches, community groups, cultural activities. He may also need to engage in more formal interactions outside the culture, including schools, community activities, and care professionals for the children. Each system provides contexts that convey specific values and will require specific functioning. The multidimensional interactions are not occurring just in cultural inside environs or formal outside environs; there are various dimensions of interactions that play out between inside and outside cultural environs. Barriers to care or obstacles are also noted as they emerge in the caregiver's story. The degree of influence and meaning these have for the caregiver depends upon the caregiver's story and perspective. Some of the interactions may give rise to more negative experiences, others may give rise to more positive experiences, and still other interactions may be considered more normative by the caregiver. Using the ethnocultural ecomap provides the social worker and the caregiver with an organized illustration or map that helps to make sense and give meaning to the interactions. There are many elements discussed here, so it is important to note that while the goal is to capture the essential elements of the context in which the caregiver functions, it is important not to make this so complex that it becomes confusing for all involved. Keeping the documentation as simple as possible yet capturing the multiplicity of interactions important to the caregiver's story are essential. After capturing the various elements in the ethnocultural ecomap, the social worker and caregiver jointly prepare an ethnocultural ecomap with four basic domains as the focus for the development of the care plan.

In order to provide a framework that incorporates the ecological context and experiences in various contexts of the caregiver's biopsychosocial functioning, this text identifies the following four domains as essential for the Black and Latino ethnocultural ecomap. The four caregiver domains essential to assessment in the ethnocultural map are (1) the caregiver context, (2) family member dementia care recipient context, (3) family resources context, and (4) community formal resources context. The biopsychosocial functioning and problem location within one of these four domains is based on the caregiver problem identification and formulation as communicated to the social worker.

Applying this ecological framework to the case example of Juan and his mother, the social worker would identify his household, the systems he is interacting with, including his neighborhood, his job, the immigration and naturalization office, his attorney, law enforcement in Rhode Island, and in Connecticut, the airlines, the prison in Connecticut, and his girlfriend, her job and her contact systems in the Dominican Republic who helped her find Juan's mother's extended family members and the credit union that lent her the money to buy the airline ticket to the Dominican Republic for Juan's mother and herself. For Juan's mother, the ecomap would identify the local clinic she has visited, the Alzheimer's Association, her other son in Florida, his work situation, the airlines, and the extended family networks in the Dominican Republic and El Salvador. Appendix B at the end of this chapter is an ethnocultural ecomap illustrating some of the content that should be recorded from the case example.

It is important to insert lines with arrows indicating reciprocal power, energy, stress, and/or support relationships, as well as one-sided relationships identifying the origin of the relationships and the direction of the power, energy, stress, and/or support (Hartman, 1978; Hartman & Laird, 1983). Ideally positive events should be noted with a plus sign (+) next to the arrow indicating the nature of the positive relationship and a minus (–) sign to indicate a negative relationship (Hartman, 1978; Hartman & Laird, 1983). The large circle identifies the household members, and the smaller circles are other significant social systems with which the caregiver, the afflicted family member, and household members interact in their social context (Hartman, 1978; Hartman & Laird, 1983).

The familismo and fictive kin networks are identified and grouped together with a focus on the relationship energy, direction, and status. This provides the social worker with a clearer ethno cultural perspective thus enhancing the social worker's ability to more effectively assess the caregiver, the afflicted family member, and the resources or lack of resources available within the environment.

REFERENCES

Auerswald, E. H. (1968). Interdisciplinary versus ecological approach. *Family Process, 7*, 202–215.

Auerswald, E. H. (1990). Toward epistemological transformation in education and training of family therapists. In M. P. Mirkin (Ed.), *The social and political contexts of family therapy*. Boston: Allyn & Bacon.

Becerra, R. M., & Iglehart, A. P. (1995). Folk medicine use: Diverse populations in a metropolitan area. *Social Work in Health Care, 21*, 37–58.

Cournoyer, B. R. (2008). *The social work skills workbook* (5th ed.). Belmont, CA: Thomson Brooks/Cole.

Delgado, M. (2007) *Social work with Latinos: A cultural assets paradigm*. New York: Oxford University Press

Dilworth-Anderson, P., & Anderson, N. B. (1994). Dementia caregiving in Blacks: A contextual approach for research. In E. Light, N. Niederhe, & B. Lebowitz (Eds.). *Stress effects on family Alzheimer's patients*. New York: Springer Publishing.

Dixon, P. (2007). *African American relationships, marriages, and families*. New York: Routledge Taylor & Francis.

Dixon, P., & Osiris, K. (2002). *TLC: Talking and listening with care: A communication guide for singles and couples*. Decatur, GA: Oji Publications.

Fajardo Ortíz, G. (2002). *Los servicios sociales par alas personas mayores en Iberoamérica: Estructura, avatares y necesidades*. Washington, DC: National Hispanic Council on Aging.

González Sanders, D. J. (2003). *Confidential ethnic family caregiver assessment*. Unpublished assessment document.

Gray, J. (1992). *Men are from Mars, women are from Venus*. New York: Harper-Collins.

Hartman, A. (1978). Diagrammatic assessment of family relationships. *Social Casework, 59*, 465–476.

Hartman, A. & Laird, J. (1983). Family centered social work practice. New York: The Free Press.

Kilgannon, C. (2005, April 15). Immigrant populations with native remedies. *New York Times*, p. 1.

McGoldrick, M., & Gerson, R. (1985). *Genograms in family assessments*. New York: W. W. Norton & company.

National Association of Social Workers. (2007). *Standards for cultural competence in social work practice*. Washington, DC: Author.

Roff, L. L., Burgio, L. D., Gitlin, L., Nichols, L. Chaplin, W., & Hardin, M. J. (2004). Positive aspects of Alzheimer's caregiving: The role of race. *Journal of Gerontology, 59B*(4), 185–190.

Schensul, J. J. Wetle, T., & Torres, M. (1993). The health of Puerto Rican elders. In M. Sotomayor & A. Garcia (Eds.), *Elderly Latinos: Issues and solutions for the 21st century* (pp. 59–77). Washington, DC: National Hispanic Council on Aging.

Zapata, J., & Shippee-Rice, R. (1999). The use of folk healing and healers by six Latinos living in New England: A preliminary study. *Journal of Transcultural Nursing, 10,* 136–142.

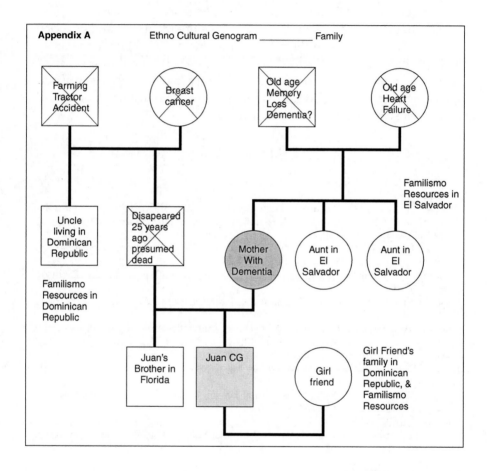

Appendix A   Ethno Cultural Genogram _____ Family

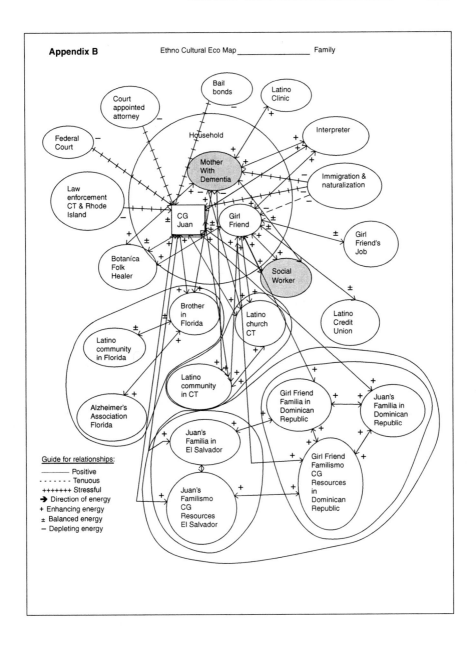

Appendix B   Ethno Cultural Eco Map _____ Family

7

Identifying the Social Work Role and Problem Domain for Ethnic Caregivers

CASE EXAMPLE

I tell myself all she [Adriana] needs is to go back to Peru and she will be fine. I think she just misses her other family and life in Peru that's why she is confused. The family members call and write but she doesn't talk to them anymore. I don't think she remembers or knows who they are. She has three sisters and many other family members in Peru. We have a big family. They want to see her. But the boys don't want to go back. They are in school and they like it here. I don't know what to do. She is getting more and more confused. The boys are worried. I don't know what to tell them. I feel worried all the time. My husband and I both work but now I can't. I have to stay home to watch her and make sure she is fine and that she eats. The boys can't take care of her. They have to go to school. They are both having trouble in school. One was suspended for fighting and he had to stay home. The little one [age 11] cries when his mother gets out of control and we have to help control her behavior. I speak and understand some English but I can't go to the school to find out what is happening to the boys and their grades because I can't leave her alone. They want to help her but they can't and she can't help them and the boys don't understand. They don't know what Alzheimer's is. My husband and I don't know much about it either. We want to help her but don't know what to do.

It is hard because my husband doesn't understand what is happening to her either. The boys are sad, and sometimes they get angry with her when she doesn't understand them, or when she forgets what she is doing. We all need help. I can't work anymore. I can't do anything but stay with her at home. I feel sick sometimes but I don't go to the doctor because I can't take her with me on the bus and I can't leave her home alone. I'm worrying about everyone all the time. I can't sleep and if I do fall asleep, I don't rest.

I wake up a lot. My husband is angry because we have more bills, and it costs more to feed everyone. He is stressed. He worries about me because I can't sleep. Adriana and I used to go to church, but we can't now. She has had accidents because she doesn't say she needs to go to the bathroom. It is has been embarrassing for us that I can't help her. The church helps me, when I go. It helps me to feel better. I know I am not alone. God can help me. I miss my friends from work and from church. I'm too embarrassed to tell them.

Manuela, a 55-year-old caregiver, was born in Peru. She and her parents traveled to the United States 15 years ago. She is married but has no children. Shortly after her arrival in the United States, her maternal cousin Adriana, a single mother with two small boys, immigrated to the United States to care for and live with an elderly aunt in a large urban city nearby. When her cousin arrived they were informed their elderly aunt had been a victim of an armed robbery and had been killed. Having no money, no way to return to Peru, and needing a place to live, they contacted Manuela and asked for assistance. Her cousin and the two boys settled into life with Manuela and her husband. In time all became naturalized citizens of the United States.

Three years ago Manuela assumed care for her cousin and the two boys, now ages 11 and 13, due to her cousin's increasing memory loss and confusion. Initially, Manuela attributed the memory problems in cousin Adriana to leaving Peru, migrating to the United States, and the past trauma of sudden and violent loss of the elder aunt. Nothing was done in terms of assessment. As time passed it became clear to everyone, especially the boys, that Adriana had confusion and memory loss issues. Three years ago Manuela took her cousin Adriana to the doctor who diagnosed her with early-onset Alzheimer's disease.

CATEGORIZING ETHNIC CAREGIVER PROBLEMS IN FOUR DOMAINS

This section introduces a simple framework to assist caregivers in sorting problems into four domains of care. The four domains are (A) caregiver self-care, (B) family member dementia care, (C) caregiver family resources, and (D) caregiver community resources. Each domain is discussed, and a case example is provided. The letters assigned to each domain (A–D) provide the circular focus identified and illustrated in the concept map provided in Chapter 4.

Rationale for Use of Four Domains

The use of the problem domain illustration form described in this section tends to help caregivers separate problems, compare the problems by domains, and apply appropriate thinking in terms of the problem itself to better identify possible solutions or resources. To help facilitate the process the social worker has in hand the four domain forms to help the social worker and caregiver identify the problem and the particular domain in which it best fits. As the social worker and caregiver assign the problem a domain, the caregiver is better able to assess the problem and ability to tap into his or her own resources or the resources of others in hopes of resolving the problem. In short, the use of the forms tends to help caregivers sort problems, then partialize them, which often leads the caregiver to gradually experience less dread and anxiety about failure, and feel more competence, hope, and confidence in his or her ability to resolve the problems.

The second step requires the social worker to introduce and explain the six-step problem-solving process and the four-domain problem-solving approach. In this section the four domains (A–D) are defined, and the problem identification process is discussed in detail.

To fully understand the rationale for the use of the four domains in the problem-solving process, one must begin at the standard paradigm of problem solving and how effective problem solving can be for dementia caregivers. Some evidence-based practice research has shown that caregivers tend to engage in more "attentive listening, self-exploration and self-expression" when working with individual social workers (Toseland, Rossiter, Peak, & Smith, 1990, p. 214). In addition, social workers "tended to keep clients more focused on specific problems and problem solving, and to take more responsibility for problem solving during and between sessions" (Toseland, Rossiter, Peak, & Smith, 1990, p. 214). The use of the four domains (A–D) helps the social worker to focus the caregiver by the domain, types of problems and issues specific to an individual caregiver in order to take specific problem-solving actions. In order to resolve the problem, the problem must first be identified effectively.

Social workers know that the experience of dementia and dementia caregiving means different things to different people. Every ethnic group, culture, family, and individual caregiver gives meaning to the experience in a way that adequately enables them to conceptualize and operationalize the caregiving role for their unique situation. By providing a domain-specific paradigm, the caregiver is taught a specific way of thinking about and organizing the problems. With this new cognitive shift, social workers can help foster caregiver self-exploration and self-expression in terms of engaging the caregiver to focus on specific problems, specific problem-solving solutions, and problem-solving responsibility during and between sessions. Keeping the intervention specific and simple helps the caregiver learn the process, and repeat the process as new problems emerge. The hope is that the caregiver will have learned and practiced this simple four-domain process and therefore can implement it after intervention with the social worker ends.

Defining Four Domains

The four domains are defined as follows. The *caregiver self-care (CGSC)* problem domain includes identifying the individual and/or interpersonal self-care needs of the caregiver in physical, mental, emotional, health, and social interactions. It also includes financial, transportation, and home needs. Often caregivers experience depletion of self-care resources in multiple ways in both the short-term and long-term caregiving role. Generally family caregivers are committed to care for their family member regardless of the cost to themselves. Driven by love and loyalty, caregiver acts of selfless care seem to grow stronger with each new symptom presented by the afflicted family. While there are many diverse caregiving experiences, what has been described as a common experience is the increase in the unpredictability, intensity, and complexity of the caregiving role as the dementing disease progresses, bringing new symptoms for the caregiver to manage. The longevity of the caregiving experience often has many turning points and can be described as an emotional rollercoaster ride with the caregiver as the lone passenger traveling up peaks of hope one moment, then traveling into deep valleys of self-doubt, anger, loss, and grief the next. Caregivers living in this uncertain, long-term, changing lifestyle often experience a loss of sense of self, and a change in inner equilibrium and energy. Fear, worry, and stress may become companions to caregivers regardless of the love and devotion they have for their ailing family member. Some caregivers experience loneliness. This is often the case with all caregivers, even those who have family members or fictive kin they can turn to for sympathetic, understanding listening and support. The magnitude of the caregiving task is such that caregivers do benefit from a supportive consultation with a knowledgeable and sensitive social worker that can recognize and respect caregiver needs and strongly encourage caregivers to actively work at providing themselves with elements self-care.

The next problem domain is *family member dementia care (FMDC)*. This domain includes problems associated with assistance the caregiver may need to obtain information about Alzheimer's or other dementing diseases, assistance in obtaining education about their relative's diagnoses, or assistance in determing strategies to manage the day to day disease symptoms appropriately. Similar to caregiver self-care, this domain includes the physical, mental, emotional, and social needs of the care recipient. It also includes financial, transportation, and home needs that may be a problem for the caregiver or the family member with dementia. Because the ethnic caregiver and the afflicted family member are often spouses, partners, daughters, or sons, or family members who might be sharing the same household, the needs are often intertwined. For this domain the social worker and caregiver seek to identify changes or decline in the family member's memory that are creating problems. One example is assessing the afflicted family member's ability to complete activities of daily living. Another is assessing the emergence of new Alzheimer's disease symptoms and the lifestyle adjustments the family member and caregiver need to make to maintain safety. Understanding the problematic dementia symptom type, origin, and severity is an essential function of both the caregiver and the social worker in order to know how to intervene to ensure sustainability of adaptive functional levels in the family member. Often caregivers need to apply new strategies and shift their approach to respond to different symptoms. Having the help of a social worker enables the caregiver to use the expertise of a professional to help determine when the physician should be contacted to reassess the family member, or make a referral to case management. Social workers can also help caregivers pursue legal guardianship or consider options in terms of adding additional multidisciplinary medical, legal, or supportive team care assistance.

The third domain is *caregiver family resources (CGFR)*. This domain focuses on identifying familismo, kin, or fictive kin family members who want to help and can help the caregiver provide care for the family member. Often caregivers are so busy with the day-to-day care that they tend to overlook the availability of family members or extended family as resources for additional help. In previous chapters the discourse included information about ethnic cultures having designated roles for specific family members. This domain is created with the ethnic caregiver in mind and with the needs identified by the literature as possibly culture specific such as family kin involvement in multiple levels of care. The role of the social worker is to attentively listen for underlying cultural nuances as the caregiver expresses the problem. Valle (1998) first used the phrase "listening with a culturally attuned third ear" when assessing culturally diverse dementia caregivers (p. 123). "Listening with a culturally attuned third ear" helps the social worker begin to gather problem-related information identifying beliefs, values, and impressions within the ethnocultural context (Valle 1998). By attentive listening, the social worker is better able to understand the caregiver's unique perspective of the problem, and the cultural responses of significant members including the caregiver, the family member and the perspective of other essential kin regarding the problem. The social worker is seeking to identify the family members in the family constellation that may be of support to the caregiver by providing concrete help such as respite care, shared care responsibilities for a few hours or for a couple of days a week, transportation assistance, financial support, or other familial social support services.

The social worker is also seeking to understand the family protocol to see if there are issues that are impacting the caregiver or the care recipient. Finally, family relationships and care concerns are identified that may be causing additional problems to the caregiver because they are causing obstacles to self-care or appropriate care for the afflicted family member. Because often the family knows little about the disease, the lack of knowledge and understanding may cause other family members stress and worry from underlying cultural misunderstandings. The caregiver might have to also provide care for other family members in order to help them cope with the changes in the afflicted family member. This adds an additional layer of care and communication to the already-taxed caregiver who finds it necessary to split his or her energy, attention and care toward other family members in need of assistance. Helping other members of the family to understand the meaning of the disease, the symptoms, and symptom management can overwhelm the caregiver. It is here that the social worker can best assess ways to accommodate the unique culture-of-origin traditions and perspectives identified in the family resource domain. The culturally competent social worker becomes directly aware of the reality of the family relationships and protocols, and the accompanying impact of the dementing illness on the family system. By assessing the family situations, the social worker is able respond to multiple requests for services coming from family members by using various skills including counseling, education, and family interventions via an intercultural engagement perspective to assess strengths and resilience in order to provide support for the caregiver, the afflicted family member, and other significant family members or fictive kin.

The fourth domain seeks to identify *caregiver community resource (CGCR)* involvement or lack thereof in the provision of support for caregiver self-care (CGSC), support for family member dementia care (FMDC), and/or for caregiver family resources (CGFR) domains. In this domain the social worker explores the caregiver's knowledge of community resources, and the interest of the caregiver, afflicted family member, and family in seeking and using community resources.

Often what occurs when discussing this domain is that the caregiver offers information regarding community resource-engagement history in terms of agencies that have been successfully or unsuccessfully contacted for assistance, and the caregiver's perspective regarding engagement success or lack of success. If it does not happen naturally in the discussion, the social worker should actively engage the caregiver in this discussion. The social worker should explore how the community resource, agency, hospital, or institution was perceived as being helpful or harmful to the issue, person, or situation involved, paying close attention to note the reason for the caregiver's inability to access community services. Basically this is a discussion of what has worked and what has not worked in service access and delivery. It is essential for the social worker to identify if language, culture, ethnicity, or race prevented access to care services on the part of the community agency or from the perspective of the caregiver or family.

Costs not only in terms of finance but also in terms of time, effort, and family scheduling or conflict because of proscribed family roles are also important to identify in order to reduce these issues and increase service utilization. While challenging, pinpointing ways in which services can be tailored to meet the specific needs of the caregiver can also be cost effective, especially if the caregiver and social worker can work together to develop a list of helpful services that might be used to deal constructively with problems.

The discussion should be designed to focus on how much the caregiver thinks the service is able to enhance the quality of life for all persons involved. Efforts to identify gaps between what caregivers identify as service needs and what the agency provides in terms of service availability should be noted. The social work role is to listen without judgment and to allow each caregiver to find a solution that best fits their cultural and personal value situation. In a family that places a high premium on caring, concern, and mutual support, the social worker can further convey that exploring this community resource history can provide essential information to make services more accessible as well as culturally appropriate and acceptable to the caregiver, the afflicted family member, and to the family kinship network.

If the caregiver, afflicted family member, or family has experienced a negative interaction with a community agency(s), the social worker will have to assist in the processing of this critical event before moving on to the help-seeking/help-receiving problem-solving actions. This is the point in which step two of the process (thoughts and feelings) provides the opportunity to use cognitive behavioral theory to assist the caregiver in communicating the painful past experience to examine the feelings and thoughts associated with the negative event and the meaning given to the experience. The social worker's role should be to encourage the caregiver to share his or her story and to convey the thoughts, feelings, and meaning given to the situation. Next, the social worker should assess the ability of the caregiver to let go and move forward. Some caregivers may find that the experience was too painful and may not be ready to try again and reconnect with an agency. The social worker will have to work with these caregivers to help them begin to make a paradigm shift enabling them to begin to think differently about the situation in order to change the outcome. However, if that is not an option at this time, the social worker may have to identify an alternate service agency or community resource for the problem situation. What is key is that the social worker ensures that the caregiver receives the needed help by referring the caregiver to an alternate but appropriate agency if necessary.

Other caregivers may simply need to process the incident with the social workers by sharing what occurred, how they felt, and the meaning given to it. Once this has been done, some caregivers may feel ready to develop a new relationship with the agency. Not all caregivers will be at the same place in terms of the ability to reengage with an agency after a hurt that has been felt very deeply. If that is the case, the social worker should not force the caregiver to work through and let go. Rather, the social worker should meet the caregiver where the caregiver is, and value client self-determination. Respect can go a long way in solidifying the relationship with the caregiver. Encouraging the caregiver to identify the right time to get past the issue with the agency and offering to help in the future facilitates the birth of new reasoning in the caregiver by allowing time and space to rethink the possibility of cognitive change. It also enables the social worker to move away from a procedural prescriptive approach to serving the unique needs of the individual ethnic caregiver. If the social worker and caregiver have established an appropriate working relationship, the caregiver will not be apt to experience discomfort in saying no to the social worker, nor will either think it inappropriate to say no if the caregiver thinks that is best. Again, the right balance in power between the social worker and caregiver facilitates the collaborative work in the therapeutic relationship tailoring the problem-solving approach to the caregiver's need.

Most caregivers need a combination of informal and formal community services to help them provide care for the ill family member. Ethnic caregivers tend to rely longer on the family and kin network to help and will utilize community resources such as in-home, respite, and other community care and health care services only when absolutely necessary. However, this may not be the case for all ethnic caregivers. Some may prefer or need specific formal service care assistance. For that reason, social workers should provide a variety of care options just in case the caregiver decides to consider these options. Social workers should also provide guidance to caregivers regarding how to access resource guides that describe a variety of appropriate services available for dementia care in their community.

LEARNING THE PROBLEM IDENTIFICATION PROCESS

I have often used an overflowing laundry basket metaphor to describe to caregivers their feeling of being overwhelmed by the sheer size of the mountain of laundry. One needs the content in the laundry basket, which is, after all, necessary, useful, and has meaning and purpose. But when the garments are all intertwined and mixed together, it is often difficult to see what they are, whose they are, and where one garment ends and the other begins. Another reaction to the overflowing laundry basket is a sense of feeling intimidated, because the job of sorting through everything looks daunting. Just looking at the job, time, and effort required may cause dismay for some. It is important to partialize the problem into more manageable pieces. As the social worker helps the caregiver to identify the problem and to sort the problem to place it in the specific domain, the caregiver will perceive the problem as more manageable. The hope is that by partializing the problem, the caregiver will be less intimidated and become more invested in problem solving as clearer problem specificity is given to the problem-solving process. Once the problems have been identified, the social worker then seeks to enter the culture frame by engaging the Black or Latino caregiver in identifying the culture-specific values, skills, activities, and resources. Understanding the caregiver experience will provide greater insight into the caregiver's personal and interpersonal cultural perspectives and considerations that are important for the caregiver to proceed. Exploring the caregiver's need to provide cultural perspective to the problem-solving process normalizes the process and significantly increases the caregiver's cultural empowerment in the problem-solving intervention relationship with the social worker.

The social worker should make every effort to encourage the caregiver to take a proactive role in decision making throughout the process, which in some cases may be experienced as culturally dystonic. This is another reason why the social worker and caregiver need to jointly consider the impact of the culturally constructed experience care process. It should not be generally assumed that the caregiver is functioning in a culturally syntonic framework and is therefore capable of identifying and assessing generational differences. If the caregiver indicates that cultural values are important, then identifying problem-solving options helpful to dementia care that are a good fit with the culture will further encourage the caregiver to be active problem-solving efforts.

However, it is important to note that often caregivers convey problems the same way they experience them, which is often intertwined and within the context of the caregiving narrative. The social worker should take notes as appropriate, and should explain to the caregiver that note taking is a part of the process to ensure active listening and understanding of the caregiver problems, and enables the social worker to highlight issues and address the problems the caregiver conveys. Finally, note taking helps to decrease the need for the caregiver to have repeat information. Ethnic caregivers are generally interested in knowing what is being written so it is best that the social worker take the lead and explain the procedure to decrease concern about what is being written down and why. Sitting in close proximity to the caregiver also helps the client see what is written and often helps the client alter perceptions if there is concern about documentation. This added sensitivity communicated by the social worker conveys respect to the caregiver who may have experienced less sensitivity with providers in the past.

The four domains (A–D) are discussed next in linear order for clarity. Refer to Table 7.1 in this chapter; the problems identified in this section will be noted vertically in the problem domain sections. The six horizontal columns will show the six-steps in the cognitive behavioral problem-solving self-efficacy process that the social worker is helping the caregiver to learn (see Chapter 4). The rationale is that as the social worker repeats the six-step process with the caregiver, the caregiver will make a paradigm shift, learning and implementing the process.

COMPLETING THE PROBLEM-SOLVING PLAN

Once the initial client and social worker introductions are compete and the social work role is clarified, the social worker gives the caregiver an opportunity to discuss what has brought him or her to the social worker for assistance. This sets the tone for the next step where the social work role is succinctly reviewed with the caregiver, and the caregiver role is clarified in preparation for engagement in the helping relationship. If the caregiver agrees to accept the intervention with the specified role responsibilities, the social worker provides a brief explanation of ways in which caregivers have been helped to acquire skills in problem solving by focusing on specific domain problems. The social worker uses a blank problem-solving form to refer to as they work to clarify the identified problems and how the problems will be addressed. Next the social worker introduces the problem-solving plan form and describes the A–D problem domains noted on the form with the caregiver. The social worker explains that while most problems that caregivers experience seem to overlap and cause multiple concerns, many problems can be placed into one of the four domains in order to identify the context of the problem. In the beginning it is important for the social worker to be patient and to help the caregiver orient into the agency, the work with the social worker, and the problem-solving paradigm. For most caregivers, this problem-solving method requires new learning. Kindness can go a long way in helping the caregiver engage with the social worker. Social workers must be open to ways in which the caregiver presents the ethno cultural family member group, as the collective coping abilities of family members and fictive kin may be involved in diverse ways in the care of the family member. First impressions are important and lasting. Beginnings often influence future encounters. Therefore, social workers should not rush this beginning phase, especially when seeking to assess what is and what is not culture and to understand the caregiver's cultural expectations around the help-seeking and help-receiving practices.

Using a blank problem-solving plan form, the social worker explains each of the six steps of the process. By clarifying the caregiver's participation as essential in communicating the necessary information and the required action for each step in the problem-solving process, the caregiver and social worker together learn and understand the extent and scope of each problem and the impact the problem is having on the caregiver. Together both learn how the caregiver is thinking and feeling about the problem (cognitive) and how the causes and effects have led toward inaction or specific maladaptive or unsuccessful action (behavioral). In the brainstorming step, the overall social work strategy is to validate the caregiver's participation by conveying genuine respect toward the caregiver and the afflicted family member. This will foster a culturally attuned understanding and will encourage the caregiver to convey problem-solving ideas and resources without fear of shame, embarrassment, or judgment by the social work professional.

WORKING THROUGH THE PROBLEM-SOLVING PLAN

The most effective use of the problem-solving plan is to enter information left-to-right beginning with the domain. With social work assistance the caregiver is guided through the problem-identification process in order to help the caregiver find key words or phrases that enable the caregiver to identify which of the four domains best describes and fits the problem. Once the first step is completed, the social worker moves horizontally to the next step in the problem-solving process until all six steps have been completed and the required information has been obtained from the caregiver. By defining clear boundaries for each domain problem, the caregiver is able to identify how the problem will be addressed and who will be involved in the problem-solving process apart from him-/herself.

GETTING THE INFORMATION FROM THE CAREGIVER AND WORKING THROUGH THE PLAN FORM

If the social worker presents the activity of filling out the form simply as "information gathering," the caregiver is likely to understand and to cooperate easily. It is important for the social worker to be aware that obtaining a complete picture of the problem requires patience and kindness in order to keep the caregiver from feeling blamed for the problems. Often caregivers perceive themselves as walking a tightrope between doing what they think is right, doing what everyone who is close to and cares for the afflicted family member thinks should be done, and adhering to cultural values, beliefs, and traditions. The initial meetings are aimed at understanding the caregiver and the problems experienced. Therefore, the social work effort should be a balance between the need to get to know the caregiver, to building the working relationship, and to understanding the root of all the difficulties surrounding each of the identified problems including the cultural aspects.

WHERE THE SOCIAL WORKER NEEDS TO HELP

Some caregivers may not initially be cooperative and may object to disclosing personal and private information. Others may be reluctant to violate cultural norms and values. Still other caregivers may be experiencing a sociocultural-based crisis such as poverty, legal issues or some other combination of embarrassing difficulties. If the social worker does not know enough about the cultural norms and values, sociocultural issues, or the disease process, the social worker will likely feel backed into a corner and forced to talk the caregiver into engaging in the process. This may come across to the caregiver as unconvincing, and sounding pressured and/or defensive. This is not a comfortable situation for either the social worker or the caregiver. Therefore, it is important for the social worker prepare in advance by doing research about the caregiver's cultural norms and values and about the disease process. By being aware of the possible risks associated with the information-gathering task, the social worker can take the lead and explain the initial discomfort that the caregiver might experience in the beginning, but can also note that the social worker is prepared to help the caregiver maintain cultural values and norms by fostering information gathering and problem-solving strategies that would be culturally appropriate. It is here that professional humility, respect, and empathic attunement skills are essential for social workers in order to communicate a genuine interest in helping and an openness to gaining a better understanding about the ethnic caregiver's experience. Dealing with such challenges are a critical and demanding point in the information-gathering task, but if handled professionally, overcoming the challenges will help to establish the necessary problem-solving working alliance.

BEING AWARE OF HOW PROBLEM SOLVING IS DEFINED BY CULTURAL GROUP

The intent of the problem-solving process described in this text is to focus the caregiver on each step of the problem-solving process rather than allowing the caregiver to focus on the success or failure dualistic thinking. Dualistic success-or-failure thinking can lead caregivers to a feeling of inadequacy and may cause the caregiver to delay, avoid, or refuse to try to resolve the problems for fear of making mistakes. This state is often worse for caregivers than failure itself because it may paralyze the caregiver, resulting in the problems increasing or worsening due to lack of action. Dualistic thinking can also cause anxiety and stress, which will impacting caregiver's health. Hence, fear of failing has more pernicious effects than failure itself. Therefore the social worker's first step is to assess the caregiver's problem-solving approach or avoidance behavior and thinking in terms of the fear of failure, worthlessness, anxiety, or basic inadequacy.

While there are significant adverse life conditions and circumstances that affect portions of the Black and Latino caregiving population that represent significant challenges and have potential for negative consequences, it is important that social workers refrain from identifying ethnic cultural caregivers with the sociocultural problems that they face and recognize that ethnic cultural caregivers are capable of change, adaptation, and resilience in response to internal and external demands of life and of caring for a dementia-afflicted family member. The reality of sociocultural problems—both historical and current—and their effects on many ethnic caregiving families cannot be forgotten, ignored, or denied. Social work ethics and cultural competence perspectives mandate that social workers adopt an attitude of respect for ethnic caregivers' possession of strengths and capabilities to cope with these challenges (NASW, 2007). It is crucial that social workers think critically about the individual caregiver and the vicissitudes of their unique caregiving context when seeking to understand, interpret, and assess the family phenomena. To do less is to be professionally and ethically irresponsible.

WHO ARE THE OTHERS THAT THE CAREGIVER MAY SEEK OUT AS PRIMARY PROBLEM-SOLVERS (FAMILY, FRIENDS, CHURCH)?

Unlike many White middle-class families, Black and Latino families often have a wellspring of family, friends, and church members who represent a significant source of problem-solving resources and support. Both cultures, regardless of immigration status, have been purported to value interdependence and extended family values associated with specific family practices (Hill, McBride Murry, & Anderson, 2005, p. 33). Understanding the family structure (i.e., married, partnered, widowed, single parent households), context (i.e., urban or suburban, senior housing), and socioeconomic level (upper class, middle class, lower class, or poverty level) informs the social worker about the particular caregiving context and the nature and functioning of the family.

Identifying factors such as the particular role assigned to members within families (familismo) and to friends (fictive kin) is a means to identifying the formation of patterns of association, assistance, and social support. Church or spiritual relationships within the ethnic community and cultural context that affect caregiver functioning is another important asset. "The church, the most prominent social institution second only to the family, continues as a major source of support for the African American community" (Carlton-LaNey, 1999, p. 319).

Understanding family, friends, church, or spiritual contexts, neighborhoods, health, community, and macroeconomic factors and interactions by systems, even though well removed from ethnic caregivers, must be understood so that the social worker and caregiver can use the resources in problem solving. The degree that these systems provide support resources and/or protective factors can help facilitate positive outcomes. Conversely the factors from these same systems that impinge on the caregiver by creating additional risk factors and stress must be identified and taken seriously in the contextual analysis and assessment when seeking to advance the ethnic problem-solving process.

DEFINING PROBLEMS PRECISELY AND CONCISELY

In previous chapters communication styles were discussed. Here, processing styles will be discussed to learn factors that need to be taken into consideration when seeking to define problems precisely and concisely.

Processing styles are important because if the social worker is not aware of the differences in processing styles, he or she may miss important problems and cultural communication cues, or may try to make the caregiver communicate problems from the social worker's own communication template, which may be entirely different from the caregiver's style. Lack of awareness regarding communication and processing styles may cause unenlightened social workers to misunderstand caregivers who need extra assistance in order to identify problems for step one and talk about thoughts and feelings for step two of the problem-solving process. The misunderstanding may also result in the caregiver either successfully avoiding the problem-solving process or may inadvertently cause the caregiver to experience some discomfort in this step of the process. As mentioned previously, often caregivers convey problems the same way they experience them, which is often intertwined and within the context of the caregiving narrative or story.

If the caregiver is an "inner processor" one that experiences problems more inwardly and is more inner oriented or introverted, the caregiver may tend to process problems and thoughts and feelings inwardly as well, and therefore may require more time to think, work through, and process problems thoughts and feelings before being able to talk about them (Dixon, 2007, p. 198). This does not mean that the caregiver cannot engage in the problem-solving process; it means that culturally competent social workers need to be cognizant of this difference in processing style and be proactive, viewing it as a strength and validating the caregiver's processing style. Social workers can also be flexible about the time needed to engage in each step of the discourse by being guided by the caregiver's processing style rather than insisting that the caregiver supplies all the needed information up front, so to speak, and moves forward according to the social worker's timing.

On the other hand, "outer processers" are more apt to talk about problems, thoughts, and feelings as they work through them (Dixon, 2007). The culturally competent social worker will need to think critically about what particular processing style the ethnic caregiver is presenting and, similar to the previous example, view it as a strength and validate it. These caregivers may also require additional time in order to fully tell their story with the detail they perceive necessary to fulfill their processing style. Again, social work timing flexibility is key in order to allow the caregiver to move to the next step in a culturally appropriate manner.

Identifying the particular processing style and allowing the appropriate time may not be the only social work challenge when seeking to assist the caregiver in defining the problem precisely and concisely. Teasing out information from caregivers who might be "avoiders" may also be challenging for social workers. "Avoiders are people who do not deal with problems at all-internally or externally...because working through their thoughts and especially their feelings might open wounds...and cause them to have to deal with themselves and or/the other person" (Dixon, 2007, p. 198). They may request assistance, but may function in denial about the problem realities and/or may just not want to assume the problem-solving responsibility. The skilled social worker will have to employ additional clinical skills using insight-oriented perspectives in order to engage and sustain the caregiver in the problem-solving process. These caregivers may also require more time to work through past wounds, learn to rely less on the use of the avoidance psychic defense, and learn to employ a more adaptive psychic defense in order to engage in the problem-solving process.

Social workers should use various strategies to help the caregiver. First, social workers should be self-aware in order to employ the skill of use of self in the problem-solving process. As noted in previous chapters, the one constant element in the problem-solving process with the caregiver is the social work role. Therefore social workers should balance empathic attunement with a positive, confident, and enthusiastic attitude in order to communicate hope that even though the afflicted family member's intrinsic dementing disease cannot be controlled, decreased, or stopped, the caregiver's problems can. By learning this multiple-step process, the caregiver can define the relationships between the problem and the particular domain, and then identify solutions the caregiver can use to begin to control, decrease, or resolve the problems. Using inductive reasoning, asking questions, and using probing prompts when it is appropriate to encourage caregivers to retrieve information from their experiences and from the familial, sociocultural, and environmental systems context are all strategies social workers can employ to help the caregiver define the problem precisely and concisely. By tapping into previous problem-solving knowledge, experiences, and strategies that have worked in the past, and by identifying the relevant starting point or conditions for the problem help define the problem concisely.

CASE EXAMPLE

Using the case example at the beginning of this chapter, the following illustration shows what the social worker and caregiver interaction and the sorted problems might look like when placed within the four domains of care. The social worker may find that there may be multiple issues identified as fitting within a particular domain. If that is the case, it is suggested that the social worker and the caregiver prioritize the problems according to what the caregiver decides should be the priority unless an issue of the caregiver's or the dementia-afflicted family member's safety arises. Then every effort should be made to communicate to resolve the safety issue as soon as possible. If the social worker is unsure of the safety risk, it is important to explore the situation fully with the caregiver to establish a clear safety or risk assessment to ensure that the required critical care assistance is provided. As in all social work interventions, safety takes precedence. In this case the social worker would set aside the problem-solving and four-domain procedure to focus on what is necessary to ensure safety for all. The next section provides the case examples sorted into domains using the subjective experience as communicated by the caregiver to the social worker.

CAREGIVER SELF-CARE (CGSC)

I don't know what to do. I don't know what to tell them. I feel worried all the time. We all need help. I can't work anymore. I can't go to the school. I can't do anything but stay with her at home. I feel sick sometimes, but don't go to the doctor. I can't take her with me on the bus. I can't leave her at home. I'm worrying about everyone all the time. I can't sleep. I don't rest. I wake up a lot. I can't go to church. I miss my friends from work and from church. I am too embarrassed to tell them.

Summary: The caregiver feels helpless, hopeless, stressed, tired, lonely and alone. She seems to be under the mistaken impression that work only involves outside of the home paid work. The social worker should help the caregiver understand the meaning of her new role as caregiver and the work involved, and to explore ways in which the experience in this role has changed and is currently impacting her life. Additionally the importance of self-care should be explained to encourage the caregiver to take care of herself, to rest and relax, and to reconnect with family and friends. The caregiver should be encouraged to see her doctor for a complete physical to rule out any physical issues and to give peace of mind regarding her own health. If she does not currently have a physician, the social worker should help her identify a physician and encourage her to make an appointment as soon possible. Finally, the social worker should encourage the caregiver to re-engage with her friends, coworkers, and church members in order to help her feel better emotionally and spiritually and re-energize the faith strength she verbalized. The social worker can engage the caregiver in role-playing activity to help her get over her concerns or fears about discussing the illness with others and provide her with answers in anticipation of questions that may come from coworkers, friends, church members or others in a way that is comfortable for her.

FAMILY MEMBER WITH DEMENTIA SYMPTOM MANAGEMENT (FMDC)

Adriana needs supervision. She cannot be left home alone nor can she be in public or use public transportation due to incontinence issues. Adriana forgets to eat. Her confusion and memory loss has increased. She doesn't understand her boys, which is causing conflicts. Her behavior becomes agitated and out of control.

Summary: Family Member with Dementia symptoms are as follows: incontinence issues, increased confusion, memory loss, forgetting to eat, conflicts, agitated and out of control behavior, isolation at home. The social worker should refer the caregiver to the physician caring for the family member for an updated physical and assessment for possible medication to help manage memory and behavior. The caregiver should advise the physician of incontinence, eating, and any other physical, mental, and emotional symptoms observed in Adriana to rule out other causes. If there is a language issue, the social worker should either arrange for an interpreter to accompany the caregiver or teach the caregiver to advocate for the interpreter.

CARE CAREGIVER FAMILY RESOURCES (CGFR)

I think she just misses other family in Peru. She has three sisters and many other family members in Peru. We have a big family. The boys [age 11 and 13] want to help. We want to help her but don't know what to do.

Summary: There are family members in Peru who are possible resources and are interested in helping. It is a big family with many possible resources. The boys and the caregiver and husband also want to help. The caregiver should be encouraged to consider family members as resources for care especially since family members are concerned about her. Another option is for the caregiver and social worker to determine if returning to Peru would be in Adriana's best interest. The family should be encouraged to discuss a variety of care options in the United States and in Peru or other locations if family is available.

CAREGIVER COMMUNITY RESOURCES (CGCR)

I speak and understand some English. The boys go to school. They want to help her but don't know what Alzheimer's is. My husband and I don't know either. I don't go to a doctor. The church helps me. I miss my friends from work and from church. I am too embarrassed to tell them.

Summary: The social worker should discuss ways the caregiver and family can access information about Alzheimer's disease in the Spanish language they can understand. This will help the family understand the disease process, know what to do, and how to help themselves, each other, and Adriana. Knowing more about Alzheimer's disease will also help all to understand (and explain) the disease to correct any misunderstanding and to reduce shame. The social worker should identify resources available for the caregiver to pay for various services for the afflicted family member. Also, the social worker should help the caregiver with information on available respite and day care resources, as well as in-home or home health aid resources.

The following example of the completed problem-solving plan in Table 7.1 illustrates the content in each of the four domains noted earlier and steps one to six of the problem-solving process. The content is simple, clear, and self-explanatory. By entering the information into the required sections on the form, there is less risk for the social worker and the caregiver to make different interpretations about the problems, proposed solutions, available resources, or how or when the problem-solving plan will be implemented. Here communication is transparent, and easily verifiable by both parties. In using the form there is also less risk of the caregiver feeling he or she has done something wrong in communicating the information. Because it is a required form used as a helping tool, it is much easier for the ethnic caregiver to view it as just that, a tool to assist in obtaining a complete picture of the problem and the impact of the problem on the caregiver and ill relative. It places some of the attention on the use of the tool itself and less on the disclosure of information that might make the caregiver uncomfortable.

TABLE 7.1   Caregiver Problem-Solving Plan

Caregiver Name			Social Worker		Date:
1. Problem	2. Thoughts/feelings	3. Causes/effects	4. Possible solutions	5. Resources available	6. Problem-solving plan implemented
A—CGSC "I don't know what to do, need help, can't go to doctor, school, work, or church"	Helpless/hopeless, stressed, worried lonely, alone	Tired, sick, can't sleep, can't rest	See doctor, get physical exam	Church members, friends	Contact doctor, make appointment ASAP, set action date
B—CGDC Unsafe actions, conflicts, supervision necessary, incontinence	Confused thoughts, memory loss increasing	Agitated/out of control behavior, forgets to eat	See doctor for updated physical medication assessment and memory exam	Church members and friends available to drive both to doctor	Contact doctor, make appointment ASAP, set action date
C—CGFR Sons (aged 11 and 13) want to help, need disease information Caregiver's husband and family in Peru also want to help	Don't know what to do, don't know about the disease, get worried, mother gets agitated or is unsafe, family members in Peru worried	Sons are stressed, worried, having difficulty in school with grades and behavior	Have family members come to visit and help with care, support sons and caregiver	Family in the US. and Peru Sons with help of family	Caregiver contacting family in US and Peru to ask for members to come and help, set action date Getting social worker to help sons
D—CGCR Language barrier, needs Alzheimer's disease information in Spanish, needs doctor, misses friends from work and church	Feels embarrassed about language barriers, lack of knowledge about dementia illness, and conflicts with familismo cultural values regarding privacy, family honor, protecting family, caring for family values	Isolated and lonely, unable to seek help from doctor, community resources, church, or friends	Identify bilingual doctor/clinic and make appointment for self and cousin, discuss ways to adhere to cultural values with social worker and family	Social worker, church, community clinic, husband's physician	Will contact clinic in community to locate bilingual doctor, will ask pastor in church for help, Alzheimer's association for Spanish disease information for boys— set action date

As mentioned earlier, culturally competent social workers are aware that communication styles for ethnic caregivers are often not linear but rather circular and may include a great deal of essential detail, hence the need to take notes. When completing the form what often works best is to use the notes taken during the information-gathering meeting to fill out the form with the caregiver. This will lessen the challenging effort to record and track the content while the caregiver is providing information. Using an erasable writing tool also helps, as often the problem is perceived to be in one domain when in fact it is better identified in another domain.

EXAMPLE OF A COMPLETED PROBLEM-SOLVING PLAN

After completing the assessment process the social worker and the caregiver together engage in identifying the problems for work. The social worker allows the caregiver to take the lead, encouraging the caregiver to state the reason the caregiver is seeking assistance. Identifying problems for work can be challenging if the caregiver has avoided the problem issue or is facing a fear of failure in problem solving. Some caregivers may have to overcome fear of failure and irrational beliefs related to their perceived ability to resolve problems. Additionally, some caregivers may have the irrational notion that humans have value only based on their accomplishments and that if they lack some competence or adequacy, then they are worthless and therefore might as well give up. Other caregivers may attribute their self-worth to achievement and success measured by successful resolution of the problems at hand. The problem with all of these examples of irrational thinking is that dementia care problems are, for the most part, very much a part of the caregiving reality and many problems are not easily resolved. Some problems, such as adding locks to prevent a wandering family member from leaving the house in the middle of the night, do have an immediate solution.

Other problems like the behavior disregulation demonstrated by the afflicted family member when the lock cannot be opened are caused by emotional changes that occur in the afflicted family member's brain as the dementing process progresses. These intrinsic problems emerge subtly and gradually, and over time tend to intensify. As the level of intensity increases, new strategies need to be implemented at each level to either manage or resolve the problem. If the caregiver's goal is to achieve complete resolution of the problem immediately or when the first symptom emerges, then generally speaking the caregiver may have some false thinking that is certain to cause the caregiver to experience some serious disappointments in problem solving.

Social workers play a pivotal role in the lives of caregivers and their afflicted relatives not only in teaching the problem-solving process, but also in validating the caregiver reality and validating the learning caregivers are accomplishing. This problem-solving intervention is crucial especially when caregivers experience multiple domain issues and emotional overload. The overwhelming feeling experienced by the caregiver can be the result of the various individual role requirements and conflicts including the following: (1) the increasing care need for self, family, and afflicted family member, (2) the demands being made on the caregiver by the various systems that the caregiver interacts with or fails to interact with, and (3) insufficient disease knowledge. Added to this are cultural values and expectations that the caregiver is required to function within, and the caregiver can't but feel overwhelmed. Hence, helping caregivers effectively sort through this quagmire of problems improves coping, enables caregivers to understand the cultural components that may be influencing the problems, and may foster problem-solving success. A copy of the completed problem-solving plan can be given to the caregiver to use as a reference and reminder in between sessions to help implement the problem-solving plan effectively.

REFERENCES

Bandura, A. (1991). Self-efficacy mechanism in physiological activation and health-promoting behavior. In J. Madden IV (Ed.), *Neurobiology of learning, emotion and affect* (pp. 229–269). New York: Raven Press.

Bandura, A. (1977). Self-efficacy: Toward a unifying theory of behavior change. *Psychological Reports, 84*, 191–215.

Bass, D. M., Clark P. A., Looman, W. J., McCarthy, C. A., & Eckert, S. (2003). The Cleveland Alzheimer's managed care demonstration: Outcomes after 12 months of implementation. *The Gerontologist, 43*, 73–85.

Beck, A. (1976). *Cognitive therapy on emotional disorders.* New York: International Universities Press.

Brandell, J. (1997). *Theory and practice in clinical social work.* New York: The Free Press.

Carlton-LaNey, I. (1999). African American social work pioneers' response to need. *Social Work, 44*(4), 311–321.

Compton, B. R., & Galaway, B. (1989). *Social work processes* (4th ed.). Belmont, CA: Wadsworth Publishing.

Cuéllar, J. (1990). Aging and health Hispanic American elders. Stanford Geriatric Education Center, *Number 5 Ethnogeriatric Reviews.*

Dilworth-Anderson, P., Williams, I. C., & Williams S. W. (2001). Elderly of African descent. In L. K. Olson (Ed.), *Age through ethnic lenses: Caring for the elderly in a multicultural society* (pp. 95–102). New York: Rowman & Littlefield.

Dixon, P. (2007). *African American relationships, marriages, and families.* New York: Routledge Taylor & Francis.

Ellis, A. (1962). *Reason and emotion in psychotherapy.* Secaucus, NJ: Lyle Stuart Publishers.

Fortinsky, R. H., Kercher, K., & Burant, C. J. (2002) Measurement and correlates of family caregiver self-efficacy for managing dementia. *Aging & Mental Health, 6,* 153–160.

Fortinsky, R. H., Unson, C. G., & Garcia, R. I. (2002). Helping family caregivers by linking primary care physicians with community-based dementia care services, *Dementia, 1,* 227–240.

Furstenberg, A. L., & Rounds, K. A. (1995, December). Self-efficacy as a target for so-cial work intervention. *Families in Society: The Journal of Contemporary Human Services,* pp. 587–595.

Giachello, A., Bell, R., Aday, L., & Anderson, R. (1983). Uses of the 1980 census for Hispanic health services research. *American Journal of Public Health, 73,* 266–274.

Goldstein, E. G., & Noonan, M. (1999). *Short-term treatment and social work practice: An integrative perspective.* New York: The Free Press.

González Sanders, D. J. (2004) *Theoretical perspective concept map: Cognitive behavioral, prob-lem solving and self-efficacy process.* Unpublished theoretical concept map document.

Haley, W. E., Roth, D., Coleton, M. I., Ford, G. R., West, C. A., Collins, R. P., et al. (1996). Appraisal, coping, and social support as mediators of well-being in Black and White family caregivers of patients with Alzheimer's disease. *Journal of Consulting and Clinical Psychology, 64,* 121–129.

Hayes-Bautista, D. (1983). On comparing studies of different raza populations. *American Journal of Public Health, 73,* 274–276.

Heppner, P. P., & Hillerbrand, E. T., (1991). Problem-solving training: Implications for remedial and preventive training. In C. R. Snyder & D. R. Forsyth (Eds.), *Handbook of social and clinical psychology: The health perspective* (pp. 681–698). Elmsford, NY: Pergamon.

Hill, N. E., McBride Murry, V., & Anderson, V. D. (2005). Sociocultural contexts of African American families. In V. C. McLoyd, N. E. Hill, & K. A. Dodge (Eds.), *African American family life: Ecological and cultural diversity.* New York: The Guilford Press.

James, I. A. (1999). Using a cognitive rationale to conceptualize anxiety in people with dementia. *Behavioral and Cognitive Psychotherapy, 27,* 345–351.

Marriott, A., Donaldson, C., Tarrier, N., & Burns, A. (2000). Effectiveness of cognitive-behavioral family intervention in reducing the burden of care in carers of patients with Alzheimer's disease. *British Journal of Psychiatry, 176,* 557–562.

Olson, L. K. (Ed.). (2001). *Age through ethnic lenses: Caring for the elderly in a multicultural society.* New York: Rowman & Littlefield.

Pearce, J. (2002). Systemic therapy. In J. Hepple, J. Pearce, & P. Wilkinson (Eds.), *Psychological therapies with older people: Developing treatments for effective practice* (pp. 77–102). New York: Taylor & Francis.

Pearlin, L. I., Mullan, J. T., Semple, S. J., & Skaff, M. M. (1990). Caregiving and the stress process: An overview of concepts and their measures. *The Gerontologist, 30*(5), 583–594.

Perlman, H. (1970). The problem-solving method in social casework. In R. Roberts & R. Nee (Eds.), *Theories of social casework* (pp.129–180). Chicago: University of Chicago Press.

Perlman, H. H. (1957). *Social casework: A problem-solving process.* Chicago, IL: University of Chicago Press.

Perlman, H. H. (1979). *Relationship: The heart of helping people.* Chicago, IL: University of Chicago Press.

Sanchez, C. D. (2001). Puerto Rican elderly. In L. K. Olson (Ed.), *Age through ethnic lenses: Caring for the elderly in a multicultural society* (pp. 86–94). New York: Rowman & Littlefield.

Spark, G. M., & Brody, E. M. (1970). The aged are family members. *Family Process, 9,* 195–210.

Toseland, R. W., & Rivas, R. (1984). *An introduction to group work practice.* New York: Macmillan Publishing.

Toseland, R. W., Rossiter, C. M., Peak, T., & Smith, G. C. (1990). Comparative effectiveness of individual and group interventions to support family caregivers. *Social Work,* 35(3), 209–217.

Valle, R. (1998). *Caregiving across cultures: Working with dementing illness and ethnically diverse populations.* Washington, DC: Taylor & Francis.

Wilkinson, P. (2002). Cognitive behavioral therapy. In J. Hepple, J. Pearce, & P. Wilkinson (Eds.), *Psychological therapies with older people.* New York: Taylor & Francis.

Weintraub, S., & Mesulam, M. (1993). Four neuropsychological profiles in dementia. In F. Boller, et al. (Eds.), *Handbook of neuropsychology* (Vol. 8, pp. 253–282). Amsterdam, Netherlands: Elsevier Science.

8

Target Problems and Problem-Solving Goals

CASE EXAMPLE

I can't do it all. I feel burned out. I'm trying to keep sane but I am so sad and nervous. I'm afraid my mother has a brain tumor. I don't know what is wrong with her. Maybe her Alzheimer's disease is getting worse. What else would be causing her to pass out? I need to keep watch on her to catch her if she falls. I can't be with her all the time. I can't take her with me when I go to the store for groceries. I have high blood pressure that I think is worse now.

My stepbrothers don't talk to me and don't help. It is just me here with my mother. I am alone. They make me so angry. It hurts to see her sick, and not to be able to get my brothers to help. They haven't talked to me since I moved into my mother's house to take care of her in 2007 a few months after my stepfather died. She wasn't eating. She locked herself out of the house several times. The neighbors have helped us so much. Each time someone saw her they kept her at their house until I could get there. My brothers just left her alone. I could tell she had changed right away. But they didn't know. Not even my sisters-in-law. They work and are busy with their families. Sometimes I think they don't care at all. My father died in World War II. I was little and never really knew him.

My stepfather died in 2006. Everything changed after he died. Everybody got angry with me. Like they wanted me out of their life. But she is my mother and I love her. She is all I have. I tried talking with them but they just argue and yell at me. It upsets my mother so I don't ask them to come to the house anymore. My mother was an only child, so there is no other family for me. I am an only child too except for my stepsiblings. They have never accepted me. My skin is lighter like my mother's and they would always make fun of me because I was different and had a different last

231

*name. My stepfather loved me. He helped us all get along. Now I feel so
alone. I cook for my mother and make her eat or she won't eat. I'm so angry
at my siblings that I can't sleep. I worry all the time about everything.*

The adult daughter caregiver and her mother who has dementia were
both born in Brazil and moved to the United States when the caregiver
was 2 years old to live with her biological father's parents after her father
was killed in World War II. The caregiver self-identifies as a biracial
Black and Latina and is trilingual, speaking Spanish and Portuguese
fluently and some English. During their early years, mother and daughter (who never married) spent time both in Brazil and in the United
States until her mother met and married a Puerto Rican man and they
had four sons. The caregiver's four stepbrothers are married; two live
in the same town and two live in another state with their families. The
caregiver has always worked out of her home as a seamstress. After the
death of her stepfather in 2006 conflicts arose as the male siblings ques-
tioned her legal right to their parent's property. It was not until these
conflicts arose that the caregiver found out her mother and stepfather
had altered their will in 2001 to leave the house to the caregiver.

Because two brothers had married and moved out of state, she
recalls the parents assumed the other two would do the same. The caregiver believes that the parents left her the family home not only so that
the mother could remain in the home, but also because she is the only
daughter (step-daughter), had never married, and always kept an apartment nearby to assist her parents. The mother's fainting spells require
immediate medical evaluation and care and seem to be causing caregiver stress and insomnia possibly impacting the caregiver's blood pressure, another urgent medical issue. The caregiver worries all the time
about her mother falling and about her inability to help her mother and
control her own blood pressure.

SELECTING TARGET PROBLEMS AND
ESTABLISHING PROBLEM-SOLVING GOALS

This case study is provided to point out that ethnic family functioning is not always congenial and functioning purely out of familismo
or kin values. There are situations that can cause a rupture in family
interaction patterns creating adversarial battles, initially over roles and
responsibilities and later over attitudes of trust and respect. Family
members trying to convince, persuade, or cajole another family member

FIGURE 8.1. Ethnic Theoretical Perspective Concept Map: Cognitive Behavioral, Problem-Solving, and Self-Efficacy Process

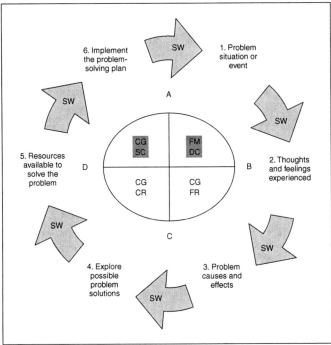

Problem-solving focus is on four domains of care: (A) CGSC—Caregiver self-care, (B) FMDC—Family member dementia care, (C) CGFR—Caregiver family resource, (D) CGCR—Caregiver community resource.

SW-Arrow flow (SW) represents role of the social worker relationship as the constant factor in the caregiver (CG) problem-solving process

1—Caregiver is experiencing high blood pressure, stress, inability to sleep at night because dementia-afflicted mother passes out and falls down.

2—Social worker helps caregiver to clarify the thoughts and feelings about her blood pressure, inability to sleep, and mother's passing out, and thoughts about this experience.

3—The problem causes and effects for CG are escalating blood pressure, stress, being tired, fatigue, inability to sleep at night, having to watch mother all the time to catch her if she passes out; causes and effects for ill mother are safety, hitting head when she falls or risk of injury.

4—Social worker and Black and Latino CG jointly explore ways to solve the problems.

5—SW & CG jointly set up a plan for each to see their own physician as soon as possible and arrange for an interpreter to help communicate.

6—Jointly CG and SW set a date to implement the problem-solving plan for CG: contact physician(s) that day and set urgent care appointment for both. CG instructed to tell the physician to evaluate blood pressure and to explain impact of caregiving role and mother's health issues. Takes mother to her physician to discuss frequent passing out, falling and hitting head. Physician hospitalizes mother to complete medical tests.

Black and Latino CG experiences relief and can rest while mother is hospitalized; feels she is complying with responsibility outlined in cultural values to care for mother with Alzheimer's disease. With the problem-solving plan successfully implemented, the Black and Latino family caregiver experiences empowerment and self-efficacy.

© 2011 d j gonzález sanders

into accepting the need to include other family members in property ownership or to remove herself from a bestowed parental gift has many cultural implications related to values, roles, and traditions, not to mention the high premium on caring, concern, and support for the afflicted mother. Hence, the need for a multilevel assessment of the caregiver, afflicted family member, and of the family functioning to understand the siblings' involvement in the presenting problems and the adversarial situation to enhance the family members' ability to help.

However, when selecting target problem for work, the *first priority* is to always target problems that are a *safety risk* for the caregiver or the ill relative. In the case example, the caregiver indicated her mother is passing out and she fears she will not always be there to catch her. The priority problem domain is *family member dementia care* (FMDC). Assessing safety for the Alzheimer's afflicted relative is the focus for the social worker. It is unclear if the physician has been told about the problem of the mother's fainting or passing out, so the social worker should clarify that with the caregiver. If the physician has not been advised, or if the physician needs to be re-contacted for an update, the social worker should help facilitate this. The *caregiver self-care* (CGSC) problem domain is also a priority because of the caregiver's escalating blood pressure. The six-step problem-solving process actions presented next provide a checklist to help the caregiver assess each problem domain and the problem-solving plan in an efficient manner.

LEARNING A NEW PROBLEM-SOLVING PROCESS

The major reason that this approach is ideal for ethnic caregivers is that it focuses on multiple, prime aspects of care that Helen Harris Perlman (1957) found essential to success when engaging in problem-solving casework. Brandell (1997) citing Perlman (1957) notes that the problem-solving approach seeks to "maintain the relationship on the basis of reality," cognizant of "their separate and realistic identities" focusing the work toward the goal of "a better adaptation between the client and his current problem-situation" (p. 41). Perlman's problem-solving model developed at the University of Chicago in the 1950s continues to be used today by social workers (Brandell, 1997).

The approach developed by Perlman (1957) is in fact timeless and the most appropriate model for ethnic caregivers whose goal is to provide loving care for their dementia-afflicted family member. It focuses on the here and now day-to-day problems of helping ill relatives suffering from the impact of memory loss illness in their lives. Perlman (1953) views the model as a "parallel to the normal problem-solving efforts of the ego" (p. 308–315).

As the memory loss disease progresses in the ill relative, the caregiver assumes more and more of the problem-solving task. Because the caregiver also has to resolve problems in his or her own life roles, the added level of problems originating from the ill relative's memory loss can result in significant challenges for the caregiver. Therefore, introducing a simple problem-solving approach to assist with the problem-solving tasks can help to significantly lessen the problem burden and psychic energy depletion in the caregiver and family.

A helpful analogy depicting the difference between a decreasing physical ability and a decreasing memory capacity can be to consider someone who is gradually and progressively losing the ability to balance properly. In the beginning this person needs a cane or walking stick for necessary balance and support. Later, as ambulation decreases, that same person may progress to a walker, and finally, when the ambulatory ability declines even more, the person may require the use of a wheelchair for safety and full physical support.

Next consider the demand made on the caregiver's psychic energy function by the dementia-afflicted family member. They begin by gradually using shared memory assistance from various family and friends, or perhaps from one family caregiver to make up for the memory deficits experienced. As the dementing illness progresses, decreasing the afflicted relative's cognitive function in other intrinsic brain functions apart from memory, including problem solving, language, vision, spatial process and behavior regulation, the attuned caregiver automatically steps in to provide the needed brain functions to assist the ailing member. Gradually, the caregiver assumes more and more of the relative's care by providing the required cognitive functioning support until the ill relative becomes incapacitated and requires full care. In the former example, the support needed is physical and can be provided with an adaptive device. However, in the latter illustration, the cognitive support of another person is needed. We know that problem solving is a normal function of the ego. Unless some effort is made to assist the caregiver with problem-solving strategies, it is likely that the caregiver will experience significant ego energy depletion, exhaustion, and stress as he or she engages in thinking for two, remembering for two, and so on, over an extended period of time regardless of the influence of cultural values.

Therefore, the timeless problem-solving process introduced here helps the caregiver to partialize the problems into smaller, more manageable problems, helping caregivers decrease the feeling of being overwhelmed by problems. Additionally, the efficient methods in which problems are identified and assessed, incorporating the family's own cultural attitudes and beliefs into the appraisals and assessments, can add problem-solving success to the process with the guidance and direction of the social worker. A significant step added in the model presented in this text and adapted specifically for ethnic caregivers is the sorting of problems by domain and the emphasis on tapping family resources for assistance. Most have found this extremely helpful.

UNDERSTANDING THE NEW PROBLEM-SOLVING PROCESS

In the beginning caregivers may find the problem-solving process different. However, as the social worker explains the process and normalizes the required actions, emphasizing that they are already doing some form of problem solving, the caregiver will likely experience interest in learning more. The social worker validates the caregiver's past problem-solving capabilities and clarifies how learning the new the problem-solving process works to enhance the caregiver's strengths. Because the social work role is flexible in terms of method of assistance and guidance to the caregiver, it is the ideal counseling model to implement for the dementia caregiver. The caregiver may wonder why a new process is necessary. The main reason for most social work counseling is that some caregivers experience problems they are not able to solve by themselves. Therefore they seek social work assistance. Heppner and Hillerbrand (1991) state, "How people cope with their personal problems and process information—how they think, feel, and behave when grappling with a real-life problem—is a complex and dynamic process" (p. 380). As mentioned previously the caregiver is often seeking to resolve problems for at least two people and originating from different domains of care; therefore, it is likely that the caregiver will encounter problems he or she cannot solve alone and needs assistance. The social work role is based on this premise.

The goal of the social worker is to help guide and direct caregivers resolve their own life problems, the dementia care problems, and problems of the afflicted relative by helping them learn the new problem-solving process. The caregiver learns by doing. Therefore, the social worker engages the caregiver in a problem-solving process behavior to put actions in motion to assist in the resolution of problems in the four domains—between the caregiver and his or her own self care; the caregiving situation; the family system; and the social and community resource environment.

"Problem solving is a rational process including actions to define the problem, actions to collect information on which to base decisions, actions to engage the client in goal setting and decision making, actions to produce change, and actions to evaluate progress. All of these actions, however take place within a context of values and relationships and the problems presented are usually situations containing a mix of feelings, thinking, and action" (Compton & Galaway, 1989, p. 11). Problem identification within the context of cultural values is important for the social worker and caregiver and will establish appropriate goals that will help ethnic minority family caregivers of dementia-afflicted relatives cope with the secondary effects of their problems. The problem-solving frameworks used here are adapted from the combined works of Helen Harris Perlman (1953, 1970), Toseland and Rivas (1984, 2009), and Valle (1998). These frameworks focus on addressing ethnic minority family caregiver problems as they emerge in day-to-day life either in their own life situations or in the caregiver role when caring for their dementia-afflicted relative.

Helping family caregivers identify, understand, and resolve problems for themselves, their dementia-afflicted relatives, and the family can present many challenges. The goal of this social work problem-solving model is to provide social workers and caregivers with a simple, clear model of problem solving to reduce the stress and to help caregivers, patients, and families focus on the target problem in a way that helps facilitate resolution. Because of the variety of problems, including the caregiver's physical, mental, and emotional health issues, insufficient knowledge regarding the disease, and maladaptive coping patterns related to the disease symptoms presented by the dementia-afflicted family member, the social worker regards the caregiver as the expert in his or her life situation and in terms of identifying the particular problem to target. Additionally the social worker is aware of the caregiver's feelings of grief related to changes or losses in the caregiver's own life dreams, such as loss or postponement of career goals or life aspirations, social activities, and interests. The increased dependency by the dementia-afflicted relative on the caregiver, resulting in the caregiver feeling resentment, anger, frustration, and hopelessness and helplessness, can also negatively impact the caregiver's ability to understand and to manage the dementia symptoms emerging in the afflicted family member. For most ethnic minorities, their family member's transition from home care to day care, respite or alternative out-of-home care can be a traumatic experience. By working collaboratively with the caregiver to make the paradigm shift from primary caregiver to collaborative caregiver, the social worker provides support and guidance in addition to concrete guidance and information. By developing a problem-solving plan, the social worker helps the caregiver to think about and identify the most appropriate problem resolution to facilitate the best care possible for the afflicted family member while maintaining important family and cultural values.

Grief related to anticipated loss is a reality family caregivers are faced with as they provide day-to-day care and treatment of their relative afflicted with this life-threatening illness. Caregivers stand by helpless as the afflicted family member slowly succumbs to the dementia disease. Each phase of the disease brings unique family circumstances and problems. Caregivers and families are often faced with the daunting task of making end-of-life decisions. The role of the social worker is to provide support during these many difficult decision-making situations. The social worker, physician, and other members of an interdisciplinary team often are all involved in educating the caregiver and family on treatment options. It is vital for the social worker to advise the caregiver and family to keep the physician informed of care concerns and symptom changes in their relative.

In the cyclic illustration of this intervention process, the social worker and the caregiver function together throughout the process. The caregiver is fully involved and takes the lead in all of the decisions. The function of the social worker is to engage the caregiver in applying the problem-solving process, thus strengthening the caregiver's own ability to resolve problems by learning and mastering the six action steps process, thus developing a sense of efficacy and mastery. The next section will provide concrete examples applying the problem-solving process action steps.

APPLYING THE NEW PROBLEM-SOLVING PROCESS

In this section, the examples provided in the illustration are discussed with the problem strategy applied. Using the information taken from the assessment form, the social worker engages the caregiver in filling out the problem-solving plan. It is optional who should write it out. Generally the caregiver prefers the social worker to fill out the form the first time; however, the social worker should encourage the caregiver to write out the content if the caregiver is able and willing do to so. This tends to enhance learning and mastery of the process, tends to foster ownership, and also empowers the caregiver, giving confidence to move forward. It must be kept in mind, however, that both the assessment process and the problem-solving process are a dynamic activity that can change with new information provided by the caregiver about the situation. Additionally, caregivers may not always understand or acknowledge the seriousness of their problems. Because caring for a dementia-afflicted relative is often a new learning experience, caregivers may be uncertain about the trajectory of the disease process, the symptoms, and the impact of both on the afflicted relative.

When the caregiver's role changes as noted in earlier case examples, the social worker provides support according to this new role, taking into account the shifting needs required by the afflicted family member. Adjustments are made to the roles, authority, and responsibilities of all those involved. To move the problem-solving process to the next step of social work assistance, it is necessary to link the cultural information to frameworks of family care, fostering empowerment, problem solving, and mastery. The problem-solving process is one of the tools the social worker employs to help the caregiver think about and identify the most appropriate problem to target for work while maintaining important family care and adherence to cultural values.

CASE EXAMPLE OF ETHNIC CAREGIVER PROBLEM SITUATION OR EVENT

1. The caregiver is experiencing high blood pressure, stress, inability to sleep at night because the dementia-afflicted mother passes out and falls down.
2. The social worker helps the caregiver to clarify the thoughts and feelings about her blood pressure, inability to sleep, and mother's passing out and her thoughts about this experience.
3. The problem causes and effects for CG are escalating the blood pressure, stress, tiredness, fatigue, inability to sleep at night, having to watch mother all the time to catch her if she passes out. The causes and effects for the ill mother are safety, hitting head when she falls or risk of injury.
4. The social worker and Black and Latino caregiver jointly explore ways to solve the problems.
5. The social worker and caregiver jointly set up a plan for the caregiver and her mother each to see their own physician as soon as possible and arrange for an interpreter to help communicate.

6. Jointly the caregiver and social worker set a date to implement the problem-solving plan for the caregiver to contact the physician(s) that day and set urgent care appointments for both. The caregiver is instructed to tell the physician to evaluate blood pressure, explains impact of caregiving role and mother's health issues. Takes her mother to her physician to discuss frequent passing out, falling and hitting head. Physician hospitalizes mother to complete medical tests.

The Black and Latino caregiver experiences relief, can rest while the mother is hospitalized, feels she is complying with her responsibility as outlined in her cultural values to care for her mother with Alzheimer's disease. With the problem-solving plan successfully implemented, the Black and Latino family caregiver experiences empowerment and self-efficacy.

Problem Situation or Event (Sorted by Domain)

In directing the problem-solving process, social workers must also guide caregivers through the essential steps outlined in the illustrated process. It is essential to teach caregivers the process of problem solving while guiding them through the action steps. Teaching caregivers the process of thinking about problems in ways that facilitate the separation of issues and sorting them into domains is the *first step*. All six steps of the process are vitally important as each step promotes caregiver self-growth, self-actualization, self-determination, and mastery.

Thoughts and Feelings Experienced

In *step two*, thoughts and feeling experienced, the attempt is to elicit information about the caregiver's interpersonal self in relation to the problem. The more the caregiver is aware and knows about him-/herself in relation to the problems, the better informed the caregiver is and the more realistic the caregiver will be about his or her ability to care for others. Self-aware caregivers are better able to identify self-strengths and capabilities as well as self-deficiencies. Conversely, the less aware the caregiver is about all of the above, then less able the caregiver is to seek and engage in appropriate solutions to problems. Also, the less able the caregiver is to engage in self-reflection and self-awareness, the more thorough the social worker will have to be in guiding and directing the caregiver around deficiencies in competency and capacity to other supportive measures to assist the caregiver. This is part of the art of social work, in that it involves the social worker creatively assessing the caregiver to determine which strengths and capacities for resourcefulness in self and others are known to and present for the caregiver to manage the care process safely promoting well being. And those strengths that are absent require the social worker to identify other supportive care resources to ensure care that has safety and well-being as the outcome for all. The application of each step will be discussed here.

Caregiver self-awareness is key for caregivers to identify feelings and thoughts about the problem required in step two. All too often caregivers don't know what they don't know. They are so busy focusing on the looming issues that they do not take time to self-reflect to identify how they are thinking and feeling about the problem. The omission of this vital step muddles the process and can inhibit the ability of the caregiver to tap into strengths and capacities, and to work toward resolving the problem. If caregivers are not self-aware they may not be aware of the overall impact of the problem of self on the afflicted relative or on the family.

It should be noted that some ethnic caregivers may be reluctant to consider the impact of the care process on the "self" in this process for fear of being judged as being selfish or operating contrary to cultural expectations. It is in this area that this intervention provides a new perspective for most caregivers. Often caregivers know they are feeling overburdened or overwhelmed but communicating how they really think or feel about the problem is not something they allow themselves to do. The truth is that this intervention not only gives caregivers permission to self-reflect, but also strongly encourages them to do so by making self-awareness and self-reflection a required process in this step in the context of improving the care of their afflicted family member.

With social work guidance, this step also provides the opportunity for caregivers to expand their self-reflection to include learning how thoughts and feelings tend to either foster or hamper problem solving. For example, some caregivers have shown remarkable resourcefulness and creativity in attempting to resolve problems, whereas others demonstrate a lack of knowledge about resources or they minimize or ignore problems or give up. Therefore, the information the social worker gathers about the aspect of self-awareness of the caregiver's functioning is an important indicator of the caregiver's ability to apply the problem-solving process to resolve problems.

Another example of the need for step two and caregiver self-reflection is to determine to what degree the caregiver is able to identify his or her role or contribution to the problem and to generate the possible solution (Goldstein & Noonan, 1999). Other concerns are whether the caregiver is sufficiently self-aware of his or her own values and how these values might be contributing to the problem, and whether the caregiver is able to use feedback provided by the social worker or significant others to make changes to problem solve. All of these factors must be explored and assessed by the social worker to help caregivers employ the most appropriate problem-solving solution.

Problem Causes and Effects

In applying *step three* of the problem-solving process, identifying problem causes and effects, the social worker is seeking to identify additional or underlying problems that exist that might be directly or indirectly related to the caregiver-identified problem in step one. This step develops the ability in the caregiver to assess the degree in which the identified problem can be linked to other problems, or the degree in which the problem has infected, damaged, or caused pain to the caregiver, the afflicted family member, the family, or the others in the social context. It also provides the social worker with information regarding the extent that problems identified in step one are developing causes and effects, leading to other problems that might be impairing safety or the successful implementation of problem solving. Another reason for this step needs is to see if the solutions being considered for application to the identified problem will serve to exacerbate an underlying problem or influence the underlying problem in a positive manner.

This step also involves caregiver self-awareness because it prompts the caregiver to assess his or her ability to engage in critical thinking skills about step one, the identified problem, and step two, thoughts and feelings about the problem, and to identify other links to other problems that may not have been previously discussed or included in the problem identification. These could be underlying problems. Step three also provides essential information to the social worker about the caregiver's ability to understand the full scope and impact of the problems, and about the caregiver's ability to apply critical thinking skills to problems.

Exploring Possible Problem Solutions

Exploring possible problem solutions in *step four* is largely concerned with helping caregivers learn how to think about alternatives to solving problems. This is considered to be brainstorming solutions and is done to not only expand the caregiver's ability to think about problems, but to think about problem solutions out of the box if you will. This step is helpful in that it creates an opportunity for the caregiver to engage in several actions that foster assertiveness, self-efficacy, and mastery. Caregivers are guided by the social worker to freely engage in thinking of solution options, and weighing the implications or consequences of the options while avoiding impulsive, inappropriate behavior. Here, caregivers also learn to be more assertive by using their voices to communicate options, assess the pros and cons of the options with the social worker, and assume power and control of the problem, all with the guidance and direction of the social work professional. Because of the proclivity of ethnic older adults and populations to generally convey respect toward professionals in authority positions, the social worker can assist caregivers expand their skills to help identify the best solution for the identified problem. Again, encouragement coming from the social worker will help the caregiver be open to understanding how culturally sensitive options can be used to avoid obstacles generated by confounded cultural values and still provide solutions to the problems.

For some ethnic caregivers this may be too freeing at first, especially if it is an older adult female whose generational functioning has been somewhat disempowered through historical socialization processes unique to the culture and family patterns. Developing assertiveness may cause increased stress and may even paralyze actions by caregivers. Exploring emotions that may be preventing caregivers from taking action is essential here. It reverts back to step two of the process, which addresses thinking and feeling. Some caregivers may not realize that they are thinking in a particular way until this step is taken. At times deeply felt emotions stemming from painful situations experienced in the past may still come forward. Often, these emotions are caused by deep-seated mistaken beliefs formed by irrational thinking. Social workers need to help caregivers process this irrational thinking to reach the root of the mistaken beliefs. In this instance beliefs does not refer to cultural beliefs discussed in earlier chapters. Rather, it refers to beliefs that were formed with mistaken information and/or misconceptions no longer realistically apply. Caregivers may have only a vague or limited knowledge of the irrational beliefs especially if formed years before. Culturally competent social work skills need to be employed in this step.

The guidance and support of the social worker will help the caregiver to identify the irrational beliefs and thinking and the associated emotions, and replace all with realistic conceptions (Hepworth & Larson, 1990, p. 432). Social workers can also help the caregiver to perceive and adopt a strategy that is relevant to the successful intercultural care relationship for the ethnic disease-afflicted family member.

Resources Available to Solve the Problem

Resources available to solve the problem come into action in *step 5*, and involve a parallel process with both the caregiver and the social worker perceived as experts and each contributing to the resource gathering information action. Resource options generated from this step should include the full spectrum of the problem-solving resources needed in all four domains. Some caregivers bring different expectations about what they would like in terms of resources to help problem solve. Therefore, it is important for the social worker to have a discussion with the caregiver to gain a clear understanding of the expectations especially, when working with ethnic caregivers. Even though the problem-solving process described here is simple and succinct, it still requires learning a number of concepts and skills, plus applying self-discipline, time, effort, and diligence. So it is in everyone's best interest to make sure that the caregiver is clear about the process and has indeed signed on to the process. Goldstein and Noonan (1999) note the following.

> Clients vary with respect to whether they want symptom relief, access to resources, advice, information, and guidance; sympathetic listening and acceptance; encouragement and support; someone who will help them in problem solving, interpersonal conflict resolution, and self-understanding; immediate relief or a more reflective process; or an authority who will unilaterally solve the problem or a more mutually participatory process. Many clients do not have a clear understanding of what to expect or what is expected of them. (p. 89)

Caregivers are largely unaware of the various roles and professional practice skills social workers possess. So clarifying the expectations to ensure that the social worker and caregiver are in agreement in terms of working-relationship expectations is a vital step in the initial engagement. Caregivers of dementia-afflicted relatives expend a great deal of energy and time providing care and managing all other life duties. Social workers should make sure that caregivers understand their investment of time and energy in the problem-solving process can be both challenging and rewarding. It requires persistence and determined effort, but the outcome may significantly enhance problem-solving, equipping caregivers with new and more effective problem-solving skills.

Knowing the influence of ethnic cultural values on the caregiver and the afflicted family member often determines whether the caregiver wants informal or formal resources. Informal resources are resources provided by immediate, extended familismo, kinship, and fictive kin members, which often include close friends and spiritual or godparent. In some families informal care resources include neighbors or members of the community or church group. Formal resources, on the other hand, are resources where there is a fee for service paid directly to the agency or to the individual providing the formal service. Included in formal services are physicians, social workers, visiting nurses, respite care, day care, senior centers, nursing homes, attorneys, or agencies providing education, individual or group support, training or other care resources. Clarifying caregiver expectations regarding resources needed for problem solving should be explored to ensure there is indeed a desire on the part of the caregiver to use either informal or formal resources, a combination of both, or neither. To do this, the social worker should elicit the caregiver's knowledge of community resources, interest in obtaining community resources, identifying community resources previously contacted for assistance, past experiences seeking help from community resources, inability to access community services, and desire not to access community resources. Generally, ethnic caregivers prefer to seek assistance from the informal resources especially when it involves direct care of the ill relative or support with activities of daily living. Informal providers, although competent are often viewed by ethnic caregivers as outsiders or strangers that may not provide the quality care that a family or kin member would provide. This step is concerned with generating numerous resource alternatives that are vital in working with caregivers; therefore, clarity up front is necessary to develop solutions to achieve problem solving.

Implement the Problem-Solving Plan

It is crucial to help caregivers commit to a date to implement the problem-solving plan, which will enable them to transfer the learning to the circumstance, hence the need for *step 6*. The rationale for this step is to assist caregivers to begin to accept and assume responsibility for action and to clarify their role and participation in the problem-solving process. By taking steps (however small) in alleviating care difficulties they practice the problem-solving process while still receiving the guidance of the social worker. This provides opportunities for the social worker and caregiver together to monitor progress (or lack thereof), and if necessary make changes.

Implementation involves active collaboration of both the social worker and caregiver. The social worker uses multiple roles and skill sets during this step. One social work role is to observe the caregiver's efforts when implementing the plan to assess the caregiver's strengths, weaknesses, the ability to assess use of self in the process, the ability to move forward, and the capacity to overcome challenges. Another role is to discuss the latter with the caregiver to enhance the caregiver's ability to self-reflect, weigh progress and outcomes, and affirm progress and identify challenges. A third role is to keep the caregiver focused on the problem-solving goal, making sure the caregiver is moving in the right direction. The social worker needs to balance urging the caregiver forward with the need to allow the caregiver move at their own pace. At least three factors tend to contribute to balancing the pace: (1) caregivers capacity, (2) urgency of the need to resolve the problem, and (3) the complexity of the problem. A caregiver making too little forward progress or making impulsive leaps forward will require additional assistance from the social worker to overcome implementation challenges.

It is recommended that the social worker and caregiver negotiate the implementation date to ensure a realistic timeframe based on the ability of the caregiver to achieve the date. Except for problems involving caregiver or afflicted family member safety or urgent medical care needs, the social worker should avoid pushing or forcing the caregiver to provide a date that he or she may not be able to meet. It is best to allow the caregiver to select the date that gives the caregiver sufficient time to do what is necessary to implement the problem-solving plan. For example, if the caregiver plans to use formal resources, the caregiver often has to wait for an available date to secure the services. Trusting the caregiver to manage the circumstances to make this decision is an important endeavor, not only to strengthen the work relationship between the caregiver and the social worker, but also to enhance caregiver self-confidence. It is better to reinforce the caregiver's efforts to take the lead than to inadvertently set the caregiver up for failure.

To enhance caregiver confidence and reinforce implementation efforts, the social worker should reflect back to the caregiver the steps the caregiver takes or has taken on his or her own behalf or on behalf of the ill relative (Hepworth & Larson, 1990). Receiving feedback from the social worker helps the caregiver recognize gains and gauge his or her efforts in the process. It is only by implementing the problem-solving process within the context of daily problems that the caregiver will see and experience the benefits of the actions. Often, once the caregiver begins to experience benefits from the implementation of actions, the caregiver's efforts may tend to positively influence and reinforce these implementation efforts, which in turn will tend to build confidence and increase motivation in the caregiver.

HELPING ETHNIC CAREGIVERS LEARN NEW WAYS TO THINK ABOUT THEIR PROBLEMS

In the previous section implementing the problem-solving plan was discussed to emphasize the actions steps the caregiver needs to take to participate in the process. In this section the emphasis is on the caregiver's need to transfer learning the problem-solving process, beginning with sorting problems by domains and ending with demonstrating skills into real-life care situations. In the beginning the caregiver may resist efforts to learn the process simply because it is new and unfamiliar. Like most new endeavors it takes extra effort in the beginning to reduce tenuous feelings to develop a comfort level. The added facts that each step in the process requires specific thinking never before consciously considered may, in the beginning, pose challenges to the caregiver. The social worker can assist in reducing these uncertainties and lingering doubts by normalizing the steps through engaging the caregiver in a discourse about how problems were solved in the past. As the social worker explores the steps the caregiver has automatically taken in the past and points out similarities and differences with the new problem-solving process, the caregiver will realize that he or she is simply using more self-awareness in applying discrete concepts and expanding the range of conscious actions and options in a more focused manner.

The social worker should avoid giving the impression that the past actions the caregiver has employed to solve problems are wrong, defective or a complete failure. The unwitting communication of the latter message to the caregiver could result in increased doubt, hesitation, and fear of failing. In an extreme case, ethnic caregivers may also feel insulted or disrespected resulting in an irreparable rupture to the working relationship, leading the caregiver to sever ties with the problems solving process and the social worker and agency.

To assist caregivers to learn new ways to think about their problems, social workers need to teach them the process while guiding them through it. At first the process, form, and concept map (Figure 8.1) may appear to overwhelm the caregiver. Selecting the concept map first to describe the process involved using a visual illustration of what the overall process looks like will benefit the caregiver. Assuring the caregiver that the social worker will help the caregiver to learn and apply the process also reduces anxiety and helps the caregiver know that he or she is not alone in the process. Explaining the problem-solving plan form also helps because the social worker partializes each required step while explaining the rationale for the step. The social worker should then identify the components involved, explain what the concepts mean, and give examples of the responses. The social worker should discuss the rationale and provide a description.

The social worker can use modeling or role-play strategies to communicate what the action might look like and to help caregivers understand the desired activity or behavior. Both of these strategies enable the caregiver to practice the action with the social worker before applying it in the respective life situation. These two strategies have been used by social workers for years and are proven in terms of their ability to enhance learning, build confidence, self-efficacy, and mastery.

Modeling for this problem-solving process involves the social worker demonstrating the particular behavior while the caregiver observes. The social worker could model the skill of identifying thoughts (cognitive or thinking component), and identifying feelings (emotional component). After modeling, the caregiver is encouraged to ask questions or critique the activity demonstrated. Next the caregiver is asked to participate by engaging in the previously modeled action. A discussion and critique follows and if necessary both the social worker and the caregiver repeat the process until the caregiver experiences self-efficacy.

Role play can assist the caregiver's learning by practicing how the caregiver might handle unfamiliar or uncomfortable situations. For example, if a caregiver decides to implement the use of family resources and a rift in the relationship is the identified problem, the social worker and caregiver can role play a particular script to help the caregiver practice how he or she would apply the previously identified action to achieve the desired outcome. Both would discuss and critique the role play and repeat the skill until the caregiver feels comfortable applying it. This strategy can be especially helpful when working with clients who are engaging in help-seeking behaviors with a community resource agency for the first time. What often occur during both modeling and role play are noticeable decreases in caregiver anxiety and tension and an increase in humor and self-confidence. Again, repeating the role play until the caregiver experiences self-efficacy is important. A simple way of determining whether the caregiver has achieved self-efficacy is to ask the caregiver to rate his or her ability to apply the task on a scale of 1–10 with 10 representing mastery or full confidence and 1 the extreme opposite or complete lack of confidence (Hepworth & Larson, 1990). Caregivers will vary in terms of amount of time needed to learn the new ways to think about the problems.

Selecting the target problems and establishing problem-solving plans can be complicated in an ethnic family where multiple levels of family issues may be impacting the caregiver and the afflicted family member in problematic ways. Sometimes even the well-rehearsed and planned solutions to problems do not succeed. Therefore it is essential to communicate to the caregiver that the problem-solving plan, while effective, is not always perfect. The desired solution may not be achieved especially if the implementation plan falters. If this occurs, the social worker and caregiver should be encouraged by the fact that the plan was attempted. Next, both should engage in reviewing the process to assess which action step was deficient and to brainstorm a new action step. The failure of the first attempt should not be minimized nor overemphasized. Rather, it should be placed in the context of a normal part of the learning experience when new ways to think about problems and resolve them are sought. Although caregivers may decide to learn to apply the problem-solving process and may desire the begin the learning immediately, the social worker should delay beginning the learning process if the caregiver needs to address urgent or safety related problems.

In the case example provided in the beginning of this chapter, the safety of the ill relative that is fainting and the caregiver's blood pressure problem require immediate medical attention and action. Both are high risk problems and therefore the problem-solving steps presented earlier need to be expedited by the social worker. Although the social worker should be careful not to cause alarm, the social worker should also assist the caregiver to move the work forward expeditiously by (a) explaining the risk, (b) helping to set a reasonable time frame that requires the caregiver to take prompt action, (c) monitoring progress, and (d) assisting the caregiver as necessary by advocating for prompt medical assessments for both the caregiver and the afflicted family member.

This bears repeating: Addressing safety problems *always* takes precedence over learning new ways to think about the problems and also takes precedence over addressing family relational problems. In the case example, it is not likely that the caregiver would be able to effectively concentrate on learning a new problem-solving process if these two urgent problems were not resolved first. Once the safety issues are addressed and the problems successfully resolved, the next step is for the social worker is to begin with the full evaluation and assessment of the caregiver and the afflicted family member as noted in earlier chapters. If sibling conflicts are clearly implicated in the presenting health care problems or are contributing to the health problems, an assessment as to the frequency and intensity of impact of the family problems should be made to plan for resolution as soon as possible. Helping caregivers learn new ways to think about their problems is designed to help caregivers learn to apply these problem-solving steps as a life long process. It is a useful process that can help caregivers in their relationships with others beyond the immediate caring responsibilities.

APPLYING THE NEW PROBLEM-SOLVING PROCESS TO FUTURE CAREGIVING PROBLEMS

As mentioned in previous chapters, for most Black and Latino families the caregiving role is often informally assigned to the oldest or youngest adult daughter. Often the role designation may be attributed to females simply because it involves a knowledge and expertise of various domestic tasks that most females are automatically trained to learn and develop as young children through the gender family values socialization process. In the case example provided, the Brazilian caregiver automatically assuming the care role may be a natural extension of the role modeling she witnessed as a child demonstrated by her mother in the home. On the other hand, the four younger siblings are Latino males from a second family that generally tends to defer caregiving duties to the females in the Latino family. Why is this an important consideration? It is important because understanding how this particular family has internalized the values from both cultures requires historical family interaction assessment information. Finding out what it was like growing up in the biracial family as the oldest child and only daughter who was also a stepdaughter and stepsister to four younger male siblings, and the only member of the family who had a different last name from her siblings can provide key information about the complexity of the role designation, the upbringing of the caregiver, and how the caregiver has thought about and internalized her identity and place in the family system. Her brothers probably had a different extended family interaction as they had access to familismo members from Puerto Rico. She, on the other hand, stopped traveling to Brazil and due to distance and time, and had less contact with family in her home country. Knowing the historical background of the caregiver and the afflicted family member is vitally important to understanding the interaction with the siblings, and the care for the mother that has occurred over time.

Family members react in various ways to loss, grief, and pain. Due to the recent loss of the father and now the diagnosis of Alzheimer's disease in the mother, the siblings could all be reacting to multiple losses in maladaptive ways. Therefore, this could be a mixed bag of care concerns about the past loss and the mother's cognitive decline, misplaced toward a tangled and passionate interwoven historical sibling problem and legal property ownership. The social work role is to gather the information including to clearly define the implications of the siblings' attitude and behavior effects on the caregiver and the afflicted family member. The historical assessment will allow the social worker to get to know the situation, access boundary breeches, and determine how and when this change in sibling interaction originated and progressed reaching the current adversarial state.

Some families function adaptively (for them) in chronic verbal volleys that can seem like arguments to an outsider. Therefore, assessing the communication patterns in the family is also an important social worker task. The differences in family members' formal education, socioeconomic status and class are pertinent as well. Completing this comprehensive assessment is essential for the social worker to have a clear understanding of how the caregiver experiences the care context.

Why is all this being reviewed again? The social worker has to fully assess all aspects of the problems with which the caregiver is requesting assistance to help the caregiver identify which problems to prioritize for timely resolution and which problems to use for learning purposes so that the caregiver will have the necessary acquired skills to be able to implement the problem-solving plan once the social worker's and caregiver's work together ends. It may not be feasible to tackle a problem that will require long-term work if the social worker and caregiver agreed that the intervention time is of short duration. The family conflicts described in the case study seem to be more than just squabbles over sibling favoritism by parents or sibling rivalry. The problems may in fact have a long evolving history with fixed patterns of interaction, and therefore may require more than just an overview of the family history. Additionally, the family is a biracial, step-family who recently suffered trauma and loss and therefore a more detailed historical, cultural, racial and acculturation information gathering process is needed to include information about father/stepfather, the caregiver, the dementia-afflicted mother and members of the immediate as well as extended family. Hence, sorting out family issues and sibling conflicts are important and can be complicated to understand due to the vicissitudes of life and the vast familismo and kinship network patterns of interaction. For all of these reasons, social workers should focus on helping the caregiver to learn the problem-solving process so that the caregiver can continue the work after ending with the social worker. Complicated family patterns often require an understanding that resolving long standing family conflict problems may be a lengthy process with increments of growth by caregivers and family members over time. Thus participation in corrective strategies may involve family members' willing participation in the problem-solving process to collaboratively resolve problems.

Using logs to document the caregiver's progress in learning and implementing the six-step problem-solving process that resulted in resolving problems will allow the caregiver and social worker to assess steps at each level, identify what worked and what did not work, evaluate outcomes, engage in productive discussions about what actions the caregiver found helpful, and where the caregiver needed assistance to stay on track or to reconsider certain steps such as thoughts and feelings, or causes and effects, or perhaps how he or she sorted the problem into a particular domain. Social workers are encouraged to provide the caregiver with copies of the initial problem-solving plan noting the implementation date so that the caregiver can refer to it as a guide and reminder of the necessary steps the caregiver needs to complete outside of meetings with the social worker to ensure work is completed in between meetings. It is important to remember that some caregivers may never have had to ask for help before, or may never have had to give an account of their efforts to solve problems to a social work professional. Therefore they may feel somewhat anxious about carrying out the problem-solving process requirements, such as remembering what to do for each step or when to begin to implement actions to meet the established date, another reason to provide a copy of the problem-solving plan.

The following samples of documentation logs (Examples 8.1 to 8.3) are provided as options for the social worker and caregiver to use to record caregiver progress or notes for future reference. Reviewing favorable outcomes tends to enhance the caregiver's self-confidence and reminds the caregiver of efforts used in the past that may be able to be reapplied in the future. By the same token, reviewing problematic or unfavorable problem-solving outcomes are equally important. These discussions of what didn't work tend to pave the way for increased learning and may also help caregivers avoid making the same mistakes in future problem-solving efforts. It is recommended that the social worker keep meeting notes to document discussions on progress made by the caregiver. As always, social workers should be guided by individual caregiver's capabilities and learning needs. Keeping the problem-solving process simple is what makes this intervention attractive and effective for both social workers and caregivers.

Example 8.1 Problem-Solving Plan

Caregiver Problem-Solving Plan

Caregiver Name _____Social Worker _____Date: _____

1. Problem	2. Thoughts / Feelings	3. Causes / Effects	4. Possible Solutions	5. Resources available	6. Problem-solving plan implemented
A—CGSC					
B—CGDC					
C—CGFR					
D—CGCR					

Example 8.2 Problem-Solving Plan Spanish Translation

Plan Para Solucionar Problemas

Nombre de Cuidador _____Trabajador(a) sociale _____Fecha _____

1. Problema	2. Pensamientos/ Sentimientos	3. Causas/ Efectos	4. Soluciones Posible	5. Recursos Desponibles	6. Implementando plan de soluciones
A—CGSC					
B—CGDC					
C—CGFR					
D—CGCR					

Example 8.3 Problem-Solving Process Progress Notes

PROBLEM-SOLVING PROGRESS NOTES

Confidential

Caregiver Name_____ Social Worker _____
Date _____

_____
_____
_____
_____
_____
_____
_____
_____
_____
_____
_____
_____
_____
_____
_____
_____
_____
_____
_____
_____
_____
_____
_____
_____
_____
_____
_____
_____
_____
_____
_____
_____
_____
_____
_____
_____

© Delia J. González Sanders

REFERENCES

Brandell, J. (1997). *Theory and practice in clinical social work.* New York: The Free Press.

Goldstein, E., & Noonan, M. (1999). *Short-term treatment and social work practice: An integrative perspective.* New York: The Free Press.

Heppner, P. P., & Hillerbrand, E. T. (1991). Problem-solving training: Implications for remedial and preventive training. In C. R. Snyder & D. R. Forsyth (Eds.), *Handbook of social and clinical psychology: The healthy perspective.* Elmsford, NY: Pergamon.

Hepworth, D. H., & Larson, J. A. (1990). *Direct social work practice: Theory and skills.* Belmont, CA: The Wadsworth Publishing.

Perlman, H. (1970). The problem-solving method in social casework. In R. Roberts & R. Nee (Eds.), *Theories of social casework* (pp. 129–180). Chicago, IL: University of Chicago Press.

Perlman, H. H. (1953). The social components of casework practice. In L. Parker (Chairman), *The social welfare forum. 1953.* New York: Columbia University Press.

Perlman, H. H. (1957). *Social casework: A problem-solving process.* Chicago, IL: University of Chicago Press.

Perlman, H. H. (1979). *Relationship: The heart of helping people.* Chicago, IL: University of Chicago Press.

III

Foundations and Future Care

9

Financing, Workforce, and Dementia Care Trends

CASE STUDIES IN CONTEXT

This chapter does not begin with a case study, but rather calls attention to the fact that all case studies in previous chapters could be expanded to include issues regarding information and help seeking once a family caregiver reaches the point when he or she can no longer provide or coordinate all the family-provided or other non-paid care needed by their relative with dementia. In many published studies of family caregivers, Black and Latino family caregivers are found to delay or avoid admitting their relative to a nursing home as a permanent living arrangement much more frequently than White family caregivers. When social workers encounter families at this point and by using the problem-solving model explained in this book, they will consider the domain of family caregiver community resources. This chapter is intended to help social work professionals understand financing and service delivery trends when working with Black and Latino families to plan strategies for linking these families with appropriate resources.

OVERVIEW

This chapter provides a timely review of health and social care financing policies in the United States that influence social work practice with ethnic dementia caregivers. Medicare, Medicaid, and the Older Americans Act (OAA), all passed into law in 1965, are the principal means by which federal and state governments pay for health and social services for older adults with disabilities and their families.

259

Family caregiver support programs financed by the OAA are emerging at the federal level as well, some of which are specifically designed for families caring for relatives with dementia. The Affordable Care Act of 2010, also known as the Health Care Reform Act, opened the way for innovations in care delivery financed by Medicare and Medicaid that could improve opportunities for social workers to work with families caring for older adults with disabilities caused by dementia. States are in the midst of re-engineering their long-term care systems to reduce reliance on nursing homes and to increase the availability of home- and community-based services for older adults with disabilities and their families. The chapter then turns to trends in the American work-force in the context of an aging society, with a focus on the need for more social workers specializing in gerontology. Finally, the chapter addresses timely trends in dementia care, including earlier presenta-tion and diagnosis of dementia symptoms and new home- and com-munity-based services that respect the rights and dignity of people with dementia.

FINANCING AND SERVICE DELIVERY TRENDS

Medicare

When we consider ongoing debates in Congress and public concern about the future of the Medicare program, it seems that Medicare has always been a part of the public policy landscape in this country. In fact, Medicare was established only in 1965 as Title XVIII of the Social Security Act. Since its passage as a national health insurance program for older Americans, and for certain younger Americans with disabili-ties, Medicare has been both lauded for its reflection of "health care as a right" for its covered population and condemned for its relentlessly growing cost and the economic burden it places on the national econ-omy and future generations of Americans.

Regardless of one's political or economic position regarding the current and future solvency of the Medicare program, there is broad consensus that Medicare has provided a solid foundation of health insurance security for America's older population. Before 1965, most older Americans could not afford to purchase health insurance poli-cies because the cost of premiums was prohibitively high due to their advanced age and the financial risk their health problems represented to private insurance companies. Medicare was initially structured to help pay for the most costly health care services, particularly hospital and rehabilitation services, and over the years has expanded to include partial or full coverage for a range of other medical services.

Medicare includes four different coverage areas: Part A (Hospital Insurance); Part B (Medical Insurance); Part C (Medicare Advantage); and Part D (Medicare Prescription Drug Coverage). The terms "enrollee" and "beneficiary" are used interchangeably in this chapter to refer to a person who has any type of Medicare insurance. Visit www.Medicare.gov for more details about Medicare than provided in this chapter.

Who Is Eligible for Medicare and How Many Americans Are Covered?

Most Americans are automatically eligible for Medicare Part A coverage when they reach their 65th birthday. Because Medicare Part A is financed through payroll taxes, eligibility at age 65 is based on having evidence of payroll taxes of any amount deducted from pay for at least 40 quarters (the equivalent of 10 continuous or noncontinuous years) over a lifetime. Spouses of eligible Medicare Part A beneficiaries are automatically eligible for Medicare Part A at age 65 even if they did not contribute the required minimum payroll taxes, upon providing evidence that their spouse is also a Medicare beneficiary. If these criteria are fulfilled, no monthly premium is required; for those who do not qualify based on these criteria, the premium amount depends on how many quarters they did contribute payroll taxes, with the minimum amount in 2011 set at $248/month. Only about 1% of Medicare enrollees pay their own monthly premium (AARP, 2009).

Americans younger than age 65 may be eligible for Medicare Part A due to acquiring specific diseases or long-term disability. End-stage renal disease or amyotrophic lateral sclerosis (or Lou Gehrig's disease) at any age qualifies an individual for Medicare Part A benefits. Evidence of disability for at least 24 consecutive months also qualifies a younger American for Medicare Part A coverage.

In 2010, a total of 46.6 million Americans were enrolled in the Medicare program, that is, enrolled in Medicare Part A, B, or C. As Figure 9.1 illustrates, nearly 39 million of these Medicare enrollees were eligible due to age, while nearly 8 million under age 65 were eligible due to disability. Figure 9.1 also shows the steady growth in the Medicare enrollee population since 2001 in both the "elderly" and "disabled" population groups.

FIGURE 9.1.   Growth in the Medicare Population, 2001–2010

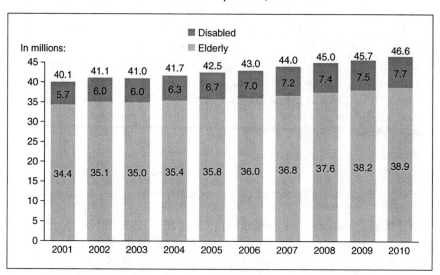

What Does Medicare Part A Pay for?

Even though Medicare Part A is called Hospital Insurance, it also pays for skilled care in a nursing home, at home, and through the hospice benefit. For *hospital care*, Medicare Part A pays nearly the entire hospital bill if the hospital stay is 60 days or less; however, the enrollee is responsible for a deductible amount, which in 2011 was $1,132. Hospital stays longer than 60 days are quite rare, but an enrollee is responsible for a daily cost-sharing fee starting on day 61; in 2011, this cost sharing amount was $283.

For *skilled nursing facility (SNF) care*, an enrollee is eligible for Medicare Part A coverage if he or she experiences a hospital stay of at least 3 days and is then transferred to the SNF within 30 days of hospital discharge for a health problem directly related to that hospitalization. Skilled nursing and/or rehabilitation therapy needs also must be demonstrated for Medicare Part A to cover SNF care. Individuals with Alzheimer's disease or other dementia may qualify for SNF care if they have skilled nursing needs related to the dementia or another health problem requiring skilled nursing or rehabilitation therapy. Medicare Part A pays the entire cost of SNF care for the first 20 days of a qualified SNF stay, but the enrollee is responsible for a daily cost sharing fee beginning on the 21st day; in 2011, this fee was $141.50/day. The Medicare SNF benefit ends at 100 days; beyond which the enrollee is responsible for the entire cost of care.

The Medicare *home health benefit* is also covered under Medicare Part A if a beneficiary is homebound, needs skilled nursing and/or rehabilitation therapy, and has a physician's approval to receive care. The current definition of homebound focuses on a beneficiary having considerable difficulty leaving his or her own home without assistance. Covered services include nursing, home health aide with nursing supervision, rehabilitation therapy, and medical social work. Unlike SNF care, a prior hospital stay is not required to qualify for home health care under Medicare. However, care must be provided by a Medicare-certified home health agency, which sends a nurse to the home for an initial assessment to determine Medicare eligibility. Beneficiaries are certified to receive home health care for up to 60 days at a time; recertification is required every 60 days to determine if the beneficiary still requires skilled care. Medicare pays for the entire cost of an approved 60-day episode of care; no cost sharing is required. As with SNF care, persons with dementia may qualify under the home health benefit if they show clear evidence of skilled care needs related to the dementia disease, or if they have another health problem that requires skilled care.

Finally, Medicare Part A pays for *hospice care*, which is available for enrollees who are projected by physicians to live for 6 months or less. Hospice care must be provided by a Medicare-certified provider in a free-standing hospice facility, in the home setting, or in a nursing home; in the latter two settings, hospice care is most often provided by a division of a Medicare-certified home health agency. Many beneficiaries in advanced stages of dementia disease qualify for Medicare hospice benefits and could receive hospice care in any of the settings noted.

What Does Medicare Part B Cover and How Much Does It Cost?

Medicare Part B covers outpatient diagnostic and therapeutic services, including physician office visits, hospital clinic visits, physician visits to the bedside during a hospital stay, outpatient mental health services, laboratory and diagnostic imaging tests, and selected clinical preventive services. Part B is financed by individual premium payments and by federal general revenues; therefore, there is a required monthly premium charged to join Medicare Part B. In 2011, the cost of the monthly Part B premium was $96.40 for beneficiaries with lower or modest income. However, this monthly premium cost is higher if an individual's annual income is greater than $85,000 or a married couple's annual income exceeds $170,000 (in 2011). This Part B monthly premium is presently the only Medicare fee that is based on income. Despite the monthly cost, most Part A enrollees (93%) also purchase a Part B Medicare insurance policy (AARP, 2009).

Many Medicare beneficiaries with dementia can benefit from receiving clinical preventive services to screen for or help prevent other health problems, so it is very important to ask such individuals or their family members if they have received these services. Clinical preventive services covered by Medicare Part B include influenza, pneumococcal, and hepatitis B vaccines; cardiovascular screening tests (every 5 years); mammograms (annually); cervical, colorectal, prostate, and vaginal cancer screening tests (frequency varies by type of screening); diabetes screening (up to twice annually depending upon results); bone mass measurement to screen for osteoporosis or osteopenia (every 2 years); and tobacco use cessation counseling for smokers. The 2010 Affordable Care Act (described in detail later) included a provision to remove the cost-sharing requirement for these clinical preventive services as of January 1, 2011; therefore, there is now no cost to Part B beneficiaries for receiving these critical screening services.

Mental health services available under Medicare Part B deserve special mention in this book. As discussed in Chapter 2, many individuals with memory problems may actually have depression due to situational grief or more serious psychological problems that may mask as dementia. Social work professionals working with such clients with Medicare Part B insurance should consider discussing the possibility of their client seeking the services of a social work mental health professional, especially with special training in geriatrics, such as a geriatric social worker working with a geriatric psychiatrist. In addition, family caregivers who are Medicare beneficiaries might show signs of depression and anxiety due to the stress of providing care to loved ones with dementia, and they might benefit from referral to a clinical social work mental health professional.

What Is Medicare Advantage or Medicare Part C?

Social workers working with older adults need to be knowledgeable about how Medicare Advantage plans represent an optional way for Americans to receive Medicare coverage. These plans are offered by Medicare-approved private insurance companies, which receive a set amount of payment per enrollee from the Medicare program and must provide a minimum of all Medicare Part A and B services to individuals who choose to join their private plans instead of the government-administered Parts A and B. In effect, beneficiaries "trade in" their Part

A and B membership cards in order to join a Medicare Advantage plan. Many Medicare Advantage plans offer more benefits, such as lower premiums and reduced cost sharing for certain services, and for this reason they have become increasingly popular in recent years (Health Policy Brief, 2011).

Figure 9.2 shows the fall and rise in Medicare Advantage enrollment over the past decade; in 2010, more than 11 million Medicare enrollees (24%) were members of a Medicare Advantage plan, the highest number and proportion ever. After a decline in enrollment between 1999 and 2005, the rapid rise since 2006 coincided with an increase in the amount paid to Medicare Advantage plans per enrollee by the Medicare program, an average of 10% more per enrollee than Medicare spends in the Parts A and B programs, resulting in much more extensive marketing of expanded benefits by Medicare Advantage plans across the country.

As Figure 9.3 illustrates, Medicare Advantage plans have widely varying penetration rates across the states. Enrollment rates vary from 41% of Medicare beneficiaries in Oregon and Hawaii to less than 1% in Alaska (Health Policy Brief, 2011). As a general trend accentuated by the key to Figure 9.3, states containing insurance companies with extensive experience managing large, insured, working-age populations through managed care arrangements are the states where insurance companies became Medicare-approved Medicare Advantage plans, and therefore where larger proportions of Medicare beneficiaries are enrolled in Medicare Advantage plans. More than half of these beneficiaries are enrolled in plans offered by just a few companies, including Blue

FIGURE 9.2.   Recent Trends in Medicare Advantage Enrollment

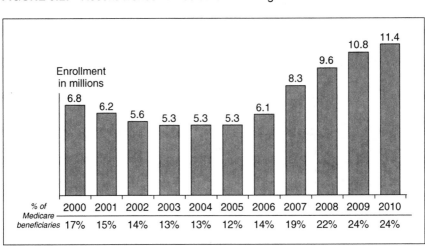

FIGURE 9.3.   Medicare Advantage Penetration Across the United States, 2010

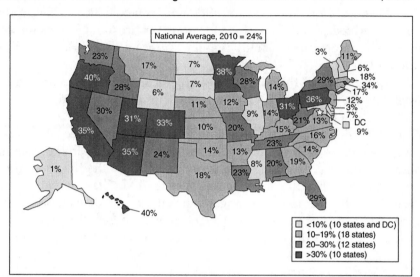

Cross-Blue Shield affiliates, Humana, Kaiser Permanente, and United Healthcare.

An important trend to note for this book is that Black and Latino Medicare beneficiaries are disproportionately enrolled in Medicare Advantage plans. It is believed that some ethnic groups may join in order to receive expanded Medicare benefits such as vision and dental care offered by some plans that use their payment surpluses from Medicare to make their plans more attractive than Medicare Parts A and B. In addition, lower income beneficiaries are less likely to be able to afford private insurance policy supplements to Medicare (referred to as Medigap policies), so these beneficiaries view Medicare Advantage plans as the best way to obtain a maximum benefit package under Medicare alone (Health Policy Brief, 2011).

The major debate regarding Medicare Advantage plans is whether they are too costly and unfairly offer expanded benefits to members compared to those in traditional Medicare A and B programs, or whether it is precisely the direction Medicare should be headed, offering choice to consumers and more coordinated care through strategies aimed at controlling the provider supply and encouraging members to engage in healthier lifestyles and take full advantage of clinical preventive screening services. In the short term, it appears that payment levels to Medicare Advantage programs will be reduced; this is described later under the Affordable Care Act of 2010. Based on legislative proposals before Congress in 2011, Medicare Advantage policy directions range from requiring future Medicare beneficiaries to enroll in Medicare Advantage plans, to weakening Medicare Advantage plans and strengthening traditional Medicare by offering expanded benefits to Part A and B enrollees.

Little is known about how well Medicare Advantage plans work for Blacks and Latinos with Alzheimer's disease and other dementia. Because consumers must make a proactive choice to enroll in Medicare Advantage plans, it is possible that fewer Blacks and Latinos with dementia join these plans, especially if the families do not know about the different plans in order to help them decide whether to remain in Medicare Parts A and B or switch to an Advantage plan. Social workers assisting Black and Latino caregivers having dementia-afflicted relatives should provide information to help determine the best option to pursue for Medicare coverage.

How Does the Medicare Prescription Drug Program Work?

Medicare Part D is the final component of Medicare health care financing, and it pays part of the costs for prescription drugs through contracts Medicare has established with private plans. Part D began operation in 2006, and by 2010 Medicare Part A and B beneficiaries in most states could choose from at least 45 stand-alone Part D plans. Most Medicare Advantage plans offer their own choices of prescription drug plans. As with Medicare Advantage health insurance plans, social workers need to help with this as the amount of choice for prescription drug plans can be bewildering to persons with dementia and their families, especially if they have lower levels of health literacy due to socioeconomic circumstances.

The amount of coverage provided by Medicare prescription drug plans depends on the amount of expenses for medications accumulated throughout the year. In addition to the monthly premium required to be a member of a plan, the typical plan requires an initial deductible payment, which was $310 in 2010. For expenses up to a coverage limit ($2,830 in a typical plan in 2010), the plan will pay 75% of medication expenses and the beneficiary pays the remaining 25%. Then, there is a large coverage gap, known as the *doughnut hole*, within which the beneficiary is responsible for paying all medication expenses. Once an upper expense limit is reached in this gap ($6,440 in a typical plan in 2010), the beneficiary is responsible for only 5% of drug expenses. This is clearly a very complex insurance arrangement, and the *doughnut hole* has caused a great deal of uproar among consumer advocacy groups. As a result of widespread discontent with this arrangement, the Affordable Care Act of 2010 included provisions to begin closing the *doughnut hole*, so that by the year 2020 all Medicare prescription drug plans will be required to pay 75% of drug expenses up to the limit where the beneficiary pays only 5%.

What Health Care Services Are Not Covered by Medicare?

It is important for social workers to know the health care services that not covered by Medicare. Contrary to popular belief, Medicare does not pay for long-term nursing home care or for in-home care that is provided for chronic illnesses that do not require skilled nursing or rehabilitation therapy. If a beneficiary has Alzheimer's disease or other dementia, but does not hold the prospect of improving in health status by the delivery of skilled care services, then it is highly unlikely that Medicare will pay for those services. Medicare also does not pay for assisted living facility care, eye or hearing examinations, dentures or other dental care, or for orthopedic shoes. The only exceptions are that some Medicare Advantage plans may pay for vision, hearing, dental, and/or orthopedic shoes as part of their expanded benefits, as noted earlier in this chapter. The critical message here is that people and families living with dementia must understand that if long-term care is required in a nursing home or at home, without the prospect of improved health or function, then Medicare will not pay for these services.

How Does Having Dementia Affect Beneficiaries' Medicare Expenses?

We close this section on Medicare by showing how a diagnosis of Alzheimer's disease or other dementia influences Medicare expenses accumulated by beneficiaries during the course of a year. Figure 9.4 compares average per-person Medicare payments in 2006 for selected types of health care services for Medicare for beneficiaries with and without dementia. This figure further classifies beneficiaries according to selected medical conditions such as heart disease and diabetes. Results indicate that, with one exception (physician services for patients with congestive heart failure), beneficiaries with dementia generated higher Medicare payments for all types of services than beneficiaries without dementia; for example, among those with heart disease and dementia, total Medicare payments in 2006 were $24,275 per person, compared to those with heart disease but not with dementia, for whom the average

FIGURE 9.4. Medicare Payments for Beneficiaries With and Without Dementia

Selected medical condition by Alzheimer's Disease/ Dementia (AD/D) status	Average per person Medicare payment				
	Total Payment	Payment for Hospital Care	Payment for Physician Care	Payment for Skilled Nursing Facility Care	Payment for Home Health Care
Coronary Heart Disease					
With AD/D	$24,275	$9,752	$1,690	$3,587	$1,748
Without AD/D	17,102	7,601	1,462	1,124	868
Diabetes					
With AD/D	24,129	9,417	1,598	3,586	1,928
Without AD/D	15,162	6,279	1,277	1,078	884
Congestive Heart Failure					
With AD/D	24,900	9,999	1,663	3,740	1,756
Without AD/D	20,722	9,384	1,696	1,663	1,198
Cancer					
With AD/D	21,933	8,110	1,503	2,905	1,498
Without AD/D	15,887	5,637	1,293	822	583

From Alzheimer's Association Facts & Figures (2011), p. 39.

Medicare payments were $17,102 per person. Looking at Figure 9.4 it can be seen that dementia care adds considerably to total Medicare payments regardless of coexisting medical condition.

Medicaid

The Medicaid insurance program was passed into law in 1965 as Title XIX of the Social Security Act, immediately following passage of the Medicare program. Because of Medicaid's official standing within the Social Security Act, individuals with Medicaid insurance are often referred to by health and social work providers as *Title 19 patients*.

Medicaid is a health insurance for Americans of any age with limited income and assets, and was established because poor Americans in the 1960s were unable to purchase private health insurance due to the prohibitive cost of monthly premiums. When the U.S. Congress enacted Medicaid, the typical beneficiaries were young families with dependent children, often headed by single mothers, and Medicaid covered medical expenses related to physician visits for prenatal care and pediatric health problems as well as catastrophic expenses related to hospitalizations. However, amendments to Medicaid legislation in 1968 for nursing home care, and in 1981 for long-term care at home through the Home and Community-Based Waiver program, opened Medicaid coverage for older adults with chronic health problems such as Alzheimer's disease.

Visit www.Medicaid.gov for more details about Medicaid than are covered in this chapter.

How Is Medicaid Administered and Financed?

Medicaid is jointly administered and financed by state and federal governments. States administer their own Medicaid programs on a daily basis, while the federal Medicaid program (part of the Centers for Medicare & Medicaid Services) provides broad guidelines requiring state provision of certain Medicaid services such as nursing home and hospital care. Medicaid eligibility is based on a *categorical test*, where individuals must be classified as aged, blind, disabled, or a member of a single-parent family with dependent children; an *income test*, where states apply their own threshold for income eligibility (often lower than the federal poverty level); and an *asset test*, where states assess the value of real and personal property. States have wide latitude in establishing income and asset levels for individual and family financial eligibility for their Medicaid programs. Generally, states in the southern U.S. have established lower levels of income and assets for Medicaid eligibility, while states in New England and the upper Midwest have established higher levels of income and assets.

Medicaid financing is shared between the federal and state governments. A formula based on state per-capita income is employed to determine the federal share of Medicaid financing for each state. In states with the highest per-capita income the federal Medicaid share is 50%, while in states with the lowest per-capita income, the federal Medicaid share is as high as 76%; nationwide, the federal government funds about 57% of all Medicaid costs (Kaiser Commission, 2010a). Once individuals and families are deemed financially eligible for their state Medicaid programs, they may or may not be responsible for cost sharing and deductibles at the time services are used, depending upon the state in which they reside.

Over the decades since Medicaid was established, older adults and adults with disabilities have consumed ever-growing proportions of total Medicaid expenditures. Figure 9.5 shows how the Medicaid enrollee population is distributed much as Congress envisioned when Medicaid was first established, with 85% of all enrollees in 2007 being adults and children in families with limited income and assets; however, these enrollees are responsible for only about one-third of all Medicaid expenditures. Conversely, older adults and adults with disabilities made up 25% of all enrollees but consumed 67% of all Medicaid expenditures

FIGURE 9.5. Medicaid Enrollees and Expenditures by Enrollment Group, 2007

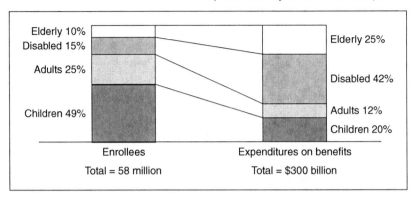

in 2007. This discrepancy is due largely to the fact that Medicaid programs in states pay primarily for much more expensive nursing home care and long-term in-home care for older adults and adults with disabilities, while paying primarily for much less expensive ambulatory care (with occasional hospital care) for younger families with dependent children.

What Are Medicaid Waiver Programs and Why Were They Developed?

By the late 1970s, it became quite clear to state and federal Medicaid program decision makers that the most expensive Medicaid-funded service for individual beneficiaries over time was nursing home care, and that the population most likely to use nursing homes, older adults, was projected to grow in size into the future. Even though most of these older adults entering nursing homes were covered by Medicare insurance due to their age, as we have seen Medicare does not pay for long-term nursing home care. Moreover, even if many of these individuals paid for nursing home care from their personal assets and savings when they first entered, the high cost of nursing home care (nationwide average of $72,000 per year; Kaiser Commission, 2010b) led them to quickly spend their personal resources, and they soon became sufficiently poor to qualify for Medicaid in their states. From that point until they died, Medicaid paid for their long-term nursing home stays. The policy solution was to develop home- and community-based services so that individuals with moderate to severe disabilities could remain in their homes (where most preferred to stay in the first place) rather than enter nursing homes.

This Medicaid policy change led to the Home and Community Based Waiver Program option enacted in 1981. States were invited under this legislation to apply to the federal Medicaid program for a Waiver Program and to demonstrate how the Waiver Program would result in cost savings to their Medicaid program compared to providing nursing home care to their disabled populations. Medicaid Waiver programs specifically target home-dwelling individuals who are so disabled due to their medical conditions and related symptoms that they would qualify for nursing home-level care in their states. States were permitted to develop Medicaid Waiver programs for defined populations, such as older adults, younger adults with disabilities, and individuals of any age with developmental disabilities. States were also permitted to establish higher Medicaid financial eligibility thresholds for Medicaid Waiver Program enrollees than for their other Medicaid programs; for example, income limits for Medicaid Waiver eligibility might be 150%–200% higher than income limits for other Medicaid program eligibility.

Over the past 30 years, Medicaid Waiver programs have proliferated throughout the country. By 2009, 44 states had Medicaid Waiver programs in place for older adults and younger adults with disabilities, and 49 states had Medicaid Waiver programs for individuals with developmental disabilities (Eiken et al., 2010). Medicaid spending for Americans with long-term care needs has shifted quite dramatically as a result of the growth of Medicaid Waiver programs; in 1990, only 13% of all Medicaid long-term care spending was for home- and community-based services (87% went to nursing home care), but by 2008, spending on home- and community-based services accounted for 42% of total Medicaid long-term care spending (58% to nursing home care). As with most Medicaid spending patterns, states differ greatly in the proportion of their long-term care spending devoted to home and community-based services. In 2008, for example, Mississippi spent only 13% of its Medicaid long-term care budget on home- and community-based services (same as the national percentage back in 1990), while in New Mexico 73% of all Medicaid long-term care spending went to home- and community-based services (Kaiser Commission, 2010).

For individuals enrolled into Medicaid Waiver programs, available services include personal care assistance, homemaker and chore services, adult day care, and transportation to medical appointments. Social workers need to know these are precisely the types of services that families often provide on a daily basis to older relatives with dementia and other chronic medical conditions, so the availability of these services also helps Black and Latino families keep their relatives at home for a longer period of time than if these services were unavailable. In most states, social workers are commonly employed as care or case managers to develop service packages for clients enrolled in Medicaid Waiver programs. People with dementia and their families have benefitted greatly from Medicaid Waiver programs by receiving home- and community-based services to delay or avoid nursing home admissions. Blacks and Latinos, who prefer to keep their older relatives at home as opposed to placing them in nursing homes, have been particularly helped by the availability of Medicaid Waiver programs.

Dual Eligibles: Americans Enrolled in Medicare and Medicaid Programs

When individuals are enrolled in both Medicare and Medicaid, they are referred to as *dual eligibles.* Nearly 9 million Americans are dual eligibles; they represent 15% of all Medicaid enrollees, and 16% of all Medicare enrollees. Consider what we have learned in this chapter about eligibility criteria for Medicare and Medicaid. If someone is age 65 or older, or younger than age 65 and disabled (Medicare-eligible) *and* has limited income and assets (Medicaid-eligible), he or she is at great risk for having or developing multiple health problems requiring extensive health and social services. Indeed, dual eligibles are among the sickest and poorest Americans; they are more likely to be hospitalized, use emergency rooms, and require long-term care than other Medicare beneficiaries. Social work assistance is greatly needed to help these health disparities populations.

Figure 9.6 illustrates how dual eligibles compare to all Medicare beneficiaries on a number of characteristics salient to the topic of this book. More than half (54%) of all dual eligibles have cognitive impairment or other mental health problems, compared to 24% of all Medicare beneficiaries. Nearly half (46%) of all dual eligibles are Black, Latino, or members of other racial and ethnic groups of color, compared to only 17% of all Medicare beneficiaries. The much higher proportion of dual eligibles with low income and low levels of educational attainment compared to all Medicare beneficiaries echoes the disadvantaged socioeconomic position of Blacks and Latinos compared to Whites, as detailed in Chapter 1.

Social workers are highly likely to work with dual eligibles if they are providing care to Blacks and Latinos with dementia, and the positive news is that these individuals are eligible for the widest array of health services, ranging from acute care to rehabilitation therapy to long-term care at home (through Medicaid Waiver programs), than any other segment of the American population. The biggest challenge for

FIGURE 9.6. Dual Eligibles Compared to Other Medicare Beneficiaries, 2008

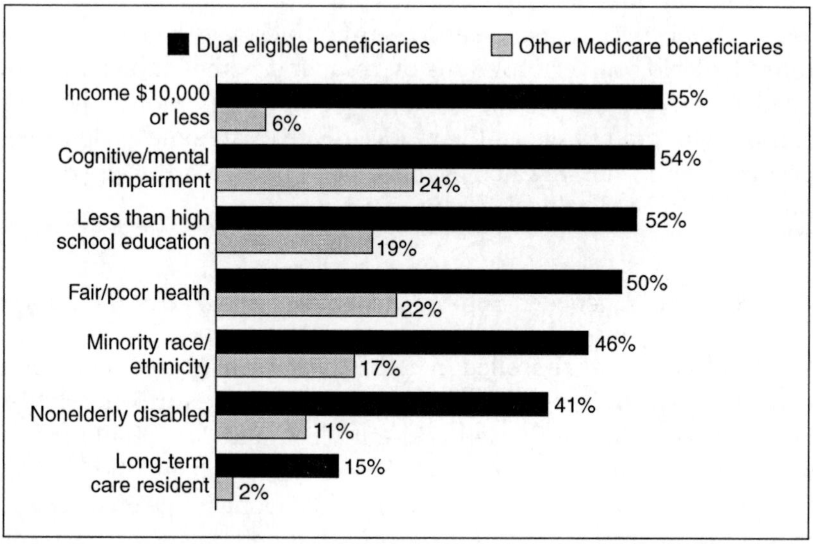

From Kaiser Commission (2010c).

social workers is to help coordinate all available services, because it has been found that dual eligibles often use the same types of services paid for by both Medicare and Medicaid at the same time, especially in-home care, which could result in duplication and fragmentation of services received by dual eligibles (Fortinsky et al., 2004).

The Patient Protection and Affordable Care Act of 2010

The Patient Protection and Affordable Care Act (PPACA) was enacted March 23, 2010. The Council on Social Work Education (CSWE) enlisted the services of Lewis-Burke Associates, LLC, to prepare the Patient Protection and Affordable Care Act of 2010: A Resource Guide for Social Workers (Lewis-Burke, 2011). The guide contains seven chapters "on the health care reform law, specifically highlighting many of the provision that relate to social work education and training, and changes to the health care system that, in some cases, will fundamentally alter how services are provided in this country" (Lewis-Burke, 2011, p. 2). Regarding the guide, Lewis-Burke (2011) state the following.

In addition to ensuring coverage for more Americans, ending insurance discrimination, and closing gaps in Medicare and Medicaid, the law creates new and expands existing federal programs aimed at enhancing the health professions workforce. This includes many new provisions that, if funded, would assist with recruitment, retention, and specialized training of social workers. (Lewis-Burke, 2011, p. 2)

The PPACA included many components that directly affect Americans enrolled in Medicare and/or Medicaid, and social workers providing care to Blacks and Latinos with dementia might find several opportunities within provisions of the PPACA to link these clients and their families with newly available services and program initiatives. This section briefly highlights selected PPACA components that could most directly affect Medicare and dual eligible beneficiaries, especially those that could help reduce racial and ethnic disparities in the use of Medicare-funded services. Most of these Medicare and Medicaid changes started January 1, 2011. Social Workers need to be aware of the content in the CSWE Patient Protection and Affordable Care Act of 2010: A Resource Guide for Social Workers (Lewis-Burke, 2011) and on the PPACA. Visit http://www.cswe.org for the CSWEHealthCareReformGuideMar11Final.pdf and http://www.kff.org/healthreform/upload/8061.pdf for more details about PPACA.

Medicare Changes in the PPACA

- Clinical preventive services under Medicare Part B are available at no cost to beneficiaries; before the PPACA, beneficiaries were responsible for paying 20% of the cost of these services. As discussed earlier in this chapter, these services prevent or help detect through screening tests the most serious medical conditions of adulthood and later life, including cancer, diabetes, and heart disease. Removing the financial barrier is expected to increase the use of these important screening procedures for all Americans, especially Blacks, Latinos, and other racial and ethnic groups of color.
- Free "Welcome to Medicare" physical examination for new beneficiaries, during which physicians provide several screening tests, including a set of screening questions to help detect memory or other cognitive problems. Normally, Medicare beneficiaries are responsible for paying 20% of physician office visits under Part B, so this free visit with screening examinations is expected to increase checkups throughout the Medicare population.

- Annual free wellness visit starting 12 months after the Welcome to Medicare exam.
- Reduction in Medicare payments to Medicare Advantage plans, which may result in reduction of plans participating in Medicare Advantage and the need for covered individuals to find other Medicare Advantage plans or enroll in Medicare Parts A and B. There is early debate about whether racial and ethnic groups of color will be disproportionately affected by Medicare Advantage closures.
- Closing the *doughnut hole* in Medicare Part D prescription drug coverage gradually until it is completely closed in 2020. All beneficiaries with intermediately high prescription drug costs will be helped greatly by this PPACA provision.
- Establishment of *Accountable Care Organizations* (ACOs) to promote and improve the quality of health care to Medicare beneficiaries and lower or slow the increase of Medicare costs (Lieberman & Bertko, 2011). Social workers should become familiar with ACOs, because they may find themselves working for an organization that becomes an ACO partner (primary care physicians, hospitals, home health agencies, and other providers within defined geographic areas will form ACOs). Indeed, the National Association of Social Workers (NASW) voiced strong support for ACOs, and provided detailed recommendations to federal Medicare program officials about how professional social workers could help immensely in improving the quality of care while closely monitoring service costs within ACOs (Clark, 2011).

Medicaid Long-Term Care Changes in the PPACA

- Extends through 2016 the Money Follows the Person (MFP) demonstration program, an initiative started in 2006 to move Medicaid-insured nursing home residents back into the community with adequate health and social care support; states also have the option to expand the number of individuals targeted for return to community living in their MFP programs.
- Provides financial incentives to states to expand the population receiving home- and community-based services under Medicaid Waiver programs.
- Establishes the Community Living Assistance Services and Supports (CLASS) Act, a national, voluntary insurance program

intended partially to help subscribers avoid having to join the Medicaid program to receive long-term care services. In effect, the CLASS program is intended to work like long-term care insurance programs that have been available through private insurance companies for years, but because it is through a national program, it is expected that premiums will be much more affordable to working and working-age adults (National Health Policy Forum, 2010).

Changes for Dual Eligibles in the PPACA

- All the changes in Medicare and Medicaid already noted will help improve service availability and quality for dual eligibles.
- Two new federal offices have been created to help determine ways to improve care coordination and control care costs for dual eligibles—the Federal Coordinated Health Care Office and the Center for Medicare and Medicaid Innovations. As of mid 2011, 15 states had received 1-year planning grants from the Innovations Center to design integrated care models so that all Medicare and Medicaid funded health and social care services delivered to community-dwelling dual eligibles will be coordinated and streamlined. Social workers stand to play key roles in these state-integrated care models for dual eligibles given their professional experience providing care management services to populations requiring long-term care. Blacks and Latinos who are dual eligibles, especially those living with dementia, stand to benefit greatly from improved models of care intended primarily to sustain independent living at home as long as possible.

Older Americans Act

The OAA was also passed into law in 1965 to develop a nationwide network of information, referral, and direct service delivery related to nonmedical but essential health and social services for all Americans aged 60 and older regardless of income level. The so-called *Aging Network* that was constructed with funding allocated by the OAA includes the national U.S. Administration on Aging; state-level units on aging, which may be departments or divisions within departments in state governments; and more than 600 Area Agencies on Aging, the operational units of the Aging Network serving sub-state geographic regions. Core services funded by the OAA and its amendments include: nutrition (home-delivered meals and congregate meals at community sites); multipurpose senior centers; transportation; legal assistance; pension and employment counseling; and nonmedical home- and community-based support services such as personal care, homemaker and chore assistance, adult day care, and mental health services. Ombudsman services are provided to nursing home residents with OAA funds. Fees charged for these services vary widely across the country, and many are offered free of charge. All of these services could be very beneficial to supplement care provided by families. Although a similar range of in-home and supportive services is offered by Medicaid Waiver programs, as discussed earlier in this chapter, many adults age 60 or older are not Medicaid-eligible and may not be disabled to the extent of needing nursing home care. Therefore, OAA funds services for a much broader segment of the older population than either Medicare or Medicaid. For more details on services funded through the Aging Network with funding from the OAA, visit www.aoa.gov (Niles-Yokum & Wagner, 2011).

Two programs offered through the Aging Network are especially important for individuals and families living with the daily challenges of dementia: the *National Family Caregiver Support Program* and the *Alzheimer's Disease Supportive Services Program*. The National Family Caregiver Support Program, established in 2000, provides grants to states and U.S. territories to assist family caregivers to care for their relatives at home as long as possible. Federal funding is allocated based on proportion of the population aged 70 and older, and all states, as a condition of receiving this federal funding, must offer core services including information to the caregiver about available resources for their specific needs, assistance in accessing these community resources, individual counseling, support group organization, caregiver training programs, and respite care. More than 600,000 caregivers nationwide were served by funding from this program in 2008. The Alzheimer's Disease Supportive Services Program provides competitive funding to states or local areas to develop evidence-based and innovative programs to help individuals and families living with any type of irreversible dementia. Between 2007 and 2010, nearly 70 programs were funded to partnerships in 34 states and Puerto Rico to develop and carry out their programs. Information about the availability and content of these programs within states or local jurisdictions may be obtained by contacting the appropriate Area Agency on Aging serving that region.

WORKFORCE TRENDS

Now that we have seen the major financing mechanisms for health and social services for older Americans in general, and how these financing mechanisms could assist Black and Latino families caring for older relatives with dementia, we turn attention to the social work profession in America and how well equipped it is to serve an aging society. In this section, we first review where professional social workers currently practice in serving Medicare and Medicaid beneficiaries. We then discuss where social work practice opportunities are likely to emerge given the policy trends discussed earlier in this chapter. Finally, we discuss the long-recognized but not yet achieved need to infuse greater amounts of geriatrics and gerontology education into professional social work curricula and continuing education mechanisms in order to produce greater numbers of social workers with timely knowledge about health and social needs of America's rapidly growing older population.

Where Social Workers Care for Older Adults and Families

Nearly 600,000 professional social workers practice in the United States (Institute of Medicine, 2008). Of these, more than 240,000 are *clinical social workers* practicing in mental and behavioral health settings. Only about 37,000 clinical social workers are Medicare-certified providers who provide social work services to Medicare beneficiaries experiencing emotional, behavioral, psychological, and social problems related to a wide variety of health and mental health conditions, including Alzheimer's disease and other dementia (Clark, 2011). Many clinical social workers are employed by Area Agencies on Aging and other service providers that are responsible for operating state Medicaid Waiver programs. In this care management capacity, these social work professionals conduct comprehensive in-home health and social needs assessments with potential clients and family members to determine eligibility, and then design service packages for eligible recipients. Many other clinical social workers practice independently as care managers on a fee-for-service basis, offering their services to older adults and families faced with disabilities and multiple health conditions who have resources to pay out-of-pocket for these professional services. Regardless of the setting in which they practice, clinical social workers working with this clientele must possess knowledge about dementia diseases and also demonstrate cultural competence to be able to serve families from all racial and ethnic backgrounds. Opportunities for clinical social workers to practice in these settings will grow considerably over the next several years as Medicaid Waiver programs and other initiatives designed to maintain older adults with dementia and other health problems at home as long as possible expand, pursuant to PPACA-stimulated changes for Medicaid beneficiaries and dual eligibles discussed earlier in this chapter.

Medical social workers account for most of the remainder of the social work professional workforce. They practice as part of interdisciplinary health care teams in hospitals, primary care settings, rehabilitation facilities, home health care agencies, nursing homes, and hospice and palliative care programs. Medical social workers working with older adults must be Medicare-certified providers, and they play multiple roles including case management and care coordination, patient and family education, discharge planning, advance care planning, and community outreach and engagement. As the NASW recently made clear to Medicare officials, "Social workers are…the only health care professionals devoted exclusively to addressing the psychosocial needs of Medicare beneficiaries and family caregivers" (Clark, 2011). With the advent of ACOs, also pursuant to the PPACA as discussed earlier, numerous opportunities will develop for medical social workers to join interdisciplinary teams in primary care settings and hospitals to help these Medicare-approved providers improve the quality of care and contain costs for Medicare beneficiaries.

Need for Social Workers in an Aging Society

Despite these opportunities for growth in the social work profession due to favorable public policy and financing trends in Medicare and Medicaid programs, there is a growing need for more geriatric-trained social workers to practice with America's exploding older ethnic population. With this goal in mind, in 2004 the Council of Social Work Education (CSWE) Commission for Curriculum and Educational Innovation (COCEI) and Commission for Accreditation (COA) took the lead and began reviewing and revising the Educational Policy and Accreditation Standards (EPAS), the COA document to increase and improve social work curricula developing a competency-based education advanced in Gero Social Work Practice. Social workers seeking to improve Gero social work skills should refer to the competency requirements. Visit http://www.cswe.org/18949.aspx?catGroupId=6&catId=77 for the complete Generalist and Advanced Gero Social Work Practice brochure detailing information regarding the required Advanced Gero Social Work Practice guide (CSWE, 2008).

The brochure not only outlines the Gero social work required student curricula in both generalist and advanced education, but also identifies the required demonstrated practice outcome for each competency and the evaluation required by the academy and by the field agency supervisors in actual practice settings. Social workers seeing to increase Gero education skills are encouraged to visit the CSWE website for Gero education training. The authors note:

> The advanced Gero Social Work Practice Guide is an outcome of a decade of accomplishment in gerontological competency-based social work education supported by the John A. Hartford Geriatric Social Work Initiative (GSWI). Leadership for the development of gerontological competence in relationship to EPAS grew out of the collaboration of the two major GSWI gerontological curriculum projects: The CSWE National Center for Gerontological Social Work Education (Gero-Ed Center) with Nancy Hooyman and Julia Watkins, coprincipal investigators; and the Hartford Partnership Program at the Social Work Leadership Institute at the New York Academy of Medicine, with Patricia Volland, principal investigator. (CSWE, 2008, p. 2)

The need for geriatric social workers has been recognized since the 1980s; in 1987, the National Institute on Aging estimated that 70,000 social workers trained in geriatrics would be needed by the year 2020 to adequately serve America's growing older population. Social workers employed in care settings including nursing homes and home care report greater challenges than their peers in hospitals, including lower pay, higher caseloads, tasks below their skill levels, and lack of peer networks and employer support (Institute of Medicine, 2008; Stone & Harahan, 2010).

Several promising trends may help address these problems and reverse the trend of low geriatric training levels in the social work profession. In 2007, the NASW released specialty certificates in gerontology and made them available to its members. Two national foundations have supported initiatives to promote education and training in geriatric social work. In 1999, The Atlantic Philanthropies and the John A. Hartford Foundation funded the Social Work Leadership Institute at the New York Academy of Medicine. This Institute sponsors the Practicum Partnership Program, which as of 2007 had trained more than 1,000 social workers to work with older adults using a specialized field educational model for MSW students. The Atlantic Philanthropies also supported the establishment of the Institute for Geriatric Social Work at Boston University, which promotes the training of practicing social workers in geriatric care issues in partnership with the American Society on Aging and other national groups. The John A. Hartford Foundation also has supported educational initiatives to grow aging content in BSW and MSW curricula (Institute of Medicine, 2008). Finally, the Caring for an Aging America Act, (S. 1095), a bill to attract health professionals to the field of geriatrics and gerontology by providing loan repayment opportunities in exchange for agreeing to work in underserved areas, was introduced in the United States Congress. If enacted, this bipartisan bill expands the Health Resources and Services Administration's National Health Service Corps Program to include primary health care professionals with training in geriatrics and gerontology. Visit Eldercare Workforce Alliance http://eldercareworkforce.rallycongress.com/4544/tell-your-senator-to-support-cosponsor-caring-an-aging-america-ac/ for more information.

It remains to be seen whether these initiatives can help increase the supply of culturally competent professional social workers trained appropriately to care for the growing older population. Critical educational components in any geriatrics training program must include adequate education about Alzheimer's disease and other dementia, and the needs of individuals and families from diverse racial and ethnic backgrounds living with the daily challenges of these brain diseases. Social workers will have to be trained to recognize how much control older clients and their families wish to have over their care, because racial and ethnic variations in amount of desired control have been found (Sciegaj et al., 2004). This advanced level of social work professional expertise is closely related to the need for cultural competence and the highest level of ethical conduct, both topics which have been discussed elsewhere in this book.

DEMENTIA CARE TRENDS

This chapter closes with a brief discussion of emerging trends in dementia diagnosis and management that hold special importance to social workers and to Black and Latino families affected by Alzheimer's disease and other dementia. The important issues of seeking information and help as early as possible after memory-related symptoms are noticed, and seeking knowledge about risk for developing dementia, are themes highlighted in Chapters 1 and 2 regarding characteristics of Black and Latino populations in America, and scientific and clinical challenges in diagnosing memory and cognitive symptoms. Our concluding discussion about emerging trends in community services for families affected by dementia introduces initiatives in England that hold promise for replication and adaptation in America for Black and Latino communities.

Earlier Presentation of Symptoms and Asymptomatic Screening

There is substantial evidence that Blacks, Latinos, and families from other racial and ethnic groups of color face special challenges when seeking information or help after dementia-related symptoms are noticed. Individual and family-related factors hindering dementia symptom presentation at physician offices by racial and ethnic groups of color include differing cultural interpretations of dementia, lower health literacy, and language barriers between patients and their families and health care providers. Provider-related factors include diagnostic uncertainty and futility of making a diagnosis due to the lack of consistently effective drugs to treat symptoms on the part of primary care physicians, and lack of cultural sensitivity and competency training among health care social service providers more generally. Racial and ethnic disparities have been found in the prescription of dementia medications among individuals with a dementia diagnosis; Blacks, Latinos, and other groups of color are less likely than Whites to use prescription antidementia medications. The lack of available dementia care specialists in most parts of the United States further confounds efforts to seek help for dementia symptoms among all Americans (Alzheimer's Association, 2011; Fortinsky, 2008; Franz et al., 2007; Zuckerman et al., 2008).

Given this current state of affairs, social work professionals stand to play an important role in encouraging their Black and Latino clients to seek help for dementia-related symptoms, and in addressing these numerous barriers to adequate dementia care. Earlier detection and diagnosis of cognitive impairment could confer numerous benefits to families. These include allowing prompt evaluation and treatment of reversible causes of dementia, many which were discussed in Chapter 2; allowing potential management of symptoms with medications and nonpharmacological interventions for family caregivers, many which were discussed in Chapter 1; helping facilitate management of other frequently occurring medical conditions and the multiple medications often taken for these conditions; and providing opportunities for families to plan for the future (Alzheimer's Association, 2011). While there are no easy answers to the barriers hindering dementia care, raising awareness about the facts and myths surrounding dementia is an important first step in getting clients from diverse racial and ethnic backgrounds to seek diagnosis and treatment.

Regarding asymptomatic screening, current clinical practice guidelines do not recommend routine screening for cognitive impairment. However, as noted earlier in this chapter, the new, free Welcome to Medicare physical examination includes assessment for possible cognitive impairment, which could represent the critical first step toward increasing communication between doctors and older patients and their families about memory issues and concerns. Research has shown that the discussion about potential memory concerns in the doctor's office often does not occur because each member in the interaction waits for the other to bring up the issue, and all feel uncomfortable about doing (Bradford et al., 2009). Asymptomatic screening could help initiate such discussions before any crisis point is reached after subsequent dementia symptom recognition. Social work professionals could help raise awareness about the importance of asymptomatic and very early symptomatic screening as part of the Welcome to Medicare visit.

Finally, as discussed in Chapter 2, recent clinical studies have begun to determine the effectiveness of modern techniques for detecting biomarkers in the brain, bloodstream, and cerebrospinal fluid that may be strongly associated with the presence of cognitive impairment or risk for developing dementia. Such studies could also help unlock the mysteries surrounding racial differences in risk for carrying genes and proteins that greatly raise the possibility of developing Alzheimer's disease. Social work professionals could use their cultural sensitivity when working with Black families to explain why it is important to consider enrolling in these types of scientific studies. Admittedly, this issue carries serious ethical concerns, especially regarding what to do if one is found to have elevated risk for developing dementia, but these discussions are imperative if racial and ethnic disparities in screening, diagnosis, and treatment are to be surmounted.

Emerging Community-Based Services for People With Dementia

Partnerships among community organizations and innovation represent the major forces behind emerging trends in service development for people with dementia and their families. Many emerging services and programs place high priority on including racially and ethnically diverse populations, or are located within communities in which different groups of color are the predominant residents. In the United States, many evidence-based family caregiver support programs, and programs serving frail older adults including those with dementia, are being disseminated into communities throughout the country. Many of these programs were discussed in Chapter 1, including those that have included Black and Latino family caregivers in their original inceptions. With financial support from OAA funds and other funding sources, replication and customization of these programs is occurring within numerous Black, Latino, and other racial and ethnic communities. Partnerships among community organizations, as well as input from target populations within the community, are critical ingredients of these programs; professional social workers could help fuel the further development of these initiatives in their own communities.

America is far from alone among countries grappling with the growth of Alzheimer's disease and other dementia in its racially and ethnically diverse population. In England, over the past decade, several national policy directives have provided considerable guidance about how community-based dementia care services might develop in local areas and regions through organizational partnerships. As one result, the Partnerships for Older People Projects (POPPS) were established in 29 locales with funding from the national government. The guiding goal of POPPS is to provide earlier and preventive services for older people with, or at risk for, mental health problems including memory and cognitive impairment. Embedded within many POPPS projects are creative support services for people in earlier stages of the disease process.

One of the more creative services established in several POPPS locales is known as a *well-being café* or *dementia café*, where people with dementia and their families can meet in a relaxed atmosphere to learn from each other, engage in recreational, entertainment, and educational activities, and share a meal and other refreshments together. These cafes were first introduced in the Netherlands in 2000, and the POPPS initiative enabled their rapid spread throughout England; such cafes have also been developed in Australia (Capus, 2006; Fortinsky, 2008; Mather, 2007). Many of these cafés are located within existing community gathering places, often resulting in a cross-section of service users representing the composition of the community's population.

Looking to the future while considering these promising recent program and service developments at the community level, two parting recommendations close this chapter. First, these emerging programs, with social interaction and informal information sharing as a foundation, could represent an initial first step toward raising awareness about memory problems and bringing people together to discuss how to overcome the multiple barriers to seeking dementia diagnosis and treatment underscored in this chapter. While family support groups have partially served this function for modest numbers of families and persons living with dementia, these groups are less available in Black and Latino communities than they are in White communities. In contrast, cafés could help open discourse about dementia in the context of other ongoing social activities, and empower families to problem-solve together. Social workers should consider developing services such as dementia cafés in communities where they work, especially where Black, Latino, and other racial and ethnic groups of color predominate. The authors of this book are presently working with community partners to develop a café in a Latino community and there is considerable public interest in the development of this service.

A final recommendation is that professional social workers serving older adults with dementia and their families throughout defined geographic areas could lead development of partnerships in their locales to replicate, adapt, and develop new community services for this population. For reasons mentioned throughout this book, Black and Latino communities would greatly benefit from leadership in the health care professional arena to develop such services. Many more individualized and family-oriented dementia care services could then be designed and planned based on knowledge gained from sharing practice insights with professional colleagues, and from interaction with Black and Latino families during the course of working with them throughout the dementia disease process.

REFERENCES

AARP Public Policy Institute. (2009). *The Medicare beneficiary population. Fact Sheet #149.* Washington, DC: Author.

Alzheimer's Association. (2011). *2011 Alzheimer's disease facts and figures.* Chicago, IL: Author.

Capus, J. (2006). The Kingston dementia café: The benefits of establishing an Alzheimer's cafe for carers and people with dementia. *Dementia: The International Journal for Research and Practice, 4*, 588–591.

Clark, E. (2011). *NASW comments on notice for proposed rule making for Medicare ACOs.* Letter from Elizabeth Clark, NASW Executive Director, to Donald Berwick, CMS Administrator, June 6, 2011. Retrieved June 21, 2011, from http://www.socialworkers.org/practice/clinical/2011/110606%20NASW%20Comments%20on%20CMS%20Proposed%20Rule%20CMS-1345-P.pdf

Council on Social Work Education. (2008). *Advanced gero social work practice.* Washington, DC: Council on Social Work Education.

Council on Social Work Education. (2011). *Patient Protection and Affordable Care Act of 2010: A resource guide for social workers.* Washington, DC: Lewis-Burke Associates.

Eiken, S., Burwell, B., Gold, L., & Sredl, K. (2010). *Medicaid HCBS waiver expenditures FY 2004 through FY 2009.* Cambridge, MA: Thomson Reuters.

Eldercare Workforce Alliance. (2011). *Caring for an Aging America Act (S.1095).* Retrieved from http://eldercareworkforce.rallycongress.com/4544/tell-your-senator-to-support-cosponsor-caring-an-aging-america-ac/

Fortinsky, R. H. (2008). Diagnosis and early support. In M. Downs & B. Bowers (Eds.), *Excellence in dementia care: Research into practice* (pp. 267–284). Maidenhead, England: Open University Press.

Fortinsky, R. H., Fenster, J. R., & Judge, J. O. (2004). Medicare and Medicaid home health and Medicaid waiver services for dually eligible older adults: Risk factors for use and correlates of expenditures. *The Gerontologist, 44,* 739–749.

Franz, C. E., Barker, J. C., Kravitz, R. L., Flores, Y., Krishnan, S., & Hinton, L. (2007). Nonmedical influences on the use of cholinesterase inhibitors in dementia care. *Alzheimer's Disease and Associated Disorders, 21,* 241–248.

Health Policy Brief: Medicare Advantage Plans. (2011, June 15). *Health Affairs.*

Institute of Medicine. (2008). *Retooling for an aging America: Building the health care workforce.* Washington, DC: National Academy of Sciences Press.

Kaiser Commission on Medicaid and the Uninsured. (2010a). *The Medicaid program at a glance.* Publication #7235–04, June 2010. Retrieved at www.kff.org

Kaiser Commission on Medicaid and the Uninsured. (2010b). *Medicaid and long-term care services and supports.* Publication #2186–07, October 2010. Retrieved from www.kff.org

Kaiser Commission on Medicaid and the Uninsured. (2010c). *Dual eligibles: Medicaid's role for low-income Medicare beneficiaries.* Publication #4091–07, December 2010. Retrieved from www.kff.org

Lieberman, S. M., & Bertko, J. M. (2011). Building regulatory and operational flexibility into accountable care organizations and 'shared savings.' *Health Affairs, 30,* 23–31.

Mather, L. (2007). Memory lane café: Follow-up support for people with early stage dementia and their families and carers. *Dementia: The International Journal for Research and Practice, 5,* 290–293.

National Health Policy Forum. (2010). *The community living assistance services and supports (CLASS) act: Major legislative provisions.* Washington, DC: Author.

Neumann, P. J., Cohen, J. T., Hammitt, J. K., Concannon, T. W., Auerbach, H. R., Fang, C., et al. (2010). Willingness-to-pay for predictive tests with no immediate treatment implications: A survey of U.S. residents. *Health Economics.* Advance online publication. doi:10.1002/hec.1704

Niles-Yokum, K., & Wagner, D. (2011). *The aging networks—A guide to programs and services* (7th ed.). New York, NY: Springer Publishing.

Sciegaj, M., Capitman, J. A., & Kyriacou, C. K. (2004). Consumer-directed community care: Race/ethnicity and individual differences in preferences for control. *The Gerontologist, 44,* 489–499.

Stone, R., & Harahan, M. F. (2010). Improving the long-term care workforce serving older adults. *Health Affairs, 29,* 109–115.

Zuckerman, I. H., Ryder, P. T., Simoni-Wastila, L., Shaffer, T., Sato, M., Zhao, L., et al. (2008). Racial and ethnic disparities in the treatment of dementia among Medicare beneficiaries. *Journal of Gerontology: Social Sciences, 63B,* S328–S333.

10

Technology for Social Work Communication With Ethnic Caregivers

INTERNET

As a communication tool, the Internet provides unparalleled links between people. The linkages are through email, websites, and even audio and video. This section examines each of these three Internet technologies and how they might be used by social workers in conjunction with caregivers and their dependents.

EMAIL

Email has replaced the postal letter as the primary asynchronous means of communication. An email is instant, does not require the recipient to be present or awake at the time of receipt (asynchronous), and can contain attached images, photos, links, and videos along with text. For caregivers, it extends their reach in several different contexts:

- Caregivers who must work but want to keep in touch with their family
- Sending urgently needed information
- Keeping the dependents up-to-date and informed
- Providing feedback from the client communicating needs, including received instructions or information, medical supplies (prescriptions and other medical needs), and general whereabouts and self-described current health
- Direct communication between the caregiver and medical personnel

- Direct communication between the caregiver and other family members
- Direct communication between the caregiver and social worker

Email is quick and cheap and does not even require a trip to the mailbox; it is delivered exactly at the time it is sent. As a result, the caregiver can provide social support beyond the boundaries of face-to-face interaction while having many of the same qualities of such interaction.

Social workers find equal value as caregivers in the use of email for different kinds of communication. Some of the email communications are identical to those of caregivers, but a whole range of communication beyond those are important for social workers. Included are the following:

- Communication between the social worker and caregiver
- Contact with the social worker's own agency for more efficient use of time and resources
- Interaction with other resource providers outside of the social worker's own agency
- Coordination between the caregiver and other agencies who may be part of the care array that has been arranged by the social worker
- Providing a general link between a sequence of medical, social, and familial resources. A social worker's email acts as a general clearinghouse for a complex of individuals and agency personnel

One of the most important innovations in the use of email has been with mobile devices or "smart phones." Having email available on a mobile device, both social workers and caregivers have far more location flexibility than when tethered to a desktop (or even a laptop) computer. All communications using email should be linked to a mobile device in addition to any tethered technology. In this way, social workers and caregivers can achieve contact without having to be in a single location.

A possible issue with poorer populations is access to email. To a great extent, the burden will rest with the caregiver for providing email access to patient and self. Some older patients may not know how to use email and, combined with dementia, they may not be capable of learning how to use it. However, over time, use of and access to email is becoming less problematic. Prices have dropped for Internet access and caregivers can use the same Internet access for both themselves and the patient. Likewise, over time, the ability to use email is becoming as common as telephone use; so understanding how to use email in the future will be less and less problematic.

Many cities have freely available wireless network to the Internet, and such access is certainly more cost-effective for cities than individualized wireless access. Social work agencies may want to lobby for such access because it is less expensive than individual contracts with Internet providers and benefits both business as well as the needy. Not only do most computers, both laptop and desktop, come with built-in wireless connectors, so too do smart phones such as the Apple iPhone, Google Android-equipped phones, and phones with BlackBerry Internet Service. In time, the hard-wired cable connection to the Internet may become a thing of the past.

GLOBAL POSITIONING SYSTEM

The use of a Global Positioning System (GPS) is another technological innovation that has become a common consumer product over the last 20 years. Designed as a navigation system for military use, a GPS is now a ubiquitous aspect of driving to an unknown location. However, a GPS is used in a wide range of applications for keeping track of people and vehicles. Included in its use are:

- Keeping track of children
- Locating the elderly with Alzheimer's disease
- Emergency location for assistance
- Locating client's residences

With a GPS system, social workers can spend far less time attempting to find both caregivers and patients. Likewise, caregivers can quickly locate their wards who may have wandered off and thus do not have to call emergency responders or caseworkers. Many GPS are bundled with smart phones along with Internet access and email capability. As such, GPS can be part of a multiple technology solution to communication for caregivers and social workers.

INTERNET CAREGIVING RESOURCES

In part, both GPS and email are included in a general Internet resource. However, this section focuses on the resources that are available on websites. (See also the section *Enhancing the Ethnic Caregiver Social Support Network* for a discussion of blogs.) One of the most important strengths and weaknesses of websites is that virtually anyone can create one. On the one hand, this allows many different viewpoints to be expressed and possibly employed. On the other hand, virtually anyone can publish advice and prescribe a course of action that can be detrimental to both caregivers and patients.

The most important role of the social worker using Internet caregiving resources is to review the online sites and their validity. By providing a reviewed list of links to online resources, the social worker performs an essential role of filtering out unverified information and making valid resources available to caregivers. Sites such as that sponsored by the *Alzheimer's Association* (www.alz.org) have excellent information for caregivers that can be useful to both the caregiver and the social work professional alike. Other sites, especially personal ones, may have heartfelt descriptions of a loved-one's travails, but they may have little value otherwise.

An important feature of any site for caregivers is the language it is written in. Social workers should be especially cognizant of the choices they make in terms of the language of the client and the language of the website. The Alzheimer's Association's site has some materials in both Spanish and English, but most of the material is in English. When good articles are not available in the client's language, many language translation programs are available—many at no cost. For example, Yahoo's *Babel Fish* (babelfish.yahoo.com) and *Wordlingo* (www.worldlingo.com) provide free translation of sites and/or segments. Likewise, *Google Translate* is a browser extension that can be added to the *Google Chrome* browser. Then, the user can translate any page to a language of their choice. Social workers can help caregivers set up these technology aids to translation and not have to limit the resources to the few that are in the caregiver's or patient's language of choice.

TELEHEALTH INNOVATIONS

The term *telehealth* is a broad one and includes any kind of health services that include some kind of electronic communication including email and Web-based aids already discussed. However, the concept of telehealth tends to be more inclusive and planned as part of a more general health delivery system. The concept can be broken down and is best understood as two general types.

Store-and-Forward Telehealth

For the most part, store-and-forward telehealth planning has been based on client records, diagnosis, and recommendations (including drug prescriptions) that have been stored as text, digital images, video, or audio. This information is made available to an array of medical and technical personnel who are responsible for a patient's overall care. Because the data are stored, the services can be made available on an asynchronous basis, meaning that the caregiver or social worker has continuous access to the data. This allows a care model to be organized around the social worker helping the caregiver to access and use the telehealth information independent of time and location. This model is more dynamic because the caregiver is not dependent upon the social worker to be available at all times when the social worker is busy with other cases or not at work. However, much of the information may be too technical or specialized for the caregiver and may require the social worker to add real-time assistance to interpret and use the information available in a store-and-forward telehealth format. Likewise, some information may require non-social work specialization such as a physician who must write a prescription or a judge who has to issue a court order. Nevertheless, if well-organized, store-and-forward telehealth services can be used by social workers to provide other area specialists with needed information stored in a telehealth framework.

Real-Time Telehealth

More widely known and identified as *telehealth* is the real-time model where physicians work with emergency personnel to provide specific instructions in emergency care. Such telehealth services include remote monitoring of electronic readings of different organ functions (e.g., heart rate, blood pressure) to real-time video, allowing physicians to see what an emergency response team sees.

As applied to social workers dealing with Alzheimer's patients and caregivers, social workers can see what a caregiver sees and offer assistance in determining a course of action that may include providing guidance for dealing with a specific event or condition, recommending or contacting medical or emergency units, or finding care resources for a particular situation. All assistance that social workers accomplish using a telephone are available, and one can consider the phone, mobile or nonmobile, as part of a telehealth system. More robust technology such as real-time video, video conferencing, and medical monitoring round out a telehealth plan, but all telehealth implementations depend upon the caregiver's ability and willingness to use that technology when provided by the social work agency. Likewise, more sophisticated teleheath instruments may require training for the social worker, caregiver, and client in conjunction with other agencies who are linked into the same system.

ENHANCING THE ETHNIC CAREGIVER SOCIAL SUPPORT NETWORK

An ethnic social support network is by necessity and in reality defined by those who make up the network. Categories such as *Latino, Asian,* and *African American* may not reflect or be sufficient to define truly diverse categories. For example, the different groups that made up the Vietnamese Diaspora after the Vietnam War included waves of Vietnamese who worked for Americans, Vietnamese who did not want to live under a communist regime for political, social, or religious reasons, and then Chinese–Vietnamese who were purged after the China–Vietnam border war. Likewise, different ethnic groups such as the Hmong, Khmer, and Laotians who fled Southeast Asia after the war were often grouped as "Asians" or "Vietnamese." The broader categories only served to identify what general part of the world one was from or regions speaking the same language. They did not reflect ethnic networks.

> Electronic social networks are one mechanism where social workers can identify self-defined social networks and introduce clients to these networks or find ethnic-based resources for clients. Likewise, social workers can help establish such networks for their own community. However, social networks are free and open to anyone, and an essential role for the social worker may include identifying legitimate and helpful networks. One of the dilemmas of social networks is the inclusion of fraudulent information for exploitation or well-meaning but inaccurate information that may harm caregivers and their wards. (Greene, Choudhry, Kilabuk, & Shrank, 2010)

Facebook

One of the best-known social network portals is Facebook. It is a free service where users can post personal profiles, link with other users as friends and exchange messages, and automatically post notifications when they update their profile. Importantly for social workers, users may create or join common-interest user groups. For minority groups and Alzheimer's caregivers, the ability to join and participate in these discussions provides social support wherever they have Internet access.

The Alzheimer's Association maintains a Facebook site at http://www.facebook.com/actionalz for general information, and more localized Facebook sites are available in different nations (e.g., in the United Kingdom, http://www.facebook.com/alzheimerssocietyuk) and local communities. Likewise, minority groups maintain Facebook pages. For example, Facebook pages exist for African Americans at http://www.facebook.com/pages/African-American-Alzheimers-Disease-Awareness-Information/215828890235 and a more general health access for Latinos at http://www.facebook.com/pages/Latino-Health-Access/130299473681954.

More localized health forums can also be found on Facebook for support in specific locales and ethnic groups. Such local Facebook pages that share stories and advice can facilitate group meetings either online or face-to-face. For example, the Lansing (Michigan) Latino Health Alliance (http://www.facebook.com/pages/Lansing-Latino-Health-Alliance/275587797724) provides a network for health issues in the greater Lansing area for a group that may feel more isolated than areas where larger Latino populations can be found.

The most important role of Facebook for social workers, both with minority and nonminority populations, is to establish credibility for a page that can be monitored and used by the appropriate groups whose lives have been impacted by Alzheimer's. So many dubious claims have been made for Alzheimer's disease cures that social workers need to provide a social network presence where they can act as information providers and debunkers. For example, one Facebook page that included the headline *Ginseng for Treating Alzheimer's Disease* was followed by a smaller subhead indicating: *Some studies show that ginseng can improve mental functioning, but the science behind the claims is weak.* Interspersed in the post were ads for prescription drugs for depression. Similar findings were posted for diabetes (Greene et al., 2010).

Greene et al. (2010) showed that Facebook pages often contain unsupported information and were surrounded by ads for prescription drugs. Even a cursory review of Facebook pages with Alzheimer's disease topics show similar trends. Social workers and agencies who create their own Facebook pages can monitor and correct any information inserted by advertisers or others who inject dubious information.

Some of the minority groups may be especially susceptible to *folk medicines* that have no proven worth in disease treatment but are widely believed to be effective in the ethnic community. Ideally, the social worker should have a respected minority member act as a spokesperson to debunk these fables in such a way that does not attack the culture but effectively debunks the erroneous information. For example, Asian herbs have a very strong history in some Asian communities and are regularly recommended by herb sellers. A non-Asian image in a Facebook page may have little strength in convincing an Asian population that Asian folk medicine is ineffective in curing Alzheimer's or any other disease.

Twitter: Information in 140 Characters

A common mistake made in considering social networking is underestimating *Twitter*. Twitter (*twitter.com*) is an instant posting system where only 140 characters can be sent at any one time. However, within the 140-character post can be a URL to another resource. For example, the following *tweet* (Twitter message) includes an abbreviated URL (Twitter uses a URL shortener):

Alzheimer's called "defining disease" of baby boomers—The Chart—CNN.com Blogs http://t.co/W6su59L via @cnn

The original URL is:

http://pagingdrgupta.blogs.cnn.com/2011/01/27/alzheimers-called-defining-disease-of-baby-boomers/

So within that 140-character post is a much more powerful tool in the URL shortener. It is a way to easily and quickly send messages to everyone who subscribes to a Twitter category or trend.

One gauge of Twitter's power is that it has been partially credited with the overthrow of Tunisia's government. Using Twitter postings, protestors organized mass gatherings. Likewise, in Iran and Egypt, Twitter was used both to organize internal protests and gather international support for movements. If social workers can organize their caregivers around a Twitter trend or profile page, they can effectively use this microblogging tool to easily keep in touch with a wide range of caregivers, and as well, caregivers with one another. These short and quick messages can link to anything from blog posts to videos.

An important feature that any Web page or blog posting should have is a link to Twitter and other social network resources using a "share button." The share button allows readers to quickly pass on the page's information to users with a like interest. For example, if a user (including the social worker) finds a good resource online, a share button on the page provides an instant link to a Twitter application. Resource information is then sent to all who subscribe to the Twitter profile or trend. One such share button site is http://www.addtoany.com/ where the share button can be freely downloaded.

Ethnic Minorities and Trending Topics

In Twitter, a trending topic is any topic around a subject. Each trend is identified by a pound sign (#) followed by a topic or individual's profile name. For example, one topic found on Twitter was, #EnglishMadeInNigeria. Nigerians from English-speaking countries from all over the world (including Nigeria) posted thousands of tweets with sayings they identified as having Nigerian origin. The following represents a small sample:

- please off ur shoes before coming in.
- No any other way
- wetin I go chop dis morninq oh…me dey hunger
- ahh an Cold is catching me o! put off the AC nau!

In looking at trending topics, one can recognize different ethnic groups by the topic names and subject matter. Most are not health related, but they provide an interesting window into what different groups have to say and in their own voice.

Working with community members' agencies can set up any number of ethnic-centered topics that relate to caregiving and resources for caregivers and clients. Because they are short, tweets are easier to send and receive using mobile devices such as smart phones and other mobile devices connected to the Internet. By tapping into and providing Twitter trends (topics) that relate to both an ethnic identity and caregiving, social workers can optimize an entire social networking strategy.

Alzheimer's Disease Discussions on Twitter

For some unknown reason, Twitter users will adopt a topic name or profile identity that has nothing to do with what they tweet about. Alzheimer's disease is one such example. As a result, links such as http://twitter.com/#alzheimers have nothing useful or even extant, while http://twitter.com/#ALZHEIMERSread is an excellent resource for Alzheimer's information. Because topic and profile names are unique and not controlled, the first user to use a Twitter name gets it. Only by reported abuse will Twitter shut down a Twitter account that is following your tweets; otherwise, it is an uncontrolled and uncensored resource.

The most valuable use of Twitter is to use tweets to guide caregivers to resources or alert them to information that has just become available. With only 140 characters, details must be summarized and links to blogs or websites must be used as the main resource site. Tweets can be recovered from anything from desktop computers to mobile phones.

Blogs

Blogs are topic-centered websites. The only difference between a Web page and a blog is that blogs allow users to dynamically add images, text, links, and multimedia content without having to use a Web development tool. Also, blogs allow users to add comments of their own. This can be quite useful for getting feedback and forging links between users. For all intents and purposes, however, blogs and websites are indistinguishable, accessed by a Web address.

As noted elsewhere in this chapter, Web pages and blogs can be translated into any language using tools built into the browser or on the site itself. The advantage of using a translator tool built into the page is that a user on any browser can have the page translated. Again, Babel Fish is an example; it is one of the oldest Web page translators available for free (http://babelfish.yahoo.com/free_trans_service) and can be used by any browser and can translate a Web page into several different languages. So, if a client uses the default *Microsoft Internet Explorer* on a Windows computer or *Safari* on a Macintosh, it doesn't matter. Some browsers, such as Google's *Chrome,* have downloads for extensions that will do the translations, but the user has to have *Chrome* to do the translations. That can be valuable for sites where no translation tool is on the site itself. With the translations built into the Web page, anyone can easily get a translation.

The content of a blog needs to be kept current. Many blogs can be found with out-of-date information; because resources change frequently, having someone (or group) responsible for keeping the blog current is important. When working with multiethnic groups, images and messages need to reflect the different ethnicities who may use the blog. Even a simple photo of a client taken with a mobile phone can make a world of difference to those who use the blog because they see "someone like themselves."

Linking Technology

Social networking tools need to be integrated. Facebook can have links to a blog as well as a button that brings up the Web address in Twitter and Facebook that can be sent to all who subscribe to your Twitter profile or trend and get Facebook updates. Facebook has several built-in features that automatically alert users to any changes or updates, but they must be activated. Likewise, most blog applications have an option to allow users to subscribe to your blog through a *Really Simple Syndication* link that sends out announcements every time a new blog post is added. Once received, the users can easily make tweets and announcements on their own Facebook page.

While much can be done automatically using Internet technology to address diverse ethnic groups served by an agency, most must be done by the social worker. Automatic translation certainly is helpful where English is not the native language, but representations of diverse communities must be reflected in the materials presented by the technology.

REFERENCE

Greene, J. A., Choudhry, N. K., Kilabuk, E., & Shrank, W. H. (2010). Online social networking by patients with diabetes: A qualitative evaluation of communication with Facebook. *Journal of General Internal Medicine, 26*(3), 287–292. doi:10.1007/s11606-010-1526-3

APPENDIX

National Association of Social Work Standards and Guidelines: Cultural Competence in Providing Services to Ethnic Caregivers

In 1994, in view of the future projected growth of ethnic populations, the National Association of Social Workers (NASW) made the following recommendations for social workers working with older ethnic and cultural minorities who are most likely to have a need for social services due to poverty and other social and health disparities.

1. Presenting problems should be defined in terms of family and community systems and the culture, ethnicity, and heritage of the client.
2. Social work interventions should be based on the client's and the family's definition of problems, goals, needs, and solutions. Service plans should be based on the older person's strengths rather than deficits.
3. Programs should be preventive in nature whenever possible.
4. Services should be family based and community based.
5. Service planning should be designed to enhance choices offered. For example, program options should include home health services, respite care, family support groups, and in-home care, along a continuum to nursing home care. Resource and program development activities should be undertaken to ensure the availability of services.
6. Services must be tailored to fit older people rather than forcing older people to fit into categorical services.
7. Services must be accessible.
8. Development of services should reflect appropriate roles for the life cycle of the individual.

(National Association of Social Workers (1994). *Social work with older people: Understanding diversity* (pp. 17–18). Washington, DC: National Association of Social Workers)

Social work with ethnic minority older adults is becoming a priority due to the increasing number of ethnic older adults. The profession is working diligently toward developing improved practice methods with older individuals with the NASW taking the lead. The NASW defines a BSW-level social worker in gerontology as having the following credentials.

This credential specifies the following requisite competencies for the BSW-G level gerontology social worker:

- Assessment
    - Identify biopsychosocial, spiritual, and cultural diversity aspects (including race, ethnicity, language, sexual orientation)
    - Identify strengths, resources, activities of daily living (ADLs), nutrition, and presence of elder abuse
    - Utilize tools relevant to older adults
- Documentation, Report, Record Keeping
    - Monitor client progress in achieving goals
    - Record provision of service
    - Facilitate information between resources with client's informed consent
    - Protect confidentiality
- Care and Case Management
    - Have familiarity with care plans
    - Negotiate systems (including family, medical, community, religious, spiritual, etc.)
    - Provide advocacy, supportive counseling for the client and family
    - Engage in multidisciplinary teamwork
    - Utilize community resources
    - Consultation with supervisor
- Service Planning
    - Adhere to service plans with measureable objectives
    - Identify and prioritize client issues and concerns including bereavement/loss and the life cycle
    - Assist in service planning that includes both short- and long-term goals, client support, crisis prevention, and community resources
- Client Advocacy and Supportive Counseling

(National Association of Social Workers (2011). Retrieved January 7, 2011, from http://www.socialworkers.org/credentials/default.asp)

The NASW defines the clinical level social worker in gerontology as having the following credentials. This credential specifies the following requisite competencies for the CSW-G level gerontology social worker:

- Assessment
  - Identify biopsychosocial, spiritual, and cultural diversity aspects (including race, ethnicity, language, sexual orientation)
  - Identify strengths, resources, activities of daily living (ADLs), nutrition, and presence of elder abuse
  - Utilize tools relevant to older adults
- Documentation, Report, Record Keeping
  - Monitor client progress in achieving goals
  - Record provision of service
  - Facilitate information between resources with client's informed consent
  - Protect confidentiality
- Care and Case Management
  - Have familiarity with care plans
  - Negotiate systems (including family, medical, community, religious, spiritual, etc.)
  - Provide advocacy and supportive counseling for the client and family
  - Engage in multidisciplinary teamwork
  - Utilize community resources
  - Use effective communication skills with older adults and family members
- Clinical Practice
  - Diagnosis
  - Independent practice
  - Develop treatment plans that include short- and long-term goals, treatment interventions, care direction and management, client support, and crisis prevention
  - Identify and prioritize client concerns including issues of grief and bereavement across the life cycle
  - Develop advance care plans that include the following objectives: autonomy/self-determination, legal, financial, and end-of-life/palliative care
  - Assess and evaluate cognitive functioning, mental and physical health status, and physical functioning (e.g., ADLs and IADLs) of older adults
  - Assess the caregivers' needs and stressors

- o   Utilize relevant social work theories and treatment modalities including, but not limited to, individual, group, and family therapy, cognitive behavioral therapy, psychoanalytic theory, and supportive psychotherapy
- Administration
  - o   Monitor and evaluate efficacy, efficiency, and appropriateness of service plans
  - o   Collect and analyze data
  - o   Educate and teach other professionals, caregivers, and older adults about the aging process, wellness, management of health, community resources, and life transitions
  - o   Advocate on behalf of individuals and the community relative to service gaps, negative effects of social and health care policies, discrimination, and other barriers that influence the lives of older adults

(National Association of Social Workers (2011). Retrieved January 7, 2011, from http://www.socialworkers.org/credentials/default.asp)

Index